Garden of Hallucinations

Garden of Hallucinations

Rites of Mystodokos

Ryan Daniel Gable

~ Table of Contents ~

PART III – *HAND OF GOD*

Magic vs Miracle

Sacrifice & Ritual

Heka & the Cosmic Egg

Magnetism

Solar Rainbows

Four Horsemen

Exorcising Demons

PART IV – *MAGIC IN SACRED SCRIPTURES*

Jesus as a Magician

Magic & Miracle in the Bible

Rabbinical Sorcery

The Quran & The Gospel of Barnabas

The Way of Isa

EPILOGUE

The Divine Plan, Gnosticism, & Jesus the Nazarene

Keys of the Mysteries

In dealing with the products of the collective unconscious, all images that show an unmistakably mythological character have to be examined in their symbological context. They are the inborn language of the psyche and its structure, and, as regards their basic form, are in no sense individual acquisitions.

~

Mythology and magic flourish as ever in our midst and are unknown only to those whose rationalistic education has alienated them from their roots. Quite apart from ecclesiastical symbolism, which embodies six thousand years of spiritual development and is constantly renewing itself, there are also its more disreputable relatives, magical ideas and practices which are still very much alive in spite of all education and enlightenment.

~ Carl G. Jung ~

Introduction

Paradise: "heaven as the ultimate abode of the just the abode of the just: Adam and Eve before the Fall in the biblical account of the Creation; the Garden of Eden."

Hallucination: "an experience involving the apparent perception of something not present."

~

Our goal with this treatise is in no way to disparage investments in religion or spirituality. In fact, readers may come away from this work with an even stronger conviction for those things than before. We strive here instead to provide respite from dichotomy which seeks to relegate on the basis of separation. Our endeavor will provide a steady analysis of the intentional or otherwise unintended *sleight of hand* exhibited by the English language in particular, but by using the Japanese concepts of the *spirit of words* and the *spirit of sound*. Only through properly considering the power and magic of a word can we take a sure course into the mystical and address the numerous *sacred scriptures* which speak to the *Word of God*, i.e., vibration, and the *Creating of the Universe*.

This work intends to extrapolate and link the *Garden of Paradise* archetype with shamanism, altered states of consciousness, and the occult evolutionary process of man which is driven by unseen forces like consciousness. Throughout the first two sections of this text, we will explore the power of words, how they relate to the creation of the world, and how divine forces guide our development. Only then are we made familiar enough with the *forces of nature* to even attempt an understanding of *magic* and *miracle*.

In section three the basic elements of magic will be unfolded but not totally unveiled for that is the domain of powers we can only speculate upon. This section will provide an overview of *sacrifice* and *ritual* and how both just as well pertain to faith, prayer, hymns, communion, austerities, alchemy etc., as they do to literal practices of barbaric *sorcery*. We will demonstrate that a *sacrifice* is both part of *ritual* and a *holy* act that has nothing to do with harming an animal or human. However, sacrifices of the former and latter do indeed reflect the necessity in spiritually transforming oneself by *killing the beast* or *dragon* within. As we explore ancient and modern practices of *exorcism*, we will also take note of the cultural parameters by which the *demon* or *monster* is to be defined. The same determinates will be used in addressing prophecies of *eschaton*. These *last days* will be shown, along with the *apocalypse*, to be complex narratives concealing a sophisticated comprehension of the cycles of man and nature. Take note that there are four: the number of riders on the revelatory horses, the number of seasons, and the number of sections in this work.

The text will conclude in part four with an overview of *magic*, *sorcery*, and *miracle* in both major and minor world religions and philosophies. These things will be addressed in reference to Christianity, Islam, Judaism, Hinduism, Shintōism, and the like. Within all these systems we will find evidence of *secret teachings* that rest just beneath dogma and literal interpretation.

It is unfortunate that the *sacred texts* of so many traditions have been jumbled by institutional powers and perverted through both intention and ignorance by the profane. As philosopher Manly P. Hall says:

> *"...after the decline of the Mysteries, when the sacred books fell into the hands of the profane, the subtler values were lost."*

These *subtler values* may still be ascertained, however, with proper study and interpretation of the countless *sacred texts* from around the world. For if one desires to *"understand any one sacred book completely"* it is absolutely *"necessary to also understand all other sacred books."* And as James M. Pryse wrote in The Apocalypse Unsealed:

> *"Every thoughtful student of the literature of the ancient religions, including that of early Christianity, can not but be impressed by the fact that in each and all of them may be found very clear intimations of a secret traditional lore, an arcane science, handed down from times immemorial."*

~

It is our intention throughout this work to provide a better understanding of certain histories, mythologies, religious stories, and traditions which speak to all manner of *mystical practices*. Our concerns are not only with generalities of such things, but specifically with the particulars of being *resurrected* like Jesus or Lazarus from an earthly tomb. For this is the ultimate goal of the *mysteries*, to follow in the footsteps of the *Son of God* and to be *born again* as a *Sun of God*; to return to the *Garden of Paradise* from the *Garden of Hallucinations*, which, in essence, is a *dream world*.

Although we may experience parallels to the "garden" in altered states of consciousness, as we will see, life itself, while beautiful, is the ultimate and extended altered state of unconsciousness. Though many await the *second coming* of their savior, the *parousia* will not occur in any physical manifestation per se.

The *flashes of lighting* and the *opening of the heavens* refer instead to the unfolding and sprouting of the *seed* within, finally awakened, or *born again*, to its true nature and purpose. Such a process completes the mythological and theological cycle, whereby the *Paradise Tree* bearing poisoned *fruit* in the Garden relates to the *Tree of Redemption* at Calvary. Famed comparative mythologist Joseph Campbell explains the meaning:

> "The first, the Tree of the Fall, represents passage from the eternal into the realm of time. The second is the Tree of the return from the realm of time to the spiritual. So that Tree is the threshold tree, the laurel tree, which may be seen in its two aspects, going from the sacred to the profane and from the profane back into the sacred."

It is the *"bite of death to ego that opens the eye and the ear to the eternal"* and it is the offspring of the *woman* that will *crush* the head of the serpent in the end.

Campbell also explains how our acceptance or rejection of these many and varied metaphors leads to the polarizing classifications of *believers* and *skeptics*, both of which miss the point entirely. The purpose of metaphor and mythology is to align waking consciousness to the *mysterium tremendum* and to obtain *"recognition of the dimension of the mystery of being."*

Metaphor and myth provide the basis for a cosmic and moral order out of which an individual may be carried through the various stages of life. He writes further of mythology in general:

> *"A mythology may be understood as an organization of metaphorical figures connotative of states of mind that are not finally of this or that location or historical period, even though the figures themselves seem on their surface to suggest such a concrete localization. The metaphorical languages of both mythology and metaphysics are not denotative of actual worlds or gods, but rather connote levels and entities within the person touched by them."*

Along with all that is presented in the first four parts of this work, the concluding epilogue will provide the necessary *keys of the mysteries* to understand these things better; from astrolatry, astrology, and cosmogony, to the esoteric nature of the Bible, Quran, Zend Avesta, and the Revelation of St John.

~

By reading further you admit yourself as *mystodokos*, an initiate receiving the *mysteries*, whether you are neophyte, hierophant, adept, or just a little curious.

~ PART I ~

Twilight Language

KOTODAMA

The word *kotodama* translates from Japanese (Nihongo) as *spirit of a word* or *soul of a word*. Selecting no specific *word* here we are still able to understand the idea as a sort of mythical power emanating as *spoken word* and *sacred sound*. The Romans called this authority *voces magicae*, or *magic words*.

Words indeed have power. Their usage solidifies an idea and brings it from the spiritual into the physical realm. Perceptions, thoughts, and ideas shape our reality, drive our behavior, form our myths and folklore, and create the *manifest* world.

Words are by the simplest definition expressions of *consciousness* that result in *creation*. The Hebrew *gōlem,* or shapeless mass, is an illustrative physical example of this process. In one 16th century story, a man called Elijah of Chelm, with assistance from the mystic Jewish text known as *Yetzirah,* created one of these creatures. The artificial and shapeless monster came to life having had written the secret name of god on its forehead. In most stories the *golem* comes to life through intention, will, and the Hebrew word emét, which means 'truth'. In order to stop this monstrous manifestation, a letter is removed from emét so that the inscription reads mét, the Hebrew word for 'death'.

The word *tulpa* is thought to be a creation of Buddhist philosophy. These *thought-forms* are manifest either through a deliberate act of will or by unintentional thoughts. Although similar to a *golem*, the *tulpa* can form as a result of individual or collective thoughts with no need for additional physical assistance.

Non-physical entities that manifest by individual or collective thoughts are called *egregore*, from the French égrégore and Greek egrēgoros, which means 'wakeful'.

Tulpas are likewise warnings: to be wary of wandering thoughts that may lead to unnecessary suffering. Although the Shintō practices of indigenous Japan define life as the opposite of suffering, i.e., a wonderful experience made painful by wicked spirits, the idea of *kotodama*, especially in one's thoughts and expressions, remains.

Sound also has a *spirit* since it is the result of utterance, especially those of prayer or singing. The 'spirit of sound' is called *otodama* by the Japanese. When certain words have particular positive influence, and make someone happy, they are called *kotohogi* – 'celebration words'. Here we are reminded of *The Word of God*, which may be described as *vibration* and *sacred geometry* (God is the Grand Architect).

The kanji characters for **Kotodama**, the *spirit of language*.

Vibration itself is the *Word of God,* particularly as an expression of pure *consciousness*. It is the method by which divine names or words are intoned to attract their associated corresponding energies. Spoken words begin as *concepts* and *thoughts*, then are expressed as *vibrations* out of *body* and *mouth*. For *"God said, Let there be light."* These concepts and thoughts stem from the spirit/soul and the processing unit we call the brain. All of these elements are invariably associated with the head: also, dome and skull. Another name for this area of the body is the *temple,* and parallel to that fact is the Italian word *duomo*, which means *cathedral*. It is in the temple or cathedral where God, in countless forms throughout the world, is worshiped. These sacred locations are also centers of spiritual energy and *transmutation*. The *Gnostics, an* early Jewish and Christian mystical sect, likewise believed that the brain corresponded to the Garden of Eden, and as Jean Doresse points out in <u>The Secret Books of the Egyptian Gnostics,</u> *"the membranes enveloping the brain, to the heavens; the head of man, to Paradise, etc."*

The *body is a temple* (1 Corinthians 6:19-20) and therefore a *vessel*. A*lchemy* is a spiritual process, representing a transformation of our internal components of *self*. The *homunculus* forms through a process of self-internalized observation and adaptation, and in development of necessary centers of *thought* and *action*. The image of a *boat* in this context is common throughout the ancient world, representing a *vessel* for the *soul* in the *afterlife*, just as the *body* is the *vessel* for the soul in *physical life*.

Another allegory, sadly misunderstood, is the *Tower of Babel*. This tower was supposedly constructed by an ignorant group of humans unsatisfied with earthly existence and seeking to acquire divinity by circumventing *The Great Work* - alchemy. The hidden meaning here is that the artificial world that man has designed, engineered, and upheld to the highest degree, is but a mere phantasm in reality. Each step or stage of the *El-Temen-An-Ki* – a ziggurat house in Babylon symbolizing the foundational stone of heaven and earth - represented one of the seven planets, its angles being the four worldly corners.

Kurt Seligmann explains in <u>The Mirror of Magic</u> how the *"seven steps of the tower were painted in different colors which corresponded to the planets."* These were: black for Saturn; white for Jupiter; brick-red for Mercury; blue for Venus; yellow for Mars; and gray or silver for the Moon. Opposed to the black Saturn was the highest stage, a golden symbolic sympathy of the brilliant Sun. Without proper perspective or understanding, the artificial world, and all material achievements, are but attempts to rival the glory of the heavenly spheres.

Author Manly P. Hall writes on an unrelated subject: *"As man attempts to elevate himself spiritually he gradually separates himself from his material environment."* Therefore, if man attempts to elevate himself materially by subjecting *natural law* to *manmade law*, then he separates himself further from his spiritual nature. In his attempt to steal the *keys of heaven* his language is confused, i.e., the *mysteries of nature* are shrouded in darkness.

The Genesis 11:1-9 *Tower of Babel* story is by far the best-known example of the sort. However, Mexican history on the other side of the world preserves much of the same story, and amazingly in physical form. The Great Pyramid of Cholula, or *tlachihualtepetl*, is known as the *man-made mountain*. It resides in Cholula, Puebla, Mexico, and is the largest pyramid by volume known to exist in the world. Its base is 45 acres, and its height is 210 feet. It is, as author Graham Hancock confirms in his monumental work <u>Fingerprints of the Gods</u>, *"three times more massive than the Great Pyramid of Egypt."* Graham documents the work of a Franciscan named Diego de Duran, who visited Cholula in AD 1585 to collect some of the local historical knowledge. Upon interviewing a woman said to be over one hundred years old, Duran explains what sounds stunningly like the Biblical *tower* but in Mexico, not Babylon:

> "In the beginning, before the light of the sun had been created, this place, Cholula, was in obscurity and darkness; all was a plain, without hill or elevation, encircled in every part by water, without tree or created thing. Immediately after the light and the sun arose in the east there appeared gigantic men of deformed stature who possessed the land. Enamoured of the light and beauty of the sun they determined to build a tower so high that its summit should reach the sky. Having collected materials for the purpose they found a very adhesive clay and bitumen with which they speedily commenced to build the tower ... And having reared it to the greatest possible altitude, so that it reached the sky, the Lord of the Heavens, enraged, said to the inhabitants of the sky, Have you observed how they of the earth have built a high and haughty tower to mount hither, being enamoured of the light of the sun and his beauty? Come and confound them, because it is not right that they of the earth, living in the flesh, should mingle with us. Immediately the inhabitants of the sky sallied forth like flashes of lightning; they destroyed the edifice and divided and scattered its builders to all parts of the earth."

Compare this with the Genesis account:

> "Now the whole world had one language and a common speech. As people moved eastward, they found a plain in Shinar and settled there. They said to each other, 'Come, let's make bricks and bake them thoroughly.' They used brick instead of stone, and tar for mortar. Then they said, 'Come, let us build ourselves a city, with a tower that reaches to the heavens, so that we may make a name for ourselves; otherwise we will be scattered over the face of the whole earth. But the Lord came down to see the city and the tower the people were building. The Lord said, 'If as one people speaking the same language they have begun to do this, then nothing they plan to do will be impossible for them. Come, let us go down and confuse their language

so they will not understand each other. So the Lord scattered them from there over all the earth, and they stopped building the city. That is why it was called Babel — because there the Lord confused the language of the whole world. From there the Lord scattered them over the face of the whole earth."

To *confuse the language* is a description of mingling many things together in order to bring ruin. The word *confuse* stems from the Latin *confuses*, but can also be broken into *con* and *fuse*, or a fusing of a belief based on deception (i.e., having been tricked). Without understanding the origin of some words, and especially their meaning, we are subject constantly to this *con* of *fusion*. *Kotodama* was understood well by the famous, or infamous to some, Japanese author, and scientist Maseru Emoto, who documented his belief that conciseness could affect the molecular structure of water. Proof for this need not be found in a laboratory setting, however, but in the use of words like *love* and how they make one feel when intended purely and equally received as such. The word *hate* has a similar but opposite energetic strain on the body. Most would prefer to be *loved* than *hated*, and this fact is not merely a matter of the ego, morality, or the simple fact of being human. Mr. Emoto explains his in his book <u>The Hidden Messages in Water</u>:

"We all know that words have an enormous influence on the way we think and feel, and that things generally go more smoothly when positive words are used... Words are an expression of the soul. And the condition of our soul is very likely to have an enormous impact on the water that composes as much as 70 percent of our body, and this impact will in no way effect our bodies. People who are in good health are also generally in good spirits. Indeed, a healthy spirit most comfortably resides in a healthy body."

Much like Japanese, which is a unique, complex, and difficult language, Sanskrit, the sacred language of Hinduism, contains similar concepts relating to sound and vibration. *Anāhata-śabda* is an awareness of pure sound beneath audible sounds. The word anāhata means 'unhurt' or 'unstruck' and relates to the *heart chakra*, while śabda means 'speech' or 'sound'. We therefore obtain the translation of *unstruck speech or sound*. Many interpretations could be provided here but we will focus on the simplest. An 'unstruck' sound is one that resonates within or beyond. An 'unstruck' form of speech is that which requires no verbalization. Our intention here is not to linguistically break apart the *anāhata-śabda* but to demonstrate its relationship with *kotodama*. The underlying theme is that words have a powerful soul/spirit and an unstruck meaning only discernible to a student of the occult. By the fact that God spoke Creation into existence, and that we are emanations of this Source, we are to understand our innate abilities in shaping the world.

The Tower of Babel is also a prototype for Jacob's Ladder, a means by which to reach the seven planetary spheres and zodiac. It is the World Mountain, physical earth, and symbolic of man's own body. Some believe it was an actual monument, in part, likely a type of Babylonian pyramidal ladder called *ziggurat*, used for astronomical observations of the heavens. By observing the heavens one could attune himself with the *Divine Plan* and hear the vibratory harmony of the spheres.

GOD'S WORD
& THE TRINITY

The Tibetan Buddhist and Hindu concept of *OM*, that mystical syllable considered most sacred, is a powerful vibration which speaks the world into existence. It is still used in Sanskrit prayers and texts today. The sound itself is usually broken into a triune of sounds *A – U – M,* an expression of Brahma, Vishnu, and Siva, together the universal *germ* of Creation. The concept of IAO likewise draws on this cosmic *seed*. Isis, Apophis, and Osiris, whose name is further associated with "sperm," are the Egyptian equivalent of the far eastern AUM and the Christian Trinity of Father, Son, and Holy Ghost. Here you also have the past, present, future; the body, mind, soul; and life, death, and resurrection. Witches and pagans may refer to the trinity as mother, maiden, crone. The Greeks called it the *Three Graces*: Euphrosyne, Aglaia, and Thalia. Comparative mythologist Joseph Campbell explains in his book <u>Thou Art That</u>, how the "graces" represent the Holy Trinity:

> *"The first of the three Graces is Euphrosyne, or rapture, sending forth the energy of Apollo into the world. The second is Aglaia, splendor, bringing the energy back. Then, embracing the two, we find Thalia, abundance."*

According to Campbell the *word of creation* is spoken through the sexual metaphor of the teeth and tongue acting as a vagina and penis. He says, *"out of their forming words together all the gods, the heavens, and the world are brought forth."* On that same note, Manly Hall adds that the WORD is made of the seven vowels of the Elohim which are the decree that *"issues as a host of living powers from the 'lips of the Creator'."*

The written and spoken *word* are equally as powerful. When one lacks awareness of such power and subjects the self to the will of others, they are essentially agreeing to become a servant of the *magician*. Take the magician's stereotypical and known tools as an example: wand, chalice, sword, pentacle. The wand represents *will power* and the element of air; the chalice represents *intuition* and water; the sword or athame represents the fiery power of *mind*; and the pentacle represents the *bodily temple* and earth. These instruments are by no means necessary for magical practice of any kind, instead acting as mere assistants to the focusing and concentrating of *intention* and *will*. The same may be said of the magician's robes, selected colors, symbols, and locations for ritual. However, there is far more to be said about the symbols, colors, locations, etc., in that they draw on the energetic signature of that which the magician is attempting to connect with, in order to complete the work.

These symbols are tools that have significant power in carrying out a specific symbolic action. A powerful symbol, if granted its intended meaning, acts upon the imagination, and influences the observer. This may be done itself symbolically in the form of political speeches; media; entertainment of various forms, from trance-inducing music to film; certain methods of writing; and even the ritual of cooking.

The magical wand is similar to the baton used by a conductor in controlling the orchestra through tempo and rhythm. Wands also play a similar role to the scepter, an ornamented staff carried by rulers to denote their sovereignty. Upon additional consideration, the staff acts also as an umbilical cord between man and God or earth and heaven, from whence rulers derive their temporal powers.

In alchemy the *elixir of life* is "truth" found within visible nature, the sun, and in the subterranean and mineral worlds; it is perfect gold. This is the philosophical gold of religion; that absolute and supreme "reason", often referred to as the *Great Work* or *Search for the Absolute*. Gold is the metal of the sun and thus signifies warmth and light, as opposed to the coldness and darkness of hell. The *Great Work* is the ultimate goal of theurgists who attempt an esoteric journey intended to invoke an illuminating awareness of Divinity. In alchemy, this *work* is also referred to as: *god-working, ceremonial magic,* and *Divine action.* One Japanese tradition holds that the hare, which finds refuge on the moon, works with pestle and mortar to make the *elixir of life,* an appropriate symbol considering the significance of the moon in dictating human affairs, starting with menstruation and birth. In the book <u>Occult Science in India and Among the Ancients</u>, Louis Jacolliot explains what it means to be born:

> *"The first birth is merely the advent into material life, the second birth is the entrance to a spiritual life."*

The second birth spoken of here by Louis is a spiritual reawakening akin to the *second coming* of Christ. Attempting to circumvent the process to achieving such alchemical gold results in a *confusion of languages.*

In order to find *salvation* many adherents to one *faith* or another say that we must *follow in the footsteps of* [insert prophet]. They tell us that we will only find redemption by following the *Word of God,* and that this is the only *Way* to a heaven of some sort. This is utterly fascinating from an esoteric point of view. In occultism we would call this deeply esoteric concept *The Way,* that Middle Pillar *pathway of mildness* in Kabbalah, and the footpath of the Buddha. As per the Biblical description of Jesus Christ in John 14:6, we also read: *"I am the way, the truth, and the life."* For Muslims, the Quran says Allah *"will show them the way"* too (*Muhammed* 47:5-6).The Japanese practice of Shintō, which means *Kami Way,* is a parallel example of what we read in the book of John and Muhammed. The *word* itself can be broken down into *shin* and *to* (pronounced toe). *Shin* is a given name relating to *Kami* and *do/to* relates to *michi,* which means *way.* The former can also translate into the word *true.* Therefore, Shintō could mean both *Kami-Way* (kami are *divine beings*) and *True-Way.* The "truth" found in Shintō is *harmony* - just as it is the harmony of the bell (Belle) which works to calm, with love, the beast (a prince trapped in the body of an animal) in the story of *Beauty and the Beast*. Taoism, or Dōkyō, also means *teaching of the way*. These are concepts we find all over the world and throughout virtually every human culture.

The *beast* in this context is really an inverted version of *GOD*, i.e., the *DOG*, or *matter* over *spirit*. This is also the *Yin-Yang* or *Yab-Yum*. That there is a drop of man in God and a drop of God in man – who was created in His image - is represented by the black and white dots.

The Way is a path by which contradiction and dichotomy are replaced with harmony. This is one of the deepest reasons why Jesus Christ was crucified between two thieves or Odin was hung on the World Tree in like manner. Deviating from *The Way* is akin, in either direction, from either point of view, to walking on the left-hand path, which is always associated with sure destruction of self. And thus we may return more directly to our discussion of the power, energy, and influence of *Words*.

The meaning of life may be surmised into what is a simple but profound realization, and certainly a *cliché*, in English. To truly LIVE and LOVE may be stated as the point and purpose of conscious experience, or at least as those things that define our humanity. But what happens when an inversion occurs as a result of wickedness? The left-hand path inverts and distorts. Adherents of this path choose chaos because they have given up their inborn ability to create, having disconnected from Source. LIVE and LOVE therefore become EVIL and EVOL, two words that are certainly spelled differently but also pronounced the same, or almost exactly the same, with the same vibration. The same can be said of LIFE, which is reversed similarly as EFIL. This reversal of meaning is the purest expression of chaos and destruction. For it is the perversion of natural things, not power or nature itself, which constitutes evil. If "God so loved the world" (John 3:16), the opposite must be that Satan, the *great dragon*, 'hated the world'. At the very least, he loved himself more than man. Love thus becomes hatred and EVOL, things that may invert or distort but certainly never create. For "God Said" (Genesis 1:26) in spoken word and Source reached outward and Created ALL. In the book of Psalm 33:6-9 we further learn of the power of *God's Word*:

> *"By the word of the Lord the heavens were made, their starry host by the breath of his mouth. He gathers the waters of the sea into jars; he puts the deep into storehouses. Let all the earth fear the Lord; let all the people of the world revere him. For he spoke, and it came to be; he commanded, and it stood firm."*

To reverse God's Word, which Created the world, is to bring destruction upon the same. In the traditional account of Good vs. EVIL we find GOD (minus a letter from good) and the Devil (add a letter to evil). Satan, the Hebrew *śāṭān*, is the accuser or the adversary, and He who seeks to destroy God's Creation. Creation was an act of living and an imparting of life. When we LIVE each and every day it is best to *live life to the fullest*, within a moral boundary, so that we do not succumb to EVIL influences as in the *Temptation of Jesus* in Matthew 4:1-11.

After the Devil tempted Jesus in these verses with hunger and miracle, he offered *all the kingdoms of the world*. But nothing can be offered that we require and have not already been provided. It is important to realize that *temptations* will cease and the Devil will leave once his advances are rejected. He ultimately has no power except that which we allow, and thus EFIL is something we must cultivate in *sin* by rejecting LIFE:

> *"Then Jesus was led by the Spirit into the wilderness to be tempted by the devil. After fasting forty days and forty nights, he was hungry. The tempter came to him and said, 'If you are the Son of God, tell these stones to become bread.' Jesus answered, 'It is written: 'Man shall not live on bread alone, but on every word that comes from the mouth of God.' Then the devil took him to the holy city and had him stand on the highest point of the temple. 'If you are the Son of God,' he said, 'throw yourself down. For it is written: 'He will command his angels concerning you, and they will lift you up in their hands, so that you will not strike your foot against a stone.' Jesus answered him, It is also written: 'Do not put the Lord your God to the test.' Again, the devil took him to a very high mountain and showed him all the kingdoms of the world and their splendor. 'All this I will give you,' he said, 'if you will bow down and worship me.' Jesus said to him, 'Away from me, Satan! For it is written: 'Worship the Lord your God, and serve him only.' Then the devil left him, and angels came and attended him."*

Buddha was tempted in similar ways, but by rejecting such offerings was illuminated shortly after underneath the *bodhi* tree.

Whereas western traditions see this battle between good and evil as an external event to be experienced at some point in the future, some eastern traditions see it more accurately as an internal battle to be lived daily. It is during our daily routines that we are confronted with devilish temptations and vampiric forms looking to suck the life essence from our bodies. Until we come to *understand* the powerful nature and usage of *words*, then we are more dead than Lazarus, and thus highly vulnerable to the *many tricks* that deceive, along with the manipulative *satanic contracts* that offer to make life easier.

But we must be careful even with our religious and theological approach to such subjects, since the word *religion* is derived from the Latin *religare*, which means *to bind*. Although the Latin *religio* means *reverence*, as in respect for God, we must consider otherwise to what degree *dogma* has restrained our bodies and minds. Control is not necessarily a terrible thing if it provides us with guidance, structure, and civility. How control is used by institutional systems, however, is a matter separate from the latter. For *theology* comes from the Greek *theos* and *logia*, or *God* and *study* – *to study God*. It may also be interpreted as *theos* and *logos*, or the study of *God's Word*, which has certainly been distorted by false prophets for millennia. That WORD is in effect not *spoken* so much as it is the WILL of *creation* acting through the mental determinations of the *Grand Architect*. The Greeks used the term LOGOS, i.e. the WORD, to describe the god of our solar system. Within this WORD was the trinity: *First Logos*, the divine; *Second Logos*, visible universe; and *Third Logos*, the mind. It is evident by this alone that the Christian dogma is by no means unique and is as Greek as it is Oriental.

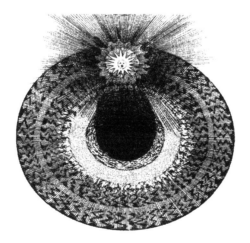

The separation of Earth and Sun by Robert Fludd,
from a 17th-century print. The *Germ* within the *Cosmic Egg* took form
and out of *The One* came *The Many* - those emanations that still
remain part of *Source*.

The dual principle of light & darkness creates the Universe,
from Robert Fludd's <u>Philosophia Mosaica.</u>

The smallest globe atop the others represents Supreme Deity or The One. It is divided in half with one segment representing *divine darkness* that hides Deity and the other a symbol of the *divine light* of God and His Creative Powers.

The larger dark globe on the left is a symbol of the darkness that was upon the face of those primordial waters as Creation began. To its right is a globe of light whence emerges the First Cause of the Supreme Deity, creating light and forming the mundane world by dissipating darkness.

In the central sphere is divided the Superior and Inferior worlds in similar fashion to the *Grand Rosicrucian Alchemical Formula.* Below the central sphere are two half spheres. The one on the left is entirely dark and represents the diurnal hemisphere of the world. The right half globe is the nocturnal hemisphere. These relate to the brain as well.

The Universal Kokoro, according to Sadashizu Yoda.

Unlike the specifics of the Holy Bible or Holy Quran, the Kujiki-72 describes the creation of ALL THINGS as occurring in five forms called WEIGHTS. These *Five Weights* are *Kami*, *Kokoro* (Mind-Heart), Principle (Nature/Behavior), Qi (Vital Energy), and Boundary (State). Avery Morrow, in <u>The Sacred Science of Ancient Japan</u>, describes these *Five Weights* as: *"kami lives, the mind rules, principles preserve, qi determines our fates, and borders create form."*

From the most eastern of traditions, or from the Land of the Rising Sun (Nihon), we acquire a slightly different view of the manifestation of matter and of Creation. This version, as could be argued for some parts of the Bible or Quran, too, is both spiritual and scientific.

In other words, it is a harmonious balancing of Creation, Life, and what will ultimately be Death. That is to say: past, present, and future. The WORD (*logos*) is CREATION out of VOID. The *Five Weights* therefore represent far more than the Creation of "heaven and earth" (Genesis 1:1), providing us with a deeper look at the Grand Architect.

The Ancient of Days by William Blake (1794).

POLY TRICKS
& SATAN'S CLAUSE

Although the word *politic* stems from the Greek *politikos*, and *politēs* (citizen), in *Twilight Language* there is another meaning. Politics breaks down into *poly* and *tics* (ticks). Since *poly* means 'many' and *tic* or *tick* means both 'muscle spasm' or 'parasitic arachnids', the word *politics* literally means 'many parasites'. A *tick* is also the sound made by a clock; and once more, as we know, *Father Time* is the god Saturn.

These *many parasites* play a game similar to the ones played in court, or on a *court*, convincing the public to take sides on different teams that have their own mascots and colors - donkey or elephant / blue or red. Countless people are so thoroughly convinced by this dichotomy that they have reverted to zealotry and tend to lean toward anarchy with no trust whatsoever in the political system. Such extreme and biased ideologies are as possessing of the mind as physical possessions are of the body.

Although people clamor on about *democracy* and voting, few stop to define the former word. A democracy is merely 51% deciding how 49% can live their lives. It is, in fact, similar to *mob rule*. The Greek word *dēmokratia* stems from *dēmos* and *kratia*, meaning *people* and *power* respectively. So, it is this *power of the people*, or *mob rule*, with no consideration for the *rule of law*, or any legalities, that consumes the political minded. Without the *law* there is total chaos and only the domination of an ever changing minority by an ever changing majority. This is one of the greatest political tricks of the blood sucking ticks we call parasites. It is a contract we make to live with a governing body that pays lip service only, it seems, to *the people* and their *rights*. For a *person* is merely "a character in a play or story," someone to be played, while a *rite* is a ceremony or act, something that is performed rather than maintained as inalienable. For more on this see my book *Liberty Shrugged*.

The contrived *uniparty*, as it is called, which operates under the guise of *choice (democracy)*, is thus like the *Old Man of the North*, bringing presents to the "nice" and coal to the "naughty." In other words, the uniparty delivers special privileges and gives protected class status to its supporters while prosecuting its opponents. It is always there to protect its supporters with its *presence*.

The character we know as "Santa Claus" is an exemplification of the above. Although "Santa" may be derived from another source, the name is an anagram for Satan, an influence associated with and derived from saturnine intelligence. His white and black characteristics are exemplified by his personification as either Santa or Krampus. His *naughty or nice list*, which grants rewards or punishments to children based on behavior, is another symbol of his persona. Rewards are granted by Santa in the form of presents while Krampus usually beats children as punishment for some cosmic transgression. If the *punishment* is coal, we therefore have a substance that is burnt and thus associated with hell, while the former *presents* are similar to divine blessing which come down from heaven.

The "Santa Claus" of this agreement is only one letter short of the "clause" in a contract: *"a particular and separate article, stipulation, or proviso in a treaty, bill, or contract."* This contractual obligation, the *clause*, is the agreement as per whether a child will receive a blessing or be damned - presents or coal. In the case of Santa Claus, or *Satan's Clause*, punishment and coal are given by Krampus.

These are all things to be *understood* in the context of esoteric and occult thought.

UNDERSTANDING WORDS & GRAMMAR

If we are to UNDERSTAND something we must first STAND UNDERNEATH of that thing, be it physically or intellectually. From the Old English *understandan*, we stand under the authority of police, judges, teachers, parents, and the like. This is not necessarily a terrible thing unless those in power abuse their authority to force a particular standing. This is why it is critical to UNDERSTAND the meanings of LIFE, LIVE, and LOVE, and their subsequent wicked inversions into EFIL, EVIL and EVOL. Although the spelling is different in both directions the word still resonates the same, and thus its meaning is similar if not identical. Here we are introduced once again to *Twilight Language.*

It is imperative we UNDERSTAND the meanings and uses of common word before we ever utter their energetic and vibratory frequency. In the *writing* of this book there is requirement for *spelling* words and organizing sentences, with an intention to convey meaning and provoke thought. Depending on the font selected on a computer, other forms of writing include the joining of characters in a script called *cursive.*

To *spell* is to write the letters that form a word in correct sequence. The German word *beech*, a type of tree, is also one of the foundations for the word *book*. In fact, it was on *beech* that the famous runes were carved. Just as Jesus was crucified on a cross (made of *Paradise Plant*) and pierced by the spear of the Roman soldier Longinus, so too was Odin in Norse mythology. Odin is the supreme god and creator, the god of victory and the dead. He was hung on the *Yggdrasil* or *World Tree* with a spear thrust into his side. The reason of his suffering was similar to the suffering of Prometheus, who took fire from the sun and gave it to mankind. Odin won the knowledge of Runes, too, by suffering for mankind. Runes become powerful magical inscriptions that were inscribed on metal, wood, stone, etc. Once their knowledge was obtained by the Odin, he then gifted them to man. This produced the first *books*, which were composites of *spells* and *curses* intended to heal or invoke. It is the same story in Egypt where the god Thoth invented writing.

Our books today tell stories, including those of myth, and are likewise composed of words that are spelled, sentences that are constructed, and so on.

The word *spell* can be understood as the writing or speaking of the letters that form a word or name. A *spell* can also be a sign or symbol of something, like with Norse runes or Chinese kanji. From the Germanic base we also derive an older definition for *spell*, which is *"a form of words used as a magical charm or incantation."* Furthermore, this version of *spell* comes from the Latin *incantatio*, or *incantare*, which means to *chant* and *bewitch*. The definition of *incantation* is *"a series of words said as a magical spell or charm"* while the definition of *bewitch* is to *"cast a spell over (someone)."*

To *spell* is to have an ability to control people through a form of *word magic*, or *voces magicae*. It is the mastery of orthography.

To *write* is to mark down coherent letters and words on a surface of some sort. Although not derived from an original based for the word *ritual*, a *rite* is a religious or other type of ceremony. It is *"a body of customary observances"* characterize and defined through social customs, tradition, and convention.

To write in *cursive* is to string or run together a series of letters into words, as from the Latin *curs*, which means 'run'. Certain symbols like the Triquetra, an ancient symbol meaning 'three cornered' in Latin, can be drawn in a single stroke without the utensil leaving the paper. Anything written or drawn in such a way is thought to have additional magical qualities, as with *cursive*. In Christianity the Triquetra symbol represents the Holy Trinity. Elsewhere it is symbolic of any three-fold concept such as heaven, earth, and hell, or past, present, and future.

To *curse* is also to speak a blasphemous word or phrase with strong emotion, either internally or audibly as an utterance intended to invoke a supernatural power to inflect harm on someone else. It is the *"solemn utterance intended to invoke a supernatural power"* and *"a coarse or blasphemous word or phrase."* Therefore, we find that if we are to *write* in *cursive* and to *spell* out a word, we are engaging with *kotodama* and *anāhata-śabda*, and practicing a ritual or ceremony with intent to conjure our ideas into material existence like a *tulpa*, *golem*, or *egregore*.

The word *grammar* has similar origins, acting as a whole structure of language in general. Grammar comes from the Greek *grammatikē*, defined as the *"art of letters,"* and *gramma*, which is a thing that is written. In Old French, *grammatica* became *gramaire* before eventually transforming into the word we know today as *grammar* sometime during the 14th-century. This is when *grammar* was only a reference to Latin. The word *gramaire* also had the meaning of *magic* or *enchantment*. This is the basis for why *grammar* in its many forms eventually led to the forming of the word *grimoire*, or the sorcerer's *book of spells*. Grammar therefore is directly linked to witchcraft and any area of study within the realms of magic. The word *glamour*, which also has a basis in magic, meaning *magical spell*, therefore relates to the enchantment of illusory beauty. In other words, it is *vanity*, which is from the Latin *vanus*, or to be *"empty, without substance."* This is something we find in abundance within politics, media, and the *Hollywood* system.

MOVIE MAGIC & CURRENCY

Consider an idea for a story that may end up being rendered as a movie. The idea flows as energy from *ethereal space* into the mind and into the brain. That idea is then transmitted by electric pulses in the body out through the hands and onto a medium like paper with the use of a graphite or ink utensil. The *pen is mightier than the sword* since the former can provoke the use of the latter.

Once on paper the story may be transferred to a computer and printed on clean white paper with fresh ink. As the idea is ritualized and purified it becomes more life-like, manifesting as a real *thought form*. The process continues throughout production of the film and is finalized with a traditional *wrap party* wherein those involved in making a movie celebrate the end of its filming. Beyond the story is consideration for the actors, set design, lighting, costumes, symbolism, colors, editing, and the like that will be placed in the film and result in its completion.

The showing of our movie is simply this: *putting on a show.* That show is projected, downloaded, loaded, or streamed as a *broadcast*. This broad *casting* involves the projection of what was *spelled* out in the script, or through handwriting as distinct from print. It is all a special type of *rite* with dialogue and garb selectively chosen.

If our movie is shown on television, it is known as television broadcasting or *television broad casting*. The *television* is what is told (what 'they' *tell*) to our *vision*. Generally, we call this *television programming*, the process of preparing something like a rite or ritual to have influence on the viewer, who in this case becomes subject to a form of mind control by means of suggestibility, propaganda, subliminal messaging, and sub-conscious rewriting.

If our movie is simply *screened* in a *theater*, there is still a ritual projection or allusion being cast. The dim lighting, selected seats, unique smells, and our food and beverages are all part of the staged production. The word *theater* itself comes from the Greek *theatron* and *theasthai*, which means to "behold" something, perhaps even with *suspended disbelief,* or the act of *believing something that isn't true*. The word *entertain* likewise has a similar meaning. From the Lain *inter* and *tenere*, which means *among* and *to hold,* respectively, we get a definition of "entertainment" that means *to be held in a form of perceptual bondage.*

Even the word *hollywood* has this deeper meaning. Holly wood is in fact a type of wood famous for its use in the crafting of magical wands. Druids, the priestly class of the ancient Celtic culture, saw holly as a magical tree, sacred for making wands. In typical parlance we refer to a movie theater as the *silver screen*, which shares a relationship with the grayish storms conjured up by the Druidic magicians. The *movie magic* of *hollywood* likewise fits into our magical lexicon. This is all a magical formula meant to influence an audience into various states of emotion - laughter, fear, tension - in order to make money (currency).

It makes no difference if the movie is screened in theaters, streamed from online services, rented in kiosks, downloaded online, or purchased on DVD. In every single instance, and others, including the discussion of the film on social media for promotional means, energy is being exchanged. When one makes a purchase, they are exchanging *money* - electrical *currency* - and therefore paying with *energy*. When one focuses their attention on the film we say that they are *paying attention*, a payment charged at the expense of physical and mental energy, which must likewise be exhausted in order to earn money, or currency, for making financial payments. We must also make these payments in *time*, though some*times* we do not have the *money* or *time* to watch a movie.

Archdruid in his Judicial Habit by Samuel Rush Meyrick and Charles Hamilton Smith, from their *Costume of the Original Inhabitants of the British Isles* (1815).

IN THE MOURNING

Money (currency) is still mostly *earned* in a traditional fashion by working five days a week, usually *weekdays* excluding *weekends*, at a *job* that few truly enjoy. For many people it is a great *undertaking* to simply *wake* up in the *morning* and go to work. A great deal of people thus drink alcohol (*spirits*) to take the edge off after a long day and to relax.

The previous three sentences are riddled with what we have termed *Twilight Language*. If *money is the root of all evil* and the latter is an inversion of LIVE, then to *earn a living* is to earn something akin to death. To *earn* is to *urn*, a container used to store the ashes of a cremated person. When somebody makes excessive amounts of money, we say they *made a killing*.

It can easily be said that we earn (urn) money (currency) on weekdays (weak days), which culminate at the end of the week (weak) with an ending of the weakness, a time for us to rest for the next week - weekend (weak end).

As we all age it is also a fact that we weaken mentally and physically, due in part to the work we undertake in our lives. Our jobs are also more than a paid position of regular employment: the Biblical meaning of the name (or word) *Job* is to *weep* and *cry*.

When we view our *job* as a stressful *undertaking* there is a parallel to *understanding* what it means to earn (urn) money (currency) on weekdays (weak days) at a job (cry) we don't much enjoy, i.e., the *undertaker* is a manager of a funeral.

Even when we *wake* up in the morning we are faced with a similar situation, since a *wake* is the holding of vigil beside the body of someone who has died. It could be said that every morning we awaken in *mourning*, an "expression of deep sorrow for someone who has died," since we open our eyes into physical realty and consciously come back into the world from an unconscious state of being. Every morning is thus a little death of the soul brought about by consciously regaining our physicality.

Lastly, when we choose to drink alcohol in any amount we are essentially engaging with *spirits* and making temporarily contracts and agreements with them to feel better, numb ourselves, or get a simple 'buzz'. We do this because our *undertakings* make us *mourn* and our *jobs* are unpleasant.

MARITIME LANGUAGE & THE GOOD SHEPHERD

Perhaps we are far too possessed by spirits to recognize the perception altering nature of the English language in particular. Since money is currency and we pay for things with these various forms of energy, it is no surprise to find similar wordplay in general financial matters too. For how does a current flow but between two riverbanks, where the movements of energy, currency, and water rush along like an electrical line transmitting power from a substation to residential community.

The *bank* is where we keep our currency or *current-you-see*. When most people decide to buy a house, they go to a *currency bank* and obtain a *mortgage*, by which the creditor lends money at interest in exchange for taking title of the debtor's property, with the condition that once the debt is paid the title becomes void. The word *mortgage* stems from Old French and literally means 'dead pledge'. It is no wonder so many people awake (a wake) in the morning (mourning) and stress about their job (weeping) since they have to work in order to pay their *death pledge*. When the mortgage is turned upside down, or a home loan has a higher principal than what the house is worth, it is said the pledge is *underwater*.

When a company or firm is in a tough financial situation, they will convert their assets to money and pay off their debts. This is called *liquidation*, or to *liquidate*. Obviously, the word *liquidate* contains the word *liquid*, as in the water flowing by a *current* along a riverbank. When assets are turned into liquid, they are called *liquid assets* and include things like cash, or simply the available balances of accounts. When a *bank* decides to foreclose on a house, they seek to take *possession* of a mortgaged property (*dead pledge*) since the debtor is unable to make their payments. The word *foreclose* comes from Old French for 'to close' and Middle English to 'shut out'. This foreclosure is a *four-closure*, or the closing in of four walls to oust what is inside and perhaps replace it with a new possessor.

This relationship to water is also found with the influence of the moon on earth's oceans. The cycles and phases of the moon, from whence we acquire the word *moonth* or month, are the basis for our 12-month calendar. They are derived from the roughly 28-

day cycle of the moon. There is also a strong connection to the female menstrual cycle with the word *menstrual* being derived from the Latin word *mensis,* which means *month.* It is indeed the element of *water* most associated with the curvature and fluidity of the female body, mind, and emotion. From the *emotion* we derive the *ocean,* which can be both calm and turbulent, and is often referred to as 'her' or 'she'.

The Trident from Eliphas Levi's *Transcendental Magic*

Although the trident is a common symbol associated with Satan, it is actually a powerful tool of creative influences. It is a pentacle expressing the synthesis of trinity in the monad, which forms the sacred *tetrad.* The trident was a three-pronged spear and in classical mythology associated with the Roman Neptune, or Greek Poseidon, god of the seas, water, and earthquakes. Because of the trident being associated with water it became the alchemical symbol of this element. The trident is also a tool of fire since its three-prongs resemble flames. It is therefore a symbol of thunderbolts and lightning. Unfolding the outer prongs of this staff creates the cross, which is representative of all four elements. Also called the *Trisula* this staff gave its possessor triune powers. It is a symbol of the Hindu God Shiva, representing the threefold qualities of Creator, whose followers wear a trident-like symbol called *Tilaka.* When Shiva wielded this staff, it represented the three phases of time: past, present, and future; and the three conceptual worlds: heaven, earth, and hell. It also represents the *Three Jewels* of the Buddha, the Dharma, and the Sangha. The Scandinavian Thor, god of thunder, weather, and agriculture, also carried this staff. Much like the *Mjolni,* a magical hammer belonging to Odin, the *Gungnir* is a tool like the trident that always strikes its target and then returns like a boomerang. It is also called *Odin's Spear* or *Odin's Javelin*. As a symbol of water universally, and thus with the moon due to its pull on our oceans, the trident is a symbol of *emotions* or em-oceans. Our emotions furthermore trigger bodily responses to emit moisture in the form of tears.

We find the same references to water in the leftover fragments of maritime law and the Roman empire. The *Holy See*, or *the See of Rome*, is the jurisdiction of the Pope and his authority as bishop of contemporary Rome. The *Holy Sea* and the *Sea of Rome*, or the entire world, should be obvious. And what comes out of the ocean if not fish, one of the primary symbols of Jesus Christ. Christians still use the simple fish outline with the letters IXOYE, a combination of the first letter of five Greek words which translates to "Jesus Christ Son of God Savior." In Hinduism it is Vishnu, the preserver in the sacred trinity, who incarnates firstly as a fish. In Mesopotamian mythology the fish-god Oannes, not unlike the Chinese ruler Fohi from around 2,752 BC, came up from the water and taught civilization. The Pope's *mitre* hat still mimics the headdress of Oannes while his ring caries the fisherman motif. Early Christians were seen in this manner, as fish being born out of the baptismal waters - dangerous illusions to those who lack *faith*.

It was on the open ocean, away from the *law of the land*, that pirates would attack and rob ships. The flying of a friendly flag, or *false flag*, would convince other ships to get close enough before they were ruthlessly attacked and pillaged. The Knights Templar famously flew the *skull and crossbones* flag as they raided British ships, thus providing the iconic image of pirates to this day.

Many also suggest that Matthew 28:20 has some reference to the Roman Empire, too, when Jesus says, *"I am with you always, even unto the end of the world."* Since Rome was, and still is in many ways, both the world and ocean, Jesus will be with us always, even until the end of man's empires. In astrological terms this idea is equally as relevant. In Luke 22:8-11 we read the following about preparation for Passover:

> *"Jesus sent Peter and John, saying, 'Go and prepare for us to eat the Passover. 'Where do You want us to prepare it?' they asked. He answered, 'When you enter the city, a man carrying a jug of water will meet you. Follow him to the house he enters, and say to the owner of that house, 'The Teacher asks: Where is the guest room, where I may eat the Passover with My disciples?'"*

Since Jesus and his disciples are interpreted as the sun and twelve signs of the zodiac, and the Passover was the Last Supper before the crucifixion, the *man carrying a jug of water* is possibly Aquarius, the water bearer. This means that Jesus, the sun, is about to die and that a new *sign* will soon replace him. The age of the bull, Taurus, was ended when Mithra(s) plunged his knife into the bull's back. The age of the ram, Ares, also depicted as a sheep for which Jesus was the shepherd, was ended by the birth of the latter bringing in the age of Pisces.

There is much overlapping between symbols of one age to the next with Jews to this day still blowing the ram's horn and Christians adorning the *Agnus Dei* and the fish. From Pisces we are approaching the age of Aquarius. This is called the precession of the equinoxes, which occurs because of the spin of earth's axis, marked with a 2,160-year cycle. It is processional because it takes the sun roughly 25,000 years to move counterclockwise through all 12 houses of the Zodiac with each passing marked roughly by 2,160 years. Each house is of course constructed by the *Grand Architect* or *Earthly Carpenter*. The redeemer is always born of an immaculate conception in the sign ascending at the vernal equinox. For Pisces the savior is associated with fish and for previous ages it is Aries the ram or lamb, and Taurus the bull or *golden calf*. This is why Jesus is the ALPHA and OMEGA, or the end of one age and beginning of another, i.e., Aries and Pisces – the *Lamb of God* and *Fisher of Men*. Shiva, the supreme creator in Hinduism, is also called *he who is without beginning and without end* in the Sanskrit text *Upanishad*.

The First Incarnation of Vishnu from Picart's *Religious Ceremonials*.

Water is also the primary element in the ultimate expression of femininity, i.e., birth. But before birth there obviously must be an act of copulation. Before that there must be, at the very least, the simplest of interactions resulting in some form of mutual attraction. Whether it is one-nightstand (seeing a *nightstand* only once before leaving) or a long-term connection, there exists a *relationship*, and where does a relationship (relation *ship*) reside if not on the tempestuous waters of passion.

Although many refer to their significant other as a *partner*, this is a word best utilized to describe short-term relations since a *partner* will soon *depart* from port like a ship. In Middle English the word is *pautenere*, which means "promiscuous woman" or *prostitute*. As such, a prostitute is temporary engaged in the activity of whatever the person making payment desires.

When a *couple* choose to marry, they are essentially merging their lives into a *cooperation* in terms of companionship (companion ship) and economics. Thus, they *board* the ship and usually move in with one another as part of their agreement to share their lives together. They will sleep in the same bed in the same room in the same house, thus sharing *room and board* on their *companion ship*.

They obtain a *marriage license*, perform a ritual, and then leave for the honeymoon. The latter word can be broken into *honey* and *moon*, a reference to the sweetness of love and sex (honey), which is a *desire* (the moon) of the couple. At this point they get in each other's *business* officially after obtaining their license. The *marriage contract*, ceremony, and honeymoon act as a series of business arrangements to produce a familiarity and bond going forward with future business. The sexual euphemism of *getting busy* is a reference to the traditional requirement of procreation, to re-produce goods by *showing each other the goods*. Copulation of sexual organs is the *merging of assets*, alongside the merging of physical and financial assets through legal marriage. The process of re-*production* to create more *goods* is the method by which a baby is born. We call that baby a *bundle of joy* and a *product of love*.

The process of birth follows the same esoteric pattern. When a woman is set to go into labor her *water breaks* and contractions come in *waves*. The baby then proceeds down the *birth canal*, defined as a waterway allowing for passage of boats or ships. These ships, we assume, must *dock* at some point to offload their *goods*, take on new *goods*, and replenish their supplies. When this occurs there is a manifest of the ship's cargo that changes appropriate hands. Who else but a *doctor* has *docked* (tie up at a dock, to load or unload cargo) in the waterway and is ready to issue a *certificate of birthed* 'goods'.

Before any of this can even happen, however, a woman must be impregnated with *semen* (sea men) that enter her *vessel*.

Formal and legal marriage is thus the creation of a *business* partner-*ship* filled with waves of ecstasy and tempest. If the latter becomes too severe one may choose to leave the marriage and their *partner*, which by the word implies separation from the start. A *divorce* is the legal *dissolving* of the marriage, just as certain things dissolve and part ways in water. Some may finally say a *marriage* is then nothing more than a *mirage*, or an optical illusion created by certain atmospheric conditions like those often encountered by sailors (*Fata Morgana*).

When we focus our attention on the *goods* offloaded at the *dock* and certified *alive*, we are faced with the manifestation of spirit in *corporeal* form. We get this word from the Latin *corporeus*, which means 'body'. The *corporeus* is obviously the base for *corpse,* a dead body, and *corporation,* a group of people acting as a single entity by giving up - killing - their individuality. A *corporation* is thus the corpse of many people authorized as a single entity to legally act in matters of business.

Most businesses rely heavily on *contracts*, not unlike that of a marriage, for selling and buying goods, or hiring and retaining employees. The *contract* is a written or spoken agreement enforceable by law. In both etymological terms and *Twilight Language* it is a *con-tract*, i.e., the *tract*, or the drawing up of an idea to use deception (con) in persuading someone to do or believe something. Businesses often hold *con-ference calls* and *con-ferences.* Much of what goes on in the business world, and finances in general, could be said to *confuse,* or *con-fuse,* the average person. It blends together various forms of deception in aim of achieving a specific end – the acquisition of *currency* and the obtaining of more oceanic territory.

Legalese is one of the main vehicles for such deception. As the formal and technical language of legal document it is openly difficult to understand and thus very *confusing*. There is a major different between what is *legal* and what is *lawful*. The former is concerned with the *law* itself and the latter with what is permitted by law. Something can be *legal* but not necessarily *lawful*. Something may be against the *law* but not necessarily *illegal*. One of the best examples of *legalese* comes in the form of a statement of intention. In order to exercise certain *inalienable rights,* one must *declare* rather than *request* an exemption or right.

Legal courts are also expressions of *Twilight Language* to the point of being humorous. Firstly, a *court* is where a game is played, like basketball or tennis. Secondly, each side, both defendant and plaintiff, are organized into *teams*. Thirdly, the judge acts as *referee*. The defendant and plaintiff attorneys pass the ball back and forth on the court, passing the argument around like the striking of a tennis ball with a *racket*, which is arguably what the whole thing is all about. The *ball is in your court* now.

~

One may also wonder why formal legal proceedings are overseen by a person in the same garb as a high school or college graduate. Both wear black robes (colors vary for schools), graduates wear square hats, and judges bang a gavel as a symbol of authority. When we are dealing with what is legal or lawful, and with squares and the avoidance of color in black, then it must be symbolically the planet Saturn being called upon. Saturn is the father of time, necessary evil, agriculture, rule, and dissolution, as with those things that dissolve in water - perhaps the waters of chaos. Saturn is known as the *lord of the rings* and we adorn everything from our ears to fingers with his symbol. For royalty they wear his crown. As an elder god of ancient pantheons, who goes by many other names, Saturn is a cornerstone of powerful forces. He is also Capricorn, the goat which has typically been burdened with superstitious fears, doubts, and sins, and then sacrificed for atonement. Here we find part of the basis for the "scapegoat," originally an actual goat stressed with all of the sins of a community, driven from the town, and then killed in the belief that all wrongdoings or thoughts would be forgiven. The Hittite's, whose kingdom lasted from approximately 1800 to 1175 BCE in the near East, used a similar method to protect their military. Rams and a woman carrying beer and bread would be taken through the army camp before being driven from Hittite territory. From Saturn's elder form (EL) we also obtain the word elite, election, electricity, and even angelic. EL is also the Hebrew name for God, and further means *power* and *might*.

We are reminded of the Elohim and elementary particles that comprise our physical (physics-EL) world, for which Saturn is the Grand Architect with tools such as a hammer or gavel. As *Father Time*, who is represented by a square and cube, Saturn is rightly at home in New York City's Time Square. In fact, since New York is called *The Big Apple*, the *fruit* of deception and enlightenment, we can surmise that the patron of this world-famous place is indeed the *Lord of the Rings*. It is also from the Greek god *khronos* that we get Cronus and chronology, the arrangement of events or dates in the order of their occurrence. From this we order our days, weeks, months, years, decades, ad infinitum.

The Good Shepherd, 1878 by Bernhard Plockhorst.

Jesus Christ is the Alpha and Omega, i.e., the end of Aries and beginning of Pisces. He is thus called both the *Lamb of God* and *Fisher of Men*. Aries is the lamb. Pisces is the fish. Bacchus is often depicted with a lamb in his arms, and it was the *Unconquered Sun*, Mithra(s), who was met by shepherds when he was born in a grotto. Hermes, the Greek "guide of souls," or *psychopompos*, is commonly depicted as a *Good Shepherd* carrying a goat. The Greek musician and poet Orpheus was also known as the *Good Shepherd*. Egyptian Pharaohs are famous for holding the *crook* and *flail*, objects to herd the bull (Taurus), a previous age, and the ram (Aries), the age preceding Pisces. Author and forensic geologist Scott Wolter writes of the Egyptian King Akhenaten, who is often depicted with the crook and flail: *"Akhenaten's attempt to unite the followers of both religions is one of the multiple meanings symbolized by the crook and flail. The flail herds the bulls or the followers of Taurus, and the crook was used to herd the sheep or the followers of Aries."*

LANGUAGE AS MAGIC

Languages and *Alphabets* are composed of symbols we call letters, a written or printed communication, which resonates to certain frequencies or vibrations as expressed visually or verbally. The sounds of animals, insects, the human voice, and the playing of instruments, are all an expression of symbols in auditory form. Spoken words and music utilize the vibration of symbols in auditory form.

The sound of music or the uttering of incantations are felt in mind and body to have profound energies that provoke people into a state of ecstasy or, if used for nefarious purposes, anger, and depression. As Pythagoras defined harmony as the essence of God, songs and dancing have always been used to evoke the presence of Creator and align oneself with the energies of the planetary spheres, as is the case of *whirling dervishes*. In the case of the largely imagined *Black Mass* we learn of witches invoking infernal powers by aligning themselves with diabolic forces through profanity and sacrilegious behaviors.

The utterance of certain words with proper intention can produce powerful influences. This is why the names of people and places can be powerful forces. This is the reason why many associate themselves with gods or planetary intelligences by name. It is the sympathetic reason why some attempt to call upon heavily energies with sigils. It is the reason that one may feel energetically drawn to an individual, location, or a specific text. Certain philosophic truths resonate at frequencies that attract those ready to understand them but repel those yet to develop the capacity for understanding such information or having such thought.

In reciting magic incantations, especially in Egypt, it was believed that not only names, but also every spoken word had a powerful effect. But to have such an effect a word must be spoken correctly with proper intonation. To master this quality one must study rhythm too.

Words are incredibly powerful, because they not only retain the power of a symbol but also the deeper meaning of that image. In this way words can be substituted for other things and those things can then be commanded as per their name. This is why having the name of an angel, demon, spirit, etc., and especially their energetic signature, has always been thought necessary in magical practices.

To have the name of something is to have power over whatever it may be. This is the meaning behind Genesis 2:19-20 where it is described that the Lord God formed wild animals and birds, and then allowed man to name each of these living creatures:

> *"Now the Lord God had formed out of the ground all the wild animals and all the birds in the sky. He brought them to the man to see what he would name them; and whatever the man called each living creature, that was its name. So the man gave names to all the livestock, the birds in the sky and all the wild animals."*

In this way *man* was given *dominion*, and with it *responsibly*, over Creation. As the intellectual principle, Adam's dominion is equated to his observation and understanding of the manifest world. Later we will learn the significance of this in relation to the zodiac, or *animal wheel*.

As Heinrich Cornelius Agrippa writes in his masterpiece Occult Philosophy of this power:

> *"For hence voices and words have efficacy in magical works: because that in which nature first exerciseth magic efficacy, is the voice of God."*

Therefore, letters derive their efficacy from the harmony of the voice, and their value by their written symbol, as is the same with numbers. In occult studies we learn that a word is considered twofold; that there is expressed an internal and external form. Internal expressions are conceived by the mind and soul, and those of an external nature are expressed by the bodily senses. Names are also twofold; at physical birth man is given a name, but like the body it is only an identification with an infernal experience - only God retains man's true name.

~

Some words are considered too sacred and powerful to be uttered by the tongue of man and so the name of God has many minor variations; God's personal name being composed of four Hebrew Letters - YHVH.

Words with multiple meanings, or those with different methods of spelling that still retain the same pronunciation, are thought to have a more powerful influence on the physical and spiritual realms. In casting a *spell*, words written out of order as an anagram, or those written backwards, are believed to direct darker and more malevolent energies. Writing the name of God backwards is meant to invoke His negative - what is known as the Black God. For the White God is merely a reflection of the former and vice versa. Writing backwards the name Aphrodite, the goddess of love in Greece, is perhaps useful in invoking hatred rather than love. Any writing or speaking of magical phrases in reverse is believed to invert their intended effects. This is why some recite the Lord's Prayer in reverse or sign contracts specify details written the same. A famous case of this came in 1634 with the accusation against Father Urbain Grandier, who supposedly signed a contract with several demons, and Satan himself, in both blood and in reverse.

~

Sometimes a powerful word may be extract from another word, or a name from a name, as is the case of *Messia*, משיה from *Ismah*, ישמה, and *Michael* from *Malachi*, מלאכי. Words are powerful, especially when performed with a specific intention through the *will* or *desire* of the operator. They are the instruments of enchanters and occult vehicles for attracting or repelling those things we desire. As philosopher Alan Watts writes of the power of language and words:

> *"Language in its broadest sense, including words, numbers, signs, and symbols of all kinds, is what peculiarly distinguishes men from animals, and enables us to know that we know. Language is the symbolic echo of direct experience, lending to it resonance that enhances it - as a great cathedral, with its subtle reverberations, lends an other-worldly magnificence to the voice of a choir."*

Francis Barrett further explains in <u>The Magus</u> how *"the virtue of man's words are so great, that, when pronounced with a fervent constancy of the mind, they are able to subvert Nature, to cause earthquakes, storms, and tempests."* The most barbarous and unintelligible words are said to have the most powerful nature in *black magic*. But, likewise, elegance and beauty in language has a power unlike that of the darker arts. Roger Bacon (1214-1294), the English philosopher and scientist, writes on the power of words in relation to the soul:

> "We must consider that it has great force; all miracles at the beginning of the world were made by the word. And the peculiar work of the rational soul is the word, in which the soul rejoices. Words have a great virtue when they are pronounced with concentration and deep desire, with the right intention and confidence. For when these four things are joined together, the substance of the rational soul is moved more quickly to act according to its virtue and essence, upon itself and upon exterior things."

As David Frankfurter further explains in his essay, 'Narrating Power: The Theory and Practice of the Magical Historiola in Ritual Spells', the power of narration is *a 'power' intrinsic to any narrative, any story, uttered in a ritual context, and the idea that the mere recounting of certain stories situates or directs their 'narrative' power into this world.* This is why *spells, curses, incantations, utterances,* and even *intonation* are considered so powerful. The naming of a *disease* or *demon*, often the purveyor of the former, is so important because it gives the magician, or doctor in this case, a knowledge of the evil to be exorcised. The power of words, or *word magic*, is intrinsic within the reservoirs of ancient thought and creation, existing as gods, goddess, heroes, heroines, archetypes, and the like. Using iconographic images or quotations from scriptures are commonalities in ritual magic and spells in particular. As Frankfurter puts it, *"the power of a story was also accessible through the concrete letters that told it."* The magician attempts to draw on the power of certain words, names, stories, and myths into the present operation by endowing a current idea with a past energy which has proven its reliability. The Romans called this magical practice *voces magicae*, the use of *magic names* and *magic words* that can be written in Greek or Latin. Perhaps nowhere in the world, however, was this more important than in Egypt. Here it was the *word*, spoken, inscribed, or etched, which birthed creation in likeness to Genesis.

In Japanese magic there is a magical grid comprised of nine lines drawn one at a time, starting with a horizontal stroke, then vertical, and so forth moving right and then down. Each line corresponds to a concept within the sacred Japanese system of *Kuji*, defined as a series of simple *mantras*. It is broken into four parts that include the nine basic 'words of power', the *Kuji In* (mudra) hand gestures corresponding to the nine words, the protective grid known as *Kuji Kiri*, and a tenth symbol known as *Juji*. In numerology, there are also nine forces connected to the numbers one through nine. These *nine words of power* remind us here of the Eight Immortals of China and Egypt's Ra, whose descendants are known as *Ennead*, or the Nine Gods of Heliopolis. The *Nagas* of Hinduism, or semi-divine serpent beings, are likewise thought to be eight or nine in number.

OPERATING SYSTEMS

Language and grammar are the systems by which our society operates; they are the basis for communication, relationships, business, etc. Without *understanding* conflicts easily arise as a result of *confusion*.

In the Biblical book of Genesis, we read that *"the whole world had one language and a common speech"* - (Genesis 11:1). The people, however, angered the Lord for attempting to build *"a city, with a tower that reaches to the heaven."* So, the Lord said, *"Come, let us go down and confuse their language so they will not understand each other."* So, the Lord did go about confusing their languages and then scattering *"them from there over all the earth."*

Such a story conveys and implies far more than the confusion of mankind over *languages*, which are not specified in the story to be verbal communications. Perhaps the *confusion* stems from the introduction of vastly different languages into the human world. The *"one language and a common speech"* therefore could relate to a universal language of symbols and intuition, or simply *knowing*.

After the introduction of *language*, by our modern definition, mankind became confused and unable to communicate. This story could also refer to a cataclysmic event which toppled man-made technologies and resulted in the resettling of different groups of people *"over all the earth."* The *"one language and a common speech"* separated and thus developed into the different forms of communication we have today.

Furthermore, having a *"common speech"* implies that there were uncommon forms of speech in use at the time when *"the whole world had one language."* The idea that man would attempt to build a *"tower that reaches to the heaven"* is also relatable to the Chiram Abiff story in masonic lore.

The three ruffians responsible for the Grand Master's death are only guilty because they attempted to circumvent the processes of initiation by stealing the secrets of the master mason, just as man attempted to reach heaven by theft with the construction of the *tower* in the first place.

Out of Egypt we can observe the same idea, as told in a story by the philosopher Socrates. In the myth is Thoth, Egyptian god of writing, who approaches Amon, King of all Egypt, and urges him to introduce the practice of writing for all people to enjoy:

"O King, here is something that, once learned, will make the Egyptians wiser and will improve their memory; I have discovered a potion for memory or wisdom."

Amon quickly responds with great wisdom, asserting that a written language in particular is in fact a destructive force against memory and wisdom. He says, *"it will introduce forgetfulness into the soul of those who learn it."* Amon concludes his comments with respect to the great god Thoth:

"Your invention will enable them to hear many things without being properly taught, and they will imagine that they have come to know much while for the most part they will know nothing."

If the world truly had o*ne language and a common speech* in the remotest of human existence then perhaps it was an ability to connect with the *divine* in a way, we are unable to conceive of today, at least without the assistance of conscious altering substances.

As the world crystalized even further from the point of Creation, according to esoteric tradition, that connection with *Source* was increasingly severed and man was rendered lost and abandoned, kicked out of the preverbal Garden *paradise*. The gods of antiquity effectively ceased direct communication with the world. This process can be explained by the unfolding of mind into thought, feeling, impulse, and finally crystallization into solid form.

~

It is fascinating today to *understand* the difference between *science* and *intuition*. It is of the first matter critical to recognize that *science* is merely the observation and study of the natural world, which is in essence what all the greatest *mythologies* document from the earliest to most recent times. Furthermore, science is a system that is evidence based, even if 'evidence' can be flawed, distorted, or altered. We get the word *science* from the Latin *scientia,* which comes from the word *scire* - to *know*. This means that *science* is not mere *observation* but is in fact defined etymologically in the same capacity as we define *intuition* - to *know*. The word *intuition* stems from the Latin *intuitio,* from the Latin *intueri,* which means *consider.* This means that *intuition* is essentially a process of consideration, something more akin to our view of science, while the latter is an ability to simply *know* – what we call *intuition.* By using both *intuition* and *science,* however they are defined, it may be said with confidence that humans have developed increasingly complex machines to assist in daily duties.

We rely so heavily on many of these devices that without them the very substance of society might erode overnight. The most relied upon of all technologies is certainly the synthetic computer, as distinct from the biological computer of our body and brain. Be it a cellular phone or a laptop, a computer is simply an electronic device for storing and processing data. It is given instruction in the form of a *program*. Note that it is through our television, tablet, phone, laptop, etc., that we receive entertainment and news in the form of *programs* that tell-our-vision (television) what is funny, sad, important, or newsworthy.

The two most popular computer operating systems (OS) outside of Linux are Microsoft Windows and macOS, or Apple. Here we are presented with a sort of *twilight imagery* in both the names and logos of these companies.

Take Windows, for example. Microsoft has utilized a colorful window for their logo since 1992. Over the years it has transformed slightly but retained its original design until today it resembles a sort of modern window. Throughout the 1990s the logo looked as if it were moving, having been pixilated on its left side. These pixels are like dots that form a geometric grid, which implies movement.

Now take the Apple logo. Although it has gone through many phases, from rainbow and translucent to monochrome, aqua, and chrome, it was originally much more than a simple apple that had been bitten by some hungry engineer. In 1976, One of Apple's founders, Ronald Wayne, had originally designed a logo depicting Sir Isaac Newton sitting under an apple tree. The crest featured a quote from English poet William Wordsworth: *"Newton... a mind forever voyaging through strange seas of thought."*

This logo changed relatively quickly, however, since Steve Jobs believed it was too old-fashioned for a computer company. Enlisting the help of a graphic designer named Rob Janoff, we today have a variation of the rainbow bitten apple. The missing bite comes from an attempt to make it clear that the logo was really an apple, rather than a cherry, and to refer to the computer term *byte*. Just as humans choose to *bite* or forgo a piece of food, i.e., make a binary decision, a *byte* is a group of binary digits. Former Apple executive Jean-Louis Gassee called the logo a symbol of lust, knowledge, and anarchy, obviously referring to the Garden of paradise story:

> *"One of the deep mysteries to me is our logo, the symbol of lust and knowledge, bitten into, all crossed with the colors of the rainbow in the wrong order. You couldn't dream of a more appropriate logo: lust, knowledge, hope, and anarchy."*

The Microsoft Windows logo, with its original grid pattern and dots, is far more than a simple household window. It is an opening, gateway, portal, and the like, into your personal space at home or in the office. It is a link between the computer operator and terminal, and the digital universe we often call a sub-reality. There is no doubt incredible esoteric energy in the fact that its  co-founder in 1975 was Bill Gates. Bill is a traditional name for the Devil, and refers to the King of Hell, Ba'al, while the Gate is perhaps one leading to hell.

The Apple logo is far more than a reference to a computer *byte*, instead symbolizing, as Jean-Louis Gassee said, lust, knowledge, hope, and anarchy. The most appropriate place to find these ideas in relation to the apple is in the Biblical story of the

Garden of Eden. From GARDEN we acquire EDEN. For it is here that lust, the temptation of knowledge, hope for a more potent experience, and anarchy were first told. The apple invites us to take another bite (byte) and the serpent promises *"that when you eat from it your eyes will be opened, and you will be like God, knowing good and evil"* (Genesis 3:5). We may find these identical esoteric themes in the overhyped *metaverse,* which promises us an internet as a single, universal, immersive virtual world. *Meta* means "beyond" in Greek, and thus indicates a *synthetic* world beyond the *organic.*

In other words, a synthetic world to rival organic Creation. Reversing the letters of *meta* gives us *atem.* In German "atem" means "breath." Going back to Genesis 2:7 we are reminded:

> *"Then the Lord God formed a man from the dust of the ground and breathed into his nostrils the breath of life, and the man became a living being."*

It was from the *breath* of God that Man (Adam and Eve) became a living thing. This means that Meta is Atem (Adam), the first man, in reverse, and included in his name is the *breath of life.* The Hindu Manvantara is the Day of Brahma when he let out a similar Great Breath. As the macrocosmic universe breathes so too does the microcosmic universe breath, a symbol of motion and heat. Cabalists and magicians will also be aware of *Adam Kadmon,* he who is the first of four worlds that came into being after the contraction of God's infinite light. He is the microcosmic universe inside all of us, and we are an extension of him externally in our thoughts and actions.

If we take the name Adam and reverse it, we get Mada, which is also similar to Meta. Either way we are dealing with *Twilight Language* once more wherein the word *meta* may be reversed to share a direct relationship with the *breath* (atem) given to *Adam* in the Garden. The meta-verse is therefore the Adam-Verse, or *Adam's Curse,* a synthetic reality created and breathed into by man - not God - who long ago learned how to control the *atom* with the atomic bomb. From the sub-atomic, to man, to the breath of life, the atom, Adam, and atem are all at work in the *metaverse.*

Finding these parallels compels us to consider the "verse" in its relationship with the previous inversions. For a *verse* is a writing arrangement with a rhythm, which therefore makes it a magical *spell.* The idea of a *curse*, or an utterance to invoke supernatural power, is also relatable since curses are typically magical *spells* read in reverse. Man's attempt to replace the organic world with a synthetic reality begins with a *window to beyond* and a *poisoned apple.* It proceeds with the promise of everlasting life, sold within the cult of *transhumanism* - see my book *The Technological Elixir.* The *metaverse,* as discussed by the transhumanist professor Yuval Noah Harai, is a place where light, gravity, and the laws of physics are totally different, and where your senses must be retrained – something akin to Neo when he wakes up and uses his eyes for the first time in the *Matrix* movie. The metaverse is therefore a meta-curse. It is the eighth sphere, the sphere of downward development set aside from the other seven planetary intelligences. It is in opposition to God's Creation and thus the essence of *black magic.* It is the divine *adversary* and the domain of His Infernal Majesty. It is *"lust, knowledge, hope, and anarchy,"* or all the things that HIM promises to detractors of GOD. We are also reminded of the *golem* when we examine the *metaverse* and its inversions. The Hebrew word emét, or truth, is placed on the forehead of this shapeless monster in order to bring it to life. To destroy the creature one letter must be removed from the forehead, thus leaving mét, which means death.

What this all means is that man has attempted to recreate the Garden of Eden and replace God's Creation. Man sees himself and nature as imperfect, blaming these imperfections on God. The line of thought goes that imperfect man can usurp the authority of an imperfect creator and thus redesign himself and nature into a more perfect form by reflections of an imperfect source.

~ PART II ~

Garden of Paradise

THE GARDEN

First Iteration

The *Garden of Eden* is described by Abrahamic religions as the *Terrestrial Paradise*, though it is everything but a physical place. As Joseph Campbell explains:

> "The Garden is a metaphor for the following: our minds, and our thinking in terms of pairs of opposites - man and woman, good and evil - are as holy as that of a god."

The *fruit* mentioned in Genesis is not necessarily an apple either and just as well may be a pomegranate. But it is the *temptation* of Eve itself - by the serpent with *fruit* from the forbidden *tree* - that we will put special emphasis on here. Genesis 3:1-7 describes the scene as such, referring to a very common motif about *the one forbidden thing*:

> "Now the serpent was more crafty than any of the wild animals the Lord God had made. He said to the woman, 'Did God really say, 'You must not eat from any tree in the garden'? The woman said to the serpent, 'We may eat fruit from the trees in the garden, but God did say, 'You must not eat fruit from the tree that is in the middle of the garden, and you must not touch it, or you will die.' 'You will not certainly die,' the serpent said to the woman. 'For God knows that when you eat from it your eyes will be opened, and you will be like God, knowing good and evil.' When the woman saw that the fruit of the tree was good for food and pleasing to the eye, and also desirable for gaining wisdom, she took some and ate it. She also gave some to her husband, who was with her, and he ate it. Then the eyes of both of them were opened, and they realized they were naked; so they sewed fig leaves together and made coverings for themselves."

It is an oversimplification to reduce this account to pure mythology, theology, and the like, without first considering the numerous esoteric aspects of the story. The apple and pomegranate are fruits that have come to represent desire and degeneration, along with knowledge and wisdom. The apple is poisoned with *desire* and the *realization* of individuality; a temporary and perceived separation from Source, a droplet of water in a vessel floating in the sea, or the amnesia of our divinity. There is separation between *man* and the *divine* just as there is separation of man's inner and outer life, the former representing Eden and the latter a fallen state.

Apples usually are symbols that represent wisdom, but their consumption symbolically bestows mortality. In the *Garden of Eden* these apples grew *from "the tree of the knowledge of good and evil."* In Genies chapter 2, verses 17-18, the "Lord God" warned man that if he ate from this tree he would "certainly die." In the Biblical account Eve is tempted to eat of the poisoned fruit. The serpent tells her: *"For God knows that when you eat from it your eyes will be opened, and you will be like God, knowing good and evil."* Being "like God" would be to become immeasurably wise, realizing good and evil. It would mean having the power to create.

Wisdom is an attribute given nearly everywhere in the world to serpents. In the story of the *Quest for the Golden Fleece* a serpent described as "terrible" guarded the "Golden" fleece, which was hung on a tree in a sacred grove. In this story the serpent was described as "subtle" or "shrewd". Serpents are true symbols or wisdom, for they tempt man with knowledge of self and *desire*, which results in man's disobedience of God – sin - and his eventual death. In India there are semi-divine serpents called *Nagas* which, according to Buddhists, guard sacred texts. In general Hindu mythology these serpents *guard the treasures of the earth*. In Egypt, Ammon Kematef was a serpentine deity who swam in the cosmic ocean and helped to create the Universe and all the knowledge contained therein. Hindus venerate the seventh avatar of Vishnu as a deity called Rama, similar to the Egyptian god Ra and the universal feminine principle *ma*. In Greek Hermeticism the god Pymander fashioned Seven Governors out of himself. Gnostics likewise believed in seven creators that emanate from Sophia, or wisdom. The Greeks, and particularly the Gnostics, saw the Pleiades constellation as the *seven sisters* or the *seven pillars* of Sophia, who is portrayed with a blue light much like the Creator is described in the sacred Maya book of *Popul Vuh*. We are reminded also of the powerful Hindu gods with blue skin. The Central American god Quetzalcóatl or Kukulcán was a civilizer and known as the Plumbed Serpent. Another creator deity from the same area named Itzamná was also part serpent. Some Hopi believe that snakes are their elder brothers. In China there is the Lung or Long Dragon which symbolizes the balancing of all things in the universe. The founder of Chinese civilization, according to the mythological record, is a man named Fohi. With the head of a man and body of a serpent, not unlike the Chaldean Oannes, he was, as manly Hall wrote, *"the first educator of the Chinese."* Fohi was also born of a virgin over 2,750 years before Christ. The founder of Japan, Jimmu, took on a more radiant form as a "son" of the "sun" goddess Amaterasu.

The Greek legend of *Hepera (Hespera)*, a paradise-like *Garden of Eden* at the western end of the world, also included serpents guarding golden apples of wisdom on a *Tree of Knowledge*. The Greek myth of the *Hesperides*, or nymphs of the sunset, describes their job in caring for this garden, which belonged to Hera, the wife and sister of Zeus. If consumed, the apples that grew in the garden would grant immortality. Anyone eating of this fruit would surely "be like god." Hera did not trust the nymphs, though, and instead sent a one-hundred-headed dragon named *Ladon* to protect the garden.

In the Garden of Eden, the apple initiates downfall while in the Greek *Hepera* it gifts immortality, the very thing that Lucifer or Lilith promises to Eve. The word *immortality* likely has little to do with physical life, however, and more to do with the experience of bliss found in paradise, or the *ultimate adobe of the just*. The *ability to live forever*, granted by the *fruit*, is therefore a reference, as shall be clear to students of the occult, to an *afterlife*. Immortality in the ancient *mystery schools* meant a physical resurrection and the *realization* – "they realized they were naked" – that life is but a mere sample of infinite Creation.

Some ascribe the serpent, fruit, and the embarrassment Adam and Eve felt in the Garden to the awakening of sexual desire. In this case the serpent is the phallus, the fruit is sexual pleasure, and the shameful nakedness of the two is guilt. The *fruit* could simply be the *realization* of *sexuality* within an individual unit, not beholden to Adam or God, or an attempt to destroy the blissful state of the Garden as it existed before *desire*.

Disobedience and spiritual pride contributed to both the fall of Lucifer from heaven and to the fall of man from the Garden. Philosopher Alan Watts explains in <u>Beyond Theology: The Art of</u>

<u>Godmanship</u> that Adam was prideful because he, like the serpent, *"aspired to become as a god 'knowing both good and evil."* Despite being warned, *"not to eat form the Tree,"* Adam and Eve became guilty with the same sin that cast Lucifer from heaven, i.e. he saw himself as God's equal: *"Lucifer would then be the force against creation, the agent of death to all that is not pure spirit."*

Second Iteration

The Garden of Eden narrative also shares close parallels with countless other religions, cultures, mythologies, etc. The Egyptians believed in an island paradise, or Garden of the Gods, called *Ta-Neteru*, which was destroyed by cataclysm. Another heavenly paradise in Egyptian belief was *Aaru*, or the *Field of Reeds*. It also went by the name *Sekhet-Aaru*, a place where the dead went to live. Egyptian mythology relates that this place was the domain of Ra, the sun god, who traveled there each night in rest. Such a paradise was the domain of the gods, but also called *amdwat*, the *land of shadow*, or simply *duat*. It is said to be located in the west where the sun *sets* (Set is the Egyptian god of storms and disease) each evening. In contrast, Japan is known as the "land of the rising sun." It is on the *horizon* (Horus is the Egyptian god of the sky and sun) where the sun resurrects each morning. In Welsh mythology this land was called *annwn*. In Mayan mythology this land is called *Xibalba*. Images found in the tomb of Double Comb, an eighth-century ruler of the Mayan city of Tikal, depict an underworld with similar features also found throughout the Valley of the Kings in Upper Egypt. In both these versions of the underworld there is a *"dog or dog-headed deity, a bird or bird-headed deity, and an ape-headed deity,"* as author Graham Hancock documents. In Central America one level of the underworld was called *Teocoyolcualloya*, or *"the place where beasts devour hearts."* This is similar to stages in the ancient Egyptian *Hall of Judgment*, which includes an almost identical series of symbols and also a great beast that consumes men's weighted hearts. It was here during the *final judgement* that the brain was discarded, and the *heart* was weighed against that of a *feather*, representing cosmic truth and justice. If the heart (*desire*) was *heavy with sin*, the balance of the scales would be tipped and the judgment written by the god Thoth in his book, before a beast part crocodile, hippopotamus, and lion, known as the "eater of the dead," would devour the heart. A less detailed story is told in Matthew 12:36-37 wherein we read:

> "But I tell you that everyone will have to give account on the day of judgment for every empty word they have spoken. For by your words you will be acquitted, and by your words you will be condemned."

Hence we say *speak your mind* or *speak your heart*, for the words we speak are expressions of the *heart* which will be judged against our soul/spirit. If the feather (*soul*) were to be heavier than the heart, then the *dead* would *pass on* to the next stage.

The bird (avian)-crocodile-reptile motif is also present in Japanese mythology with the sea monster/dragon *Wani*. Generally seen as a monster, the kanji 鰐 is translated as *crocodile*. Being an ocean-locked country, the ocean is especially akin to *maya*, or illusion, for the Japanese. In fact, *maya* means both illusion and mother, and it is the *land of mother* or the *land of the eternal* in Japan which exists beyond the ocean like *Ta-Neteru* or the *duat*. This land is where the soul/spirit receives *eternal life* according to Shintoists, and thus it makes sense that there is an association with the crocodile *Wani* in this under-or-parallel world.

Egyptian Hall of Judgement

Third Iteration

We may be familiar with Adam and Eve, but according to Hebrew legend another woman was created before Eve to act as Adam's wife. Lilith was a therianthropic creature, portrayed as part snake and part woman, often wearing wings. In Mesopotamian mythology she was known as the demon goddess Lamashtu. It is difficult to understand why more scholars have not pointed this out from both texts and depictions of the Garden, that Lilith is the serpent on *Tree of the Knowledge of Good and Evil*. This obviously equates Lilith with Lucifer. The God YAHWEH even blamed her for having tempted Eve, while also revealing the *mysteries* of the Garden to Adam. Arthur Cotterell and Rachel Storm describe Lilith in <u>The Ultimate Encyclopedia of Mythology</u> as such:

> *"The Serpent in the Garden of Eden is frequently portrayed with the face of Lilith, who in Hebrew legend was Adam's first wife. She considered herself his equal and left him – and Eden – rather than submit to him. She was often depicted as winged, with the body of a snake, and was said to be the temptress of Eve. She acquired the character of a wicked demon who killed new-born babies and was the enemy of men."*

When Moses came across the Midianites or Kenites, he found them worshiping the god of storms and war, i.e., YAHWEH. He found that these people wore a Tau cross in veneration for their god. This god of storms and war is also Ialdabaoth to the Gnostics, the *adversary* of *wisdom* and the distorter of creation. To the Egyptians he was *Maahes*, the solar god of war personified by a lion. *Sekhmet* is the female version of this solar god of war, but she also provides medicine. In Mesopotamia, *Nergal* was the god of death, pestilence, and plagues, much like those brought down upon Egypt. But the sun god of Mesopotamia was *Shamash*, who likewise provided medicine and healing powers. The solar *rays* of the sun also give it the ability to *raise* crops from the ground and to *raise* the dead back to life like Lazarus. Such power likewise allows the sun to *raise* man out of the abyss and death – often seen as winter – and back into the true light of the *mysteries*.

It must be noted with care that Lilith's name literally means "Storm Goddess." According to Talmudic legend, she was created at the same time as Adam but refused to be submissive to him in the same why Lucifer refused to honor Adam, God's Creation. Instead of lying beneath him, Lilith flew away into the desert where she consorted with demons and became the mother of monsters. When God sent His angles to subdue her, they were unsuccessful due to her increasing power and her violent threats aimed at innocent children. After interacting with the angles, although she refused to return to her place in the Garden, she agreed to leave children alone under the condition that: *"whenever I shall see you or your names you images on an amulet…"* Lilith then began searching for unprotected children to punish them for the sins of their fathers. She haunted men in their dreams, causing nocturnal ejaculations which were used to birth more demons. One myth explains how Lilith only became a demon because YAHWEH made her from filth and sediment instead of pure soil and clay. Hoping to make Eve less monstrous, God then took a *rib* directly from Adam. This is told in Genesis 2:22 as such:

> *"Then the Lord God made a woman from the rib he had taken out of the man, and he brought her to the man."*

Fourth Iteration

Much of the Garden narrative, particularly the *fruit* from a *tree* given by the *serpent* to make one *like God*, bears a striking resemblance conceptually to the hallucinogenic experiences brought on by *ayahuasca* and other similar substances. In fact, the idea of a talking snake, or serpent body with the head and upper body of a woman, parallels directly shamanic experiences with a spirit called *Mother Ayahuasca*.

According to the theory of Professor David Lewis-Williams, prehistoric cave and rock art around the world preserves the record of mankind's oldest concept of an otherworld of souls and supernatural beings – perhaps a *Garden* or *Land of the Gods*. It is theorized by David, and author Graham Hancock in his book <u>Supernatural: Meeting with the Ancient Teachers of Mankind</u>, that explorations of these worlds were initiated through ASCs, or altered states of consciousness, specifically brought about through the consumption of psychoactive plants. ASCs can also be entered through dehydration, starvation, hyperventilation, rhythmic dancing and drumming, illness, and self-mutilation. These rituals and actions have been performed by man for thousands of years, often for dangerous and erratic reasons. One terrible example is the focusing of the eyes on the tip of the nose until ocular damage occurs and one begins to hallucinate. According to Hancock, *"these trances may have been achieved through physical stress such as body-piercing, starvation or sensory deprivation in the caves where the paintings were created."* From the work of Dr. Rick Strassman, who documented how patients given various does of DMT saw cells, DNA, geometric designs, and strange creatures, we can derive a theory that the Biblical Garden of Eden narrative is focused on the same type of experience. Add *ayahuasca* trips with talking serpents, especially those that have female attributes, and the story becomes even more clear. We are dealing with a therianthropic tempter hanging on a tree, offering forbidden *fruit.* Such an image conjures up the symbol of modern medicine known as *caduceus,* which features two serpents entwined on a staff. When the image is a single serpent wrapped around a staff we call it the *Wand of Aesclepius,* the Greek god of healing and the son of the Apollo. The staff with a single serpent, or serpents, is also an umbilical cord connecting heaven and earth. This is why the *messenger of the gods,* the Greek Hermes, and Roman Mercury, carry the winged staff.

Caduceus   **Wand of Aesclepius**

In Greek myth it is the god Phanes, an embodiment of reproduction and new life, who is depicted with a serpent coiled around his entire body. His staff is surrounded by the twelve signs of the zodiac and a *mandorla,* or the almond shaped *vesica piscis* which represents the vaginal opening and a portal to the spiritual realm. The *mandorla* is essentially the *cosmic egg,* providing protection for new life resting inside. Within all of this imagery, as if it were the outer shell of a mysterious egg, we are talking about altered states of consciousness, which are very likely to be the basis of not just prehistoric cave and rock art but of modern myths we interact with daily. One of the most famous of these botanical sources of ASC is known in the Quechua language of the Incas as *ayahuasca* - *Vine of the Dead* or the *Serpent Vine*. The plant *psychotria viridis,* a bush of the *Rubiaceae* family, releases psychotropic quantities of Dimethyltryptamine (DMT) when cooked for certain periods of time in water. However, *monoamine oxidase*, which occurs naturally in the stomach, effectively destroys DMT on contact and renders it useless if consumed orally. Through some yet-to-be-discovered source, the ancients were able to find a seemingly random plant that counteracted this neutralizing substance in the body. *Banisteriopsos caapi* is a member of the *Malpigia* family and contains *monoamine oxidase inhibitors*, which allow for DMT from the *psychotria viridis* to become active when the two are prepared together. Such supposedly primitive people were obviously very sophisticated and extremely scientific in their approach to pharmacology.

Other substances that induce similar states of altered awareness include the famous *Psilocybe Semilanceat*a (liberty cap fungus) and *mescaline*, which is a psychoactive alkaloid derived from peyote cactus. *Psilocybin* is also very closely related to *Dimethyltryptamine* (DMT) on a molecular level and to *serotonin*, which carries messages like Hermes or Mercury between nerve cells in the brain and throughout the entire body.

Fifth Iteration

In the *Quest for the Golden Fleece* there is an ointment bestowed upon the leader of the group of Argonauts by a female magician, which makes the wearer safe from all harm. Edith Hamilton writes in her book <u>Mythology</u> how this special ointment would make *"him who rubbed it on his body safe for the day; he could not be harmed by anything."* The plant from which this magical substance was derived supposedly grew from the blood drops of Prometheus when they struck the ground. The philosopher Apollonius wrote that this herb grew from the flowing of blood out of Prometheus' wounds, which dripped to the ground like the blood of Jesus gathered in the *Holy Grail.*

When the bee nymph Melissa was dismembered like Orpheus, Osiris, Chiram Abiff, and the brilliant philosopher Hypatia, her body parts birthed bees instead of sacred plants. However, the bees produce honey and when mixed properly could provide a medium for other substances. From the honey we are to further understand alchemical or spiritual gold, and thus the phrase: *Dat Rosa Mel Apibus* or *The Rose Gives Honey to the Bees*. This "honey" is a symbol of the *mysteries* and parallels the golden apples on the *Tree of Knowledge* in the Greek legend of *Hepera*.

Blood of the youthful Attis also fell upon the ground and redeemed the earth like the blood of Jesus. The blood drops of Adonis likewise caused a crimson flower to sprout where they struck the ground. Perhaps this flower is the red rose that *gives honey to the bees*?

When the Greek god Cronus attacked his father, the resulting wound produced blood drops that spawned a race of monsters known as the Giants. The Hindu goddess Kali, an embodiment of time and death like Cronus and Saturn, or the Tibetan mKha'sGroma, is commonly depicted with a protruding tongue. In the story of a battle between the goddess Durga and the demon Raktabija, Kali acts to prevent the further birth of demons by licking up each drop of blood as it falls.

The blood of Dionysus, Greek god of wine, or the Roman Bacchus, produces the pomegranate, which many believe was the actual *fruit* in the Garden of Eden. The pomegranate is also the food that Persephone partook of in Hades, forcing her to stay in her imprisoned state for the amount of time each year equivalate to the amount of food she consumed. Persephone's trip to the underworld, from *paradise* above, parallels that of Adam and Eve being cast out of the Garden for eating an *apple*. Demeter is so distraught that her daughter is trapped in such a hellish place that she refuses to allow the crops to grow all throughout the fall and winter months. The *fall of man* in this context is obviously an analogy to explain the changing of the seasons. This allegory is at the heart of most *mystery* traditions. In like manner, the blood of Taurus ushers in a new age when he is stabbed by the solar deity Mithra(s). The falling blood, or *nama sebesion* (sacred fluid), is the redeeming blood of Christ drank as the wine of Dionysus and Bacchus. It is not only redeeming per se, but *eye opening* and *unveiling* to "the way, the truth, and the life."

The word *unveiling* is meant to call to mind the goddess Isis and her famous inscription: *"No Mortal Man Hath Ever Me Unveiled."* Once one has been initiated into the *mysteries of nature and life* they are no longer "mortal" in any sense of the word. They have obtained what John 3:16 calls "eternal life." The full verse says:

> *"For God so loved the world that he gave his one and only Son, that whoever believes in him shall not perish but have eternal life."*

In Mesopotamia an ointment was used to perform incantations with ghosts. Witches are also thought to have hallucinated the entire ordeal of the *Black Mass* with a similar substance. Reportedly, they rubbed the salve on their broomsticks and then performed sexual acts with them.

Whether an ointment, salve, blood, wine, or psychoactive substance the case is made just the same: these substances provide healing and redeeming powers against death and disease. They allow us to *"walk, even as he walked"* as we read in 1 John 2:6, and as we believe was the original state of man in the *Garden of Paradise*.

Sixth Iteration

Ayahuasca has been utilized as a sacred substance for exploring altered states of consciousness for thousands, perhaps even tens of thousands, of years; it is ritually derived from the forest using an equally sacred process. *Peyote Cactus* is also sacred, as are many forms of mushrooms, for inducing ASCs.

Entopic phenomena (abstract geometrical patterns) and therianthropic beings (half-animal half-human) are two of the most common visions documented by shamans when taking these psychoactive substances. Graham Hancock explains that from cave art to rock art, and occurring all around the world, we find the same *"enigmatic geometric patterns such as grids, nets, ladders and zig-zag lines."* This is all documented in Dr. Rick Strassman's book, <u>DMT: The Spirit Molecule</u>.

Now let us consider the Microsoft Windows logo once more with its grid of dots, or pixels, along with its obviously symbolic interpretation of being a *window* or *gateway* to the *other side*. Such an image, and the company it represents, is parallel to the visions of a machine world that is often experienced with DMT usage.

Now let us consider the Apple logo once more with a single bite (byte) removed, along with its original color scheme that the former Apple executive Jean-Louis Gasseeall called: *"colors of the rainbow in the wrong order."* The apple is poisoned with *desire* and *realization*, elements of physical materiality and consciousness to be explored from a human experience after passing through the *window* and into the *other side*. This *window* is most often symbolized by a *mirror* which can be used to talk with spirits and ghosts, or to both enter and leave the dreamworld. It is as Lewis Carroll wrote in *Alice's Adventures in Wonderland*, which is packed with LSD, mirrors to the upside down, and bizarre characters:

> *"If I had a world of my own, everything would be nonsense. Nothing would be what it is, because everything would be what it isn't. And contrary wise, what is, it wouldn't be. And what it wouldn't be, it would. You see?'"*

These are all themes we can find in popular television shows like *Stranger Things*, movies like the *Matrix*, and countless music videos pumped out of the entertainment industry.

Ayahuasca is, for all intents and purposes, akin to the *"the tree of the knowledge of good and evil."* The brewed mixture of *psychotria viridis* and *Banisteriopsos caapi* produces an unpleasant and sickening experience before, under the right conditions, one slips into an altered state of consciousness.

Experiences will become clearer the more one *undertakes* such a journey, especially depending on to what extend the mind is opened from the start. This unpleasant substance will almost certainly make you vomit, defecate, and feel extremely sick as if it were pure poison with an administered intent to kill.

Instead, after the body adjusts to the substance, you are taken to the underworld, parallel world, or to a place seemingly beyond physical reality. In this altered state of consciousness an experiencer will inevitably see and interact with entities. One of the most common is *Mother Ayahuasca* who invariably appears as a serpent with a female head. Among other things, she is *Mother Earth*.

Paintings of window-like devices and dots (pixels) from El Castillo Cave in Spain, compared with Microsoft Windows logo.

This serpent with female head is also how Lilith is both described and depicted in her role as the *tempter* of Eve in the Garden of Eden. Michelangelo's *The Temptation and Expulsion* on the Sistine Chapel (1508-12) shows the scene: a female serpent reaching out to hand Eve what we assume is *poisoned fruit*. Adam is above Eve on the left, gripping the tree and possibly reaching for something else, or for the serpent. An angel hovers behind the serpent and to the right casts Adam and Eve from the Garden with what appears to be a sword. Some believe that the painter of this fresco chose to depict Adam and Eve in their positions on the left as an implication that the second woman (Eve) was performing oral sex on the first man. This state of bliss was interrupted by the *temptation* of the *Storm Goddess*, who is half serpent, named Lilith.

Perhaps she was attempting to elevate Eve above her lower position in relation to Adam, precisely why Lilith left the Garden in the Hebrew myth.

Many likewise believe the *old serpent* was likewise simply trying to help mankind. But the story is far more complex than these initial notions suggest.

Seventh Iteration

According to Coptic tradition, and traditional Judeo-Christian narratives, the *old serpent* was evicted from heaven for one of two, or both, of the following reasons.

Firstly, it was the powerful angel's pride in aspiring to be equal to God. For as Proverbs 18:12 informs: *"Before destruction the heart of man is haughty, and before honour is humility."* Pride, therefore, comes before the *fall*, which is archetypical in that it relates to Lucifer's fall, Adam and Eve's banishment, and the actual period of the year we call autumn, or the *Fall* before *death* arrives riding a pale horse.

Secondly, the story goes that when Adam had been created and God gathered all the angels to adore his work, Satan refused. As a powerful angel the Devil believed he was superior to man, due to his spiritual nature and his existence prior to the formation of man and matter.

The Temptation and Expulsion by
Michelangelo, from the Sistine Chapel, (1508-12).

In using the names Lucifer, Satan, and Devil we can learn something esoteric of their meanings.

Satan comes from the Roman and Greek gods of agriculture, debauchery, chaos, and time, known as Saturn and Cronus respectively. Saturn's image has been painted differently in many cultures but remains the foundation for *Father Time* and *The Grim Reaper*. Saturn is the god of time and is said to speed up and then reverse this construct, often watching flowers die for amusement before bringing them back to life. This spirit of destruction is also one allowing for creation, as by death there is availability for new life to sprout. He is also the *Grim Reaper* because he is *death*, the oppositional and balancing force of birth and life. In Hebrew the name śāṭān means "accuser" or "adversary." It is said that Saturn/Satan "plants" (an agricultural analogy) into each of his children the seeds of their own destruction, and this is why you commonly see the grossly misunderstood images of Satan eating humans – his children. Philosopher Manly Hall explains how Satan *"is the cold demon of ice that freezes the spirit in the blood and is given dominion over the tomb of unrealized hopes."*

Saturn Devouring His Son by Francisco Goya, early 19th-century.

Devil is a composite of many cultural and religious traditions, the name coming from Greek *diabolos*, which also means "accuser." In English the DEVIL is a reversal of LIVED. He is *opposition* and *adversary* for certain but is also the epitome of EVIL in all of its forms, especially as a reversal of LIFE and LOVE - EFIL and EVOL. Hall writes that the *Devil* is *"the spirit of perversion or negation, the created principle of misuse."* In essence, evil, or the Devil, is an abuse or misuse of power.

Lucifer is a slightly different character, representing the Devil and Satan before his *fall* when he was a powerful angel of light. The name *lucifer* is Latin and refers to the morning appearance of the planet Venus. This *Morning Star* is Lucifer, the "bearer of light," known by the Greek word "phosphorus," which is broken down into "phos" (light) and "phoros" (bringing). Venus rises in the western hemisphere for four years as the *Evening Star*, and then rises in the eastern hemisphere for four years as the *Morning Star*. As opposed to the *"demon of ice,"* or Satan, Lucifer is the spirit of excess and, according to Hall, *"the heat that incubates the soul"* and a power man uses *"as a flame to burn up reason."*

The Devil and Satan provides us with opposition and Lucifer with hardships to overcome. The differences between these characters are summed up in the detailed narrations of Jonathan Black, as told in his book The Sacred History:

> "The Saturn snake – Saturn – attacks from the outside, while the Venus snake – Lucifer – insinuates itself inside us. Because of Satan, the spirit of opposition, life is often hard to bear. Because of Satan, we are attacked. Because of Satan, we – like Mother Earth – are tested to our very limits, to the point where we want to give up. Lucifer attacks us in different ways. Lucifer makes us liable to make mistakes. He endowed matter with a glamor that would dazzle people and blind them to higher truths."

Hall explains further in Magic: A Treatise on Natural Occultism the differences between Satan and Lucifer:

> "Between these two thieves of excess – Satan (utter coldness) and Lucifer (blazing heat) – hangs the spirit of man, crucified like the Christ of the sublime allegory, seared by the burning fire of one, chilled to freezing by the negation of the other."

After the *fall of Lucifer*, the Devil is identified as a rebel, military deserter, and as being responsible for waging the First War in Heaven, which can then be equated to the Final War in Revelation 12:7-9 - *"And there was war in heaven: Michael and his angels fought against the dragon; and the dragon fought and his angels, And prevailed not; neither was their place found any more in heaven. And the great dragon was cast out, that old serpent, called the Devil, and Satan, which deceiveth the whole world: he was cast out into the earth, and his angels were cast out with him."* In both cases it is St. Michael the archangel who defeats Satan and twice casts him upon the earth. This narrative is also equally relatable to astronomy in the case of Venus and the Moon. The first light of Venus (Lucifer) is cast down onto earth by the Moon (the God Jehovah).

Lucifer's *fall* from God's grace was a prelude to the *fall* of humanity. Just as God casts Lucifer from the heavenly paradise so too does He cast man from that same state and into a life of work: *"therefore the Lord God sent him out of the garden of Eden to till the ground from which he was taken"* (Genesis 3:23). Just as Adam's birth provided the event by which the *light bearer* fell to earth, the Devil now wished to poison God's Creation with *false light*.

The Fall of Lucifer (1866) by Gustave Doré,
from John Milton's poem *Paradise Lost*.

In the Apocryphal books of the *Life of Adam and Eve* and *Questions of Bartholomew* the Devil literally poisons man with cursed water. Jacques van der Vliet explains in an essay titled 'Satan's Fall in Coptic Magic' how the Devil *"collects sweat from his breast and armpits and mingles it into the source of the rivers of Paradise."* When drinking from this tainted water, Eve becomes aware of *desire*, which the *Life of Adam and Eve* text calls *"the root of all sin."* As the occultist and author Magus Incognito (pseudonym) writes of man and desire in <u>The Secret Doctrine of the Rosicrucians</u>:

> *"The more he knows, the more he desires; and the more he desires, the more does he suffer from the pain of not having... He has not only the pain of unsatisfied desires for possession of material things, and physical wants, but also the pain arising from the lack of intelligent answers to the ever-increasing volume of problems presenting themselves for solution to his evolving intellect; and lie also has pain of unsatisfied longings, disappointments, frustrated aims and ambitions, and all the rest of the list.*
>
> *"And many men are but little above this stage – they are easily satisfied; they are ignorant of the unsatisfied desires which*

render others unhappy. They have no unanswered questions —
they do not even dream of the existence of such questions."

The *disease of desire* brought down upon Paradise, like the plagues visited upon Egypt by God, essentially force humanity to perform acts of *sin*. Although it is easy to assign a helpful nature to Lucifer (i.e., to say he freed man from God's bondage) we must not forget that St. Michael the archangel, who replaced Lucifer as head of God's army, was the one who defeated the *old serpent* and therefore extinguished the darkness of *false light*. This makes Michael somewhat akin to Prometheus, Odin, and certainly makes him a prototype for Jesus Christ. Kurt Seligmann writes in The Mirror of Magic how Lucifer transformed into his current alchemical state:

> *"The evil serpent of paradise was transformed by the Gnostics into the beneficent Ouroboros. The Ouroboros was changed into the alchemist's dragon, and its body being light and dark found a chemical interpretation."*

The *dragon* which must be slain to acquire treasure in folklore and fairy tales, is the beast that stands between a rough man of lead and his transformation into gold. It is this *"spirit of opposition,"* as Jonathan Black puts it, which is the driving *"glamor"* that acts to *"dazzle people and blind them to higher truths."* In the *Book of Jubilees* this *"opposition"* is called Prince Mastema, or the fallen archangel who is responsible for the Pharaoh's refusal to abide by God's will in the Exodus narrative. Prince Mastema is the Prince of Darkness, the Devil, Satan, *ad infinitum*.

The life and wisdom bestowing authority of the Nile River, associated with the fluids of Isis, are anathema to the poisoned waters of Paradise. This poisoned water is obviously another version of the *fruit* from the Garden, and it is by either form of consumption that Adam and Eve feel *desire* and discover *realization*. We can point out more clearly now that *realization* is the *birth* of *consciousness*, which is painful but also pleasing.

Since Adam and Eve represent the primordial couple or androgyny, symbolized as a hermaphrodite - male and female attributes - and as depicted by the *Rebis*, Goat of Mendes, and by Eliphas Levi's Baphomet, we find that *desire* and *realization* are also evidence of further separation from *Source*. The more conscious we become the less institutive we are, and thus the more hardened our experience is in *maya*.

We can therefore say that the moment in which *"the eyes of both of them were opened, and they realized they were naked"* was their awakening from a deep dream-like slumber, such as *Sleeping Beauty*, or that of a divine hallucination, into physical existence by way of consciousness. Birth into a physical body implies limitation of the spiritual body. Only *realization* of the true self and a *desire* to transcend matter will provide the proper internal setting of the temple for one to be *born again*. There is often confusion here as per the difference between the *ego* and what it means to be *self-centered*. The former is concerned with physical affairs while the latter is concerned with the superphysical, and more akin to the Greek maxim *know thyself*. As Manly Hall explains:

> *"Birth into the physical world results in a limitation of internal consciousness. When the eyes of the body are open, the sight of the soul is obscure. Living unfolds on the plane of form until the person becomes so immersed in material concerns that he is unable to maintain the clarity of inner vision. By the mystical experience, he is released from the powers of mortality. He is reborn in the light and can know again the kingdom of heaven."*

If this is the case, then the *old serpent* is nothing more than the *necessary evil* of Saturn. Misunderstood aspects of the Roman Saturn and Greek Cronus, along with fertility gods like Pan, have become the quintessential elements for the anthropomorphic Satan. This character, as the father of time, is a *necessary evil* that both gives and takes away life at the appropriate time. It is from the Greek *khronos*, meaning time, that we get Cronus and chronology, the arrangement of events or dates in the order of their occurrence. For without this *necessary evil* there would be no opportunity, temptation, or sin. Man would be vacant of the passions which drive excess and evil, but have no awareness of this fact or *source* itself. He would thus become impoverished of any chance of redemption.

Outside of time, or the Leviathan serpent *Ouroboros*, there is no linear progression as we understand it; thus, the experience would be something akin to an altered state of consciousness as was clearly being experienced in the Garden of Eden. However, we should note, it is important to recognize that ASCs simply bring one into another perception of reality, under the best controlled circumstances, and that the Garden narrative was the original awakening to consciousness.

When we *awake* to conscious thought we find suffering, since our spiritual nature has been separated from Source. This takes us back to the meaning of *a wake*, the holding of a vigil beside the body of the physical dead: a person spiritually rebirthed.

Eighth Iteration

Although many people taking *ayahuasca* must embark on several experiences before having anything resembling a positive spiritual revelation, the ultimate feeling of bliss, warmth, peace, etc., is akin to the Garden Paradise. Expulsion from the latter, therefore, is akin to *coming down* from the *high*.

Dr Rick Strassman documented in notes on patients given DMT how they saw *"spirals of what looked like DNA,"* things that looked *"like the inside of a cell,"* and DNA spirals made of *"incredibly bright cubes."* What we call DNA can be seen all throughout the world in the form of a symbol called *caduceus*, or a staff with entwining serpents. Scepters or staffs, even without serpents, are umbilical cords connecting that which is *above* with that which is *below*. They represent the works of God accomplished through the hands of man. The staff is also related to the symbol of a triangle and pyramid. If a triangle is ascending it represents man's attempt to connect with the heavens, and when descending, it signifies God reaching down to man. More abstractly these triangles represent the superior and inferior worlds touching at a single point like God and Adam in Michelangelo's famous painting *The Creation of Adam*. The inverted pyramid or triangle, known as the chalice, has its base in the heavens. It is analogous with water and woman. Symbolically it is similar to the Hanged Man Tarot, walking in the superior world with head or spirit in the inferior. The upright triangle, known as the phallus, has a base in the inferior sphere, which is analogous to fire and man. Often a serpent is seen moving between these two worlds, signifying the importance of the staff of Moses, which turned into a snake. The serpent, defined as *astral light* in magic, assimilates both superior and inferior periods of time. What this all means is that in altered states of consciousness, in this case from DMT, people are seeing the geometry at the basis of Creation. They are seeing the fundamental building blocks of life, from DNA to cells.

Ninth Iteration

Other entities encounter during *ayahuasca* experiences are therianthropes - human and animal hybrids - which are often seen as shapeshifters moving from one form to another. From the Americas to Africa and the far east we find underworlds (sometimes parallel worlds) with dog, bird, and ape deities, or with half-human versions of the previous. These are precisely what the entire pantheon of Egyptian gods and goddess seems to be based upon. It is especially interesting to note that the Egyptians were fascinated and obsessed with life, rather than death. Everything in Egypt was focused on the life-giving powers of the Nile River, as embodied in the *mysteries* of Isis. Life itself was embodied in a symbol called *ankh*.

Also known as the *Crux Ansata*, or *Ansata Cross*, it symbolizes the head or spiritual nature of man protruding from the bindings of material, depicted in the partially mummified Osiris. The head of *ankh* is the head of man, and the three additional protruding points are the spiritual arms and legs nailed to matter by illusion – like Jesus on the cross. The head rises forth, however, much like the fifth point does from the other four in the pentagram. These five points also represent the five wounds of Christ - *stigmata*.

The passive principle of a circle, or female, combined with the active principle, or male, of the lower portion of what is a Tau cross, symbolizes *generation* and *life*. In the philosophical language of the ancients, the *ankh* was more accurately defined as *The Life Bestowing* and it was worn always by Egyptian Adepts and carried by many gods and goddesses.

Depictions of the underworld trials in Egypt, and elsewhere, reinforce this reality of the obsession with both life and therianthropic beings.

Although Egypt did not have *ayahuasca* there was a possible equivalent in the *blue water lily*, or *Nymphaea Caerulea*, a psychoactive plant used to relieve anxiety and assist in sleep. So popular was this substance that it was placed on the tombs of some pharaohs. It may have even been used as a tranquilizer in small doses, thought in larger amounts psychosis could be induced.

The Greeks had something similar in their use of *ergot*, a fungus appearing on cereal crops which produced psychoactive effects if consumed. This is the same fungus that Albert Hoffman used to synthesize LSD in 1938.

Eleusis was sacred to the cult of Demeter, the agricultural goddess often referred to as *Erysibe* – meaning *ergot*. It was here that the Eleusinian Mysteries were carried out each year. The purple color of the fungus explains the robes of the same color worn by the goddess and her initiates, as does it explain the divine nature of the color itself. Purple is usually associated with Jesus Christ and colored cloth of this nature is often draped over a cross at many churches. Colors like purple, violet, and of course blue, are colors of royalty and even enlightenment. In the final rite of initiation in the Greek Mysteries a cup with some type of psychoactive or narcotic substance was given to the initiate. The ceremonial cup is called *kykeon* and the substance was made from a distillation of ergot.

Poppy Goddess, patroness of healing.

But consumption of *ergot* could also cause *ergotism*, resulting in severe sickness like *ayahuasca* or the *poisoned apple* in the Garden. We can assume the same of the *blue water lily*. It has been further documented that many ancient Egyptian mummies were found to have been preserving psychoactive drugs, and even narcotic substances like nicotine and cocaine.

Mandrakes and poppy also assist in producing such altered states of awareness. In fact, the Poppy Goddess appears all over the ancient Greek world. Her Minoan form dates from 1,300 BC on the Greek island of Crete. Mandrake root can be used to induce delusions, seizures, and hallucinations. It is so powerful that it is often called the *scream of death*.

The Middle East is home to *acacia* and *Syrian rue*, that when combined produce a biochemical mixture like that of the plants from which *ayahuasca* is derived in the Amazon. Libations from the Persian cult of Zoroastrianism were possibly made from the herb *Peganum harmala*, the seeds and root containing psychoactive alkaloids that induce psychedelic experiences. In Mithraism the herb used for this purpose was called *haoma*.

Mandrake Root must be uprooted by its intended user, but caution should be exercised due to the supposed death-inducing scream emitted when it is removed from the ground. It is used for support in everything from finances and sexuality to general mental and bodily health.

A similar water lily to the Egyptian variety grows in Central America and it was possibly used by the Maya, much like their famous stone mushrooms record their interest in the more *magical* kind. The Maya of Central America also partook of a mildly intoxicating beverage called *balché*, made with the bark of a leguminous tree. If fermented with honey for several days, the drink becomes powerful enough to distort perceptions of reality. The Aztecs were known to have used *ololiuqui*, Morning Glory seeds with LSD-like qualities, as well as *teonanactl*, or mushrooms known as the "flesh of the gods." Intoxication by psychoactive plant is similar to the inebriation reached by drinking the wine of Dionysus or Bacchus. Let us not forget that Christ's blood comes in the form of wine and that he also turned water into the latter. Manly Hall writes of the significance of grapes and their unique juices for which Dionysus and Bacchus were representatives:

> *"The juice of the grape was thought by the Egyptians to resemble human blood more closely than did any other substance. In fact, they believed that the grape secured its life from the blood of the dead who had been buried in the Earth."*

In various traditions all over the world wine was consumed as the blood of a fallen god, whose flesh was consumed in the form of bread or cake, made from the last harvested wheat - the origin of the Christian *Last Supper*. The concept of eating flesh and drinking blood is a practice from the most ancient times and is accepted today as a metaphor that some interpret literally. The grapes and wheat are nourished by sun and rain. Grapes are turned into wine and wheat into flower and bread. Grapes and wine, and wheat and bread, are then translated metaphorically into blood and flesh as symbols of the transformations of nature. These qualities are then imparted sympathetically to the person consuming the ritualized and consecrated items. Manly Hall adds that many ancient cultures believed grapes *"first sprung out of the earth after it was fattened with the carcasses of those who fell in the wars against the God."* These fallen carcasses are those form the First War in heaven, which was a prelude the fall of man from God's grace – *paradise*.

Tenth Iteration

When a shaman enters these altered states of consciousness and returns, often after having experienced considerable suffering like Christ, they bring with them knowledge from the other side. This is precisely the purpose of the ancient *mystery* traditions and their associated symbols like the ankh. As with *ayahuasca*, after Adam and Eve had consumed the *fruit* they were immediately subject to expulsion and sickness. The promise from the snake that Eve would certainly "not die" and that her "eyes will be opened" sounds strangely like an *ayahuasca*, or similar, experience. When *the eyes of both of them were opened* and they *knew* good and evil, Adam and Eve were cast from paradise into suffering - out of paradise into material reality and cut-off from Source. It is only through certain austerities and the usage of certain plants (if used properly and responsibly) that man is in any way able to reconnect with God. This is a fact and reality that indigenous shamans, like the *mystodokos* (initiates receiving the mysteries), have known and have been experiencing for thousands of years. This is what is told in Luke 8:8-11 which reads:

> "'Still other seed fell on good soil. It came up and yielded a crop, a hundred times more than was sown.' When he said this, he called out, 'Whoever has ears to hear, let them hear.' His disciples asked him what this parable meant. He said, 'The knowledge of the secrets of the kingdom of God has been given to you, but to others I speak in parables, so that, 'though seeing, they may not see; though hearing, they may not understand.' 'This is the meaning of the parable: The seed is the word of God.'"

Desire Brings Death by Sebald Beham in the 15th-century.

The serpent coiled upon the tree, in this case a skeleton, is symbolic of the formation of the human spinal cord in the *mysteries*, and further represents *kundalini energy*, literally meaning *snake* in Sanskrit, rising through the blossoming flower-like chakras of the plant body.

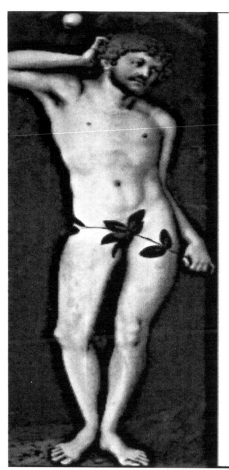
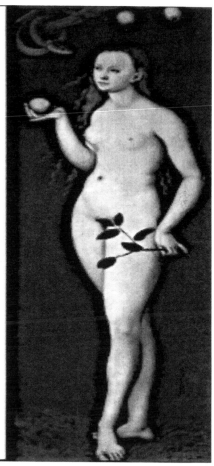

(Above) **Adam and Eve** by Lucas Cranach the Elder (1528).

(Left) Engraving by unknown artist.

Satan Presiding at the Sabbath from Paul Christian, from *Histoire de la Magie*. In many ways, the *black mass* is the antithesis to the *Garden of Eden*. It is filled with debauchery, sin, and death, which makes it a real *Garden of Hallucinations*. For the witches do everything backwards: they eat salt to quench thirst, dance back-to-back rather than -face-to-face, abort babies instead of birth them, and give in to every temptation.

Man as the Five-Pointed Star with Spirit Above –
illustrated by M. D. Logan, from Manly P. Hall's book <u>Magic: A
Treatise on Natural Occultism</u>.

MESSENGERS OF GOD

Deoxyribonucleic Acid is a self-replicating material that is mostly present in a cell's nucleus. It is the carrier of genetic information in the body. RNA is a nucleic acid in all living cells. Its role is to carry instructions from DNA to control the synthesis of proteins and cellular replication. When genetic information transcribed from DNA is transferred to a ribosome it is called mRNA or MESSENGER RNA.

Dr. Strassman's study demonstrated that under the influence of DMT it was common for his patients to sees various forms of geometry, along with bodily cells and what can only be described as DNA. Francis Crick, who co-discovered DNA, was famously on LSD when he witnessed the biological *caduceus*. Usage of *ayahuasca* usually produces similar images in the form of talking serpents, or Edenic serpents that are therianthropic. Images of Phanes, the god of new life and birth in Greece, depict him with a staff and a serpent wrapped around his body. Beyond that are the twelve signs of the zodiac. Phanes resided inside the *Cosmic Egg* and his birth represented not only new life in general but a fundamental cornerstone of basic biology and chemistry in particular. Phanes could thus be identified with DNA and the *egg* may be seen as a cell. Therefore, the Garden of Eden and *seven days of creation* become the story of copulation and reproduction at the microscopic level. For as God created by *separating* and *dividing*, so too do cells divide after fertilization of the egg with sperm. The *Wand of Aesclepius,* like the *caduceus*, is not only a symbol of modern medicine but of health in general throughout human history. Modern science and medicine are fixated on precisely what the *caduceus* represents, i.e., genetics – DNA. Since healthy DNA and cellular cycles are needed for a healthy life, it makes sense that the entwined serpents are a symbol of health and new life. As messengers of the Gods, or liaisons between heaven and earth, Mercury and Hermes carry information just like DNA and mRNA do to parts of the body. Within the body it is the baby (spirit) and placenta (substance) which share information and nutrition via an umbilical cord, i.e., the staff of Moses. These images are not confined to Greece or Rome either, as may be assumed from popular culture. Some version of the *caduceus* or double-helix can be found in ancient Sumer, Ireland, Turkey, China, and South America. In Asian countries the *Yin Yang* is of similar relationship. It is known as *Yab-Yum* in India, a symbol of the universal couple having sex. The image of *rebis* likewise shows us the primordial couple embracing each other in bliss. It is copulation and the spark of life, or orgasm, which culminates in the drawing down of spiritual forces into a new body. Thus, we have the *caduceus* as symbol of communion between heaven and earth, God and man, and baby and placenta. It is a symbol of healing; those arts learned by shamans when they take a trip into other worlds and are ferried by messengers across the rainbow bridge. Crosses are used to ward off *evil* for similar reasons relating to the medicinal nature of *caduceus*. They are, first, the basis of the medical symbol, and second, such *evil* was traditionally a disease personified as a demon. These diseases could be literal or even figurative in the cases of Jesus healing the sick.

Libation Cup of King Gudea of Lagash, Sumer (2,000 BC).

Yab-Yum - man and woman embrace in this painting from a
Tibetan temple banner, 19th-century.

Caduceus on a coin from Turkey (140-144 CE).

Aztec **Altar of the Caduceus** from Codex Fejérváry-Maye.

Nü Wa and Fu Xi as twin serpents
from Han Dynasty (c. 206 BCE – 220 CE).

The Right Hand of God (*Dextra Dei*)
designed from a stone cross in Ireland.

The Brazen Serpent by P. Ball,
from "Royal Academy Prize Designs."

Out of the Orphic Egg was birthed Phanes, the Greek god of procreation and new life. He is typically depicted inside of a *mandorla*, or almond-shaped opening, with a serpent coiled around his body. The *Universal Germ* within the Egg of Creation established the worlds and generations by three "gestures," according to philosopher Manly Hall. He says that it fashioned the souls of things by *Virtue*, the bodies by *Beauty*, and the laws of souls and bodies according to the *Necessary*. Together these concepts embody what is called *The Good*. Phanes and his staff and serpent are also the DNA inside of a cell's nucleus, i.e., the *cosmic egg*.

Known as *Twofold Matter*, the **Rebis** is a symbol of the universal hermaphrodite, an image similar to common drawings of Baphomet. It comprises the male and female, and sun and moon, in perfect harmony. The androgynous figure stands upon the back of a fire-breathing dragon just as Isis stands upon snakes or Mary upon Satan – Eve upon the Edenic Serpent. The dragon is the *great beast* that must be defeated before the *soul* can rise above *matter* – it is the ego  which drives the animal nature of man. The globe is provided wings to signify its relationship between heaven and earth in like manner to the winged solar disc and caduceus. Inside of this figure is a cross, its four arms denoting the four directions and elements, the fifth of which is found within the central dot. This point, or crossroads, is what leads into the Otherworld where initiates communicated with spirits before they were resurrected while still living. The 3 signifies the Holy Trinity and 4 represents the four elements, their combination giving us the sacred number 7. Above the man and woman is a hexagram, which symbolizes the hermetic statement: "as above, so below." This axiom conceals another truth, though, that there is no "up" or "above," nor "down" or "below."

The divine is present *within* and *without* the space we all inhabit. Inside of the hexagram we find Mercury, messenger of the gods, as with mRNA and DNA, the double helix sharing a relationship with Mercury's staff. Mercury is the extractor of gold, the spiritual substance found within the bodily vessel which is in a constant state of decay. It is here, as with literal external vessels said to be placed in something like horse dung, that the *elixir of life* will be found. For the body is the essence of the mysteries, but still only a temporary container – *in sterquilinis invenitur*: in filth it will be found. The oval shape of the symbol is representative of the egg, a symbol of regeneration and the birth of the cosmos. Here we find the *MATERIA PRIMA*, that substance from which matter and spirit, and all else, emerged. Some say this material is symbolized by the winged sphere in the lower portion of the image. That symbol is known by alchemists as *ROUND CHAOS*, which is as Jordan B. Peterson wrote in <u>Beyond Order</u>: *"the container of what the world, and the psyche, consists of before it becomes differentiated."* This takes us from the *round chaos* of *lead* BELOW to the mercurial hexagram of *gold* ABOVE. The transmutative process merges all things together again; for *ALL* is *MANY OUT OF ONE*. The hexagram therefore is a merger of the upright and downward triangle, or masculine fire and feminine water. The dragon can thus be understood as the archetypical evil, perhaps a necessary evil, and certainly the guardian of knowledge and the more precious gold of wisdom – an extremely common motif in fairy tales and other mythologies. Peterson says the dragon *"perched on top of the round chaos, represents the danger and possibility of the information within."* Only by slaying the dragon (ego) can the animal self (beast) be conquered, and emotion controlled. We are thus looking at a symbol with many layers of meaning, stemming from ancient alchemy to transcendent occultism and modern psychology. *"The Rebis,"* Peterson points out, *"is a symbol of the fully developed personality that can emerge from forthright and courageous pursuit of what is meaningful (the round chaos) and dangerous and promising (the dragon)."* It is from out of this unknown that there can be a merger of our two halves, the positive and negative, or the compass and square in the image, and the symbols of *ordered* Jupiter and *chaotic* Saturn.

Carl Jung has this to say about the archetypes of apparent opposites:

> *"The masculine-feminine antithesis appears in the long and round objects: cigar-form and circle. These may be sexual symbols. The Chinese symbol of the one being, Tao, consists of yang (fire, hot, dry, south side of the mountain, masculine, etc.) and yin (dark, moist, cool, north side of the mountain, feminine). It fully corresponds, therefore, to the Jewish symbol mentioned above. The Christian equivalent can be found in the Church's doctrine of the unity of mother and son and in the androgyny of Christ, not to mention the hermaphroditic Primordial Being in many oriental and primitive religions, the 'Father-Mother' of the Gnostics, and the Mercurius hermaphroditus of alchemy."*

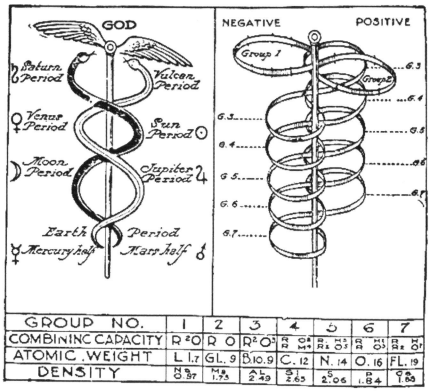

GROUP NO.	1	2	3	4	5	6	7
COMBINING CAPACITY	R²O	R O	R²O³	R O² R M⁴	R. H³ R₂ O⁵	R H² R O³	R. H R₂ O⁷
ATOMIC .WEIGHT	L 1.7	GL. 9	B.10.9	C. 12	N. 14	O. 16	FL. 19
DENSITY	Na 0.97	Mg 1.75	Al 2.49	Si 2.65	S 2.06	P 1.84	Oa 1.83

The world, the man and the atom are governed by the same law. Our dense earth is now in its 4TH stage of consolidation. The mind, the desire body and the vital body are less solid than our 4TH vehicle, the dense body. In the atomic weight of the chemical elements there is a similar arrangement. The 4TH group marks the acme of density.

The Seven Days of Creation & Caduceus, presented alongside of the atomic world with its negative and positive, or female and male, charges, from Max Heindel's *The Rosicrucian Cosmo-Conception*

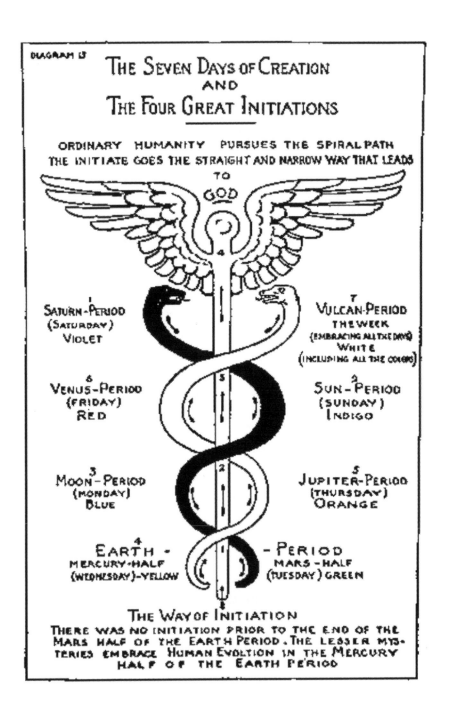

The Seven Days of Creation as *caduceus*, with obvious Kabbalistic features, from Max Heindel's *The Rosicrucian Cosmo-Conception*

BLACK CUBES & ROCKS

Black Rock, the powerful investment management company overseeing trillions of dollars, was founded in 1988 by 8 people. Today they control an immense amount of real estate, businesses, entertainment, etc., with their tentacles thrust into countless other things. A quick glance into theology and mythology will provide an altogether different view on this financial Lovecraftian Old One, however, and provide the background perhaps on why the firm chose such a name from the start. Although the purpose of this section is to examine the *black cube* as it relates to a *caduceus,* it is still nonetheless important and beneficial to look at such a contemporary company like *Black Rock*.

In Hawaii the black rock is a sacred place where souls of the dead can enter the spirt land. In Greek myth we learn that when Prometheus is tied down as punishment for bringing fire to mankind he is chained to a black rock. In the Islamic city of Mecca, we find Al-Masjid Al-Haram, or the Grand Mosque, which encloses the black cube called *Kaaba*. Said to have been built on a pre-Islamic shrine constructed by Abraham, this sacred cube contains a black stone resting within its southeastern corner. Muslims embarking on a pilgrimage to this sacred site find it customary to walk around the structure seven times, mimicking rotating rings like those of the planet Saturn - the *Lord of the Rings*.

It is not as well known that the cult of Cybele, a goddess worshiped in Phrygia, Greece, and Rome, also venerated as an icon a similar black rock. A small black cube known as *Tefillin* is also a symbol of the Jews. The word means *prayer*. This small black box contains parchment paper with written inscriptions from the Torah. The Jewish mystical tradition called *Kabbala* also so happens to be nearly identical in name to the Islamic *Kaaba*. Christians have their own cube in the form of a cross which folds ups into a box with four sides and a top and bottom. These six sides further relate to the planet Saturn for two reasons: one, a hexagram (two intersecting triangles – six sides) is the star or seal of that planetary body, and two, because the astrological sign of Saturn is a cross with an extended lower portion forming a curve.

In a seemingly and totally unrelated instance, we find the sacred Central American text *Popol Vuh* containing an interesting account of a majestic temple being constructed, which preserves a square black divining stone. The name of the stone and cubical temple is *Caabaha*, a word that means *House of Sacrifice*. Many scholars have pointed out the similarity of this particular example to the *Kaaba* at Mecca. In Arabic the word comes from *al-ka'aba*, meaning "the cubic house."

These temples are expressions of the physical world itself and the human body and head. Here we find the head-temple wherein the *middle pathway* is found and known as *bindi, uraeus,* or *third eye*. Whereas the earthly temple is square and cubical, the bodily temple is round and spherical. In modern day Azerbaijan, located in southwestern Asia, is a temple dedicated to a fire god, which is also built in the form of a cube much like the *Holy of Holies* which housed the Ark of the Covenant.

~

In mysticism we find the *magic squares* of the planetary bodies, each containing a series of vertical and horizontal columns that support all of creation, with numbers adding to the same outcome in every direction. The *magic square* of the sun adds up in every direction to 111, but since there are six columns the number 666 could be derived. The *magic square* of Saturn has only three columns vertical and horizontal, and each adds to 15, which in numerology equals 6 and can therefore add up to 666 as well. From these *squares* can be derived planetary symbols called *sigils*. Saturn's sigil is identical to the symbol of the metal lead, and likewise is the basis of the *Star of David* and *Seal of Solomon*. This *star*, or *seal*, is famous for its merging of upright and inverted triangles. The upright represents fire, activity, and man. The inverted represents water, passivity, and woman. When merged they symbolized the *alchemical marriage* and the what is known as *yab-yum*, yin-yang, or caduceus. In fact, this latter symbol is nearly identical to the concept embodied in the alchemical symbol for lead - the black stone or rock to be polished - and the sigil of Saturn, i.e., two entwined lines or serpents. We call this DNA and it is in our cells while our brains are comprised of a reptile portion akin to the seven forms of consciousness. Some call these *chakras* but others know them as *bodies*: elemental, mineral, plant, animal, human, demi-God, and God. They are seen famously in Frank Baum's <u>The Wonderful</u>

Wizard of Oz where we meet a tin man (mineral), scarecrow (vegetable), and lion (animal). In this particular story Dorothy is sent into an altered state of consciouses through the vortex (cyclone) of a tornado, something she shares in common with Alice and her mirror. Manly Hall explains this unfolding of consciousness in Magic: A Treatise on Natural Occultism, describing how man developed from mineral, plant, and animal states:

> "As the universe began as a dark nebula of mind stuff, so man, the little universe built in the image of His Father and bearing witness to the functions of his creative pattern, also began his physical manifestation as a mineral thought-form. Later he appeared as a fiery plant, and gradually, after many ages of transition, this plant became a sacred animal composed of a body and humid ether. Later, like his celestial archetype he incarnated into physical substance as a human creature."

The *Sigil of Saturn* is characteristic of another powerful pair of symbols in the form of the masonic square and compass, which are usually accompanied by the letter "G" to signify the *Grand Architect*. These two overlapping symbols, or triangles, comprise the four elements of the four corners of material creation. From another point of view they are the two (XX) chromosomes of a biological female, who carries the *matrix* or *womb* of creation within her body. It is through her *waters* that we have reproduction and growth, and just as *fire* empowers *emotion*, *air* provides us with *thought*, and *earth* is the groundwork for our physical *body*.

~

In Japan we find the recently cracked *sessho-seki*, or killing stone, at the Nikko National Park just north of Tokyo. This dark stone supposedly held a shape-shifting female spirit called Tamamo-no-Mae. In the story she transformed herself into a beautiful woman and got close with the emperor who then became sick. A court astrologer used divination to determine that Tamamo-no-Mae was the cause of his illness. Although she fled from the emperor's presence, the samurai caught and killed her, leaving only her spirit to transform into the stone. Her original form is a nine-tailed fox, which is notoriously a trickster spirit. Saturn is also the archetypical trickster as can be seen in his *magic square* which deceptively conveys the number 15x3 instead of 6x3: *the greatest trick the devil ever played was convincing the world that he did not exist.*

The nine tails once more relate to the *Ennead* of Egypt and the *Council of Nine* that Gene Roddenberry supposedly channeled as inspiration for *Star Trek*. It cannot be coincidence that one of the most popular antagonists of the show, the BORG, flew around in large black cubes. It also cannot be a coincidence that their prime directive was *to* assimilate *"biological and technological distinctiveness"* into their own through computerized technology. There is furthermore no way that pure chance lead MIT Technology Review to publish an article in 2017 using a black cube to represent 'The Dark Secret at the Heart of AI'. A New York Times article from 2023 did something similar, asking 'Why an Octopus-like Creature Has Come to Symbolize the State of AI'. The article subtitle reads: *"The Shoggoth, a character from a science fiction story, captures the essential weirdness of the A.I. moment."*

~

The 1920 German movie *Algol: The Tragedy of Power* features a coal miner who meets an alien from the planet Algol. The alien bestows upon him a prototype device to be used for harnessing unlimited energy. In the 1950s the name ALGOL was used to refer to computer programming languages such as ALGOL 58 and 60. From ALGOL we also acquire the word *algorithm,* which MIT relates to a black cube. Perhaps this is why IBM put their Q System One quantum computer inside of what amounts to a shiny black cube.

Originally the name Algol comes from the Arabic *al-ghul* and is the basis for the name of the real star Algol. The Greeks marked this star as the *blinking eye* of the Gorgon Medusa and therefore we still refer to it as the *demon star*. Is it not strange that artificial intelligence is "A" "I" or *an eye*? In the *Lord of the Rings* it [the eye] is the powerful dark lord *Sauron* whose name is derived the Latin *sauria* for lizard. From this "eye" we also acquire the *Eye of Providence* which often is depicted with *divine rays* emanating downward to create the physical world. Sometimes there are seven and other times there are eight; in the latter case, Source is the eye and the eight sphere is itself an emanation from the divine.

This "eye" is what we see when we turn the planet of Saturn on its side so the rings outline the planet itself in the center. Otherwise known as a *monad* - the substance that reflects the order of the world from which materiality is derived - this dot surrounded by a circle is the egg fertilized by sperm and the alchemical symbol for gold.

~

The black cube of Saturn furthermore relates to the geometric and mathematical designs of our world and beyond into infinite space. If you draw seven lines as emanating rays from a single eighth point what you find are the *seven days of creation* and the *eighth sphere* that Blavatsky called *"furnace of nature."* The eighth sphere is also called *death*, a place the soul visits to be recast before being sent back into the mortal world. The seven rays stemming from the eighth sphere thus produce a cube in three dimensions or a hexagon (six sides) in two, wherein there are six points like the Star of David or Seal of Solomon, with an eighth in the middle. This is creation personified. The downward flow of creation in this example also mirrors the spheres Kether, Tifareth, Yesod, and Malkuth on the kabbalistic *Tree of Life*. Since Saturn is the *Grand Architect* or *Ancient of Days* he is responsible for calculating the corners and angles of our physical reality. He is not necessarily evil, but he is *necessary evil*. As *Father Time* he plants in us the *seeds* of our demise and when that time arrives, he is ready to cut us down with the scythe of the *Grim Reaper*. Saturn's rings are a parallel macrocosmic symbol to planets orbiting a star and electrons orbiting the nucleus of an atom. In fact, as the architect of *form* he gives man a certain mark as described in Revelation 13:18, which says:

> *"Here is wisdom: Let him that hath understanding count the number of the beast, for it is the number of a man; and his number is six hundred threescore and six."*

The number 666 is that of carbon, i.e., 6 protons, 6 neutrons, and 6 electrons. The fact that this is "wisdom" and not a "warning" is perhaps an indicator that we are dealing with things internal rather than external. The *second coming*, being *born again*, the *apocalypse* - that great unveiling of nature - and the *"number of a man"* all relate to an internal alchemical process. In fact, the *animal self* is akin to the blinking demon eye of *algol* and the lizard god *Lord Sauron*, partially in relation to our reptile brain. This is the great beast or dragon that must be overcome. It is present in our very serpentine DNA to the extent that we exist in the physical world or cube. The black cube is furthermore lead or a slab of ashlar, those large square-cut stones representing that which must be turned into gold.

Christians see the cube as the perfect measurement of Christ and Freemasons see the perfected stone as the proper figure of man, being square, upright, and true in stature. In his intriguing book <u>How To Understand Your Bible</u> Manly Hall describes the cube as such:

> *"It is the most perfect of the geometric solids, being equal in all its parts. It consists of six faces which represent the days of creation, and of twelve lines which symbolize the zodiac. If each of the feces be open to the core, the result will be a cruciform design consisting of six pyramids."*

Each of these pyramids will have four faces for a total of twenty-four, the number of hours in a day. When this number is added to the six faces of the cube the resulting number thirty provides us with the degrees of a zodiacal sign, the houses constructed by the carpenter. The perfect cube is called the *New Jerusalem,* that sacred city within all the children, not just Jews, of Israel.

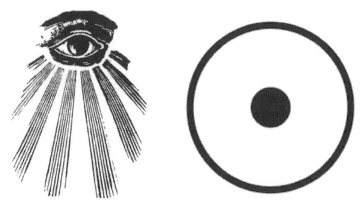

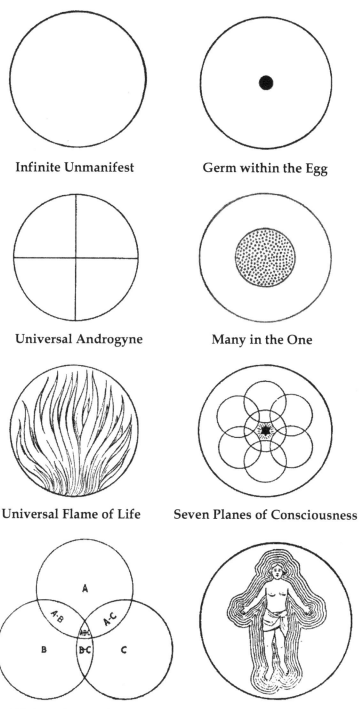

Infinite Unmanifest

Germ within the Egg

Universal Androgyne

Many in the One

Universal Flame of Life

Seven Planes of Consciousness

Three Higher Planes of Consciousness

Sevenfold Soul

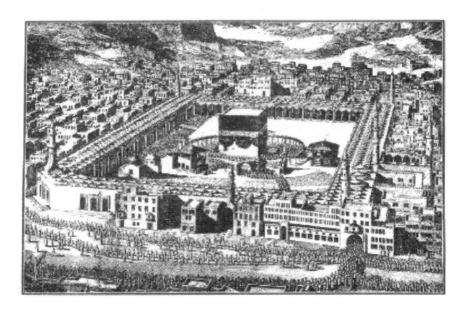

The Kaaba – located at Al-Masjid Al-Haram,
the sacred site of Muslims at Mecca

Tefillin

4	9	2
3	5	7
8	1	6

Magic Square of Saturn

Day: Saturday

Color: Black (the absence of or
complete absorption of light)

Sign: Capricorn

Metal: Lead

Hexagram Star of David / Seal of Solomon

Sigil of Saturn

Symbol for Lead

Astrological symbol of Saturn, often described as a scythe.

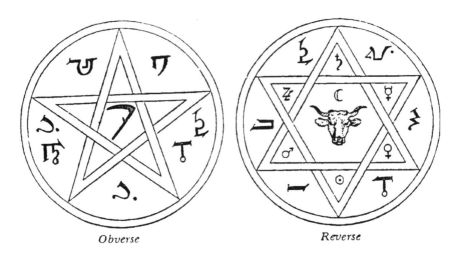

Obverse *Reverse*

**Talisman of the planet Saturn,
otherwise known as the *Star of Remphan* (Moloch)**

The *House of Israel*, a term referring to the twelve houses/tribes of the zodiac and all living things in general, was accused in Acts 7 of taking up the "tabernacle of Moloch" and the star "Remphan." Today we refer to that symbol as the Star of David, but this is incorrect. The "Jews" did not have a star, besides the one they adopted in the wilderness as a false idol – some refer to this idol as Chiun (Saturn), Apis (an Egyptian bull deity), and others as the brass bull-headed deity Molech.

Remphan is simply another name for **Chiun**, which translates to **Saturn**. The Babylonians worshipped him as **Kiyun**, a word referring to a "statue" or "idol," as did the Arabs, Assyrians, and many others.

In Hebrew the word *melech* means "king" and it is usually translated as *shameful king*, a variant for the name *Baal*. The Encyclopedia Britannica says: *"Moloch is a foreign deity who was at times illegitimately given a place in Israel's worship as a result of the syncretistic policies of certain apostate kings."*

As per the laws given to Moses by God, the "Jews" were strictly forbidden from doing what they had done in Egypt or Canaan, i.e., worshiping this deity. As Leviticus 18:21 preserves:

> *"'Do not give any of your children to be sacrificed to Molek, for you must not profane the name of your God. I am the LORD."*

This may help us to understand what Revelation 2:9 really means when it refers to the *Synagogue of Satan* as being comprised of people claiming to be "Jews" in "poverty" when they are neither:

> *"I know thy works, and tribulation, and poverty, (but thou art rich) and I know the blasphemy of them which say they are Jews, and are not, but are the synagogue of Satan."*

Jacob Frank was an extension of this "synagogue" in the 18th century, claiming to be the Jewish Messiah while laying waste to traditional religious and cultural values. Frank encouraged his followers – **FRANKISTS** - to transgress against as many moral boundaries as was possible, essentially promoting debauchery (i.e., Satanism) as the true way of the divine (infernal). He also claimed to be a reincarnation of both the Biblical patriarch Jacob and another self-declared messiah named Sabbatai Zevi in the 17th century, a cabalist whose followers - **SABBATEANS** - converted to Islam outwardly within the Ottoman Empire while retaining their Jewish faith in private (dönme). Virtually every vile insult and stereotype of the "Jew" today is derived from these Sabbatean Frankists: greed, usuary (outlawed in Christianity and Islam), pornography, bestiality, child abuse and sex, and mockery of the sacred etc., (*see* Weimar Germany 1920s).

 * **Acts 7:41-44 -** *"And they made a calf in those days, and offered sacrifice unto the idol, and rejoiced in the works of their own hands. Then God turned, and gave them up to worship the host of heaven; as it is written in the book of the prophets, O ye house of Israel, have ye offered to me slain beasts and sacrifices by the space of forty years in the wilderness? Yea, ye took up the tabernacle of Moloch, and the star of your god Remphan, figures which ye made to worship them: and I will carry you away beyond Babylon. Our fathers had the tabernacle of witness in the wilderness, as he had appointed, speaking unto Moses, that he should make it according to the fashion that he had seen."*

 * **Amos 5:25-27 -** *"Have ye offered unto me sacrifices and offerings in the wilderness forty years, O house of Israel? But ye have borne the tabernacle of your Moloch and Chiun your images, the star of your god, which ye made to yourselves. Therefore will I cause you to go into captivity beyond Damascus, saith the Lord, whose name is The God of hosts."*

The Dark Secret at the Heart of AI

No one really knows how the most advanced algorithms do what they do. That could be a problem.

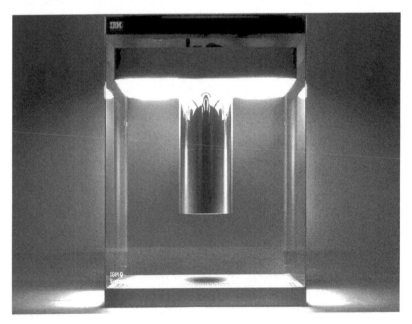

The IBM Q System One Computer

The Tower of Babel from Athanasius Kircher's <u>Turris Babel</u>.

The *tower* is a symbol of man's attempt to usurp from God the keys
to heaven. But in his arrogance and pride man finds his ability to
communicate confused. Some compare Kircher's depiction with the
internal components of the IBM Q System One quantum computer,
a similar technology seeking to raid heaven.

(image inverted)

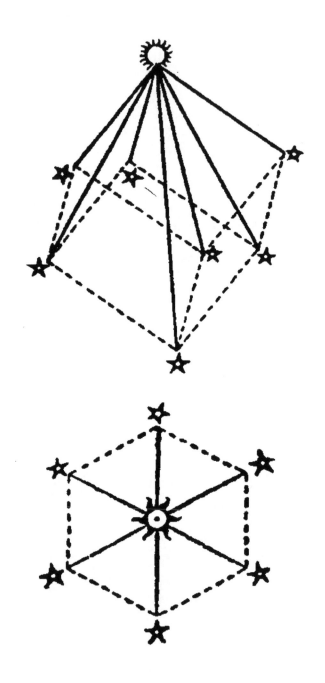

The Seven Days of Creation
from David Fideler's <u>Jesus Christ Son of God</u>.

The Transition of Matter as illustrated by Hieronymus Bosch. Depicted are the various stages of esoteric evolution that include a solidifying of a matter even finer than light, which gradually hardened into the state of nature we know today. Human bodies passed through the same stages with bones becoming solidified from a pink waxy substance, as written about by the Rosicrucian philosopher Jacob Boehme. The plant nature of man can still be seen in his nervous system. For more on this subject in particular, readers should consult Max Heindel's *The Rosicrucian Cosmo-Conception*.

SHAMANISM, FAIRIES & UFOs

First Iteration

Shamanism is a very old practice linking the practitioner with supernatural places and experiences. Shamans may, either at *will* or through *psychoactive substances*, enter into altered states of consciousness and commune with spirits on the *other side*. Their goal is to use these experiences for learning the art of healing, which is most often the information provided by entities encountered 'over there'.

Although the entities and beings interacted with vary, shamans usually obtain specific *spirit guides* that bestow this knowledge and guidance. Some receive guides at a young age that call on them to become shamans later in life. With these powers, the shaman may freely travel to the spirit world, hold communion, learn about the self, obtain knowledge of healing to help his or her people, and even influence the weather.

Although many today claim they are shamans because they carry staffs like a fantasy story character, or wear crystals and clothing they feel expresses their connection with Mother Earth, the actual practice of shamanism is anything and everything but what these people exude. Shamans almost always must go through a process of suffering, pain, and death, even torture, before they are reborn as healers. Luckily, and despite these realistic experiences, much of this occurs in the spirit realm.

Shamans are pierced by spears like Odin and Christ, levitate in the air like countless prophets, climb invisible vines or ladders like Jacob's in the Bible, and interestingly suffer from what sounds like the same medical experimentation experienced by 'UFO abductees'.

Shamanic experiences were also carried out in lesser degrees within localized tribes. As Joseph Campbell points out regarding mythology, the point of *"socially ordered cutting, branding, and cropping was to incorporate"* the person and their *"mind and body, into a larger, more enduring cultural body whose explanatory mythology became their own."*

Second Iteration

Many also relate shamanism, and particularly artic shamanism, to Santa Claus, his clothing, and reindeer, and the presents he brings to be placed under a tree. The tradition goes that these intellectual and spiritual figures of the arctic, known as *angakkuq*, would take *magic* mushrooms on the winter solstice. Since *magic* mushrooms, and particularly the red and white Amanita Muscaria (*fly agaric*) variety, are typically found underneath trees, and impart gifts through visions, the idea for wrapped presents under a pine tree began.

The red and white clothing of these medicine men also mimicked the Amanita and Santa Clause. The *red* relates to the universal female essence, menstrual blood, love, sex, passion, and magic. It is also the color of thunder and of the Germanic god Donar and the Norse god Thor. The *white* symbolizes snow, light, spirit, purity, and semen, making it *phallic* in parallel to the *yonic* qualities of red. Some alchemical myths also state that mercury is red and white. This is appropriate seeing that alchemy is a transformative spiritual process just like the one that can be experienced in the proper ritualistic taking of certain kinds of mushrooms. Many speculate that the hallucinations induced by *fly agaric* allowed for the abundance of reindeer nearby to appear as if they were flying. Spirit creatures like elves were likewise seen on these 'trips'. Furthermore, to dry the mushroom, Shamans placed them on tree branches, thus creating ornaments. The mushroom cap itself also mimics the *Pileus* worn during Saturnalia in ancient Rome, where the roles of wealthy and poor would be reversed. Are the worlds of the physical and spiritual not turned upside down by *fly agaric* mushrooms and other similar substances?

It is said that from the lighting and thunder generated from Thor's hammer, thunderstones would fall upon the ground and initiate the sprouting of mushrooms – particularly the *fly agaric*. In legend, this mushroom is called "raven's bread" due to the bird's association with both shamans and the god Odin, who was accompanied by his famous ravens *Huginn* and *Muninn*. The mushroom itself is also phallic and said to resemble the helmets worn by Viking warriors and Odin. The stone mushrooms of Central America are clearly phallic in nature too.

According to a book called <u>Pagan Christmas,</u> the Greek Zeus was considered the father of mushrooms. The *fly agaric* in particular is seen as a lucky symbol while the mushroom itself acts as a gateway to other worlds.

Odin and Jesus play the part of *shaman*, as does the great hunter Osiris. Anthropologist Felicitas Goodman explains how Osiris *"underwent a typical shamanic initiation in which his body was dismembered and then reassembled by his sister before he made his spirit journey to the Upper World."* The mythological dismemberment of Osiris also resembles the story of Huhnapu and Xbalanque, the "hero twins" from the ancient Quiche Maya book <u>Popul Vuh.</u> The pair descend into an otherworld or underworld called *Xibalba* after being abducted from their homes by messengers that arrive in the form of animals. Typically, they are owls, a symbol of wisdom and the temptress Lilith who provides the *fruit* of wisdom to Eve in the Garden. Huhnapu and Xbalanque are then transformed into therianthropes in order to have the tools necessary to conquer the trials of the *other world*. After much pain, suffering, and transformation, the pair return with wisdom and supernatural powers of healing. Egyptians called this otherworld the *duat* and said it existed in the western sky. The Maya referred to it as *Xibalba* and said it existed in an underworld, which certainly relates to the entombment of the sun each evening as it dies at sun set. In either case, this otherworldly spiritual realm is that of the pre-historic shamanic practice that continues up into contemporary times and has even been documented in Upper-Paleolithic cave art dating back 40,000 years. The Egyptians and Maya shared other similarities, too, such as believing the Pharaoh or King would ascend into heaven to be born again as a star. The only trivial difference is that the *duat* has twelve divisions and *Xibalba* has nine layers, like the nine circles of Hell described in Dante's Inferno. In both Central America and Egypt, the afterlife voyage was made in a boat with entities that ferried the soul from one level to the next – these *beings* were comprised of a dog, bird, and monkey. The bird (avian)-crocodile-reptile motif is also present in Japanese mythology, as noted earlier, with the sea monster/dragon *Wani*.

Generally seen as a monster, the kanji 鰐 is translated as *crocodile* and may therefore relate to the *eater of the dead,* the part crocodile, hippopotamus, and lion creature from the Egyptian *Hall of Judgement.*

Serpents featured prominently in not only these three seemingly different cultures but in virtually every mythology and spiritual description and depiction from ancient to modern times. Not only do we see therianthropes, or half-human/animal beings, but there are also *"spirit beings, disembodied eyes, and an extraordinary menagerie of gigantic serpents, many of which are coiled around each other, or have multiple heads, or spit fire, or are elaborately winged and feathered,"* writes author Graham Hancock in his book <u>Supernatural</u>. The Central American god Quetzalcóatl or Kukulcán was known as the *feathered serpent.*

Third Iteration

What we find in all these stories from around the world is parallel through hunter-gatherer societies and their shamans, to Medieval European fairies and their human abductions, all the way to contemporary UFO encounters in western society and beyond. There obviously are less-spiritual explanations to solve the riddle of so much similarity, but that is not our focus here.

The story is essentially the same: whether contacted at an early age or not to be a shaman or abductee, the individual will be floated into the sky, or climb there themselves, or be taken to an underworld, where they will interact with therianthropes, serpents, and spirits, experience what we may term 'medical experiments', have crystals or other objects implanted, be dismembered, be given special knowledge, and then finally returned home after having willfully sacrificed themselves like Jesus Christ or Odin for the betterment of their people. In fact, when one compares shamanic experiences with the experiences of those claiming to have been abducted by 'aliens', there is a baffling alignment of the two. Keep in mind that the latter UFO experiences are relatively recent in human history, at least in terms of how we know them in ufological history and mythology. The former, on the other hand, we presume dates back to a time when there was no religion or higher power other than what could be tapped into with the right combination of plant-based psychotropic substances, or other ceremonial and ritual performances. Animism, like Shintoism, is a *knowing* that all things have spirit and even a soul, something that shamans learn quickly. These concepts go back to the remotest periods of human history and likely before.

A shaman may experience lances or arrows penetrating their body, or other sharp objects cutting their flesh, body parts and organs being removed, and the implantation of foreign objects like crystals into their head or neck. Such sensations are also documented as a direct result of having taken DMT. These seemingly torturous experiments and experiences typically take place after the shaman has levitated or climbed on an invisible rope, vine, or ladder into the heavens. In parts of Australia these are called *"ropes of air"* and in southern Africa they are threads or strings. Sometimes shamans are taken underwater, but the most common locations apart from the sky are underground caverns. As Graham Hancock explains: *"...most accounts of shamanic initiations also begin with a sky journey (because the realm of the gods and spirits is located in the sky - for example Viho-mahse, the Tukano god of hallucinogenic snuff, lurking in the Milky Way)."*

Whatever the location a shaman is then subjected to medical experimentation just like UFO abductees. Alien/UFO abductees experience much of the same torment that shamans experience upon initiation. They are levitated out of cars, houses, and even through walls and windows, to ships in the sky, or to facilities underground or underwater. Once there, abductees usually suffer medical experiments involving long needles, sharp objects, the removal of organs, utensils inserted into their nostrils, and implants. Some interpret their experience with these beings as an enlightening one that they then utilize to help others. Many even see the 'aliens' - like shamanic spirits, spirit-animals, and therianthropes - as healers, helpers, and teachers. This has been a common theme for decades in ufology. As confirmation, Graham Hancock adds, 'alien abductees' are victims to *"the humiliating and traumatizing experience of being subjected by the abducting entities to forced medical examinations and to painful and incomprehensible surgical procedures that often leave behind permanent visible scars and sometimes even mysterious implants..."*

Alien abductees most often report seeing small beings between two to four feet in height - the *greys*. Although these *small* beings, or little people, are described as having ashy, pale, smooth skin, they are sometimes called *little green men* in popular culture. How appropriate is it then that within folklore and legend the *fairy*, a very tiny person of the same height and body as a *grey*, is most often seen wearing the color *green*? It is further interesting to note that not only are these tiny fairies often seen dressed in green - *little green men* - they also are known to shape-shift into black goats and are sometimes seen with furred cloven hooves. This further connects the spirit world and fairies with images of the Devil and the infamous Black Mass. Jacques Vallee confirms this in his book <u>Passport to Magonia</u>. He says that the UFO phenomenon is *"identical to the earlier belief in the fairy faith."* He adds, *"The entities described as the pilots of the craft are indistinguishable from the elves, sylphs and lutins of the Middle Ages."*

There are also 'screen memories' wherein the abducted individual remembers not the experience but instead the disturbing image of an owl staring with large black eyes through their window. Again, we have a reference to "She of the Night" - Lilith. Others may see insect-like creatures called *insectoids*. Timothy Leary saw something similar when he experimented with DMT, but he called them "magnificent insects."

The same phenomenon is further found in the field of cryptozoology on the subject of *dog man* or *wolf man*, both of which often stare in windows or somehow obtain entrance into a home where they watch the experiencer from their bedroom, usually in a corner or at the foot of their bed. Associate professor of History at Temple University, Dr. David Jacobs, records this exact story for one of the interviews he conducted with an abductee:

> *"The wolf was standing squarely on her bed, looking her in the eyes. She clearly remembered its fur, fangs, and eyes. Other abductees have claimed to have seen monkeys, owls, deer, and other animals."*

In popular culture and folklore, the *hat man, smiling man,* and even the *sandman*, all play similar roles. For the shaman, these are usually guides and teachers.

The late Dr. John Mack, former Harvard University psychiatrist, made a career out of helping 'alien abductees' - as far back as 1989 - understand their 'experiences' despite the immense ridicule he received up until his death. He believed, from a psychological perspective, and one that makes logical sense:

> *"...the aliens assume a form or forms that are familiar or comprehensible within the individual's own perceptual background or framework."*

Some 'alien abductees' are even taken from their home at a young age and experience being abducted repeatedly throughout their lives, just like shamans. Hancock details this in his book too:

"These spirit guides almost always appear in the form of animals or therianthropes, and frequently begin to play a role in the future shaman's life while he is still a child, long before his initiation. In this respect, too, there is a parallel with UFO abductions, which also often begin in childhood and continue into adulthood."

Mack further confirmed what Hancock and Jacobs found, that *"the aliens appear to be consummate shape-shifters, often appearing initially to the abductees as animals - owls, eagles, raccoons and deer are among the creatures the abductees have seen initially."* Although he was not entirely convinced that UFOs were 'nuts and bolts' craft, he did take a mostly objective approach in gathering data and submitting theories:

"What kind of matter is the alien abduction phenomenon? ... It seems to belong to that class of phenomena, not even generally accepted as existing by mainstream Western science, that seem not to be of this visible, known material universe and yet appear to manifest in it. These are phenomena... that seem to 'cross over' or to violate the radical separation of the spirit and unseen realms from the material world."

Fourth Iteration

Although these 'experiences' are virtually identical for shamans and modern UFO abductees, there is a slight difference between what is experienced by biological men and women. In all cases, it seems that the spirits, aliens - and especially *sprites* in folklore - are interested in human genetics and breeding. The methods used by these entities also seem to be adapting and progressing alongside human development. People no longer claim that their child was replaced by a *fairy child* or *changeling*, and when someone is taken to what they see as the otherworld or a UFO, although they may experience a few minutes or hours of *missing time,* they no longer spend what appears to be a few hours away only to be returned home years into the future. These were common reports in the past. Whatever the reasoning, and considering that some interactions with therianthropes, spirits, aliens, etc., are purely hallucinatory, there may be a more concrete reality to such potential *breeding experiments* that are usually focused on women. Shamans and 'alien abductees' both report entities coming into their room at night to have intercourse with them, or to take them elsewhere for the same reason, while plunging any nearby family or inhabitants of the home into an *unnatural sleep* – thing of the *sandman*. Traditionally we have called the beings, in these covert sexual encounters, incubus (for women) and succubus (for men). The original succubus was, again, Lilith. Shamans are even known to have spirit spouses and children in the *other world*. Some travel to visit these children, and women are often requested or demanded - usually telepathically - to breastfeed them. The same is true for 'alien abductees'. Some women have the feeling that these are actually their children, while others, even if they feel such an emotion, are so repulsed by the child that they reject contact entirely. The aliens usually insist, as do spirit companions and the fairies of old.

Although men reportedly have semen extracted from their bodies, women are used more like incubators and wet nurses. Hancock elaborates on these details:

> *"Where male abductees are concerned, sperm samples are repeatedly taken, and hybrid babies are displayed to them with the strong mental suggestion that these are their offspring. Like female abductees, who are sometimes artificially inseminated and sometimes impregnated directly in acts of sexual intercourse with 'the alien beings,' male abductees also have sex with alien females."*

Fairies are just as interested in breeding with humans as shamanic spirits and aliens. Hancock says that *"it seems that not only do fairies and aliens have a shared need for sexual and reproductive contacts with humanity, but also, in both cases, they seek these contacts in order to bring about some desired transformation in their own condition."* It would further seem that these beings have improved their "conditions" over thousands of years, since the phenomena has progressed beyond abducting humans and both stealing or replacing children.

Otherwise, hybrids between humans and spirits/aliens/fairies, are still thin, pale, have white-gray skin that is dry and ashy, and larger heads in relation to their bodies. These details may be nothing more than coincidence or a form of supernatural pareidolia, but they certainly are more than interesting. Both shamans and 'alien abductees' also report seeing what amounts to breeding pods with hybrid beings inside. Siberian shamans are made aware of how souls are incubated in nests on a shamanic world tree. Alien abductees sometimes are shown rows of compartments containing embryos or babies. Reverend Robert Kirk shared accounts from the seventeenth century of Scottish mothers abducted during pregnancy to wet nurse the babies of fairies. Hancock points out that the rooms in which these mothers were taken *are virtually interchangeable with modern descriptions of rooms on board UFOs, where women are taken to wet-nurse hybrid children.*

Mr. Hancock also points out an interesting parallel of a shaman's experience in the 1950s with that of one of the first alien abductions involving Betty and Barney Hill in 1961. Maria Sabina was a Mazatec Indian shaman who practiced in the village of Huatla de Jimenez in Mexico in the 1950s. She explained how she could not read, but upon traveling to the spirit world she was given a book and immediately learned to read it, learning information on how to help her people. This is closely related to the prophet Muhammed who was illiterate until he was contacted by the divine:

> *"A duende, a spirit, came toward me. He asked me a strange question: 'But what do you wish to become, you, Maria Sabina?' I answered him, without knowing, that I wished to become a saint. Then the spirit smiled, and immediately he had in his hands something that he did not have before, and it was a big Book with many written pages. 'Here,' he said, 'I am giving you this Book so that you can do your work better and help people who need help and know the secrets of the world where everything is known.' I found through the leaves of the Book, many written pages, and I thought that unfortunately I did not know how to read. I have never learned and therefore that would not have been any use to me. Suddenly I realized I was reading and understood all that was written in the Book and that I became as though richer, wiser, and that in one moment I learned millions of things. I learned and learned."*

Fifth Iteration

The story of divine knowledge, or even technology, being imparted to mankind from spirits, gods, goddesses, teachers, therianthropes, aliens, etc., is also preserved in the mythological story of Prometheus bringing fire to mankind and suffering a severe punishment, akin to Jesus Christ, as a result. Major world religions have their origin in such events. Muhammed was visited by the Angel Gabriel and revealed the text of the Holy Quran. Moses famously talked to God by means of a burning bush and later met him face-to-face to receive the Ten Commandments. The *Revelation of St. John* was received in similar manner, through what some would likely call hallucinations. Joseph Smith, the founder of Mormonism, received golden plates from the angel Moroni which contained the Book of Mormon. Hinduism, Buddhism, Shintoism, Animism, and so many others, likewise maintain a belief in realms beyond the physical that are inhabited by various entities and beings – call them angels, demons, ad infinitum. The Bible itself is the *Word of God* and Ezekiel, like the Prophet Enoch, experienced communications through direct contact with the Source. Ezekiel's famous "wheel" itself may be attributed to *fairy circles, fairy lights,* and *flying discs.*

These famous *fairy circles* also share a curious relationship with UFOs, seeing that both *fairy dances* and *flying saucers* tend to leave physical, often radioactive, traces of their presence. The rings of *fairy lights* seen on the ground or in the air parallel unidentified flying objects with their rows of rotating lights. As John Mack wrote about aliens assuming forms that are *"familiar or comprehensible within the individuals own perceptual background or framework,"* the same may be said of their modes of transport. What was once a floating boat, shield, etc., has turned into a spacecraft in contemporary times. However, this is not necessarily an exclusive experience of the twentieth or twenty-first century. Perhaps our ancestors also witnessed certain such things without the ability to even make a comparison to a boat or shield.

Sixth Iteration

The possible weapons used by UFOs and their occupants are also akin to *elf shot* from Anglo-Saxon medical texts. This is a condition believed to have been caused by invisible arrows fired at the body, obviously reminiscent of DMT and ayahuasca. Also called *fairy blast*, the 'weapon' can paralyze victims without causing external injuries. This all may be related to what neuropsychologists call *somatic hallucinations,* where a person experiences shorter limbs, extra limbs, and stabbing sensations, but it also may be something else entirely. These *somatic hallucinations* are probably just a contemporary name for something humans have been experiencing for thousands of years.

Depictions in cave and rock art from around the world depict what is called the *wounded man*, or a man pierced by many arrows or spears. We find this in the stories of Prometheus, Jesus Christ, Odin, and many others. Prometheus is punished by the gods for bringing fire (wisdom and knowledge) to mankind. He is tied down to a rock and daily experiences the pain of a bird eating his liver out of the side of his body. In other cases, it is a cross or pole, much like the ones shamans climb into the sky. Jesus was pierced in his side while hanging on the cross by the Lance of Longinus. Quetzalcóatl and Orpheus were likewise crucified in similar manner, and it was also the birth of the former which was signified by an angel coming down from Orion to inform the mother that her son, like Jesus, would be a savior. Interestingly, the Mayan Kukulkan or Aztec Quetzalcóatl is crucified in legend with a bird, not unlike the dove of the Holy Spirit, perched on top of the cross. We find this same exact image, but with an eagle perched on the *ash tree*, in Norse myth. It was here that the supreme god Odin was crucified to the *World Tree* (Yggdrasil) and had a spear thrust into his side like Jesus. His story is told in the Icelandic *Edda*:

> *I ween that I hung of the windy tree,*
> *Hung there for nights full nine;*
> *With the spear I was wounded, and offered I was,*
> *To Othin, myself to myself,*
> *On the tree that none may ever know*
> *what root beneath it runs.*

Other similar stories are found in Tibet, circa 700 BC, when the god Indra, born of a virgin with an ability to walk on water, is crucified on a cross, dies and is resurrected. In some depictions he is seen ascending from a chest, nearly identical in nature to the chest that Set(h) tricked Osiris within Egyptian mythology. Later, Set was himself crucified, having his hands tied behind his back to a post and knives driven into his body. The archangel Michael also suffers for mankind in his battles against Lucifer, just like the crucified Prometheus, and the Chinese ruler Fohi, who was born of a virgin, concurrently brings knowledge to his people. The same may be said of Saints, too, including St. Sabastian who is often depicted as a classical *wounded man*.

Hancock explains how the *wounded man* is much more than a metaphor, and that the motif is widespread:

> "In the Amazon judge, when shamans of the Jivaro tribe enter trance under the influence of ayahuasca, they construe the same neurologically generated skin sensations as sharp little darts being fired at them by supernatural entities. Siberian Tungus shamans speak of initiatory trances, induced by ingestion of fly agaric mushrooms, in which they experience themselves to have been pierced with arrows, their flesh cut off, their bones torn out. Ju/'hoansi shamans in southern Africa often undergo great physical pain at certain stages of their trance and it is notable how frequently they... construe their neurologically generated somatic hallucinations as insect stings."

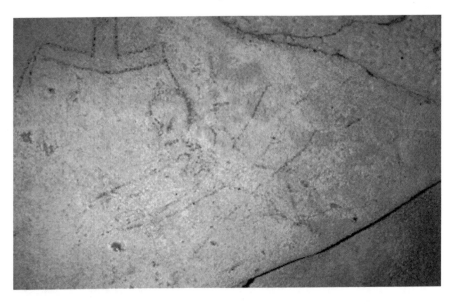

Wounded Man from Pech Merle cave in France

Like *wounded men*, symbolic crucifixions are older than antiquity. They became a common symbol in many secret societies as a part of initiation into the *mysteries*. The image below shows a hierophant holding a staff and an ankh. He is flanked on either side by participants with the heads of lions, bulls, and birds. Behind these higher degree initiates stand other participants with headdresses, signifying illumination, and an *uraeus*  serpent rising from the center of the forehead. The candidate is tied to the **X** - a common practice in Japan - above a coffin and two illuminated pillars. Upon removal from the cross, the candidate is placed in a coffin for three days before awakening and being pulled out of *death* by the strong grip of the *lion's paw*. Then, proceeding afterward, the initiate would exit by *way* of the *middle path* between the *twin pillars* and through the eastern gate of the temple to greet the morning star and rising sun. In the occult sciences of India candidates for initiation, the *Brahmatchary*, were led by a guru through a ritual facing the rising sun in the east. Afterwards, the young neophyte would be referred to as a *Douidja*, which means *twice born*.

In an article on the Cross published in the <u>Encyclopedia Britannica</u>, Thomas Macall Fallow explains the antiquity of the cross:

> *"The use of the cross as a religious symbol in pre-Christian times, and among non-Christian peoples, may probably be regarded as almost universal, and in very many cases it was connected with some form of nature worship."*

What was once nature oriented became an adopted motif of tribal groups seeking special attention from what became a regional god and doctrine.

The Crucifixion by Bartolomé Esteban Murillo (1675).
&
Odin hanging on the World Tree

The **Orpheus Amulet** – Joseph Campbell writes: *"It is clear that, in Orpheus and Christ, we have exactly the same archetype, with the motif of leaving the physical world, still symbolized with a cross in astronomy, for the spiritual. They leave the Earth, symbol of Mother, to go to the realm of the Father."*

The Crucifixion of Quetzalcóatl (Codex Borgianus)
from Kingsborough's <u>Antiquities of Mexico</u>.
&
Indra, the god of war and storms, rising out of a chest like Osiris -
page from <u>Alphabetum Tibetanum</u> (1762) by the monk Augustinus
Georgius

TIBETANUM 203

gentes præfertim in Urbe *Nepal*, Luna XII. *Badr* 𑀐 𑀝, feu
Bhadoñ 𑀐𑀤𑀺𑀡 *Augufti* menfis, dies feftos aufpicaturæ Dei
Indræ 𑀐 𑀝, erigunt ad illius memoriam ubique locorum *Cru-*
ces amictas *Abrotono*. Earum figuram defcriptam habes ad
lit.B Tabula pone fequenti. Nam A effigies eft ipfius *Indræ*
crucifixi figna *Telech* in fronte manibus pedibufque gerentis.

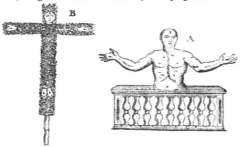

LXXXII. Statuam *Indræ* ex editis locis, pulpitifque con-
fpicuam Indigenæ Nepalkenfes adorant, peregrini vero
tanquam infigne quoddam fuperftitionis portentum mi-
rantur & obftupefcunt. *Telech* J vem forte *miniatum* ex-
hibent: notæ facræ funt *effluvia purgationum naturæ* figni-
ficant, iifque Regum pariter frontem, manus pedefque.
in folemni eorum inauguratione confignant. Sed *Indræ*
Deus eft Cæli inferioris, nubium Rector, pluviarum,
Cc 2   inun-

Prometheus Bound by Peter Paul Rubens
and Frans Snyders (1611-1618).

The Serpent Lifted Up - Annaberg, Germany 16th-century AD.

Seventh Iteration

Dr. Rick Strassman's famous medical trials at the University of New Mexico found that subjects given certain doses of DMT would report not just 'aliens' and 'fairies', but also spaceships and even clowns. Strassman explains in his book <u>DMT The Spirit Molecule</u>:

> *"These worlds are usually invisible to us and our instruments, and are not accessible using our normal state of consciousness. However, just as likely as the theory that these worlds exist 'only in our minds' is that they are, in reality, 'outside us' and freestanding. If we simply change our brains receiving abilities, we can comprehend and interact with them."*

But even before the first official cases of 'alien abductions' were reported, and long before Dr. Strassman's DMT study, Hungarian medical doctor Stephen Szara gave DMT to human subjects in an experiment to determine the substance's usefulness as a psychiatric drug. William Turner MD and Sidney Merlis MD conducted similar research, pre-alien abduction popularity, by investigating the experiences of participants in their own DMT study. Participants in both studies reported the same thing that shamans have, and modern UFO abductees still, report today.

The fact is that for at least 200,000 years when full anatomical modernity was reached - perhaps earlier - man had the brain and neurological capacity to think in similar terms to how we do in contemporary times. But something seems to have triggered an incredible transformation around 40,000 years ago in how this brain power was utilized.

Around 35,000 years ago in Europe and about 27,000 years ago in Africa, beautiful and thought-provoking art began to appear seemingly from nowhere in caves and on rocks. It appeared in an established and sophisticated form without any evidence, that we have, of pre-formation. As David Lewis-Williams suggests, and as Graham Hancock explores further, the *"catalyst was the cultivation of altered states of consciousness, most probably first experienced by our ancestors through the accidental consumption of plant or fungal hallucinogens."*

We can thus theorize that these experiences and their developments, although sudden, were probably not reached simultaneously across all cultures. It was gradual, especially considering that these timelines predate post-flood stories of civilizer gods sharing great universal wisdom.

The relationship between shamanic traditions in central and southern "*Africa, Australia, and the Amazon rain forest,*" mixed with an interest in *sprites* throughout medieval and Victorian times in Europe, and with UFOs and aliens in North America and other places in contemporary times, proves a more than sudden and coincidental connection. For them to be so consistent "*over so long a period in absence of any objective 'real world' stimulus at all is a much more mysterious matter,*" concludes Hancock.

Eighth Iteration

Psychoactive plants are not always needed to enter into these *other worlds*, however, especially considering that the vast number of 'alien abductees', even accounting for delusions, influences on the sub-conscious from popular culture, etc., do not take *ayahuasca* or anything closely related. Many have been highly trained military personnel, as detailed in my book *The Technological Elixir*. Others lose respect, relationships, their family, jobs, etc., as a result of simply telling their story. But sadly, the issue has become so convoluted at this point, largely because of the money that can be made selling fake stories, it is almost impossible to find credible information.

But a small number of shamans, including those people who will become shamans later in life, are gifted to experience these *other worlds* by slipping into altered states of consciousness without the need for psychotropics or hallucinogens. Hancock says, "*These special gifted shamans, the spontaneous trancers, obviously provide the closest parallel to UFO abductees, whose experiences are also spontaneous and not deliberately induced.*"

Strassman proposes that a small percentage of those 'abducted' by aliens, like the same regarding spirits, therianthropes, fairies, etc., experience a natural overproduction of DMT in the body. This would explain why the phenomenon has persisted from hunter-gatherer societies, and before, up until the present day.

David Lewis-Williams believes that this explains mankind's seemingly sudden development of art, religion, and societal structure. It also explains, perhaps partly or fully, the idea of *hidden masters*, non-physical *spiritual teachers*, and the meaning of taking hallucinatory substances in the *mystery schools* of Egypt, Greece, India, etc., to commune with these same parallel realities.

It is interesting to note that many DMT experiences go beyond *entopic visuals* and *therianthropes* and directly into a sort of technical or machine-based reality run by similarly described entities. These ideas are carried further by Terrence and Dennis McKenna, both suggesting in their book <u>The Invisible Landscape</u> that a sort of computer data stored in our DNA could be extracted under the right conditions or states of consciousness: *"information stored in the neural-genetic material might be made available to consciousness"* under the right conditions – hallucinogens, rituals, bodily stress, or natural abilities otherwise. Terrence and Dennis *"reasoned that both neural DNA and neural RNA were involved"* in the process of activating information stored in genes. Bruce Lamb suggested the same after researching in the Amazon, speculating that on *"some unknown, unconscious level the genetic encoder DNA provides a bridge to biological memories of all living things, and aura of unbounded awareness manifesting itself in the activated mind."* Similar ideas and theories were proposed by anthropologist Jeremy Narby, who believed there is a message, or messages, encoded in our DNA that can be read and interacted with through substances such as *ayahuasca*. All of this is compounded by the fact that under numerous methods used to reach these altered states of consciousness, serpents, a double helix, and geometry all play a key role – i.e., DNA. Narby adds that *"DNA is a master of transformation, just like mythical serpents."* It is from these serpents that man acquires much of his knowledge, and it is from these serpents that shamans have received much of their healing and botanical wisdom.

The co-discoverer of the double-helix structure of DNA in 1953, Francis Crick, also famously believed that this encoding system was akin to *"an ancient, high biotechnology."* Crick was also on LSD when he made his *discovery*, something that likely had been witnessed for tens of thousands of years in ASCs long before LSD, Crick, or modern science. Furthermore, the so-called 'junk' portion of DNA follows the linguistic parameters of Zipf's law regarding frequency and occurrence that appears in all languages throughout the world. But this is only true for non-coding 'junk' regions, whereas coding regions – the 3% – do not follow this law. In other words, the non-coding portion is like a structured language embedded in all life on the planet. Perhaps this is the information and structure being accessed in altered states of consciousness.

Both Michael Harner, one of the first Westerns to participate fully in an Amazonian ayahuasca ceremony, and Jeremy Narby in his own ayahuasca experiences, witnessed *"dragon-like creatures"* and *"gigantic boa-constrictors"* while under the influence of the plant mixture. Their experiences match Crick's assertion that the double helix is far too complex to have originated on Earth and likely came from somewhere else, suggesting that this was another galaxy from which an automated alien spaceship departed during a time incomprehensible.

It should be further noted that galaxies, like the unfolding of a flower, can also be seen to "coil" in a manner similar to snakes. In fact, galaxies rotate around a super-massive black hole mimicking a hurricane circulating around a central eye. The rotation of our spiral-armed galaxy around the center of a super-massive black hole is similar to how the planets in our solar system orbit around their star. On an even smaller scale are the electrons orbiting around the nucleus of an atom.

Comets with their tales may be harbingers of death to some, including modern man, but like any space debris they may also bring the elements of life to a barren world – *panspermia*. This understanding of micro and macro worlds – *hermeticism* - came from observing nature and applying those observations to develop conclusions based on recognized patterns. Thus, myth was an early form of science.

The Golden Mean may be observed in seashells, pinecones, flowers, flight patterns of insects, and the informational vehicle at the base of life as we know it - DNA – which spirals or coils like a great serpent. The dragon, boa-constrictor, python, and the serpent in the Garden of Eden may be quickly recalled. These are symbols and expressions found in virtually every culture, history, mythology, and otherworldly experience recorded anywhere and at any time throughout the world. Whether in UFOs, shamanic dreams, or fairy abductions, the story is almost always the same.

One interesting thought proposed by Strassman, particularly about DMT, is that our physical world is *"not dark for the denizens of dark matter, or parallel to those intelligent beings who have mastered quantum computing."*

Not only is our world an extension of their world, and their world an extension of ours, but *"those who have evolved in different universes, or according to their own unique laws of physics, actually can observe us directly with their own sense or by using particular types of technology."*

Ninth Iteration

It should become clear why modern ufology in general, but certain segments historically in particular, talk about a *reptilian* presence or species. We may extract something of meaning about this from examining the fear we collectively have over machines, robots, artificial (archonic) intelligence, and the like. All the former things are immensely transformative with dangerous potential, something we have seen unfold in highly destructive ways (cell phones, social media) without the direct dramatic shock (movies) like we would expect. It is a slow creeping (slithering) force, which has benefits, but is also a great danger.

Although the fear is justified on the surface, the worry about machines taking jobs is essentially unjustified because the industrial revolution saw a similar thing happen. Some jobs disappear and others emerge. For those afraid of some coming singularity, it must be noted that the phone you hold or computer you use is already an extension of your physical body, effectively making you a cyborg already.

We fear a dystopian science-fiction version of the future and yet find that it never happens like we imagine. That is because our brains never need to be wired to a computer when they can be symbolically wired with phones, apps, social media, and algorithms which are already *trained* machines giving us subtle commands. All the information we put online, what we interactive with in that digital world, and what we say in front of our devices, etc., builds our digital profile and avatar – that is the upload.

Moreover, the metal machines and the otherworldly computing power we often express concern with, as some coming apocalyptic event, is already here now and simply taken for granted because it is assumed as a fundamental part of life from birth. It is that metal and computing power, however, which triggers a deep reaction within our genes and psyche. Those things are literally cold and calculating and these are the traits of a reptile. Since the Garden of Eden humans have been tempted and stalked by this predator. It lurks in the dark, on the edge of light and dark – in the twilight zone. It strikes when we least expect it and rips us to pieces. It is aggressive, violent, and even bloodthirsty.

It is nature in its most extreme. But in its least extreme it drives us to eat, drink, procreate, and create order in our world.

When we apply these ideas to UFOs and space travel the predator immediately presents itself within the unknown of flying objects and the dark, limitless, endless, potential of space. The predator emerges from dreams too and altered states of consciousness, often induced by certain substances.

All these things imply danger, so we look and try to figure out what is happening. It is like sitting in a classroom and the door opens – what happens? We all turn instinctually to look at the potential threat.

The reptilian is at the core of our fears over aliens, and we are thus afraid it is going to eat us, drink our blood, torture us, etc. And yes, it is! But not the one from some other planet. The one that comprise your psychosocial state. The RED DRAGON and BEAST of Revelation are a great example of this: the dragon is your EGO guarding the treasure of internal transformative powers (philosopher's stone) and the beast is your ANIMLAL SELF which must be sacrificed for enlightenment.

In this way, the reptilian is simply the archetypical demon - and this means we need an archetypical angel too. Here we get beings like Pleiadeans, with their advanced wisdom and technology, or tall white Nordics with blonde hair. In fact, there is a deep theological dogma to ufology. It has its own history and meaning that is endlessly debated, including whether aliens are good or evil; locations like Roswell are its holy sites; and it has its own holy books, saints (many of which are living), and even heavenly ascension (rapture) versus the hell of staying on earth.

There is even a relationship between those who have been burned by a UFO, or perhaps suffered radiation burns, and the stories told about the shining face of God, or the fire that is Jesus Christ. The chanting and singing of some religions are replaced with crystal bowls, meditation, and sky watching with night vision goggles. Ufology has its own garb too, which sadly has little to do with UFOs and more to do with New Age cults. At its core there is this growing mythology which shares a direct relationship with psychic stressors on the populace, be it World War II, the fear of nuclear annihilation during the Cold War, or any similar fear about uncertainty and instability that we have today.

PSYCHIC MANIFESTATIONS, JUNGIAN UFOs & COSMIC HORRORS

First Iteration

Foo Fighters and *Ghost Rockets* are just what they sound like, i.e., balls of luminous substance and etheric cigar-shaped illusions. The February 24-25, 1942, incursion over Los Angeles and the west coast of the United States featured an object which could not be shot down or even damaged, as if it were non-physical. Across the world in May of 1943, and long before Kenneth Arnold saw his skipping 'saucers' (chevron craft - **V**) in the pacific northwest, the USAAF reported "discs" that somehow made physical contact with a military craft with no resulting physical damage. It's almost as if the military plane flew through a ghost or apparition of some sort. The story is from the USAAF 348th Group bombers, who witnessed the cluster of discs during a raid on Schweinfurt, Germany, that year. According to an intelligence report of the mission:

> *"Discs were described as silver coloured – one inch thick and three inches in diameter. They were gliding slowly down in very uniform cluster. A/C 026 was unable to avoid them and his right wing went directly through a cluster with absolutely no effect on engines or plane surface. One of the discs was heard striking tail assembly but no explosion was observed..."*

Two other A/C aircraft also flew through *"silver discs with no apparent damage."*

As the history of these things proceed, we end up with crashes, abductions, and finally a century plagued with everyday claims of alien contact. It is almost as if the entire phenomenon is based in the mind.

In fact, what Kenneth Arnold witnessed were not discs or saucers but *chevron* shaped craft. The public only began to see the former because of how the media reported the story.

In These United States

Supersonic Flying Saucers Sighted by Idaho Pilot

Speed Estimated at 1,200 Miles an Hour When Seen 10,000 Feet Up Near Mt. Rainier

PENDLETON, Ore., June 25.—(P)

NINE bright saucer-like objects flying at "incredible" speed at 10,000 foot altitude were reported here today by Kenneth Arnold, Boise (Idaho), pilot, who said he could not hazard a guess as to what they were.

Arnold, a U.S. Forest Service employee searching for a missing plane, said he sighted the mystery craft yesterday at 3 p.m. They were flying between Mount Rainier and Mount Adams, in Washington state, he said, and appeared to weave in and out of formation. Arnold said he clocked them and estimated their speed at 1,200 miles an hour.

Inquiries at Yakima last night brought only blank stares, he said, but he added he talked today with an unidentified man from Ukiah, south of here, who said he had seen similar objects over the mountains near Ukiah yesterday.

"It seems impossible," Arnold said, "but there it is."

* * *

CIRCULATION
1 ....
2 A.I.2.b ....
3 A.I.2.b ....

EKG.   TELEGRAM EN CLAIR.   4112.

Recd. AHCS. 171129a hrs Oct.43.

TO — OIAFW, OIAJX, OISHL, HBC, AMY.

From — OIPNT.

IMPORTANT. CONFIDENTIAL.

8 BC O-1079-E.
Annex to Intelligence Report Mission Shweinfurt 16 October 1943.

306 Group reports partially unexploded 20 mm shell imbedded above the panel in the cockpit of A/C number 412 bearing the following figures 19K43. The Group Ordnance Officer believes the stool composing the shell is of inferior grade.   384th Group reports a cluster of disks observed in the path of the formation near Schweinfurt, at the time there were no E/A above. Discs were described as silver colored — one inch thick and three inches in diameter. They were gliding slowly down in very uniform cluster. A/C 026 was unable to avoid them and his right wing went directly through a cluster with absolutely no effect on engines or plane surface. One of the discs was heard striking tail assembly but no explosion was observed. About 20 feet from these discs a mass of black debris of varying sizes in clusters of 3 by 4 feet. Also observed 2 other A/C flying through silver discs with no apparent damage. Observed discs and debris 2 other times but could not determine where it came from.

Copies to:-

P.R. & A.I.6.
D.B.Ops.
War Room.
D.A.T.
A.I.3.(USA)(Action 2 copies) ✓

Swiss psychologist and psychiatrist Carl Gustav Jung described some of the original sightings as a rumor that *"differs from an ordinary rumor in that it is expressed in the form of visions."* In <u>Flying Saucers: A Modern Myth of Things Seen in the Skies</u> Jung suggests that UFOs are a *"99 per cent psychic product"*, though admitting many seem to have a physical nature:

> *"The only thing we can say with tolerable certainty about UFOs is that they possess a surface which can be seen by the eye and at the same time throws back a radar echo."*

Such an idea suggests that what we may be dealing with, in large part, are psychic manifestations of a collective *desire* (or programmed *perception*) to *believe* in something – or an interacting with something beyond base-physical reality that wishes to contact us. As a result of the power found in belief, perhaps DMT and ayahuasca are not needed to merge realities. Perhaps this is why so many witnesses of UFOS, and even official investigators, report different characteristics and interactions when viewing what seems like the same phenomenon. As with *faith*, the power of the mind, or many minds, can, with intention, change reality ever so slightly. Our reality is already based on a limited number of data points out of millions processed by the body and senses every second.

In physics the *observer effect* is described as a bias which occurs when we notice what we expect or behave in ways that influence others. Therefore, the observer changes the experiment and the experimenter. The 1% allowed by Jung is a real phenomenon which possibly is responsible for the otherwise *"99 per cent psychic"* explanation for UFOs.

It is no secret that much of what we think about space and what lies beyond comes from stories told in shows like Star Trek. Although its creator, Gene Roddenberry, was certainly an intelligence guy, he did not entirely formulate ideas for the show organically. Star Trek blossomed instead as a result of channeling sessions whereby an 'alien' group calling itself the *Council of Nine* imparted detailed information to Gene and others. We are again reminded of the Eight Immortals of China, Egypt's Ennead, and the Nagas of India. This council was apparently operating from a place outside of *time* and *space*, something the Egyptians called *nun*, or the *nothingness*. In this way they are like the *cosmic horrors* of H. P.

Lovecraft, who bears a striking resemblance to Facebook's (Meta's) Mark Zuckerberg. In fact, it would seem that the Borg from the Star Trek universe are real 'aliens' operating under the guise of humans on earth today. Consider the cofounder of Singularity University, Peter Diamandis, who said of AI and brain-computer-interfaces: *"Anybody who is going to be resisting the progress forward is going to be resisting evolution and, fundamentally, they will die out. It's not a matter of whether it's good or bad. It's going to happen."* Then consider what World Economic Forum founder Klaus Schwab said about the next industrial revolution:

> *"What the fourth industrial revolution will lead to is a fusion of our physical, digital and biological identity..."*

It just sounds so inhuman, especially when you watch Star Trek and hear the famous line from a BORG: *"We are the Borg. Your biological and technological distinctiveness will be added to our own. Resistance is futile."*

Let us now explore a few more considerations on the point of such manifestations: *Poltergeists* are often thought to relate to periods of adolescence, and particularly to females, in the sense that changing emotions and hormones cause outbursts of psychic energy. Anger, frustration, confusion, sexual desire, hormones, etc., are powerful energies to contend with, and are known to interfere with electronics.

The same can be said about the UFO's apparent interest in war and nuclear weapons. War is a time of intense stress and fear. Perhaps that stress works to manifests these things, just as atomic weapons tamper with the very subatomic nature of reality and therefore may encourage interdimensional incursions. War is also a time when enemy aircraft are seen in the skies and new devices are tests, usually unbeknownst to the public or the nations involved in the conflict.

Nevertheless, encounters with UFOs, like with fairies or shamanic spirit guides, and countless other creatures or entities, including *Men in Black* or *Hat Man*, may also be a product not so much of paranoia or delusion, but of natural production of DMT in the body. The Roper Organization survey from the early 1990s, published in 1992 as 'Unusual Personal Experiences', suggested that roughly 2% of the U.S. population has experienced something akin to a shamanic or UFO abduction. But even if we were to ignore this survey and accept all the criticism aimed against it, we still must acknowledge that it is highly common for children to report seeing things that adults are unable to see. Cats are famous for this feat. Most grow out of these perceptual states, but many adults retain this ability and are usually as a result labeled schizophrenic, manic, or psychotic. One 1979 study published in JAMA, 'Increased Excretion of Dimethyltryptamine and Certain Features of Psychosis', found that the more DMT detected in the body the more likely a person was to experiences episodes of the former conditions. The study found:

> "Dimethyltryptamine excretion was greatest in schizophrenia, mania, and 'other psychosis' and tended to decline as clinical state improved. Psychotic depressives excreted smaller amounts of DMT more akin to those excreted by neurotic and normal subjects... Syndromes suggesting elation, perceptual abnormalities, and difficulty in thinking and communicating were most correlated with raised urinary DMT excretion."

What is labeled here as *psychosis*, however, has been willingly entered into by shamans around the world for tens of thousands of years. These experiences may be frightening but the result is enlightenment, knowledge, and the overcoming of fear, which is the purpose of sacred *mystery* traditions. Having any other mindset is guaranteed to produce cosmic horrors. As for UFOs, they are not only equal in age to ancient civilizations and shamanic practices, but are simply another manifestation, like fairies, of otherworldly denizens. Graham Hancock adds, that *"whether by ingesting"* certain *"plants, or by stressing our body chemistry sufficiently through extended periods of rhythmic dancing like the !Kung bushmen of southern Africa, or by means of some of the other mental and physical techniques... we all have the ability to alter our brain chemistry and temporarily 'retune' our consciousness to the same remarkable experiences as the spontaneous trancer."*

Second Iteration

Carl Jung explored the UFO subject with great interest, skepticism, and almost a since of awe. It has been suggested by many that the whole thing is a sort of *psychological projection* which thus implies the need for a *psychic cause*. One reason for this, as Jung wrote, is because of *"the apparent impossibility of the Ufo reports,"* - these defiant things *"suggests to common sense that the most likely explanation lies in a psychic disturbance."*

"The basis for this kind of rumour," Jung writes, *"is an emotional tension having its cause in a situation of collective distress or danger, or in a vital psychic need."* What better collective distress than the horrors of World War II and the detonation of atomic weapons, which made it immediately into the ufological lore – the aliens were curious or worried about us or that we may destroy other worlds too. The great war was then followed by tensions produced by the Cold War and the expanding terror of possible nuclear annihilation. Perhaps the aliens were here to save us from such destruction.

Although what we call UFOs or alien abductions have been around for thousands of years, we must note again that these facts are relatable to shamanism and substances like ayahuasca or DMT, the latter of which is produced by the body – for some in excess. Altered States of Consciousness can also be entered into through other actions like dancing or chanting, and so forth. In nearly every case wherein a person communed with the other side they return with wisdom and usually knowledge of medicine – once again, something that can save us from death or heal the body and mind.

Jung writes, *"From a fear whose cause is far from being fully understood and is therefore not conscious, there arise explanatory projections which purport to find the cause in all manner of secondary phenomena, however unsuitable."* It is not advisable to disagree with such a mind, but we should add that the "cause" is probably, although not admittedly *fully understood,* our fear of death, which is the reason we create the social intuitions we have in the first place.

It is why we reach out to god - or the gods. It is why we more commonly reach out to the stars, which is merely a modern version of worshiping the gods above us in the heavens.

The theological dogma of ufology is thus predicated on the same fears, desires, needs, and so forth that virtually every religion is founded. Now the airships are aligned with our own flying technology and rockets (space travel to other planets), rather than wooden ships in the sky, chariots, or shields. This is the basic idea behind Jung's assessment of the entire situation as being essentially mythological:

"We have here a golden opportunity of seeing how a legend is formed, and how in a difficult and dark time for humanity a miraculous tale grows up of an attempted intervention by extra-terrestrial 'heavenly' powers — and this at the very time when human fantasy is seriously considering the possibility of space travel and of visiting or even invading other planets. We on our side want to fly to the moon or to Mars, and on their side the inhabitants of other planets in our system, or even of the fixed stars, want to fly to us. We at least are conscious of our space-conquering aspirations, but that a corresponding extra-terrestrial tendency exists is a purely mythological conjecture, i.e., a projection."

Just as artifacts and art are pointed to as proof of *ancient astronauts*, such as those human figures that seem to be in space suits, we project our own desires and fears onto the UFO subject – going to the moon or mars, for example. Are we to believe that modern Apollo garb is precisely what *ancient aliens* also wore? Or perhaps it is simply a case of *pareidolia*.

Ufology is an important area of study regardless, for countless reasons, yet many in the field are unwilling to acknowledge the possibility, despite the immense liberties taken with facts otherwise, that much of what we are dealing with is without doubt a *psychic projection of our psyche*.

Jung adds, likewise, how:

"These spaceguests are sometimes idealized figures along the lines of technological angels who are concerned for our welfare, sometimes dwarfs with enormous heads bursting with intelligence, sometimes lemur-like creatures covered with hair and equipped with claws, or dwarfish monsters clad in armour and looking like insects."

In essence, 'they' are just like us, or us from the future – although 'they' are really us from the past or present. Perhaps all three. We have powerful weapons, spaceships, and aspirations to conquer other worlds and right as humanity prepares to step beyond earth, we are met with a phenomenon that happens to align with all the former. *It* or *they* mirror us precisely, even with our liberal projections of fantasy. Space is vast, dark, cold, and unknown, which are all the things that humans fear from the vicious predator hiding in the dark since the Garden of Eden. This is the ufological issue at its core:

> "Undeterred by rationalistic criticism, it thrusts itself to the forefront in the form of a symbolic rumour, accompanied and reinforced by the appropriate visions, and thus activates an archetype that has always expressed order, deliverance, salvation, and wholeness. It is characteristic of our time that the archetype, in contrast to its previous manifestations, should now take the form of an object, a technological construction, in order to avoid the odiousness of mythological personification."

Rarely considered is the *archetype* that Jung was exploring in relation to the UFO. That symbol is a nebulous unidentified flying object – often a ball, orb, or compressed ball, i.e., a disc or saucer (although this idea is a confirmable creation of media). These *"round bodies in particular,"* he writes, *"are figures such as the unconscious produces in dreams, visions, etc. In this case they are to be regarded as symbols representing, in visual form, some thought that was not thought consciously, but is merely potentially present in the unconscious in invisible form and attains visibility only through the process of becoming conscious."*

We know of these circular shapes and find them all throughout human history in the worship of the sun (sun wheels), swastikas, magic circles, and the alchemical microcosm – the *symbol of totality*. On some occasions the circle is more oval and in yet other cases it appears as a tear drop. Either way, such a model is a potentially obvious feminine symbol representing the uterus and womb.

For less common craft, such as the cigar or tubular UFO, there is no doubt we are looking at an unconscious projection of the phallus. Jung suggests the *"cigar-form may have the Zeppelin for a model."* Considering its German origins alongside the later developed rapid overwhelming surprise attacks the Germans called *blitzkrieg* - during the second global war – in addition to what transpired across Europe from Allied terror campaigns (see Dresden, or even Tokyo and other Japanese cities), it seems obvious why the UFO emerged in greater detail as a non-human explanation for the horrors cultivated by man. The UFO's fascination with nuclear facilities should be as self-evident.

When you bring secret societies into the equation, and books like <u>The Coming Race</u> by Edward Bulwer-Lytton, published in 1871, the picture gets even clearer what we are dealing with.

Of both the elongated cigar craft and tear drop or spherical craft, Jung writes:

> *"This type of explanation is, at bottom, just as mythological and rationalistic as the technological fables about the nature and purpose of Ufos."*

There is also a far more esoteric component to these commonly witnessed craft, but first we must remember that the popular culture meme of a "flying saucer" was merely an invention of the press. When Kenneth Arnold first reported what he had witnessed near Mount Baker in June of 1947 - objects *"flying very close to the mountain tops and traveling at a tremendous speed"* - he reported to the media how they *"flew like a saucer would if you skipped it across the water."* This seemingly harmless description of one set of unidentified craft became the basis for the *flying saucer* description, which would be applied to nearly all other sightings. As a result, reports would explode about their existences all over the world. When the image was put into the public mind this is exactly what they collectively conjured.

But prior to reports of reflective *flying saucers* were reports of *foo fighters* (balls of light), *ghost rockets* (etheric, elongated rockets), and a handful of usually *etheric discs*. These images are potentially related to the very archaic and esoteric concept of an individualized soul existing separate from the *world soul*. Jung writes how *"the individual soul was thought to be of 'heavenly' origin, a particle of the world soul, and hence a microcosm, a reflection of the macrocosm."* Such an idea effectively, at the very least, warrants consideration when addressing the *"lens-shaped form"* of UFOs, particularly because they may have been *"influenced by the fact that psychic wholeness, as the historical testimonies show, has always been characterized by certain cosmic affinities,"* i.e., the soul. When in the form of a tear drop there is also the implication of water descending from heaven, or what the alchemists call the *permanent water*. This substance is also called *alchemical dew* and it is the transmutative substance which both dissolves and transforms.:

> *"This 'heavenly fluid must be of a mysterious nature and is probably a conception similar to that of the alchemical aqua permanens, the 'permanent water', which was also called 'Heaven' in sixteenth-century alchemy and stood for the quinta essentia."*

> *"The 'water of the Philosophers' is the classic substance that transmutes the chemical elements and during their transformation is itself transformed. It is also the 'redeeming spirit'."*

~

"In addition," writes Jung, *"there are cases"* of UFO sightings *"where the same collective cause produces identical or similar effects, i.e., the same visionary images and interpretations, in the very people who are least prepared for such phenomena and least inclined to believe in them..."* This should be obvious proof of the collective reacting to the same stimuli, though in other cases that are more individual, witnesses tend to have a difficult time telling the same story. There is a parallel to this in the fact that the UFO can be both *"tracked by radar but remain invisible to the eye, and conversely, can be seen by the eye but not detected by radar."* Perhaps psychic projections can have some yet undetermined effect on radar or *"the appearance of real objects affords an opportunity for mythological projections."*

It is also interesting to note that the entire concept of the *flying saucer* was conjured by a pilot - with some distortion from the media - something that Jung does not point out, though he does note that the loneliness of flying a plane, when considering all of the seriousness and training, results in *"ideal conditions for spontaneous psychic phenomena, as everyone knows who has lived sufficiently long in the solitude, silence, and emptiness of deserts, seas, mountains, or in primeval forests."*

The essence of what Jung discusses in his collected works, some of which have been compiled for <u>Flying Saucers: A Modern Myth of Things Seen in the Skies</u>, is not so much the reality or unreality of the UFO, but instead the psychic aspect of its existence. He thus terms them "a modern myth" and by all metrics they must be acknowledged as such. As such, there is a great difference within ufology between the original story of Roswell and the decades of mystery and myth which has built up around the case. No rational and educated investigator could deny this fact.

We can, furthermore, certainly note that *"the motif of an extra-terrestrial invasion was seized upon by the rumour and the Ufos were interpreted as machines controlled by intelligent beings from outer space."*

It is evident that the defining characteristic and structure of a *religious experiences* is that it saves the individual, heals the individual, and makes him more complete. As Jung puts it: *"in religious experience man comes face to face with a psychically overwhelming Other."*

These are the patterns found in shamanism and UFO abductions, as already noted. The *"physically overwhelming Other"* can either be revelatory and enlightening or, if the individual is not ready or unwilling to receive the message (Holy Spirit), a cosmic horror.

Third Iteration

There are other considerations for the UFO issue, too, that are much less cosmically horrific and far more comically obvious. It is estimated that there are 10 quintillion insects on planet earth, according to the Entomological Society of America. That is a ten with eighteen zeros. This number is, again, just an estimate and likely very wrong – the real numbers, if they matter, are probably much higher. The idea that UFOs may be identified as animals or insects was proposed decades ago. Frank B. Salisbury, a plant physiologist and director of the Plant Science Department at the State University of Utah, published <u>The Utah UFO display: A biologist's report</u>, in 1974. Four years later in November of 1978, researchers from the USDA published a report called *'Insects as Unidentified Flying Objects'*. In that report, Philip S. Callahan and R. W. Mankin, a laboratory technologist from the University of Florida, conducted an experiment on five species of insects with a large electric field. The experiment found, *"each of the insects stimulated in this manner emitted visible glows of various colors and blacklight."* They then postulated that the 1965-1968 UFO display in Utah was a result of nocturnal insects that had infested the area. The idea was also discussed in The X Files, season 3, episode 12.

What this tells us is that the classic story of a glowing, hovering, humming "craft" over a house or car is sometimes nothing more than the brush discharge of an insect swarm in an electrical field which emits a hum alongside of the insect buzzing; as they hover over the lit sources of their attraction the electric fields may disturb radio and television signals and electricity in general. This electric field can likewise cause humans to feel woozy, achy, or even pass out. It has long been known that electricity usage, like the sun before, caused influenza - 'influence of the stars'. When UFOs drop off radar or disappear, they may simply have flown under the radar, disbursed, or flown out of an electric field. The abstract of the USDA report reads as follows:

> *"Five species of insects were subjected to a large electric field. Each of the insects stimulated in this manner emitted visible glows of various colors and blacklight (uv). It is postulated that the Uintah Basin, Utah, nocturnal UFO display (1965-1968) was partially due to mass swarms of spruce budworms, Choristoneura fumiferana (Clemens), stimulated to emit this type of St. Elmo's fire by flying into high electric fields caused by thunderheads and high density particulate matter in the air. There was excellent time and spatial correlation between the 1965-1968 UFO nocturnal sightings and spruce budworm infestation. It is suggested that a correlation of nocturnal UFO sightings throughout the U.S. and Canada with spruce budworm infestations might give some insight into nocturnal insect flight patterns."*

In a dream analysis provided by Jung in his UFO book - already mentioned – he also acknowledges the hypotheses that *"Ufos are a species of insect coming from another planet and possessing a shell or carapace that shines like metal."* The example provided is *"the metallic-looking, chitinous covering of our beetles."* Although our example above from the USDA refers to insect swarms, Jung references the UFO-lore itself, which says that *"each Ufo is supposed to be a single insect, not a swarm."* Perhaps both a swarm and a singular insect could be factual. He goes on to admit that, upon reading various reports:

> *"I, too, was struck by the thought that the peculiar behaviour of the Ufos was reminiscent of certain insects. To the speculative mind there is nothing inherently impossible in the idea that under other conditions Nature could express her 'knowledge' in quite other*

ways than those mentioned earlier; for instance, instead of light-producing insects she might evolve creatures capable of 'anti-gravity'."

Another particularly intriguing observation by Jung relates the technical capabilities of the UFO not to insects, but to the psyche. As a psychic manifestation, in part, and as they relate to a growing modern mythology with ancient roots, Jung says that *"the psychic 'object' and gravity are, to the best of our knowledge, incommensurable."* Therefore, he adds, *"The psyche represents the only opposite of gravity known to us. It is 'anti-gravity' in the truest sense of the word."*

It is this psyche which is responsible for our collective mythology and folklore.

Fourth Iteration

There are some other considerations for the UFO which must be considered with all seriousness.

Large numbers of people around the world take both illicit and prescription drugs, drink excessively, and are traumatized by daily news and life. These factors must play at minimal some significant part in the phenomenon today, as they must have throughout all human history. Obviously, there was no television news 500 years ago, but nonetheless we can assume life was not so easily lived for other reasons – food, disease, war, etc.

The *1518 Dancing Plague* in Strasbourg (France) is still debated today as per what caused so many people to dance for days on end until collapse and death. The *Salem Witch Trials 1692-1693* are certainly a similar display of what we call *Mass Psychogenic Illness*. Although these events have essentially nothing to do with UFOs, though there may be some relationship to them in the fear over supernatural demonic powers in the latter case, they are clear examples of how people can collectively lose control.

Two additional examples of either mas psychogenic illness or collective hallucination involves *Mariana Apparitions*, the most famous of which is the *Our Lady of Fatima* apparition that occurred in 1917 Portugal, and the more scientifically understood *Fata Morgana*, or superior mirage, by which boats or cities visually look as if they are floating in some UFO-like display of anti-gravity.

Countless Biblical stories from the Star of Bethlehem to Ezekiel have also been chalked up to UFOs today, but from another time period were called miracles, angels, or divine. As some have also pointed out, the entire story of St. John's Revelation may have been induced from consuming certain mushrooms on the Greek island of Patmos.

After major nuclear disasters, too, UFOs have been speculated upon or well-documented: Three Mile Island in Pennsylvania (March 28, 1979), Chernobyl in USSR Ukraine (April 26, 1986), and Fukushima in Japan (March 11, 2011). We know that UFOs have likewise visited nuclear installations all over the United States, UK, and former USSR. Although the leading theory is a theological form of dogma in that people believe these objects are here to protect us from such powerful technology, it is probably more likely the case that they are a modern unconscious projection of the fears we have internally for nuclear technology and especially for such weapons.

Fifth Iteration

As noted already, the UFO phenomenon is almost identical to the old stories of fairies, and to shamanic journeys. Although etheric or completely metaphoric of nature, fairies are creatures that nonetheless have a root in physical reality. Fairy lore is a branch of traditional mythology, which is ultimately one of the original forms of scientific observation - i.e., storms occur, or the wind blows, due to the influence of gods. Science and mythology both attempt to catalogue nature, particularly its mechanisms. Today we no longer blame gods for weather, but we do blame storms on politically motivated environmentalist ideology. *Fairies* are merely an anthropomorphization of nature; *elves* represent its playful, musical, and dance-like qualities; *leprechauns* are its tricky, fierce, and magical elements; pixies are a combination of the previous but with a proclivity for shiny objects and a desire to prank humans. In essence, the fairy is a generalized name for the elements - earth, fire, air, water - and their associated elemental creatures - gnome, salamander, sylph, undine. There are *woodland fairies* and *water fairies*, heavily associated with UFO sightings in the form of traditional Unidentified Flying Objects in rural areas and Unidentified Submerged Objects near bodies of water.

Women have traditionally been taken by these creatures to hidden fairy 'bases', often inside mountains, and asked to breast feed a child, or they are experimented on medically. What may to be happening here, psychologically speaking, is the rationalizing of the loss of a child, probably in the form of miscarriage. Feelings of inadequacy, loss, failure, fear, and the lack of sleep which accompanies such things, are likely the stressors, at least in part, preceding such abductions. Yet men experience something similar, but for slightly different reasons, when they are abducted by little fairies and subject to medical experimentation - we can assume, generally, to extract sperm. Sometimes a woman has her eggs removed or is forced to birth a child in this *otherworld*. Other times she is greeted in the fairy realm by her real child, whereas the earthly child back home is actually a *changeling* switched at birth. These fairy children are said to be awkward and have dry skin, perhaps attributes that would designate the child as abnormal enough to be from a world beyond our own.

In both cases we are looking at older examples of modern UFO abduction cases, and the subsequent medical, often very sexual, experiments performed by the occupants of said craft; we are looking at underground bases where little creatures experiment on humans, a common motif in modern UFO lore and perhaps background for much of the Military Lab (MILAB) abduction theory - countless military bases are underground and often inside a mountain. Nearly all these elements are found in shamanic lore too.

We also have here examples of incubus and succubus preserved in the old fairy lore and thus extended to UFOs.

~

The famous *fairy circles* may also be explained with 'science', as with the psychological aspects of these phenomenon, but they are nevertheless proof of some sort of natural process and extrapolated as evidence of the fairy or UFO. Fairy tales, or fairy lore, persevere how witnesses would see a ring of lights in a field or forest, accompanied by singing and dancing. Upon further investigation the participants would be identified as very small creatures - usually green or wearing green. If someone got too close the fairies would strike them with their *fairy shot* (also called *elf shot*) and perhaps even abduct them. The eerie similarity to UFO encounters cannot be ignored: strange lights in a forest or field, usually in a circle occupied by little green men with ray guns who just may abduct you if you get too close. The evidence leftover in both cases is found in the form of circular impressions left in the ground - often burned - where vegetation seemingly refuses to grow from that point onward. These circular marks just happen to align perfectly with the rounded structure of a *flying saucer*.

This 'ring of lights' can also be seen daily when observing the sun as it moves through the sky. An Egyptian myth tells of the *Boat of Ra* flying through the air from morning to night. From these stories we acquire the Flying Solar Disc (Winged Disc), which can be found all throughout the ancient world - most famously in Egypt and ancient Mesopotamia (Sumer and Assyria), but also found in the Americas with Quetzalcoatl. Gilgamesh of Sumer, Ahura Mazda of Persia, and Sol Invictus of the Romans were all associated strongly with the sun disc. Companies today still employ its service, too, from Chrysler, Bentley, Aston Martin, Harley-Davidson, and Southwest airlines to Mini Cooper, which is owned by BMW, a company that uses the quadrant circle for their logo.

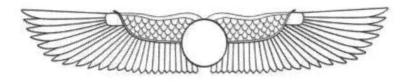

Winged Disc (*Flying Disc / Flying Saucer*)

Followers of Charles Fort (Forteans) will also be familiar with bizarre phenomenon, some of which can be explained and others not so clearly, involving strange things falling from the sky or rain that turns a variety of colors for, at that moment, unidentified reasons. The falling of circular golden coins from the sky (reported in the past, but probably more metaphoric than literal) is certainly Fortean, but shares much in common, again, with round discs coming down from the heavens like the sun god bestowing his blessings (symbolized by gold) from his boat. Heaven is likewise considered a palace filled with treasure of the same sort, a reward which commonly symbolizes wisdom, that very thing aliens impart to abductees and therianthropes impart to shamans.

Within the circle, sphere, or disc - the *symbol of totality* - we find various forms of treasure, and even the greatest gold of all in that of the *human spirit* or *world soul*. To the alchemists this would be called *quinta essentia*, the Philosopher's Stone. Jung explains this *Powder of*  *Projection* as being divided into four quadrants like the world, and like the visions of Ezekiel and his wheel found in the Bible. Comparisons to Ezekiel's wheel can also be found in the Chariot Wheel of Krishna and the Ichthys Wheel of Christ:

> *"It is the circle divided into four with the centre, or the divinity extended in four directions, or the four functions of consciousness with their unitary substrate, the self. Here the quaternity has a 3 + 1 structure: three animal-daemonic faces and one human one."*

The circle with divided quadrants is also a *nexus point* of parallel worlds. Jung adds: *"The square, being a quaternity, is a totality symbol in alchemy. Having four corners it signifies the earth, whereas a circular form is attributed to the spirit. Earth is feminine,* *spirit masculine."* One of the best examples of this *quinta essentia* can be found in the German *sonnenrad* or *sun wheel*. Better known as a *swastika*, the symbol is ancient, primitive, and powerful. It is, in essence, a cross with bent arms that signifies the straight-squared world, or with arms bent further signifies the spherical sun.

This is a 16th century woodcut of a winged sun hovering above a sepulchre filled with water, from <u>Rosary of the Philosophers</u> (Frankfurt, 1550).

Psychics stressors like war, or the more personal loss of a child, are as Jung points out partly responsible for the UFO phenomenon. The flying shields or chariots seen on battlefields in the past have been replaced with spaceships today, a result of the collective projection of our present technology and growing concerns for the future.

In the ancient world, put simply, a boat, shield, or chariot was the understood technological apex – in some cases, such as the 1561 Nuremberg, Germany, incident and the 1566 Basel, Switzerland, case, we are certainly dealing with the same phenomenon but perhaps unconsciously projected for different (but similar – culturally speaking to the context of the time) reasons.

There is also a famous case in Japan from 1803 when a mysterious boat supposedly washed ashore in Hitachi Province. Local fisherman found the object and called it Utsuro-Bune (hollow boat). Inside the boat were food, water, bedding, carpets, an unknown language, and a beautiful woman with pale skin and red hair – not exactly Japanese (depictions typically show her as being Japanese though). The woman carried a small box which she protected aggressively. What might seem like a shipwreck upon first reading changes into a UFO story quickly when one sees the later depictions of what those fishermen witnessed. The narrative of a human in a box washing ashore shares a relationship with the stories of Osiris, Moses, and the Hindu Brahmans.

As Jung points out, the ruling ideas civilization have again changed dramatically in the 20th-century, and thus, *"created a situation that resembles a tabula rasa"* where *"almost anything might appear on it."* Under these conditions, those of a blank slate, *"the phenomenon of the Ufos may well be just such an apparition."*

Although we may not be able to confirm anything concrete about the phenomenon, we do know that UFOs are social facts and that debating them transforms our politics and culture. We may ultimately learn more about them from social scientists and, as Carl Jun demonstrated, psychologists, than from physicists or UFO hunters. Imagining the origin of UFOs and their assumed occupants is also a great philosophical test which could lead us to new discoveries and a type of reverse-engineering that has nothing to do with downed unidentified objects.

The *utsuro-bune* from Matajiro Nagahashi's 1825 *Umeno chiri* (1845)

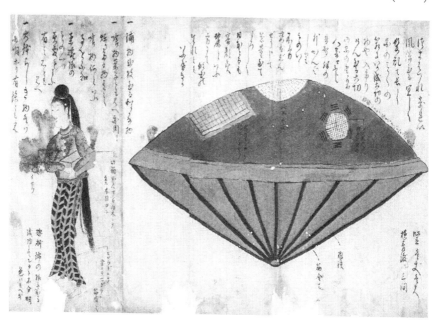

The "The Strange Boat Drifted Ashore on the Fief of Lord Ogasawara" from *Hyoryu Kishu* (Archive of Castaways), ca. 1868

Nuremberg, Germany (1561) – flying spheres, cigar-shaped 'mother-ships', and long cylindrical objects fill the sky in what some interpret as combat. As with the modern spaceship theory of UFOs, witnesses of this heavenly display likened the smaller objects to cannon balls being shot out of the larger cylindrical objects (cannons).

Basel, Switzerland (1566) – white and black spherical discs fill the sky, alongside the sun.

ANCIENT ALIENS
& DIVINE GUIDANCE

First Iteration

There is a line of thought that penetrates modern and near-modern views on the development of mankind. Whereas evolution and science have replaced creationism and God, it may be surprising or obscene to submit for consideration any suggestion that both may be as equally right as they are wrong. This is not only because of the limited records of archeology, anthropology, history, etc., nor due to the unwillingness of contemporary man, like any previous state of man, to accept that which is beyond the status quo. It may just be true due to the lack of details and context. Whatever the case, many have posited the theory of some extraterrestrial involvement in the creation and evolution of mankind. These doctrines have themselves become dogma with adherents essentially refusing to acknowledge any other explanation, or that those other viewpoints may help solidify their own.

We have already explored the links between shamans, UFO abductees, and classical archetypical myths, including those of fairies, seeing how they all suggest the same involvement of *otherworldly* entities in the continued development of mankind. If David Lewis-Williams is correct in his theory, that the catalyst for the development of civilization was the *"cultivation of altered states of consciousness, most probably first experienced by our ancestors through the accidental consumption of plant or fungal hallucinogens,"* then perhaps these entities – i.e. aliens, therianthropes, angels, demons, ad infinitum – are indeed responsible for at least the development of human civilization and perhaps even the *realization* of consciousness itself – the Garden of Eden narrative all over again.

It is certainly unfortunate that many New Age religions and psychological corruptions of culture have replaced the idea of Rapture with Ascension; they have replaced angels and demons with Nordic aliens and Reptilians; they have replaced corrupt priests supposedly acting as emissaries between man and God with corrupt gurus acting as emissaries of whistleblowers and any number of alien species; they have replaced holy scriptures with books rarely published with honest intent, and often espoused as dogma; they have turned certain abductees into cash cows and made them saints; they have turned UFO hotspots into 'holy' land to be visited in pilgrimage. Honest or otherwise, the works of authors, historians, and general researchers over the centuries have provided us with information that when interpreted slightly differently can completely alter our understanding of life and human history.

The concept of "ancient astronauts" been highly popularized by the television show *Ancient Aliens* and other similarly related productions. *The Earth Chronicles* series by the late author Zecharia Sitchen (1920-2010) has been instrumental in fanning the flames of interest in the same. Alongside Sitchen in popular culture is Erich von Däniken, who wrote the famous *Chariots of the Gods*. Both authors published their initial works in 1976 (The 12th Planet) and 1968 (Chariots of the Gods) respectively. But it was actually Matest M. Agrest who introduced Paleo-Astronautics in the 1960s, suggesting a link between ancient man and beings from other worlds. Even as early as 1910, Nobel Laureate Frederick Soddy (1877-1956), an Oxford Professor, tried to explain part of the theory on ancient civilization and its apparent inconsistencies:

> "Some of the beliefs and legends which have come down to us from antiquity are so universal and deep-rooted that we have are accustomed to consider them almost as old as the race itself. One is tempted to inquire how far the unsuspected aptness of some of these beliefs and sayings to the point of view so recently disclosed is the result of mere chance or coincidence, and how far it may be evidence of a wholly unknown and unsuspected ancient civilization of which all other relic has disappeared."

Soddy's contemporary, Charles Hoy Fort (1874-1932), is perhaps more famous in paranormal realms for his research and writing. Compiling a large assortment of reports pertaining to bizarre phenomena of the 19th and 20th centuries, Fort wrote *The Book of the Damned* in 1919 and *New Lands* in 1923. An oversimplified conclusion of his work can be extracted from the former book wherein he writes, "*I think we're property.*" Fort explained:

> "I should say we belong to something," going on to suggest, "That once upon a time, this earth was No-man's Land, that other

worlds explored and colonized here, and fought among themselves for possession, but that now it's owned by something: That something owns this earth-all others warned off."

Gerald Massey (1828-1907) was an archeologist linked to the Theosophical Society. He wrote *A Book of Beginnings*, 1881, which influenced Kenneth Grant, the secretary of Aleister Crowley. Massey's work suggested that the origin of all civilization is in ancient Egypt. Shortly before Massey published his book, Helena Petrovna Blavatsky (1831-1891) began the Theosophical Research Society that merged Hindu, Buddhist, and western *mysteries* into a single *Secret Doctrine*. Along with Meade Layne (1882-1961) from the Borderlands Sciences Research Foundation, Blavatsky introduced the concept of Invisible Masters, Secret Chiefs, or the Great White Brotherhood, into a more popular context. These Ascended Masters, as they are called, were thought to guide the spiritual progress of mankind from secret locations. They act directly to influence people and events in our world.

In 1912, the famous Austrian mystic and occultist Rudolph Steiner started the Anthroposophical society, an offshoot of Theosophy. Steiner believed, much like the purported intentions of the Invisible Masters, that "aliens" could be the saviors of mankind.

In 1935 Germany, Heinrich Luitpold Himmler (1900-1945), Reichsführer of the Schutzstaffel (SS) and a leading member of the Nazi Party, took control of the *Ahnenerbe*, which operated from this date until 1945. The group was a think-tank which searched for information on the paranormal and occult. Himmler also created the Hexen-Sonderauftrag, or the Witchcraft Special Commission, meant to recover the wisdom of the German Volk. Himmler's interest in these matters, along with others, conflicted with some prominent societies such as the Ordo Templi Orientis (founded in 1902-1903 by Carl Kellner and Theodor Reuss), of which Aleister Crowley was a prominent member; and the Hermetic Order of the Golden Dawn (founded in 1887 by William Westcott, Samuel Liddell MacGregor Mathers, and William Woodman).

The famous Vril society also operated during this time with the goal of, among other things, contacting otherworldly beings in order to channel sacred wisdom. Much of the mythos around these subjects stems from *The Coming Race*, a book published anonymously in 1871 by Edward Bulwer-Lytton.

Second Iteration

Taking a passage from the Mesopotamian creation story, as translated, and documented in Zecharia Sitchin's book <u>The Twelfth Planet</u>, we find a very ancient concept about the spiritual nature of mankind. Considering that Sumer arose in the Tigris-Euphrates River valley (Eden) between 5,000 and 4,000 B.C., it must be considered that this civilization either was in contact with a parallel but advanced Earth civilization, or that they may have been visited by 'gods' or communicated to in some manner by powerful otherworldly entities.

Perhaps they obtained their knowledge through psychoactive substances, which is definitely a leading candidate next to ancient civilizing gods. It may be as simple as classifying our evolutionary civilization across the planet today as being the result of an un-contacted tribe visited by a more advanced human civilization. There are, after all, countless similar stories of civilizing gods who restarted civilization after some great cataclysm. For more on this see my book *Occult Arcana*.

Nevertheless, these ancient stories describe the human race as essentially being produced as a byproduct of a more advanced society and technology. This story has been told in great detail elsewhere and both elaborated and embellished on as much.

Some believe that man was literally created as a slave race to mine for gold. But this story can also be explained, as Joseph Campbell points out, as such:

> "*the gods grew weary of tilling the fields and feeding themselves so they created the human race to till the fields for them.*"

From a mythological point of view Campbell's point solves the issue of the literal interpretation of man's creation as a slave species by focusing on the nature of man's ancestral *planting societies*. Furthermore, the gold that man was supposedly designed to mine for is just as likely the *alchemical gold* of the *Great Work*.

~

Within the Mesopotamian story are two factions represented by 'brothers' known as EN.KI and ENLIL. The Sumerian story essentially describes man, a spiritual force, as being created and bound to flesh as a worker:

> *In the clay god and Man*
> *shall be bound,*
> *to a unity brought together;*
> *So that to the end of days*
> *the Flesh and the Soul*
> *which in a god have ripened -*
> *that Soul in a blood-kinship be bound*

It was the EN.KI faction that wanted to see mankind as more than a brutally treated slave, and as some interpretations proceed to explain, he is represented as the serpent on the tree in the Garden offering to impart knowledge to mankind. EN.KI therefore becomes just another version of Lucifer or Lilith. Though we often depict or remember only one tree, there were two as described in Genesis 2:8-9:

> *"The Lord God planted a garden toward the east, in Eden; and there He placed the man whom He had formed. Out of the ground the Lord God caused to grow every tree that is pleasing to the sight and good for food; the tree of life also in the midst of the garden, and the tree of the knowledge of good and evil."*

The *Tree of Knowledge of Good and Evil* represents the foundation for spiritual development through ethics, morals, integrity, justice, and the like. These are the necessary elements needed to obtain the spiritual freedom and immortality found in the *Tree of Life*. This should indicate that *Original Sin* may not be the *realization* of simple nakedness, but the understanding and shame of one's condition of existence, as cut-off from Source or God. If viewed strictly esoterically, the realization of nudity represents the awakening of consciousness and has perhaps little to do with a literal interpretation of man's condition as a "slave species" – though some suggest this vehemently.

From this particular ideology, one quickly infers that the serpent may have been righteous in delivering knowledge to mankind in an attempt to free him from the chains of god, or ENLIL. However, as we have already addressed, archangel Michael fought just as fiercely to protect God's Creation in the face of Lucifer's rebellion.

Following the narrative, EN.KI's followers became a brotherhood of serpents dedicated to the dissemination of spiritual knowledge and the attainment of spiritual freedom. In response, an angry ENLIL (YAHWEH) acted to wage war on mankind's proliferation through starvation, birth control, and natural disasters like floods, then hijacked the image of the serpent and altered the method of teaching to promote the obtaining of spiritual immortality through false doctrine. EN.KI was later turned into the Prince of Darkness by ENLIL. It would be slightly more difficult, but certainly feasible, to instead see EN.KI as a tempter seeking to poison the waters of life under the guise of freeing man from the so-called bondage of Paradise, which is no bondage whatsoever. Too much information awareness, in this context, and particularly distorted information illuminated by *false light*, is sufficient to say, equally as *poisonous*.

From these ideas sprout the modern concepts of *do what thou wilt* and *you only live once*. Some point out that the former quote, attributed to the savage sorcerer Aleister Crowley, relates to love though, since the full reference in the *Book of the Law* is: "*Do what thou wilt shall be the whole of the Law. Love is the Law, love under will.*" But, as we have seen, men as wicked as Crowley distort and invert as a matter of necessity, and thus LOVE becomes EVOL, the very essence of his alcoholism, drug use, sexual perversity, and other beastly qualities. EN.KI would therefore desire for man to live outside of the dimensions of paradise by drinking poisoned water or eating a tainted apple.

Much thus comes down to interpretation and how willing one is to adhere to dichotomy as opposed to unification.

Third Iteration

Many would see this story as another symbolically laced tale of ancient man that is to be believed no more than Jonah being swallowed and surviving in the belly of a whale for three days, a story that certainly has occult leanings into the subject of *living resurrection* – three days in the belly of the beast, or womb of the earth like Lazarus, Jesus, Amaterasu, etc., before rebirth. Others see the Sumerian story as literal, though through any contemporary comparison the past can be made to look as if it relates to the present, i.e., *ancient aliens* and space travel. The theory of such extraterrestrial involvement in mankind's past explains much that has been left to the mystery of history or intentionally obfuscated to the same end. The idea suggests that a brotherhood of ideology spread from Egypt and India to the Roman Empire in many similar but distinct forms. It spread from the Egyptian source to the Americas and Asia, and eventually all over the planet. Yet the concepts embodied in this "ancient alien" account parallel, though less literally, ancient spiritual practices that involve altered states of consciousness wherein one sees aliens, demons, and therianthropic gods like in ancient Egypt.

The Egyptians maintained a belief in a spirit inhabiting the human vessel, much like we do today. They saw this non-physical essence as KA, which was the true person. Author Ahmed Fakhry wrote in *The Pyramids* about this essence and its relationship to a physical-spiritual doctrine:

> *"The Egyptian wanted his Ka to be able to recognize its body after death and to be united with it; for this reason he felt that it was very important to have his body preserved. This is why the Egyptians mummified their bodies and excelled in embalming them."*

Some suggest that having a connection to the physical world after death would merely keep one attached to matter, preventing the spirit from moving beyond. Though that may just be the point, and it may demonstrate how corrupted the Egyptian religion(s) truly were. But what we are likely dealing with here is sophisticated and advanced spiritual ideology that has survived cataclysm and war throughout all human history. Far from Egypt, Shintoists feel that material reality and life itself simply *IS*, so long as material possessions are used to serve *kami*. The Zoroastrian religion preserves a similar notion, that life is originally good, but that an evil force moved in to trigger a *fall*. Although the materiality of the Egyptians may speak more to their love of life rather than of materiality and death, William Bramley explains in his book <u>The Gods of Eden</u> how these practices nonetheless *"caused people to wrongly equate spiritual wholeness with spiritual attachment to human bodies (or to body substitutes)."* This resulted in the human intuitive drive for spiritual development and immortality being twisted into *"an obsessive quest to preserve bodies."* The preservation of bodies through mummification, however, was also practiced across the ocean in South America, where other ritual practices for freeing the soul, such as *opening the mouth,* were likewise performed. But Bramley believes that these "teachings" were the true foundation of the *mystery schools* in ancient Egypt, created by Ra, whom some feel was not as much a god as he was a physical ruler not necessarily from Earth.

These schools, as Bramley writes, *"twisted spiritual knowledge,"* while restricting public access to any remaining truth. But restriction does not necessarily mean perversion, simply because some things are so precious that they may be broken by ignorance; they may become weapons in the wrong hands instead of tools. There is no doubt that sacred wisdom has been preserved by malicious intention, but this also does not mean that the information itself is inherently dark. The Egyptian ruler Thutmose III placed many restrictions on the *mystery cults* for sure. But less than a century later, Amenhotep IV (Akhenaten) transformed these schools into repositories of symbols. Bramley believes that the intention was to *"create a secret code designed to make spiritual knowledge unattainable to everyone except those admitted"* into the elite circles, perhaps with further intention to destroy spiritual knowledge in its entirety. This would essentially place mankind in the state of existence before Eve ate from the *tree* in the *Garden.* But Amenhotep IV's organizing of polytheistic doctrine into monotheism would likely have simplified the process of understanding spiritual truths to the otherwise profane. The same can be said of the numerous stories, metaphors, allegories, parables, etc., that contain deep spiritual knowledge, and which are wildly available in world mythologies today. So, we could actually say that the literal theory of "ancient aliens" is a true perverter of sacred wisdom today, even if it is a misplaced idea.

Regardless of the validity of Bramley's interpretations, the attempt to restrict access to spiritual knowledge with a series of symbols and stories has greatly reduced its credibility and usage. However, it has also allowed for some means of preservation against further perversions. This tug-of-war between its meaning is not the intention of this writing though.

Fourth Iteration

At any rate, the Pharaohs of Egypt were as much at the mercy of the priestly class, many of which were *black magicians*, as the monarchs of the Americas or the Emperors of China. These *black* elements were distorters of ancient wisdom and did not represent the true *secret teachings* of the *mysteries*. These men, after all, conspired against the Egyptian ruler Akhenaten for his crime of turning polytheistic Egypt into a monotheistic cult.

Historian Manetho wrote that the prophet Moses (*Moshe Rabbenu* - Moshe our Teacher) had received his education in the *secret teachings* under Amenhotep IV, and that this is likely where he obtained inspiration for the famous *Ten Commandments* - from the *Confessions of Ma'at* and the *Book of the Dead* (*Coming Forth by Day*) – given on Mt. Sinai like those ancient Aryan traditions handed down from the highlands of the Himalayas.

Some even believe that Moses was Akhenaten. Interestingly, the initiation of Moses into the Egyptian *mysteries* closely resembles the same processes used in India for the highest Hindu priests, the Brahmans.:

> *"Moses, a son of the tribe of Levi, educated in Egypt and initiated at Heliopolis, became a High Priests of the Brotherhood under the reign of Pharaoh Amenhotep. He was elected by the Hebrews as their chief and he adapted to the ideas of his people the science and philosophy which he had obtained in the Egyptian mysteries; proofs of this are to be found in the symbols, in the Initiations, and in his precepts and commandments... The dogma of an 'only God' which he taught was the Egyptian Brotherhood interpretation and teaching of the Pharaoh who established the first monotheist religion known to man."*

The entire story of Moses, long before his initiation, is a repeating of the story of Osiris, who was placed in a golden coffin and floated down the Nile before being "raised" in a royal palace. In the book of Exodus Moses is placed in a small basket and put into the water where he floats to the palace and is "raised" as royalty. This story is identical, down to the bitumen used to seal the basket, to the life of King Sargon, the first great Semitic ruler of the

Akkadians. Joseph Campbell explains in his book <u>Thou Art That</u> of this account:

> *"There was a woman living up the Euphrates river who had a little child. She did not know how to care for him so she put him in a little basket of rushes and sealed it with bitumen and set it floating in the river. Pull out of the water by the gardener of the Emperor, that little boy grew up and became Sargon the First."*

According to Louis Jacolliot's book, <u>Occult Science in India and Among the Ancients</u>, the *Supreme Chief* overseeing the *Supreme Council* of occult study in India was called a *Brahmatma*. This position was only to be selected from members of the council known as *Yoguys*, who had taken vows of chastity. In order for his election to be held valid, *"he had to furnish evidence of his virile power in connection with one of the virgins of the Pagoda, who was given him as a bride,"* Any child produced from this union was then *"placed in a wicker basket, and turned adrift upon the river to float with the current. If perchance he was washed ashore he was carried to the temple, where he was at once, and by virtue of that very fact, regarded as having been initiated into the third degree. From his earliest childhood, all the secret mentrams, or formulas of evocation, were made known to him. If, however, the child floated down the stream with the current, he was rejected as a Pariah, and handed over to the people of that caste to be reared by them."*

In all these cases we are dealing with archetypes and myths that surpass common interpretation and understanding, stretching beyond such things into the symbols, and potential realities, of great deluges and arks set upon flood waters. Even Krishna was carried across the waters by his father who hoped to switch the child for a female baby due to the orders of King Kansa to kill all male babies. We also find this story of the *massacre of the innocents* in Matthew 2 with King Herod issuing *"orders to kill all the boys in Bethlehem and its vicinity who were two years old and under."*

It is clear that the Egyptian religion was beautifully complex and yet simplistic to grasp for those with intent to learn and understand. It is also clear that those beliefs were predicated on the idea that eternal life came through some form of *matter*, and that this concept bred inversion. The Egyptians, after all, were merely the inheritors of great wisdom and architecture rather than the inventors. The same ideology was, and remains, the cornerstone of the Hindu caste system today. The lower levels of society are conditioned to believe that if they behave according to the duties of their assigned caste, they will be elevated to a higher level after death and in rebirth. Roman Catholicism holds its followers on similar political grounds. It began in the Western Roman Empire with the conversion of Constantine I the Great to Christianity. After seeing a vision of the cross while marching in 312 A.D., and as documented by Socrates as *"a pillar of light,"* Constantine had another vision of what he interpreted to be Jesus the next night. Shortly after he issued the Edict of Milan, which granted tolerance to Christianity within the Roman Empire. Constantine's personal conversion to Christianity was likely far more about political control than spiritual growth, as was the case with priests in Egypt and India. Constantine is responsible for the deifying of Jesus into the physical Son of God, an idea stemming from the Nicene Creed, which does not hold water to either the Christ's teachings or the full gospel record – more on this later. This allowed the Roman State to hijack the true teachings of a real spiritual man and weaponize them into a theo-political dogma. The eastern Roman Emperor Theodosius I went further by issuing over a dozen laws intending to punish those who rejected the doctrines established by the Council of Nicaea in 325 A.D. Whereas Christians had once been persecuted under the Romans, a new Christian doctrine was used to persecute and prosecute all those who disagreed with the updated faith, including the same Christian ideology that was before persecuted. This new Christian doctrine utilized the concept of God-given laws to create a powerful worldly kingdom in the name of the divine. In effect, what the Roman Empire did to Christianity was to accept the Devil's offer to Jesus in Matthew 4:8-9, which reads: *"Again, the devil took him to a very high mountain and showed him all the kingdoms of the world and their splendor. 'All this I will give you,' he said, 'if you will bow down and worship me.'"*

Fifth Iteration

Many centuries after Moses, a man named Umayado, or Prince Taishi Shōtoku (574-622 CE), presented a series of laws for the people of Nihon to follow. As with the Laws of Moses, Prince Shōtoku, who coined the phrase *Land of the Rising Sun,* formulated his constitution from *natural law* as something that even the emperor had to follow. It should be noted, however, that there were reportedly five of these constitutions, one each for Buddhists, Confucianists, shrine workers, politicians, and common people. Although likened to authoritative dictums from the State, such constitutions held the emperor, who was in direct lineage to the Creator, and the state as subservient to the same virtues. Japan's 17 article constitution mimics the *Ten Commandments* coupled with the *Seven Deadly Sins*.

10 Commandments

thou shalt not take the name of the Lord thy God in vain
honor thy father and mother
thou shalt not kill
thou shall not commit adultery
thou shall not steal
thou shall not bear false witness
thou shall not covet

Confessions of Ma'at

I have never cursed God
I have done no murder nor bid anyone to slay on my behalf
I have not lusted nor defiled the wife of any man
I have not robbed with violence and I have not stolen
I have not spoken lies
I have not envied or craved for that which belongs to another

Coming Forth By Day

I do not offend the god who is at the helm
I do not harm my kinsmen
I do not kill
I am not an adulterer
I do not rob
I do not tell lies instead of truth
I do no wrong or mischief to other

The Kolbrin Bible

a man will not curse the sacred things
a man will not revile his parents
a man will not slay willfully
a man will not have intercourse with the wife of another man
a man will not rob another with violence or plunder or steal
a man will not utter lies to lead another into error
a man will not pander to the lusts and weaknesses of others

Prince Shōtoku's 17 Article Constitution

1. Value harmony and avoid quarreling.

2. Revere the Three Treasures of Buddha, Dharma, and Sangha.

3. Obey the imperial commands, as Earth obeys Heaven.

4. Ministers must behave with decorum, avoiding attention-seeking and flashy behavior.

5. Deal with public matters as a servant of the law, and avoid bribes and corruption.

6. Chastise evil and reward good. Encourage fidelity among your peers.

7. Take responsibility for your own affairs and do not interfere with the duties of others.

8. Come to work early, and work until late, to ensure that all matters are dealt with.

9. Observe good faith toward both superiors and inferiors.

10. Do not regard yourself as a genius and those around you as fools, but quell your anger and approach others with a calm heart.

11. Ensure that good deeds are rewarded and evil punished.

12. There is only one lord in a country. Do not allow local governors or aristocrats to doubly tax the people.

13. Ensure that all officers report for work and carry out their duty with equal diligence.

14. Do not envy those whose wisdom and genius exceeds yours, but honor them.

15. Turn away from that which is private, and be faithful to that which is public, to prevent resentment and corruption.

16. When the people are at leisure in the winter, press them into service for the state; but when they are busy producing their food and clothing, do not employ them.

17. Decisions on important matters should not be made by one person alone, but by consulting with many.

The following quotation is taken from the book <u>Beyond Order</u>, written by the influential clinical psychologist Jordan Peterson. He attempts to decipher the Ten Commandments as a universal civilizing code - although those are not his words - necessary for there to be order in the world. As with the western concept of *rights* or *civil liberties* being derived from God, these commandments, given to man by God, are extracted from a higher authority beyond the realm of man – this is not to be taken as a literal fact:

> *"The first speaks to the necessity of aiming at the highest possible unity; the second to the danger of worshiping false idols (by confusing the representation, or the image, with the ineffable it is supposed to represent); the third means that it is wrong to claim moral inspiration from God while knowingly committing sinful acts; the fourth means that it is necessary to leave time to regularly consider what is truly valuable or sacred; the fifth keeps families together, mandating honor, respect, and gratitude from children as just reward for the sacrifices made by parents; the sixth prevents murder (obviously) but, by doing so, also protects the community from potential descent into constant and potentially*

multigenerational feuding; the seventh mandates the sacredness of the marriage vow, predicated on the assumption (like the fifth) that the stability and value of the family is of paramount importance; the eighth allows for honest, hardworking people to reap the benefits of their efforts without fear that what they have produced will be taken from them arbitrarily (and, thereby, makes civilized society a possibility); the ninth maintains the integrity of the law, reducing or eliminating its use as a weapon; and the tenth is a reminder that envy and the resentment it breeds is a destructive force of the highest power."

On a separate note, the *Code of Hammurabi* is one of the most complete written legal codes in existence. It was organized by the Babylonian king Hammurabi, who held power between 1792 to1750 BC. It contains 282 rules, standards for business practices and punishments. As an extension of God on earth, it may be surmised that Hammurabi's Code was given to man by God.

Sixth Iteration

It is very clear that we find the cornerstone of many spiritual practices laid by wise souls throughout the ages, usually with assistance from God or from entities in other realms. It is also very clear that to teach such *mysteries* so freely among the public (or the profane) was to constitute a violation of the sacred and secret power of the self-described elite classes. This is one of the true reasons the priests and leadership were angry beyond measure at the *teachings of Jesus Christ,* who showed the commoner how to *walk on water, heal the sick,* and *raise the dead.* It makes far more sense to consider that Jesus learned these sacred teachings from the Hindu *Rishis,* who were famous for the same feats.

These priestly classes, therefore, used their influence and power to infiltrate, hijack, and corrupt the Edenic apple of wisdom to its core. The apple in this context represents spiritual truths obtained from the *Tree of Good and Evil*: that ethics, morals, integrity, justice, and the like, are prerequisites for obtaining what blooms on the *Tree of Life* - eternal *spiritual life.*

The *Original Sin* in this context is only the *realizing* of one's conditional state of servitude to a power pretending to be God, i.e., Lucifer who believed he was God's equal. From here we arrive at our current state of technocracy with its promises of everlasting techno-life, or transhumanism and eventually post-humanism. These ideas are even present in the Egyptian *Book of the Dead*, wherein it is explained that the "Sons of Revolt" shall forever be suppressed:

> *"Thine enemy the Serpent hath been given over to the fire. The Serpent-fiend Sebua hath fallen headlong, his forelegs are bound in chains, and his hind legs hath Ra carried away from him. The Sons of Revolt shall never more rise up."*

It is not a matter of which doctrine or dogma is true or false since the serpent is now both glorified as a wise dragon and spit upon as a slithering devil. Our primary concern should be the *truth* that no *wisdom* is ever *bestowed*; it is only *obtained* through personal workings - *The Great Work*. No belief in aliens, gods, or even God as a deity, and certainly no belief in priests or gurus, will assure everlasting spiritual life. It can be argued though, and likely concluded, that viewing existence as a cycle meant to teach certain spiritual truths for the next life, with all its sufferings, is incomprehensible since it always draws us back to the illusions of *matter*. As Jonathan Black wrote, it is this "matter" that Lucifer "endowed" with "*a glamor that would dazzle people and blind them to higher truths.*" On the contrary, viewing existence as having no purpose seems to cultivate the same outcome. Perhaps the Shintoists are the most informed about how to follow this Middle Pathway, since they tend to see no problem with *desire* so long as it serves the *Kami* – i.e., harmony with what others call nature or God. In other words, material goods are not necessarily seen as *evil* but their absence does not imply spiritual progress. Regardless of the condition of *possession* or *desire,* so long as one is serving the *Kami* then all else is secondary. However, this in no way implies, suggests, or factually states that Shintō allows for any kind of *evil*. On the contrary, it is absent of what we may call *evil*. To *serve the Kami* means to harmonize with nature and contribute to society by fulfilling your obligations to family, community, country, and your ancestors. Shintō sounds from this perspective very similar to Freemasonry and its unfished pyramid which teases personal and societal development. We may, therefore, conclude that existence is all these things and yet none of them. It is the *Middle Way* of

Buddha, just as Jesus was crucified - as the *Way and the Truth and the Life* - between two thieves. Spiritual wisdom can be guided by those figures and archetypes such as Jesus Christ or Siddhartha Gautama, but never bestowed outright. It certainly will never be granted by those speaking in the name of such figures, nor those promising to replace God with technology while encouraging you for ease and comfort to drink a black liquid we call the *technological elixir*. Others find "God" in the honoring of land, their ancestors, and the fulfillment of daily duties like Shintōists. With New Age beliefs and "ancient astronaut" theory there is a hinting that God is actually a technologically advanced alien race. But just as a man may be a mason, adhering to all the tenets thereof, without actually being a member of a lodge, a confirmed mason may not adhere to any of the tenets of the order. In other words, there are plenty of men and women who follow in the footsteps of Jesus Christ without any confirmation of their membership in Christendom, and just as many who believe attending church service once a week is the path to salvation. An ingenious shaman likewise may be as prepared to face death as the strictest Muslim, Jew, Hindu, Buddhist, ad infinitum, or a simple pious man who walks in the footsteps of no prophet or god. So long as one adheres the *secret teachings* of the ancient *mysteries* it should matter little what denomination they choose.

Most of the symbols, images, prayers, myths, etc., in virtually all religions and life-style faiths alike, are meant to provoke similar spiritual realizations not unlike the Garden of Eden narrative. Whatever feels most confrontable, be that due to culture or intuition, that is what you should utilize to focus your *intention* and *will*, the cornerstones of *magic*, in completing *The Great Work*.

~ PART III ~

Hand of God

MAGIC VS MIRACLE

First Iteration

The term *magic* belongs to various traditions and virtually every culture. It is defined in countless ways and has been redefined as many times over. For some the term applies only to those *works* carried out by religious or spiritual opposition, while the same *magic* within the confines of a particular culture or doctrine is classified as *miracle*. The Romans persecuted early Christians by this standard, accusing them of performing accursed acts. After Rome was converted to Christianity and the Catholic Church gained power, Christians began their own persecutions of pagans. During the Reformation in the 16th-century, Protestant groups again began persecuting Christians due to the centuries of abuse, at that point, which had been carried out by the Roman Catholic Church.

When Francisco Pizzaro arrived in South America and Hernan Cortez in Central America, they certainly benefited by both chance and through the study of local religious beliefs about the return of European-looking gods like Quetzalcóatl or Viracocha. The irony is that Pizzaro and Cortez set their sights on converting the locals from the very system of belief that allowed the Europeans to dominate the region in the first place. There is more irony in the fact that as the Spanish slaughtered thousands, six thousand alone at Cholula, they merely matched the bloody rituals of the Aztecs in which tens of thousands were murdered to prevent the end of the world. But the great white civilizers of Central and South America taught the exact opposite of these uncivil behaviors. Doubly ironic was the fact Pizzaro and Cortez played the part of the *trickster* Tezcatilpoca, whose cult demanded bloody human sacrifice.

Although Europeans are generally and historically condemned for what their ancestors did in Central and South America, it is important to recognize that these atrocities were only allowed by the great populations there due to religious and mythological traditions of white men with beards and robes who spread peace, love, and civility. For more on this see my book *Liberty Shrugged*.

In other words, Pizzaro and Cortez were akin to black magicians, incorporating technology, mythology, theology, and the like in their conquest of an entirely different and unique culture.

The differences between *science* and *magic* are about as fine a line as the difference between *magic* and *miracle*.

Second Iteration

Fritz Graf wrote in an essay titled, 'Excluding the Charming: The Development of the Greek Concept of Magic', that *"goēs is a complicated figure."* This is simply put, true, since *magic* goes by many names and definitions today, some seeing all magic as black, while others seeing all magic as white. Fritz says that goēs combines *"ecstasy and ritual lament, healing rites and divination"* and adds that *"the goēs has been connected with the world of the shamans."*

Healing rites, divination, and spirit communication data back tens of thousands of years and are certainly forms of *magic* as we have thus far seen in this text. These Shamans, and other earlier magicians, act as Charon, the old man who ferried souls of the dead across the rivers Styx and Acheron to Hades.

Goēs were essentially figures connected with the passage of the dead between worlds, a part famously played by the magicians and priests in Egypt. Much like the passage of the soul through various trials and gates upon death, gods like Morpheus in Greece assisted the living in traversing dreams and nightmares.

Graf confirms that *"goēs is a marginal figure connected with the passage of the dead between worlds."*

Third Iteration

The Greek philosopher, and disciple of Socrates, Plato, referred to what we call *magicians* as *agurtēs* and *mantis*, or 'begging priests' and 'seers'. Plato says that these men would visit the homes of wealthy citizens and attempt to convince them of a power they possessed and that was for sale: *"a faculty which they obtained from the gods through sacrifices and incarnations."* These men would offer *"to heal them through joy and feasts in case their ancestors or they themselves had committed some injustice; and in case they would like to harm an enemy, they would be able, at low cost, to injure righteous people as well as unrighteous ones through some incantation and decision because they were able, as they brag about, to persuade the gods to help them."* Psychic troubles, or *mania*, could be healed, say the priests and seers of Plato, at *"a low cost"* with purification rituals and mystery rites. It is still common today to believe that some daily troubles are a result of ancestral crimes, and such an idea has been turned from the world of *magic* and *goēteia* into a political zealotry which accuses current generations of ancestral guilt to derive obedience. This is done with race, gender, and the environment.

The word *magos* first appears in a Greek text at the end of the 6th-century BCE, though the word is from Persia where the *magos* or *magi* was a priest and practitioner of certain mystical rites. The 'Father of History', Herodotus, was one of the first to speak of these *magoi* or *magi* as a type of secret society. He discusses how the Persian priests engaged in sacrifices and divination, while also conducting funerary rites and dream interpretation. The Greek words *mageia* and *magos* are probably more famous in Latin as *magia* and *magus*.

Plato points out that the teachers of this art of *magoi (mageia)* derived it from *"Zoroaster, son of Oromasdes,"* who was a prophet from the Middle East. Zoroaster is known also as Zarathustra, the founder of Zoroastrianism and author of a sacred scripture called *Zend Avesta*. This commentary text is older than the *Vedas* of India, the *I Ching* of China, and many of the sacred texts from ancient Egypt. The age of the *Vedas*, however, are called into question considering the date of their writing is set from the time they were actually written down. In other words, the *Vedas*, like other sacred texts, were kept by holy men in memory long before being inscribed. Many of these sacred texts, or at least the concepts embodied within them, including the *Zend Avesta*, are pre-ancient. The *Zend Avesta* and *Popol Vuh* both tell similar stories to the *Bible*, describing the Creation of the world as beginning with *light*. All three versions are presented below:

Bible (Genesis 1:3): *"In the beginning, when God created the Universe, the earth was formless and desolate. The raging ocean that covered everything was engulfed in total darkness, and the Spirit of God was moving over the water. Then God commanded, 'Let there be Light' - and light appeared."*

Popl Vuh (Part I): *"This is the account of how all was in suspense, all calm, in silence; all motionless, still, and the expanse of the sky was empty. This is the first account, the first narrative. There was* *neither man, nor animal, birds, fishes, crabs, trees, stones, caves, ravines, grasses, nor forests; there was only the sky. The surface of the earth had not appeared. There was only the calm sea and the great expanse of the sky. There was nothing brought together, nothing which could make a noise, nor anything which might move, or tremble, or could make noise in the sky. There was nothing; only the calm water, the placid sea, alone and tranquil. Nothing existed. There was only immobility and silence in the darkness, in the night. Only the Creator, the Maker, Tepeu, Gucumatz, Fore-fathers, were in the water surrounded with light... Thus let it be done! Let the emptiness be filled! Let the water recede and make a void, let the earth appear and become solid; let it be done. Thus they spoke. Let there be light, let there be dawn in the sky and on the earth."*

Zend Avesta (I): *"Ahura Mazda, Spake unto Spitama Zarathustra saying: First I have made the Kingdom of Light, Dear to all life."*

Ahura Mazda goes on to create the Preserver, Spoiler, Eternal Life, Death, Wisdom, Ignorance, Work, Idleness, Love, Hatred, Peace, Violence, Power, Weakness, Food, Impure Food, Health, Disease, Man, Inferior Man, Joy, Sadness, Sun, Darkness, Water, Impure Water, Air, Impure Air, Earth, Barrenness. The archetypical battle between darkness and light was personified in the conflict told of by the Persian *magi* through the principles of good and evil, which were manifest like Osiris and Set under the names *Ormuzd*, or *Ahura Mazda* (creator god), and *Ahriman* (evil spirit). This epic battle between the progeny of darkness and the preservers of truth and wisdom is *Armageddon*, "the last battle between good and evil before the Day of Judgment," or the *Ragnarok* of the *Eddas* and the *Kurukshetra* of the *Mahabharata*. Author and researcher D. M. Murdoch further explains in her book <u>The Christ Conspiracy</u> the dual concepts of good and evil, god and the devil, light and darkness, and all those things Created by Ahura Mazda:

"The dualistic concepts of absolute good and evil did not originate with Christianity but are found long before the Christian era, particularly within Zoroastrianism. Satan is an adaptation of the Persian representative of evil 'Ahriman,' the twin brother of 'God,' the same as the Egyptian Set, Horus's twin and principal enemy, also known as 'Sata,' whence comes 'Satan.' Horus struggles with

Set in the exact manner that Jesus battles with Satan, with 40 days in the wilderness, among other similarities, such as the revealing from the mount 'all the kingdoms of Earth.' This myth represents the triumph of light over dark or the sun's return to relieve the terror of the night. Horus/Set was the god of the two horizons; hence, Horus was the rising sun, and Set the time of the Sun-SET."

Fritz Graf writes that *"the combination, finally, of goēteia and mageia occurs for the first time in Gorgias, in his Encomium of Helena."* In combing the Greek term for enchantment, fascination, and wizardry - *mageia* - with the word for invoking angels and demons - *goēteia* - the idea of magic took on a new form.

Dichotomy in nature was Created by God or Ahura Mazda, and therefore magic, like mythology, was an attempt to either live in harmony with nature (White Magic or Gray Magic), or to control nature (the Black Magic of Plato's begging priests and seers).

White Magic is a blending together of the *seen* and *unseen* to create what the Japanese and Shintō practitioners call *WA*, or *harmony*. It is the appeasing of forces greater than *self* with sympathetic alignment in clothing, incense, diet, exercise, ad infinitum.

Black Magic is the action of opposing such forces or of manipulating them against their natural order for selfish gain.

Manly Hall puts it simply: *"magic is the art of manipulating the unseen forces of Nature."*

The practice of *pharmaka*, or preparation of biological ingredients into medicines or poisons, was once thought to be an act of sorcery or magic due to the way such things altered the body and mind. This is the same reason alcohol is still to this day called *spirits*. Both *pharmaka* and *spirits* are from the world of the supernatural, according to those lacking scientific understanding. Thus, from this example, we see that *magic* and *science* are, in some capacity, truly the same thing.

It is as science fiction author Arthur C. Clark once wrote: *"Any sufficiently advanced technology is indistinguishable from magic."* Likewise, any sufficiently advanced *magic* is indistinguishable from *miracle* and vice versa.

Fourth Iteration

Many things we see as solely based in *science* today were but *superstition, myth,* and *magic* in olden times. The word 'superstition" itself derives from the Latin *superstitio,* and from *super* and *stare,* which mean *over* and *stand* respectively – to stand over and in awe of something. Any *faithful* adherent to their gods and goddesses is usually quite superstitious by this definition. There is also very little difference between *myth* and *magic,* as they relate to *science,* considering the two former words are designators for the manner in which we interact with and attempt to understand the world – the scientific process. As noted earlier, even the word *science,* which comes from the Latin *scientia,* means *to know.* Usually, this knowing is obtained through observation, but it shares a relationship with superstitious *intuition,* too, which comes from the Latin *intuitio,* from the Latin *intueri,* which means *consider.* This means that *intuition* is essentially a process of observation and consideration, something more akin to our view of *science,* while the latter is much more like an *intuition.*

The advent, and continued metamorphosis, of mythology, is strongly rooted in early scientific observation and understanding of how nature works. Just as we know *The Word of God* and that He spoke into existence "light," we also know that words in general have properties that need no scientific validation. Some words we classified as 'kind' and others as 'harsh' or 'mean'. As the Japanese refer to *kotodama,* the *spirit of words,* or *otodoma,* the *spirit of sound,* almost every culture in the world has a similar concept. What we call *science* today and the *magic* of technology tomorrow will eventually become pure superstition and sorcery in the past of a progressing future. What doctors and nurses perform today will be considered barbaric and ignorant in due time.

Today we 'wish' someone a "good morning" or "good night," hopefully influencing their psyche to indeed have a "good" or desirable time. In the story of <u>Beauty and the Beast</u>, published in 1740, there is reference to *Dat Rosa Mel Apibus* or *The Rose Gives Honey to the Bees.* The *rose* is a symbol of the *mysteries* and the *bees* are the initiates. This same story tells of a prince (spirit) trapped in a bestial body (matter and form). He is only to be freed through love, or the beauty and love of Belle (a bell) which rings harmoniously in resonance with the divine. In ancient Greece, an *epaoidē* or epoidē was an incantation or verbal utterance intended to ward off disease and heal the sick. Sound is a powerful force and so are the words we choose to verbalize, hence why *"even fools are thought wise when they keep silent; with their mouths shut, they seem intelligent"* (Proverbs 17:28). What we hear is the vibration of symbols transmitted through particles in the air and sent to our brains as electrical signals that are then translated into sounds.

The repetition of names with intonation in sets of three were *"united to triangular combinations in magical ceremonies,"* according to Eliphas Levi in his book <u>Transcendental Magic</u>. The physician and alchemist Paracelsus often combined the Magic Wand with a magnetized fork to create a trident for this process. Levi adds, *"The magic rod was frequently surmounted with a small magnetised fork, which Paracelsus replaced by the trident..."* He further recounts that Paracelsus ascribed to the trident *"all the virtues which Kabbalistic Hebrews attribute to the name of Jehovah and the thaumaturgic properties of the ABRACADABRA,"* the magic triangle of pagan theosophists used by Alexandrian hierophants. The 18th-century magical formula of *Ali Baba and the Forty Thieves* employs a similar magical utterance: "open sesame."

Fifth Iteration

Under the tutelage of traditional cosmology and theology certain humans were allowed a power to communicate with the gods by ritual, prayer, and sacrifice in an attempt to persuade their hand in human affairs. As philosophy crept into theology and the sciences grew in power and authority these *magicians* were transformed into superstitious atheists. For to think one could provoke the gods was as bad as thinking there were no god. Medical science also began to override the notion that the *sacred disease* epilepsy was caused by possession, suggesting instead it had a more natural cause. Magic as a word and practice began to change, at least in Greece, as a result of what Fritz Graf wrote was the *"rise of philosophical theology as a radicalization and purification of traditional, civic theology, and the rise of scientific medicine, based on the conception of nature as a homogeneous and closed system."*

In another essay, 'The Religious, Social, and Legal Parameters of Traditional Egyptian Magic', Robert K. Ritner explains how in a post-Socratic world, *"mageia was held to make use of good daimones (spirits lower than the gods of religion), while goēteia utilized evil daimones, thus producing the categories of good and evil ('white' and 'black') magic."* There is also an area of *gray magic* whereby the magician operates between the selfless and selfish. *Grey Magic* is indeed a more neutral and obscure form of the art, expressed by the descent of *White Magic* to *Black Magic*. If the former is involved in the upholding of the laws of nature by harmony, then the latter is concerned with the abuse of these laws to create chaos. But what may be considered selfish is not necessarily a dark art, unless it becomes purely perverse, centered on self at the expense of others, and abusive. Therefore, this *Grey Magic* is only a partly selfish form of action that is more obscure in both intention and meaning. Hall says that it is *"the unconscious or subconscious pervasion of power."* For there is nothing wrong with having great wealth or material possession, as in Shintō, so long as those possessions are used to serve the *kami* and follow *The Way of Truth*. Hall likewise explains that materiality and some of those things which we do *desire* are not necessarily in opposition to God's plan so long as man understands that it is his responsibility to cultivate them justly:

> *"Man was not intended by God to be rich, wise, beautiful, healthy, witty, of charming personality, or happily married. This does not mean that the Lord has any objection to his being any of these things or all of them. It merely means that if he desires these things he must go forth as Adam was directed to do, earning his bread by the sweat of his brow and not by the sweat of somebody else's."*

Being misunderstood or misidentified, nearly all forms of magic have been associated with wicked *sorcery*, likely for three primary reasons:

1) All darkness, and the unknown, is naturally attractive by its magnetism. It sparks curiosity of the instinct either by sympathy or antipathy. It attracts those souls searching for external power.

2) Darkness plays upon the imagination of the sorcerer to draw them to light like the right-hand path of the Pythagorean Y. These powerful forces of nature are easily

protected by images that act like symbolic scarecrows. The symbols ward off perverts of order and protect those who lack proper instruction otherwise. They act as repellent against the ignorant dabbling in diabolic affairs for which they cannot understand and prevent the naïve or foolish from falling victim to their own ignorance.

3) Since *magic* has been less known to the public, considered fringe, and even illegal throughout history, it has always been a scapegoat for terrible things when they should occur. The same is true today. What is a *miracle* to one is an act of *witchcraft, sorcery,* or *evil* to another.

Since "black" is void of color, and due to it being the essence of Absolute Intelligence, there is nothing evil or wrong about it in relation to magic. For there is *false darkness* and *true darkness,* just as there is *false light* and *true light.* Hall says, *"the true darkness is the womb of Light; the false darkness, the perversion of light that pours out of the true darkness."* For all *life as we know* it, i.e., all *form,* dies in the light and truly lives in darkness, and thus *"in dying really comes to life, for life as we know it is pure death."* The archetype of the Devil is but a representative gesture of this *false darkness,* symbol of inversion, perversion, and misuse. He is "not a son of Saturn" per se, *"but is a son of man and the false darkness on earth."* Hall adds, *"Man is the incarnation of the germ of mental intelligence,"* and therefore *"black magic is possible only to intelligent beings."* The nature of crystallized reality is *false darkness* illuminated by external light.

Yellow Magic is the failure, for whatever reason, to prevent these "black" perversions of the forces of nature. It is falling victim to temptation, even temporarily, while on a path of pure magical intention. *White Magic* and *Black Magic* can be summed up as such, according to Hall:

> *"A White Magician is one who is laboring to gain the confidence of the Powers That Be and to prove through the purity of his life and the sincerity of his motive his worthiness to be interested with the great Arcana (the Wand of the Magus). "*

> *"A Black Magician is one who seeks to gain authority over spiritual powers by means of force rather than by merit. In other*

words, he is one who is trying to storm the gates of heaven; he is one who is sweeping spiritual power and occult dominion with an ulterior motive."

From the Garden of Paradise story itself we get the first attempt by man to secrure occult knowledge without proper initiation. By eating the *fruit* offered by the serpent, man, working with the powers of distortion, becomes the first *black magician*.

The Pythagorean Y expresses the concept of *free will*. The Greek letter *upsilon* resembles a forked path with two possible outcomes. The left path is one of ease that ends in torment, for it signifies earthly wisdom (*vice*). The right path is one of hardships to be overcome upon obtaining enlightenment, signified by divine wisdom (*virtue*). This type of cross was also called *Forked Cross* or *Furka* during the Middle Ages and was associated with thieves due to its resemblance of the forked tongue of a serpent. The left path is the Eye of Horus or Ra, illuminating the inferior realm like the Devil's torch in tarot. Manly Hall writes of this "Y" the following: *"In Egypt the point where the arms of the Y converge was called the forking of the ways. The candidate for spiritual things always stands at the point where the three arms of the Y come together, carrying in his hand the scales of discrimination."*

In essence: **False Light** leads to **True Darkness** and **False Darkness** leads to **Tue Light**.

SACRIFICE & RITUAL

First Iteration

Suffice to say that the words "sacrifice" and "ritual" are misconstrued to mean *sorcery* unless they are in context with something like a Roman Catholic Mass. *Sacrifice* derives from the Latin words *sacrificium* and *sacrificus*, which combine the concepts of *sacra* and *facere* – *to perform sacred things*. The word *sacrificus* itself is a description of priestly functions. The Latin *sacer* also means *holy*. *Ritual* derives from the Latin *ritualis*, which comes from *rite*, or a religious ceremony. In both cases we are dealing with *holy* things or *sacra*, and thus nothing whatsoever to be anything but associated by ignorance with *sorcery*.

According to Jonathan Z. Smith in his essay 'Trading Places': "*…in academic discourse 'magic' has almost always been treated as a contrast term, a shadow reality known only by looking at the reflection of its opposite ('religion,' 'science') in a distorting fun-house mirror… Every sort of society appears to have a term (or, terms) designating some modes of ritual activities, some beliefs, and some ritual practitioners as dangerous, and/or illegal, and/or deviant.*" Despite the subjective dichotomy between *magic* and *miracle* there is no doubt that countless peoples have committed horrific crimes against innocence, nature, and all of Creation in the name of *magic*.

For those unconvinced that magic is more than sorcery, Eliphas Levi explains superbly the damage a black magician or *sorcerer* inflicts upon himself: "*This atrocious history is that of every magician, or rather of every sorcerer who practices bewitchments. He poisons himself in order that he may poison others; he damns himself that he may torture others; he draws in hell with his breath in order that he may expel it by his breath; he wounds himself to death that he may inflict death on others; but possessed of this unhappy courage, it is positive and certain that he will poison and slay by the mere projection of his perverse will.*" Levi continues, explaining the difference between white magic and sorcery: "*The more difficult or horrible the operation, the greater is its power, because it acts more strongly on the imagination and confirms effort in the direct ratio of resistance.*" Therefore, any practice that calls for the desecration of life or the literal sacrifice of animals or humans, particularly children, is the epitome of EVIL. It is wicked and demonic since a demon always seeks to cause havoc in human affairs. As Jonathan Seidel adds for the compilation text <u>Ancient Magic and Ritual Power</u>: *"Through his spells or paraphernalia the magician wounds and weakens."*

A *sacrifice*, be it of burnt offerings or the giving of flowers or fruit, is an external expression of our psyche, and often when conducted physically is either a misunderstanding or an outward symbolic action triggering an internal spiritual transformation. Its essence is found in the forgoing of gratification now for the obtaining of something more valuable in the future. This is a *burnt offering*.

Catholics are perhaps the most famous, or infamous, of religious houses in their heavy reliance on symbolic imagery, and *paraphernalia*, to praise God, though we are not proposing that Catholics are sorcerers. They are, however, magicians. Their act of communion is seen as a sacred practice to consume the 'body' and 'blood' of their savior. The Biblical book of John, chapter 6, verse 53 famously states:

> *"Jesus said to them, 'Very truly I tell you, unless you eat the flesh of the Son of Man and drink his blood, you have no life in you'."*

But for some this ritual is nothing more than a downgrading of literal barbarism, cannibalism, and the consumption of human blood. This is especially true due to the long history of Christian genocide. The Jews are not as famous for their obsession with bloody sacrifice and war, but that it did occur is a fact none the less. The same may be said of Muslims. The proof of cannibalism and vampirism in John 6:53 does not tell the entire story though, since such notions are deeply esoteric and not to be taken literally.

The blood contains "life force" and the bread is both the animated "body" we call *self* and the secondary body we inhabitant upon death. When the two are merged we obtain life of an everlasting variety. But this "life" is obtained not just with wine and bread, or the Egyptian ankh, but through agricultural symbology. The sun and water are critical for the growing of cereal crops and grapes. The essence embodied in wheat and vine is expressed as the body and blood of the *Son of Man* or the *Sun of Man*. Just as the

Egyptians ate their god as bread, the Christians take part in the same magical ceremony of sympathy. In other words, eucharist can be interpreted as literal, figurative, or purely symbolic. Depending on the *will* and *intention* of the operator, communion thus becomes either *black magic, grey magic,* or *white magic.* The ritual *communion* is the holding of sympathetic contact with the son or sun of man.

In Egypt the eucharist was called *Killing the King,* a reference to the *Green Man* Osiris, who inhabited the crops. Since Osiris is the god of agriculture he was literally depicted as having green skin to signify fertility. Osiris can also be rightfully referred to as the *Great Hunter, Great Warrior, Beast Slayer, Orion the Hunter* in Greek mythology, and *Herne* the Hunter in Norse mythology. Some may recall a connection to the Biblical Nimrod, who was also a *Mighty Hunter.* Osiris is often referred to as the "universal master" – *neb tem* – or a Lord of Beasts. The great Hindu god Siva (Shiva or Rudra-Siva) is also known in one incarnation by the name *Pasupati,* a word meaning *lord of the animals* or *Beastmaster.* Osiris, as a god of fertility, shared a connection to Orion through the name *Ourien,* which, according to Jonathan Black in <u>The Secret History of the World</u>, means semen:

> *"His [Osiris] name is connected with insemination, 'ourien' meaning semen, and what we call the belt of Orion is a euphemism. In ancient times it was a penis that became erect as the year progressed."*

There is an English legend of this sort told about a nature spirit called *John Barleycorn,* who inhabits crops. Alcohol is also derived from barley, an association we find with the wine and blood of Jesus. The Hittite people likewise drank of their god in ritual celebrations of sacrifice. In an essay titled, 'Ritual Meals in the Hittite Cult', Billie Jean Collins says:

> *"...more than simply a communion with the god, the ritual feast was a chance to sway a god or goddess to benevolence."*

In the Greek rituals of Bacchus large amounts of water would be left in the sealed temple overnight. Upon breaking the seals, the next morning, the people would find that the liquid had miraculous turned into wine - through works of mysterious forces, i.e. *spirits*. The wine would then be distributed, and it was said that anyone who partook of the drink was consuming the blood of Bacchus. Manly Hall thus states as fact:

> *"The Christian communion cup is none other than the chalice of Bacchus, whose blood was symbolized by the juice of the vine."*

Just as Jesus also turned water into wine, an homage no doubt to the Greek and Roman gods of wine, Dionysus, and Bacchus, it is also said that St. Brigid had the miraculous ability to turn her own bathwater into beer.

The mystical Muslim sect known as Sufi were pious ascetics said to share great feasts on occasion. At these meals great amounts of wine and food would be consumed. However, these things were of *spiritual wine* and *wisdom bread*.

Second Iteration

Blood has always been thought to contain the *life force* of a living creature - the soul - and was therefore forbidden for any usage by the God of Moses. According to the philosopher Alan Watts:

> *"Blood was to be the life-essence of men and animals, and thus the property of God alone, so that every animal killed for food had to have its throat slit and the blood poured to the ground."*

He adds that under the Covenant between man and God:

> *"..the sacrifice is a communion meal, between God and his people in which they take the flesh and he takes the blood. But under the New Covenant, instituted by Jesus, the people are to have both the flesh and the blood of the sacrificial lamb."*

In other case, such as Hittite military rituals, the body and bread, or bread and wine, would be offered to the gods in exchange for protection. A fire would be lit before a participant *"sacrifices bread and wine and summons the gods to eat and drink,"* writes Richard H. Beal. This ritual is called 'When the soldiers go away from the land to campaign and to the enemy land to fight'. In ritual meals of the Hittite cult the final part of any sacrificial celebration is called "drink the god." Whatever god is being consumed is the one to whom the ritual is dedicated.

Alan Watts proceeds to explain that the eucharist is more than about man communing with God, and instead symbolizes that God is within man. He writes, the "...*bread and wine offered at the altar for Mass (brought, in ancient times, by the people themselves) represent ourselves, our flesh and blood, and the work, the sacrifice, and the guilt, which they involve.*"

Third Iteration

It was believed, and now scientifically confirmed in part, that younger blood can rejuvenate parts of an older body. A 2014 article in *Science Translational Medicine* summed up the possibly in a headline 'Young Blood Rejuvenates the Aging Brain'. Another from Stanford University Magazine in 2020 says, 'Young Blood and the Search for Biological Immortality'. Columbia University asked the same thing in a 2023 article, 'Will Revitalizing Old Blood Slow Aging?'. Throughout history we have seen an obsession with blood for these and other reasons. Elizabeth Báthory was a Hungarian serial killer of young women, whose blood she used to slow her aging process and stay youthful. Vlad the Impaler was famous for just what his name implies, and for drinking the blood of his enemies. The blood of strong warriors, particularly gladiators, is sympathetically meant to impart the same strength and skill. Flesh and organs could be used the same. This definitely puts a new spin on "*eat the flesh of the Son of Man and drink his blood...*

Many took this belief to the extreme and chose to perform barbaric sacrifices of a literal nature. The sacrifices of *self* and *animal nature* degraded into literal human and animal sacrifice, and the drinking of human or animal blood.

Still, in these cases, the death of the animal and the pouring out of its blood upon the ground represented the death of vice and uncleanness, the same being poured from the body. Others undoubtedly murdered, and continue to murder, for diabolic purposes. This is witnessed in the excessive killing of animals in *Santeria*, the pantheistic Afro-Cuban folk religion. However, as with Caribbean Voodoo practices, the origins of these cults are far removed from such literal sacrifices. Voodoo itself is a combing of

African magical and religious rites with those of the Catholic Church. If Voodoo practitioners still perform bloody sacrifice today, it is likely because of their heritage in the Roman Catholic Church and its eucharist.

Fourth Iteration

If the *"more difficult or horrible the operation, the greater is its power,"* we can surmise that operations of simplicity and beauty provide a different type of power altogether. Part of this process involves overcoming the *Great Evils* known as ignorance, superstition, and fear. These things must be conquered just like the Great Dragon of *animal desire*.

The concept of an animal sacrifice, traditionally, is based on the notion of an *animal self*. There are Seven Stages of Creation ruled over by each of the seven classical planetary intelligences. According to the *Seven Rosicrucian Aphorisms of Creation*, the soul of man is sevenfold, separated into the souls of elements, minerals, plants, animals, humans, demi-god, and Gods.

The occult knowledge of Theosophist Frank Baum was preserved in *The Wonderful Wizard of Oz*, wherein the story of the different human natures in the animal, mineral, and vegetable bodies, were explained by the lion, tin man, and scarecrow. These characters also relate to the three complexes of the brain known as primate, mammalian, and reptilian. We are also reminded of Carl Jung's seven archetypes, which are the seven original planetary gods and their consciousnesses, the seven Scandinavian earth demons, or the more commonly known seven dwarfs from *Snow White*.

Today we know them as Dopey, Happy, Bashful, Sleepy, Grumpy, Sneezy, and Doc, all of which share similarities with the fairies in *Sleeping Beauty*. or the Scandinavian demons known as Toki, Skavaerr, Varr, Dun, Orinn, Grerr, Radsvid.

For our divinity to rise from the mummy bindings of the material world, it is said a *human sacrifice* must be performed; and this is not one by which a first-born must be offered up on a burning altar to a vengeful and angry storm god.

To the *profane* these are literalities, and therefore, the *dead* search for a literal fountain of youth and for literal gold. For the truly *alive* and for alchemist these are metaphors concealed by allegories; their lead is the corporeal and their gold is the spirit or soul. The transformation of self by the conquering of instinctual desires elevates *man* above that of the *animal* and into hopefully into demi-god consciousness. In this fact can be understood the true meaning of "slaying a great dragon," or the misconceptions of "human" or "animal" sacrifices.

At expense of sounding repetitive: The human and animal sacrifices are an overcoming of basic *desires* so that attention may be focused on more than generative instinct, perhaps on returning to the Garden Paradise. To these ends, Eliphas Levi writes:

> "To change lead, mercury, and all other metals into gold, to possess the universal medicine and the elixir of life such is the problem which must be solved to accomplish this desire and to realize this dream."

Nevertheless, animal sacrifices continue to be performed around the world, even when they are not prescribed by the honored deity – see the Gadhimai Festival. Although barbaric, even when invoked in the Bible, these sacrifices do have a more sophisticated meaning beyond sheer barbarism. In Hebrews 13:11-13 the animal sacrifice is performed for the absolution of sin, in parallel to the sacrifice of Jesus:

> "The high priest carries the blood of animals into the Most Holy Place as a sin offering, but the bodies are burned outside the camp. And so Jesus also suffered outside the city gate to make the people holy through his own blood. Let us, then, go to him outside the camp, bearing the disgrace he bore."

Leda Jean Ciraolo's says in her essay, 'Supernatural Assistants in the Greek Magical Papyri', that animal sacrifice has also taken on the meaning of endowing a man-made object with "*a power it did not previously possess.*" She says the sacrifice endows the object "*with sense, intelligence and mobility,*" that it otherwise does not possess. Her essay is only a documentary piece on the history of such things, though it could certainly be construed as a justification for killing animals by the excessively profane. Hence, texts of this sort are best kept for more advanced students of *esoterica*.

Fifth Iteration

If we are to perfect ourselves and complete the building of our bodily temple, we must also conquer and appropriately use certain elements, or tools of building, that may otherwise act as weapons of destruction to bring about collapse of our temple.

The unfinished pyramid is symbolic of the unaccomplished work in each individual and in each society. It represents an incomplete and imperfect structure, waiting for the final bricks to be laid. The unfinished pyramid, or capital A, is symbolic of both the body and society at large.

The *All Seeing Eye*, or *Eye of Providence*, encourages us to maintain our morality and complete our duties even when no one else is looking. This "eye" is anathema to the *Eye of Sauron*, which although made popular by J. R. Tolkien's fictional masterpiece, is ultimately derived from the qualities of a serpent, i.e., *sauria* or *saurian*. The story is, after all, called the *Lord of the Rings,* i.e., Saturn. A single "eye" can be dangerous for other reasons, too, including the abandonment of humanity to AI - an eye - or artificial intelligence, and the *blinking demon eye* of the Gorgon Medusa called Algol, i.e., algorithm.

Once the individual achieves a state of enlightenment, they act a brick in the building of *Platonopolis,* or Sir Francis Bacon's *New Atlantis.* Just as a society must operate from a solid foundation of ethics, morals, civility, and responsibility, so must each individual. The is the essence of ancient and contemporary Shintō. Each brick in this society represents an enlightened individual, and each individual builds their own temple with bricks made of personal works - the *Great Work* or alchemy.

The bodily temple must be respected through the eating of certain foods or wearing of certain clothing. A lifestyle built upon moderation and consideration for the sacred trinity of body, mind, and spirit, is essential for all initiates of the *mysteries.* It must also be built on a solid foundation with each brick an individual work of self-refinement achieved and not bestowed. Through discipline man perfects himself to become square, upright, and true, turning rough ashlar into smooth stone. This transformation is seen as an alchemical transmutation of the base metal lead (inferior self) into the superior metal of gold (higher spiritual nature); from Saturn, the black sun, to the solar saviour of the true Sun.

If we wish to unite with the Divine or with Source, we must adhere to a lifestyle and mindset which attracts such virtues.

Sixth Iteration

According to the <u>Crata Repoa: Initiations of the ancient mysteries of the priests of Egypt</u>, as reproduced in Manly Hall's <u>The Lost Keys of Freemasonry</u>, an initiate into the mysteries would be placed *"on a particular diet, interdicting him the use of certain foods, such as vegetables and fish."* Wine was limited, *"but after his initiation this restriction was relaxed."* An initiate was compelled *"to pass several months imprisoned in a subterranean vault, abandoned to his reflections he was allowed to write his thoughts. He was then strictly examined to ascertain the limit of his intelligence"* and understanding. The *magi* traditionally abstained from consuming or using the flesh of certain animals, too, and touched no blood, believing that this is where the soul resided. One of the main prohibitions of Jewish law was also against the consumption of blood based on the same belief. There is irony in the fact that *rabbis* and *magi* accused each other of the same magical crimes, while retaining that their beliefs were the *truth.* Obviously, they had much in common. As Leviticus 17:11 informs the reader:"

> *"For the life of the flesh is in the blood: and I have given it to you upon the altar to make an atonement for your souls: for it is the blood that maketh an atonement for the soul."*

Blood thus belonged to God only and was to be poured out of the animal if other parts were used. Spiritually speaking, however, even the flesh of *carnivora* is considered unwholesome due to the savage instincts of which it housed. The killing of animals likewise, we can assume from close inspection, produces much fear, and obviously death, which in no way helps one to obtain communion with Source. This is based on the idea of *magnetism* and *sympathetic magic.*

The Hindu *Bhagavad Gita* also explains in chapter 14, verse, 16, that *"Slaughtering poor animals is also due to the mode of ignorance. The animal killers do not know that in the future the animal will have a body suitable to kill them."* As a matter of fact, regardless of the various interpretations of such a statement, *"That is the law of nature."*

According to the writer Euripides, initiates of the secret *cultus* of Jupiter on Crete touched no flesh or meat and, in a chorus, addressed to King Minos, the priests spoke: *"I eat nothing which has been animated by the breath of life."* The initiates of Eleusis in Greece specifically abstained from domestic birds, fish, and certain plant foods like beans, peaches, and apples. Levi says that *"they abstained also from intercourse with a woman in child-bed, as well as during her normal periods."* This is a common theme throughout history, some believing that menstruation was impure. Although menstruation is also a cleansing process, women without child and those who were not menstruating were also forbidden. In fact, most social contact with people in general, even with men, was temporally ceased by Greek initiates and hierophants. Nevertheless, the Greek initiates had *"high standards of morality which they demonstrated in their daily lives,"* according to the philosopher Manly Hall.

In the Indian mysteries dietary restrictions were also imposed. In the third degree an initiate was also removed from social interactions for a temporary amount of time. As Jonathan Z. Smith confirms of the Greek stance on this matter:

> *"...there is a high concern for purity in both the rituals of preparation and reception. The practitioner is to abstain from sex, from animal food (including fish), and from 'all uncleanness'."*

Cleanliness in general is critical because it prepares the external body for receiving wisdom, just as dietary restrictions prepare the internal body. Both preparations help to prepare the mind and the temple which houses the brain. Hence the theme of baptism or ritual bathing was instrumental. In Shintō these purifications are called *misogi* and most commonly involve rinsing the mouth after sleep and placing the fingertips under water. The latter practice is also a common theme throughout the world since fingernails are thought to be gateways for spirits and demonic forces to enter the body. This is why a witch is often depicted with blackened fingertips and fingernails.

Perhaps these parallels will lend further credit to the parahistories, or *koshi-koden,* of Japan since the same teachings are found there in identical detail. According to Lord Amateru, the *amakami* (Heavenly Lord), who in this story is male rather than female (the sun goddess Amaterasu), one should only consume the right kinds of foods to cleanse the organs and return the body to balanced perfection - *homeostasis*. Lord Amateru's teachings are known as the *Way of Heavenly Being* (*Ame-naru-Michi*) or the *Way of Ise*, in essence another form of the alchemical marriage. The *amakami* educates his people on why they should never consume beasts or birds, since doing so would pollute the body with dead spirits. One of the only creatures acceptable to eat was a fish, but only if it had scales. For an ocean-locked people this makes logical sense. The best thing to consume were vegetables because their energy came directly from the sun, or perhaps the Sun of Man, our Heavenly Lord.

Catholics have traditionally relied on fish as well, specifically on Fridays since meat was to be abstained from on this day under the old Black Fast doctrine. Since Jesus gave his flesh on a Friday his followers honored his sacrifice by replacing meat with another food or with fish. This tradition is also found in the story of how Friday got its name, after the Norse Freya, goddess of fishing and sailing.

Augusta Foss Heindel writes in <u>Astrology and the Ductless Glands</u> of how mystics are able to peer with spiritual sight beyond the physical and into the human spinal column. Whether a person be worldly or spiritual will determine if the colors seen moving up and down the spine, *kundalini,* are red or blue. In the wise and austere the flame is blue. But for the profane and vulgar it is red: *"The color of this flame… is different in an adult who is earthly, filled with passions and desires, whose body is fed on the flesh of slaughtered animals, and which is steeped in tobacco, liquor, et cetera."*

Seventh Iteration

The *magus* or *magi* were also purified through proper regulation of sleep and abstinence from alcohol, which is equally as intoxicating as animal matter. The Bible says the same in Ephesians 5:18, commanding:

> *"And be not drunk with wine, wherein is excess; but be filled with the Spirit…"*

Proverbs 23:20-21 adds even further, speaking about alcohol and animal flesh:

> *"Do not join those who drink too much wine or gorge themselves on meat, for drunkards and gluttons become poor, and drowsiness clothes them in rags."*

The Quran 4:43 agrees with the Bible:

> *"Believers! Do not draw near to the Prayer while you are intoxicated until you know what you are saying nor while you are defiled – save when you are travelling – until you have washed yourselves."*

As for the Jews, Eliphas Levi explains how rabbinical students of the Kabbalah followed the same wisdom, especially pertaining to alcohol (spirits):

> *"...they avoided in particular all unhealthy evocations which disturb the nervous system and intoxicate reason."*

The Hindu *Bhagavad Gita* 5:22 speaks to these same ends:

> *"An intelligent person does not take part in the sources of misery, which are due to contact with the material senses. O son of Kunti, such pleasures have a beginning and an end, and so the wise man does not delight in them."*

Eighth Iteration

As David Martinez says in his essay 'Love Magic and Vows of Abstinence', the process of *"renouncing food and drink until a goal is attained solemnizes one's commitment to that goal and sanctifies its accomplishment within the supernatural realm."* He also confirms how *"certain kinds of food, certain kinds of clothing, sleep, sex, speaking, bathing, cutting hair, business dealings, entry into a house or town,"* etc., are used for the same purpose of obtaining a solemn goal. Essentially, *"anything which like fasting, produces isolation from normal society."*

By abstaining from bodily *needs* and *desires*, an initiate is empowered to focus on other disciplines such as prayer and study, usually in physical isolation, or at the very least social isolation. By rejecting daily needs and desires, *"the vow-taker protests the abnormality of the current situation"* and thus puts themself into a sympathy with the issue to be solved, understood, or overcome. Greek oracles are known to have abstained from worldly affairs before interacting with the divine, similar to how Daniel petitioned God in chapter 9, verse 9: *"So I turned to the Lord God and pleaded with him in prayer and petition, in fasting, and in sackcloth and ashes."*

We find this motif all throughout the Bible, countless other religious texts, and even in classical literature like the *Iliad*. When Moses received the Ten Commands from God, like Daniel speaking with the Lord, he went without bread or water for the same number of nights rain fell on Noah's ark, and Jesus abstained from food before being tempted by the Devil, i.e., forty days and forty nights.

Exodus 34:28

"Moses was there with the Lord forty days and forty nights without eating bread or drinking water. And he wrote on the tablets the words of the covenant – the Ten Commandments."

Genesis 7:4

"'Seven days from now I will send rain on the earth for forty days and forty nights, and I will wipe from the face of the earth every living creature I have made.'"

Matthew 4:1-11

"Then Jesus was led by the Spirit into the wilderness to be tempted by the devil. After fasting forty days and forty nights, he was hungry."

David swore a similar oath by his desire to find a dwelling place for the Lord. Psalm 132:1-5 says:

"Lord, remember David and all his self-denial. He swore an oath to the Lord, he made a vow to the Mighty One of Jacob: 'I will not enter my house or go to my bed, I will allow no sleep to my eyes or

slumber to my eyelids, till I find a place for the Lord, a dwelling for the Mighty One of Jacob.'"

In the *Iliad* we can read something similar, how Achilles vows not to eat or drink until he kills Hector:

"No, but I would now enjoin the sons of the Achaians to go into battle fasting and without food, but at sunset to prepare a great feast, once we have avenged the outrage. But until then, for my part, drink or food will by no means pass down my throat, seeing that my friend is dead."

In the above vow of abstinence, Achilles subjects not only himself to the restrictions but an entire army. An almost identical parallel can be found in 1 Samuel 14:24, which says Saul bound his "people," i.e., army, not to eat:

"Now the Israelites were in distress that day, because Saul had bound the people under an oath, saying, 'Cursed be anyone who eats food before evening comes, before I have avenged myself on my enemies!' So none of the troops tasted food."

In their desire to kill Paul, Jews took a similar vow in Acts 23:12, which states:

"The next morning some Jews formed a conspiracy and bound themselves with an oath not to eat or drink until they had killed Paul."

Although ritual abstinence, particularly of food and drink, was not extremely common outside of the *mysteries* in India, Rome, Greece, or Egypt, it certainly, as David Martinez confirms, *"played a more important role in Judaism, Christianity, and Greco-Oriental mystery religions."*

From Japan to the Americas rituals of purification and cleansing are both a common practice and a religious rite for countless *faiths*. Practitioners of Shintō fast, purify their mind, body, spirit, and personal space, and sit in seclusion with only their thoughts. This is the case in Sufism, Islam, Gnosticism, Christianity, Judaism, Kabbalism, Hinduism, Buddhism, ad infinitum. Although *fasting* is part of the *mystery* tradition it is not required as only an action thereof. Muslims fast for *Ramadan* from sunrise to sunset. In the Quran 2:183 we learn that fasting will lead to *taqwa*, or righteousness:

> *"O believers, fasting is enjoined on you as it was on those before you, so that you might become righteous."*

Orthodox Christians are supposed to fast on Wednesdays and Fridays, particularly during Lent and on Good Friday – the Catholic Black Fast. Hindus fast on certain days of the month such as the full moon and the eleventh day after both the full moon and the new moon. As with Islam, Jews are always forbidden from eating pig flesh. Seventh-day Adventists likewise abstain permanently from pork, along with alcohol, tobacco, and any type of mind-altering substance. They eat a vegetarian diet and drink clean water. Latter-day Saints eat almost exactly the same. The political movement of Rastafarians also adopted, like Voodoo, certain aspects of Christianity and mysticism, including their dietary guidelines. Rastafarians may be the strictest in their diets since they avoid all additives and chemicals too, all in an effort to reach their version of *taqwa*. We are informed of such actions relating to fasting in <u>The Grimoire of Pope Honorius</u> (published 1760) and the same is written in <u>The Greater Key of Solomon</u> (edition published in 1914 by Samuel Mathers):

> *"WHEN the Master of the Art shall wish to perform his operations, having previously arranged all things which it is necessary to observe and practise; from the first day of the Experiment, it is absolutely necessary to ordain and to prescribe care and observation, to abstain from all things unlawful, and from every kind of impiety, impurity, wickedness, or immodesty, as well of body as of soul; as, for example, eating and drinking superabundantly, and all sorts of vain words, buffooneries, slanders, calumnies, and other useless discourse; but instead to do good deeds, speak honestly, keep a strict decency in all things, never lose sight of modesty in walking, in conversation, in eating and drinking, and in all things; the which should be principally done and observed for nine days, before the commencement of the Operation."*

Ninth Iteration

In Greek mythology it is Demeter who, unlike individual or forced collective vows of abstinence in the *Iliad*, threatens the other gods directly and all of mankind with her vow of abstinence. In her Homeric Hymn, she rejects Zeus' invitation to return home to Olympus, just as David swore he would not enter his house until finding a dwelling place for Lord:

> *"For she claimed that she would never set foot on fragrant Olympus, nor let spring up earth's fruit, until she saw with her eyes her fair daughter."*

We know that Demeter threatens Zeus with the death of all mankind – starvation - if her daughter is not returned from Hades, and that this story is a wonderfully preserved agricultural metaphor. As with Demeter's story, and that of the *green god* of agriculture in Egypt, Osiris, the bread and wine of Christ are likewise the grain and grape of the whole ancient world. In Mark 14:25 Jesus provides his disciples with bread and wine, or body and blood, at the Passover feast before taking a vow of abstinence:

> *"While they were eating, Jesus took bread, and when he had given thanks, he broke it and gave it to his disciples, saying, 'Take it; this is my body.' Then he took a cup, and when he had given thanks, he gave it to them, and they all drank from it. 'This is my blood of the[c] covenant, which is poured out for many,' he said to them. 'Truly I tell you, I will not drink again from the fruit of the vine until that day when I drink it new in the kingdom of God.'"*

In Luke 22:14-16, Jesus says the same:

> *"When the hour came, Jesus and his apostles reclined at the table. And he said to them, 'I have eagerly desired to eat this Passover with you before I suffer. For I tell you, I will not eat it again until it finds fulfillment in the kingdom of God.'"*

Jesus plays the part here of redeemer for mankind, as Demeter, goddess of harvest, plays the same part in the *mystery* traditions of ancient Greece. In Egypt it was Osiris who was ritually eaten before being resurrected in his son Horus. In Japan it was the goddess of the sun, Amaterasu, who redeems the world and brings it back from the brink of annihilation. The Greek god Zeus, Jupiter in Rome, is closely associated with the Hindu trinity of Brahma, Vischnou (Vishnu) and Siva. These sacred three are part of the divided body of the "unrevealed God" and "germ of everything," known as *Zyaus*. We may recall that Osiris is linked with Orion and the name "ourien," which means semen. The "unrevealed god" in Hinduism is like the unveiled Isis, and is separated into Nara, Nari, and Viradj, like the Father, Son, and Holy Ghost.

Tenth Iteration

Manly P. Hall observes in <u>The Secret Teachings of All Ages</u> the curious misconceptions about *magic* and sacrifice, providing echo to Levi:

> *"The sacrificing of beasts, and in some cases, human beings, upon the altars of the pagans was the result of their ignorance concerning the fundamental principle underlying sacrifice. They did not realize that their offerings must come from within their own natures in order to be acceptable."*

Likewise, and contrary popular narrative, the Maya were not absolutely warlike, cruel, or barbaric. Their powerful nation reportedly lasted for nearly five hundred years without war. It was not until the decline of the empire and its domination by less advanced tribes that literal sacrifices were performed. Even then they were performed in limited capacity. Of the Maya, Manly Hall writes in <u>The Secret Destiny of America</u> that these sacrifices were metaphoric in nature and grossly misunderstood by many: *"On the altars of their gods they offered only flowers and fruit."* Jonathan Z. Smith adds on the subject of sacrifice something similar:

> *"Some of the animal materia (e.g., dung, eggs, a snake's shed skin) do not require the killing of the animal, while other materia - 'wolf's eye', 'frog's tongue' - may well be code names for plants."*

The same misunderstanding arises with the use of terms such as "kid" or "virgin" in various magical texts. Many believe these *black books* demand child sacrifice, when in fact a *kid* is a young goat, and a *virgin* is simply reference to unmarked paper or something similar. The same is true for the word *victim* which rarely denotes a human, and almost always means an animal. As noted earlier, the peoples of Central America and South America routinely sacrificed flowers, fruits, and select *animal materia*, before being driven to human sacrifice by corrupt priests who competed with civilizing gods like Quetzalcóatl and Viracocha.

Even in modern times we see horrific sacrifices and torrents of animal blood still flooding the ground. The Madheshi people living in Nepal practice *Gadhimai* every five years, slaughtering thousands of goats, buffalo, birds, etc., to the goddess Gadhimai Devi, an aspect of Kali. But in the mythology, she never asks for animal sacrifice to be performed in her honor, thus confirming the corruption of mythology and the *mysteries*.

Reportedly, the festival was finally suspended in 2015, but there is also supposedly no legal force backing those restrictions. This ritual killing may be horrific, but we must also consider that up to 100,000 cattle are slaughtered each day in the U.S. just for the luxury of what we eat.

Eleventh Iteration

Though abstinence is an important tool for communing with the divine and refining the self for *mystodokos,* and fasting is an important tool for the *faithful,* there are countless other ways to achieve the same ends. As with *ayahuasca, psilocybin* or *DMT,* acts of rhythmic dancing, drumming, bodily mutilation, etc., are commonly used. But none of these more frenzied states are to be recommended, though there is much power in the former botanical and fungal sources if used safely. Frenzied and often irrational behavior is chaotic, not harmonious, and essentially represent the distortion of the *mysteries*. Instead, we should focus on the harmony and beauty which can be found in dancing, singing, chanting, music, writing, and even reading.

In *Anacalypis,* Godfrey Higgins espouses the theory that music, poetry, and dance were the three great elements of primitive ritualism. He suggests that these elements were used before the discovery of writing and were utilized for religious and historical means. Before the invention of writing, the knowledge of ancient peoples was told in story form, often through poems, as was the case of the ancient *Vedas* and likely the *Zend Avesta* too. The famous Bards were known to have committed to memory countless narratives, even those of incredible length, and recited them verbatim at feasts and other celebrations. The practices of meditation, yoga, Qi Gong, and the like, which exist in some form, even by different names and variations, in virtually every culture, are meant to both heal and center the self. Healing is achieved through a focused mind, bodily movements organized into rhythm, and the movement of *Qi* – the life force that exists everywhere. *Centering* or *grounding* is reached in much the same way, another part of the manner by which *The Way*, or the *Middle Path*, can be followed. All of this can also be achieved through the ancient Sanskrit *Kama Sutra* and similar tantric practices such as ritually reciting *mantras*. Sex in general can certainly be healing to the mind, body, and Qi. Although it is usually scorned by very orthodox and fundamentalist religion, when not strictly used for procreation, it should only be the perversely promiscuous that is held in contempt. For, as the *Bhagavad Gita* states in chapter 2:59, the body is still in need of such world pleasures:

> *"Through the embodied soul may be restricted from sense enjoyment, the taste for sense objects remains."*

Completely denying sensory pleasures outside of rites and rituals can therefore be far more harmful to the body, mind, and spirit than allowing oneself to experience what the pagans saw, in sex, as the ultimate unification with Source. The *Sacred Marriage* is copulation between man and woman, as Eliphas Levi points out:

> *"Generation is in fact a work of the human androgyne."*

Jewish legend speaks to the action of God separating Adam and Eve, as man was on his right and woman on his left. Throughout human history, particularly in the remotest antiquity, it was already known that new life was the result of copulation. Thus, as Richard Cavendish writes in <u>The Black Arts</u>, *"all life in the universe is the result of the sexual activity of the gods."* In ancient Sumer a ritual of copulation was performed yearly, akin to modern witchcraft, by which a king would engage in intercourse with a priestess who had drawn the power of Inanna down and into her body.

As a representative of the people, land, and emissary of god, the king and priestess would ensure through copulation a fertile and prosperous year. One would be hard pressed to find a pagan sect that did not share the belief that unification with god could be reached with an act of ritual sexual intercourse.

Although Cavendish writes to the extreme interpretation of witchcraft, saying that its *"essential element"* is *"sexual union with the god (the Devil),"* we know for certain that there are just as many witches who truly find harmonious union with a Source closer to the Buddhist ethos. And they do so with sex, though this is usually performed between couples rather than in some orgy of treachery. Cavendish also writes:

> *"Magic takes a pagan delight in the pleasures of the senses, but magical theory insists that sensual indulgence for its own sake will not serve the magicians purpose."*

This is certainly true and echoed in virtually every religion and philosophy worth its weight in alchemical gold. Perhaps the *Bhagavad Gita*, closely paralleling Japanese belief, provides us with the best perspective on all such issues. Chapter 2:57 explains:

> *"In the material world, one who is unaffected by whatever good or evil he may obtain, neither praising nor despising it, is firmly fixed in perfect knowledge."*

Twelfth Iteration

The Biblical book of Leviticus, chapter 11, provides the rules about what may or may not be eaten. It is provided in its entirely here for refences:

Rules About What May Be Eaten

"The Lord said to Moses and Aaron, "Say to the Israelites: 'Of all the animals that live on land, these are the ones you may eat: You may eat any animal that has a divided hoof and that chews the cud.

"'There are some that only chew the cud or only have a divided hoof, but you must not eat them. The camel, though it chews the cud, does not have a divided hoof; it is ceremonially unclean for you. The hyrax, though it chews the cud, does not have a divided hoof; it is unclean for you. The rabbit, though it chews the cud, does not have a divided hoof; it is unclean for you. And the pig, though it has a divided hoof, does not chew the cud; it is unclean for you. You must not eat their meat or touch their carcasses; they are unclean for you.

"'Of all the creatures living in the water of the seas and the streams you may eat any that have fins and scales. But all creatures in the seas or streams that do not have fins and scales—whether among all the swarming things or among all the other living creatures in the water—you are to regard as unclean. And since you are to regard them as unclean, you must not eat their meat; you must regard their carcasses as unclean. Anything living in the water that does not have fins and scales is to be regarded as unclean by you.

"'These are the birds you are to regard as unclean and not eat because they are unclean: the eagle, the vulture, the black vulture, the red kite, any kind of black kite, any kind of raven, the horned owl, the screech owl, the gull, any kind of hawk, the little owl, the cormorant, the great owl, the white owl, the desert owl, the osprey, the stork, any kind of heron, the hoopoe and the bat.

"'All flying insects that walk on all fours are to be regarded as unclean by you. There are, however, some flying insects that walk on all fours that you may eat: those that have jointed legs for hopping on the ground. Of these you may eat any kind of locust, katydid, cricket or grasshopper. But all other flying insects that have four legs you are to regard as unclean.

"'You will make yourselves unclean by these; whoever touches their carcasses will be unclean till evening. Whoever picks up one of their carcasses must wash their clothes, and they will be unclean till evening.

"'Every animal that does not have a divided hoof or that does not chew the cud is unclean for you; whoever touches the carcass of any of them will be unclean. Of all the animals that walk on all fours, those that walk on their paws are unclean for you; whoever touches their carcasses will be unclean till evening. Anyone who picks up their carcasses must wash their clothes, and they will be unclean till evening. These animals are unclean for you.

"'Of the animals that move along the ground, these are unclean for you: the weasel, the rat, any kind of great lizard, the gecko, the monitor lizard, the wall lizard, the skink and the chameleon. Of all those that move along the ground, these are unclean for you. Whoever touches them when they are dead will be unclean till evening. When one of them dies and falls on something, that article, whatever its use, will be unclean, whether it is made of wood, cloth, hide or sackcloth. Put it in water; it will be unclean till evening, and then it will be clean. If one of them falls into a clay pot, everything in it will be unclean, and you must break the pot. Any food you are allowed to eat that has come into contact with water from any such pot is unclean, and any liquid that is drunk from such a pot is unclean. Anything that one of their carcasses falls on becomes unclean; an oven or cooking pot must be broken up. They are unclean, and you are to regard them as unclean. A spring, however, or a cistern for collecting water remains clean, but anyone who touches one of these carcasses is unclean. If a carcass falls on any seeds that are to be planted, they remain clean. But if water has been put on the seed and a carcass falls on it, it is unclean for you.

"'If an animal that you are allowed to eat dies, anyone who touches its carcass will be unclean till evening. Anyone who eats some of its carcass must wash their clothes, and they will be unclean till evening. Anyone who picks up the carcass must wash their clothes, and they will be unclean till evening.

"'Every creature that moves along the ground is to be regarded as unclean; it is not to be eaten. You are not to eat any creature that moves along the ground, whether it moves on its belly or walks on all fours or on many feet; it is unclean. Do not defile yourselves by any of these creatures. Do not make yourselves unclean by means of them or be made unclean by them. I am the Lord your God; consecrate yourselves and be holy, because I am holy. Do not make yourselves unclean by any creature that moves along the ground. I am the Lord, who brought you up out of Egypt to be your God; therefore be holy, because I am holy.

"'These are the regulations concerning animals, birds, every living thing that moves about in the water and every creature that moves along the ground. You must distinguish between the unclean and the clean, between living creatures that may be eaten and those that may not be eaten.'"

The Hermetic Dragon living in the forest, from
Lambsprinck's book *On the Philosophical Stone.*

Siegfried slaying the dragon of material desires,
as published in Jonathan Black's *The Sacred History.*

HEKA
& THE COSMIC EGG

First Iteration

Before the *time* of *creation*, there came into existence what the Egyptians called *Heka* or *Hike*. While most are familiar with Ra (Re), the chief creator, Heka was either the first emanation of Source or a direct companion to the sun god himself. The Encyclopedia Britannica says that, according to the Egyptians:

> "...heka was the primordial force present at the creation of the world, that it could be summoned up during the observance of religious ritual, and that its chief function was the preservation of the natural world order."

If not the first emanation, at the very least Heka accompanied Ra in his solar boat as it made its daily journey across the sky like Apollo and his chariot. Like the Eight Immortals of China, Ra and his descendants are known as Ennead, or the Nine Gods of Heliopolis, the city of the sun. From his illumination, Ra created Shu, god of air, and Tefnut, goddess of moisture. Their offspring were the god of earth, Jeb, and goddess of sky, Nut, who birthed Isis, Osiris, Nephthys, and Set (Seth). Isis and Osiris eventually copulate to produce from a magical ritual the sun-savior Horus, a reincarnation of Osiris. This is similar to the Hindu god Krishna being an incarnation of the god Vishnu. Horus, Krishna, and Jesus Christ all share in the knowledge of *heka*.

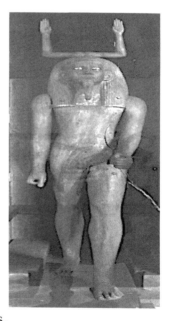

Heka from the *World History Encyclopedia*

Heka is both an attribute of Ra, or Re-Atum, and the direct personification of divinity in its first manifestation as Ra, the sun -

or *light* in general. Heka is therefore the foundation and personification of *magical power*, which is usually how the word is translated. Whether in the *Bible* or *Zend Avesta* it is God and Ahura Mazda that say *Let there be* the *Kingdom of Light*. Just as Ahura Mazda then creates the *preserver*, Heka is likewise a creator, sustainer, and protector of all things. Robert K. Ritner says that this magical force or God is *"at once creative logos and source of all cosmic dynamics."*

The Greek for word and *reason* is *Logos*, which is reference to God, the ultimate *reason*. *Logos* represents order and the knowledge obtained through our quest to understand the world by means of philosophy, science, and magic. Truth and balance come from *Logos*, which was translated to the Latin *Verbum*, and later mistranslated into "word" for the King James Bible. In the tradition of *original sin*, the *Word* or *Logos* becomes our *salvation*. In essence, God is the LOGOS, or *word made flesh*; for the WORD endows us with an ability to live life righteously. The *Word* is the God of manifested intelligence like *Heka*. Alan Watts observes of these deeper meanings:

> *"Language in its broadest sense, including words, numbers, signs, and symbols of all kinds, is what peculiarly distinguishes men from animals, and enables us to know that we know... The verbal description of the world is a simplified, albeit oversimplified, model of the world. But it provides us with a platform apart from the world itself, upon which you can stand and take a new look at the world. Words representing things make it possible to have thoughts about experiences, to deal with life in terms of symbols as we deal with wealth in terms of money."*

Logos is thus the *grand design* of a *Grand Architect*, a construct by which the work of material creation began. It symbolizes a transition from living by *impulse* and *instinct* in the Garden of Paradise to a living by internal reflections of being *consciousness*. Watts adds that this represents *"man's growing realization of the power of language and symbols, and, in particular, the stage of this growth where the power of the word is utterly fascinating."* In this way it would be easy to reinterpret the *Tower of Babel* narrative, wherein *"the Lord confused the language of the whole world,"* as a positive story conveying a multitude of different cultural and linguistic expressions. Another interpretation of the Tower can be found in the notion that any language contrary to Hebrew was *confusing* and secondary. This is a fact that can be found in most cultures: even in how modern Japanese speakers see business agreements in English as being less important, or even void, in comparison with those conducted in Japanese.

This transition symbolizes the emergence of *human ego*, reflected in the moon, and its ability to change or exercise controls over external events and internal passions by *will*. An enlightened state of understanding supported by the mastering of emotions, thoughts, and actions, was, and remains, the intent at the heart of the true *mysteries*: to conquer the three-headed beast Cerberus guarding the gate into the underworld and to obtain the sought-after *Elixir of Life*. Each head of this fierce animal represents a form of self-mastery and the vanquishing of the three *Great Evils* known as ignorance, superstition, and fear.

Logos is also purely *Heka*, the protector and sustainer of humanity and the gods they worship. There is ultimately a direct connection between this First Emanation and the goddess of truth and justice, Ma'at, who strives to bring harmony and balance to all things through a structured order. Heka is also linked to the heart and tongue, from whence we feel and speak the *Word*. Our feelings come from the heart, the seat of our personality, emotions, and our thoughts, with its connections to stomach and brain. But it is the tongue that allows us to have verbal expressions. According to the World History Encyclopedia:

> *"Heka referred to the deity, the concept, and the practice of magic. Since magic was a significant aspect of medical practice, a physician would invoke Heka in order to practice heka. The universe was created and given form by magical means, and magic sustained both the visible and invisible worlds. Heka was thought to have been present at creation and was the generative power the gods drew upon in order to create life."*

This "generative power" is the force of creation embodied in *Heka*, "*translating divine 'ideal' speech and action into its 'tangible' reflection here below,*" writes Ritner. Heka is, once more, an embodiment of speech and language. The Egyptian concept of the First Emanation was imagistic, the clear representation of something with precise images, which is at the foundation of magical practice - *visualization*. As Ritner points out, *"the conventional term of 'god' has as its root meaning 'image'."* Hence, Genesis 1:27 recounts that "God," who is plural in the original "Let Us," *"created mankind in his own image, in the image of God he created them; male and female he created them."* In John 1:1 we read:

> *"In the beginning was the Word, and the Word was with God, and the Word was God."*

Later in John 1:14 we learn how:

> *"The Word became flesh and made his dwelling among us. We have seen his glory, the glory of the one and only Son, who came from the Father, full of grace and truth."*

Logos was at the beginning like Heka, and it was this Word, or cosmic vibration, which unleashed creative forces.

The Chariot of Apollo, 1880 by Gustave Moreau.

Second Iteration

In the Egyptian creation story, the sun god RA was formed from *Atum* and sprang out of the *nothingness* called *Nun*. We can conjecture that *Nun* is *Heka*, just as this *nothingness* relates the "surface of the deep" in Genesis.

The Hopi people of Northeastern Arizona referred to the time-before-time as *Tokpela* (The First World), or the *Endless Space*. Genesis 1:1-2 provides a parallel description of this "beginning" when *"the earth was formless and empty,"* and *"darkness was over the surface of the deep."* Hopi legend describes the Creator *Taiowa* as being the only thing in existence, or what the Bible says is *"the Spirit of God... hovering over the waters."*

According to Australian Aboriginal tradition the world was created from the *Rainbow Serpent*, which emerged from a waterhole like *"the Spirit of God... hovering over the waters."* The *Book of the Hopi* describes this *nothingness* as having *"no beginning and no end, no time, no shape, no life."* It was *"an immeasurable void that had its beginning and end, time, shape, and life in the mind of Taiowa the Creator."* Here we find *Heka* with the name *Taiowa*. As the infinite mind of God conceived the finite world, Taiowa created Sotuknang and said to him *"I have created you, the first power and instrument as a person, to carry out my plan for life in endless space."* Sotuknang's duty was to lay the universes in *"proper order so they may work harmoniously with one another"* according to the Creator's plan. Genesis 1:3 describes this event as God stating: *"Let there be light."* From this creative command, God *"separated the light from the darkness"* and hatched the *Cosmic Egg*. Sotuknang is therefore comparable to Ra and Heka, as the First Emanation. The *Popol Vuh* likewise states: *"Thus they spoke. Let there be light, let there be dawn in the sky and on the earth."*

According to Scandinavian myth, the world and universe were fashioned from a hoarfrost giant named *Yimir*, whose body was comprised of clouds and mists like Shu and Tefnut. Yimir, another name for Ra, is said to have been formed from a great mess of chaos called *Ginnungagap*, a time when, as Manly Hall relates, *"primordial frost giants had hurled snow and fire."* The divine trinity of Odin, Vili, and Ve slew the giant and used his body to create the world and each interconnected part of nature. Odin then formed the Odinic or Scandinavian Olympus, a place called *Asgard,* which was built on top of a tall mountain. Upon this mountain were also the sacred and famous halls of *Valhalla*, or the *place of the fallen.*

Much like Jesus or Krishna, Quetzalcóatl, Viracocha, Osiris, etc., Odin's son Balder brought peace and love, and civilization, to the world. One of his twelve disciples was named *Loki*, in essence the manifestation of evil. When Loki had eliminated Balder, as Set did the same to Osiris, his light and love vanished form the world. However, the gods attempted to bring him back to life by resurrecting him from the underworld.

In <u>World Mythology</u> Donna Rosenberg writes of how Balder was condemned temporarily to the underworld:

> *"Balder is one of a number of fertility gods in various mythologies who are killed, go down to the Underworld, and then come back to life. The pattern of life, death, and resurrection reflects the annual, cyclical pattern in nature of birth (spring), maturity (summer), death (autumn and winter), and rebirth (the following spring)."*

In myth, Balder was struck and pierced by mistletoe, just as the Mesopotamian god Tammuz and Greek god Adonis were both killed by a wild boar. In all three cases these gods were brought back to life as a reflection of spring. In one story the Buddha dies from consuming a meal of pork. Another case can be found in the story of Cybele and her youthful consort Attis, whose death and resurrection invoked the spring, i.e., our modern Easter. Manly Hall says in <u>How To Understand Your Bible</u> the following about the holy day of increasing light:

> *"The Passover is the annual passing over of the sun from the southern to the northern hemisphere, according to the primitive ideas concerning astronomy. The sacrifice of the lamb at this period was practiced by the pagan Greeks who regarded the vernal equinox as the annual rebirth of the savior god. The ceremony of Easter is the perpetuation of pagan equinoctial rites."*

The story of Tammuz and Ishtar is close to identical with Egypt's Osiris and Isis. Such *mystery* traditions in the Norse world were organized in underground crypts which acted as temples and literal wombs inside of the earth. The chambers of these caves were usually nine, representing the Nine Worlds, as with the Nine Divine in Egypt, the Nagas of India, and Dante's nine circles of hell. Incredible parallels can likewise be found in Japan. The story of Amaterasu, goddess of the sun, involves her entombment in the earth for three days before being miraculously resurrected. Her myth is strikingly similar to the story of Jesus Christ, and of course relates to the movements of the stars and our sun. But before Amaterasu there was Ame-no-minaka-nushi-no-kami, the *Kami of the Center of Heaven*. Even before this 'universal' *Kami* was the *World-Egg* which separated into *yin* and *yang*, and here is found the influence of Chinese Taoism in Japan, an egg therefore representing Nun, Heka, Tokpela, and Yimir among others. To the Japanese this was a time called *kamiyo*, or the "age of Kami" before their descent from heaven. Then came the *kami* of birth and growth, known respectively as *Taka-mimusubi-no-mikoto* and *Kami-musubi-no-mikoto*. It was much later that the parental figures of *Izanagi-no-mikoto* and *Izanami-no-mikoto* appeared, giving birth to the High Plain of Heaven, the Great Eight Islands, which mirror the Eight Immortals of China and numerous other *Kami*. Their children are *Ama-terasu-ō-mikami*, *Susa-no-o-no-mikoto*, and *Tsuki-yomi-no-mikoto*: otherwise known simply as Amaterasu (goddess of the sun), Susanoo (god of earth), and Tsukuyomi (goddess of the moon). Here we find yet another divine trinity akin to Odin, Vili, and Ve, Osiris, Isis, and Horus, or the triune sound of *A – U - M*.

According to legend, when Izanami and Izanagi first descended from the heavens, they botched creation and had to begin again. As comical as this may seem, it relates to the Biblical God and his desire to restart mankind with a deluge. Flood myths of this nature persist all over the world to this day and they can be read about in detail within the pages of my book *Occult Arcana*. Fire was the final *Kami* born before the more well-known Amaterasu. As the final element of creation, the fire burned Izanami's body and sent her to *Yomi*, the underworld of Japan. In classical Greek Persephone fashion, or Mesopotamian Tammuz fashion, Izanagi ventures to *Yomi* to rescue his wife. But Izanami had eaten food in the underworld and was therefore bound there, a story mirroring not only Persephone and her pomegranate, but of Eve and the *fruit* offered to her in the Garden. Izanagi said to his wife:

> "The lands that I and thouh made are not yet finished making; so come back!"

Izanami and Izanagi creating the world,
from the 'Floating Bridge of Heaven'.

Woodblock Print, 19th Century.

Izanami then informs her husband to wait while she speaks with the higher powers of that land. Unable to wait patiently, however, Izanagi follows his wife and sees her in the inner sanctum covered in maggots. This story is parallel to that of Orpheus and Eurydice in Hades. As a result, Izanami is filled with shame and rage, and chases Izanagi to the surface. Izanagi then goes to purify himself in a body of water, stripping his clothes in a manner like that of Ishtar and her clothes or gates. It is here, supposedly, that Amaterasu and her siblings are born.

Amaterasu and Susanoo can be paralleled to the Egyptian sky goddess Nut and earth god Geb, but also directly with Shu and Tefnut, of the air and moisture. The usage of "god" and "goddess" here should be considered in relationship with what we already known about Shintō, however, and likewise the relationship that Heka shares with the latter.

According to the *Kojiki*, Amaterasu hid in the celestial cave because her brother Susanoo was acting violently in his capacity as the Japanese storm god. This resulted in darkness descending over heaven and earth. The *Kami* responded by performing dramas and dances for the goddess outside her cave - still integral parts of

Shintō today. Ame-No-Uzume, goddess of dawn, used erotic dance to tempt Amaterasu from her recluse.

Eventually the true sun goddess emerged bringing light, warmth, and life back to the world. In essence, after her entombment like Jesus, Inanna, Osiris, Tammuz, or Persephone, Amaterasu awakens from her deep sleep like *Sleeping Beauty* - what we call physical life - and restores light to the world like Demeter or Ceres.

She then merges with her male *Kami* and becomes *Amateru*, before descending to the shrine of *Ise Amaterasu* or *The Grand Shrine of Ise*, a slight parallel to the Egyptian city of the sun, Heliopolis, where Ra had his main sanctuary.

Amaterasu emerges from her cave to restore
light to the world, by Taiso Yoshitoshi, 1882

Amaterasu is, put simply, the sun as it transitions throughout the year, moving like Ra's boat across the heavens. In Hindu mythology we find the god Rama, one of the incarnations of Vishnu, god of protection, who shares in Ra's ability to fly through the sky.

The Japanese Kujiki-72 text informs us like all of the other creation stories how nothingness was transformed and made manifest:

> "The Creator rules over boundless infinity. Nothing existed before the Creator. No one ruled before the Creator. The Creator is without Form."

In the Mayan *Popul Vuh*, we read the same:

> "All was immobility and silence in the darkness, and only the creator, the maker, the serpent covered with feathers, they who create, were on the waters as an ever increasing light. They were surrounded by green and blue."

From the *Bhagavad Gita* 4:13 we read something similar:

> "The Lord is the creator of everything. Everything is born of Him, everything is sustained by Him, and everything, after annihilation, rests in Him."

The knowledge contained in this ancient Hindu text is much like the *Zend Avesta* since it preserves dichotomy; a cosmic conflict between good and evil, soul and body, health and disease, and knowledge and ignorance, the very things Ahura Mazda is credited with creating.

According to the Taoists of ancient China, the universe began as an egg, not unlike the Greek Orphic Egg or Universal Cosmic Egg. This *egg* symbolized the primordial state of Taiji, the *Supreme Ultimate State* of the world.

Within the *egg* is a primeval hermaphroditic giant named *Pangu*. Upon his birth the egg breaks into two halves, creating the sky above and earth below, another version of the sky goddess Nut and earth god Geb. These *forces* can also be symbolized internally by the *egg white* and yellow *yolk* of an egg.

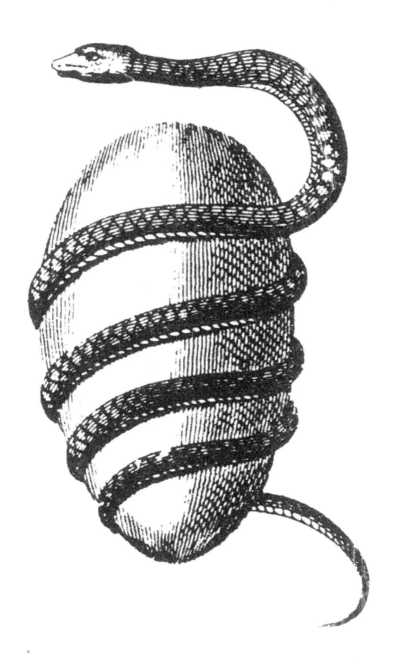

Orphic Egg, from Jacob Bryant's
An Analysis of Ancient Mythology.

Third Iteration

Heka is therefore the essence of Creator and Creation; the very thing, *magic*, which was *made* for humanity. Everything is *born of Him* and *sustained by Him*. He is the authority for *The Pyramid Texts* and *Coffin Texts* and is feared by all of the other Egyptian gods. As the personification of magic, Heka is also a god of healing. Most magical spells in Egypt were formulated to heal the sick physically and symbolically, the latter in a manner similar to Jesus Christ. Statues and depictions of this Supreme God portray Him carrying a staff entwined with two serpents. Here we are reminded of the ancient *caduceus* wand carried by Hermes and Mercury, which remains a symbol of modern medicine. The *wand* is arguably an ancient depiction of DNA, too, which directly relates to Heka as the Creator and instructor of ALL things.

Magic in Egypt, or *Heka*, was therefore the very foundation of everything, far more than just a religion or standardized practice. Although only about 1% of the population was literate, the priesthood composed and utilized the sacred texts within the temples and, when off-duty, since priests rotated, within a community. Magic in Egypt was neither good or bad, moral or immoral. It was amoral. This is utterly fascinating because the same concept can be found in faraway India and much further away in Japanese Shintō, which is much more ancient than its modern form. As quoted earlier, the *Bhagavad Gita* 2:57 explains:

> *"In the material world, one who is unaffected by whatever good or evil he may obtain, neither praising nor despising it, is firmly fixed in perfect knowledge."*

The Egyptians were thus "fixed in perfect knowledge" when considering their approach to magic as personified by Heka.

Fourth Iteration

Robert K. Ritner informs us that Heka must be *"activated by special words, acts and ingredients,"* despite its natural residence within the body and heart. Here we are reminded to 'let Jesus into your heart'. In other words, Heka is activated through magical acts, i.e., utterances and incantations, rituals and rites, and the proper paraphernalia. Heka is also one of *"the closest Egyptian lexical approximations to the English term 'miracle'."* This means that Heka is our confirmation that *magic* and *miracle* are only separated by subjective interpretation. In Egypt there was distinction between the two words. Such matters were not only amoral, but legal and the very foundation of legality itself.

When Rome officially began its rule over Egypt in 30 B.C., after the arrival of Octavian, they tolerated *magic* and Heka temporarily until it began to, by Roman standards, interfere with established theological and social dogmas. It is interesting to note that Imperial Rome had used laws in the past like the *lex Cornelia de sicariis et veneficis* to primarily prosecute murderers rather than sorcerers, though many of the latter were. Rome was, at this time in 82 BC under Sulla, more concerned with murderers than magicians.

The Imperial regime began persecuting Christians around 64 CE for practicing magic as it was seen from a pagan point of view. But, as Ritner writes, *"despite imperial sanctions, Egyptian and Roman conceptions of 'magic' did not merge until the Coptic period,* [beginning in 50 AD] *when Christian hostility stigmatized all pagan practices - Roman as well as Egyptian - with the derogatory magia."*

Christians saw Rome and Egypt as full of sorcery, while pagan Rome saw Christianity as a sorcery and Egypt as tolerable. Egypt, however, likely accepted paganism and Christianity conceptually. But sometime in-between 82 BC and 64 CE, even before establishing rule over Egypt in 30 BC, Rome had already made some attempts to eliminate parts of the Egyptian practice of *magic.* This pushed the otherwise public concept of *Heka* underground into a secretive practice. As a result of this case, but as with nearly all others, magic can best be summarized as exclusionary, *"defined by what it does not contain: piety, legality, etc."*

Rome was, however, contrary to popular belief, exceedingly tolerant of the Christian religion at one point in its history. So long as citizens paid their fair share of taxes and pledged allegiance to the state, Roman authorities cared little about individual beliefs unless they in some way threatened the status quo.

Emperor Julian, a student of classical philosophy, was known as a generally tolerant and noble man but he rapidly grew intolerant of Christianity. Although Rome generally tolerated the new Christian doctrine on the surface, as it was circulated mostly among the poor, it was orthodoxy itself at the time, often turning into fanaticism, which conjured its own persecution. Julian regarded the Church's concept of *sin*, in that of punishment and reward, sinner made saint, as an encouragement of delinquency and corruption. He strongly disagreed with the concept that all men were sinners, and that Christians possessed the sole *truth*.

For a supposedly intolerant state, Rome still welcomed Greek, Egyptian, and Persian rites, but the new Christian movement intolerantly condemned all these gods as demons and their teachings as frauds and sacrilege. If the countless battles within and outside of orthodoxy today are any indication of the past, then it surely was the Christian church itself which persecuted its own from the beginning, through both religious frenzy and political provocation. As Manly Hall points out, it is even considered among some scholars, and based on building evidence that *"it was actually the Christians who burned Rome during the reign of Nero."*

MAGNETISM

First Iteration

There is a natural sympathy and antipathy of things that we may term *Natural Magic* or *Sympathetic Magic*, and this includes the gathering of what is beneficial to achieve a desired effect: animals, plants, metals, stones, etc., are common materials. Egyptians called this nature *magicianess*, or the attracting or repulsion of things alike or different. It is similar to Heka, but not exactly the same since the latter is the ultimate expression of *magic* and not a single element thereof.

Francis Barrett writes of the hermetic axiom *as above, so below*, and of its relationship with natural sympathies:

> *"...for each mortal creature possesses a Sun and system within himself; therefore, according to universal sympathy, we are affected by the general influence or universal spirit of the world, as the vital principle throughout the universe."*

These mortal creatures, whether insects, animals, or humans possess virtue and sympathy with related elements. They also possess antipathy or repulsion with unrelated elements. The organs of the human body are believed to relate to planetary bodies as depicted by Rudolph Steiner. We already now Heka relates to the heart and tongue. This is a sort of *magical reflexology*, that practice by which reflex points on the feet, hands, and head are linked to every other part of the body. Bodily organs relate to planets and vice versa; and there are further associations to be found with stones, metals, herbs, plants, insects, animals, etc., and certain *desired magical* outcomes. As Lord Amateru (a male version of the Japanese sun goddess Amaterasu) explains in the esoteric tradition:

> *"First, the human body is a hinagata, meaning a miniature version, of the universe. Our left eye is the Sun, our right eye the Moon, and our nose is a star. The middle of our body is the world: the heart is the sovereign, the liver is the ministers, and the spleen is the common people. The lungs are the workmen, and the kidneys are the merchants. The heart is like a mirror: it shows your true*

intentions to heaven and Earth, and soon enough men will know of it. This is why one of the Three Treasures of the Emperor is a mirror, the Yaga-no-Kagami."

In Japanese mythology it is the left eye of Izanagi, acting as a sort of *cosmic egg,* from whence the sun goddess Amaterasu is birthed. After Osiris is killed by his brother Set and descends into the underworld, representing the setting sun at the end of a long day, the new sun, Horus, wages war on his father's killer. Victorious, Horus then rises in the east on the *morning* after - possibly *mourning* is father too. As the day progresses, however, he becomes stronger and the same is true for the year.

In this story, far removed from Japan, we learn that Horus lost his left eye in the battle. This became known as the *Eye of RA* or the *Eye of Horus.* Usually it is the left eye, which reflects the sun. The right eye is the moon, signifying darkness. This concept is embodied in the *Pythagorean Y* where you have the left path of ease and reflected light that leads to nothing but darkness and suffering; the right path is one of darkness and hardship that eventually leads to true light and spiritual reward. Paul Carus explains in his book The History of the Devil and the Idea of Evil that the left and right eyes represent the declining and rising sun, and their associated solstices:

> *"...the left or black eye of the decreasing sun, governing the year from the summer solstice to the winter solstice, which is contrasted with the right or bright eye of Hor, the increasing sun, which symbolizes growth of life and the spread of light from the winter solstice to the summer solstice."*

By drawing on these motifs, and those of countless religious texts, the *magician* is able to utilize the narrative power within and direct it towards an end. This is also the purpose of ritual dances, songs, rites, spells, ad infinitum, as author and artist Marlene Seven Bremner explains in Hermetic Philosophy and Creative Alchemy:

> *"Through the use of sacrifices, hymns, praises, and heavenly sounds, the powers of heaven are drawn down into the statue or idol."*

As the *Zend Avesta* likewise relates:

> *For, to all who think Good Thoughts,*
> *Who speak Good words,*
> *And who do Good Deeds,*
> *The Celestial Realms,*
> *The Best World*
> *Doth belong.*

Good Words connect one to the *Celestial Realms*; this is the purpose of prayer and hymns, especially when performed in a grand ritual space like a cathedral or any other religious building, but particularly when uttered with *faith* and *intention* to *glorify*. Hall says that there need not be a mystical effect, but that the *"repeating of beautiful words which convey a gentle and loving thought has some effect."* This is the point of *prayer*, not to demand from creation all the things you *desire*. A great example of this fact is found in Matthew 6, verses 6 and 22:

> *"But you, when you pray, go into your room, and when you have shut your door, pray to your Father who is in the secret place; and your Father who sees in secret will reward you openly."*

> *"'The lamp of the body is the eye. If therefore your eye is good, your whole body will be full of light'."*

Prayer should thus be conducted within one's self, by addressing internal consciousness. Our attention, assured by closing the door internally from the external, should then be directed not upward into the heavens but inward towards the heart, or *sanctum sanctorum*. The *lamp of the body* is the windows in Noah's Ark, the *Third Eye, Inner Eye, Eye of Horus, Eye of Izanagi,* and the eye that Odin plucks out in his conversation with Mimir, the god of memory and wisdom. For it is said that *he who watches over Israel neither slumbers nor sleeps.*

A famous drawing by Steiner associates the lungs with mercury, kidneys with Venus, spleen with Saturn, gallbladder with Mars, liver with Jupiter, and of course the heart with the Sun. Each of these planets is also assigned a color, which can be used when working with their energies. These colors are usually universal, but often vary depending upon author interpretation and culture. To attract the virtues of the planets, these are their common colors: Saturn – black; Jupiter - celestial blue; Mars - red; Sun - gold or yellow; Venus – green; Mercury - mixed colors; the Moon – silver.

Second Iteration

Sympathetic Magic, sometimes referred to as *Animal Magic*, is a consideration based on a form of *like-magnetism*. Similar things attract each other based on resonance: *like attracts like*. A parallel notion that *opposites attract* is based on the idea of *traditional magnetism*.

Animal magnetism was made very popular by the Austrian physician Friedrich Anton Mesmer, who studied the works of Paracelsus intimately. He believed that the stars had influence on human health through an invisible fluid, and thus that healing power could be found in one's own hands – *magnetism*. It is from his name that we derive the word *mesmerism*.

As the author David Conway put it:

> "From time immemorial magicians have sought to establish the natural affinity that exists between certain planets, metals, jewels, birds, beasts, herbs, colours, flowers and scents. A great deal of patience and ingenuity have been expended on this formidable task, but observation and experiment have also played their part."

Published before the time of Mesmer was a text by William Maxwell, De Medicina Magnetica, wherein it was described the following of material rays that flow from all bodies in which souls operate:

> "By these rays energy and the power of working are diffused. The vital spirit which descends from the sky, pure, unchanged and whole, is the parent of the vital spirit which exists in all things. If you make use of the universal spirit by means of instruments impregnated with this spirit you will thereby call to your aid the great secret of the Mages. The universal medicine is nothing but the vital spirit repeated in the proper subject."

This is the application of *actives* to *passives* to produce rare or uncommon effects by some magical means with use of amulets, allurements, enchantments, spells, incantations, utterances, rites, and so forth. There are some forms of this magic better left undisturbed.

By taking a new knife and cutting open a lemon while using words of expressed hatred or dislike against any individual, the absent party is said to feel an inexpressible and striking anguish of the heart, along with cold chilliness and failures throughout the body. This is merely an elementary example of what should remain undisturbed and is by no means encouraged. For as Levi wrote, a Black Magician *"poisons himself in order that he may poison others; he damns himself that he may torture others..."* We may liken this to the law of *karma*. For this is the sum of a person's *actions* in this life and previous lives, which is reflected in current *reactions*. Manly Hall writes here about such *actions* in regard to *black magic* and *magnetism*:

Animal Magnetism as made popular by Friedrich Anton Mesmer, the Austrian physician.

> *"The sending of love, hate, or similar feelings to another, in the hope of awakening a similar condition in them for a selfish or personal reasons, is also Black Magic. Mental Black Magic is far more complicated, for it includes practically all prosperity metaphysics, autosuggestion, mental suggestion, occult treatments, demonstration over environment and conditions in people, hypnosis, mesmerism, personality culture, and other varieties too numerous to mention."*

Plants and herbs are known to have medicinal properties or those that can poison. As such, herbology and pharmaka have been practices of witchcraft, magic, and science for thousands of years. Plant properties may also be determined from their corresponding colors too. We also know that colors alone can be healing or provoking. Of consciousness, intelligence, and force are the colors blue, yellow and red. Blue is soothing, yellow vitalizing and red agitating.

Sympathy and *Antipathy* are qualities of *Natural Magic* and are found in various forms of the sciences.

Although *philtres* composed of substances that induce passions and love may not be bottled and sold as a common item there are indeed natural virtues that attract these things magnetically. Pheromones are chemicals produced and released by the body of insects and animals to alter the behavior and physiology of others within their own species. They may also influence other species, including humans. Humans likewise emit pheromones that attract or repel the opposite sex.

Charms are meant to attract through sympathy and magnetism, and those items we call *enchanted* are similarly meant to delight by the casting of a *spell* or the offering of some other benefit to the wearer.

In more cultured instances the man traditionally "courts" a woman with charm by offering objects and symbols to express his feelings, or by expressing through the power of words or *spells* - as in *spelling* – written letters composed of admiration. Men and women biologically and physiologically find *attraction* to one another, even if a man or woman does not expressively find the opposite entirely attractive.

The same *magnetism* may be found in platonic friends and even in family, though the same repulsions are always near. To that which is *attractive*, from the Latin *attractivus*, is a certain magnetism that also is repulsive in nature. Those finding attraction without the desire of courtship may become close friends, bound by a magnetism that seems without direct cause, as the resulting effect is felt without consideration otherwise. The same is true for lovers feeling an effect without necessarily being aware of the causation for why they are enamored with one another.

As certain insects and mammals excrete chemical substances to attract mates, so too do these magnetic qualities exist in the plant kingdom. Herbs may be used for food while containing properties that are an aphrodisiac, those substances in food, drink, or drug that stimulate sexual passions. Not all is to be understood as being sexual in nature except only to the degree by which modern science can explain such long-held understandings on such subjects.

Third Iteration

Lions are traditionally associated with the sun, with their manes being the solar corona. Therefore, they symbolically embody the qualities of *Celestial Fire*. Serpents likewise are emblematic of the electric and magnetic currents of earth, sometimes called *telluric*, which may become an agent of the *magi*. Those conquering these elements were often depicted with a *uraeus* serpent upon their forehead in a posture poised to strike, signifying the adept's ability to change the world before them by perception. We see this famously in Egypt with royal headdresses. The *uraeus* also signifies one who has learned the secrets of alchemy and is able to control the telluric powers of the planet. Sometimes included on the brow is also a vulture, the symbol of flesh, which will be conquered upon resurrection of the soul or spirit in the *mysteries*. Both of these creatures are placed on the forehead for external association with the sacred and internal *Pineal Gland*, sometimes called the *Third Eye*. The Hindu use a small red dot, either a sticker or paint, called *bindi*, and place it in the center of the forehead. This is also a practice carried out in the occult sciences of India by *Yoguys*. The *Yahweh Mark* is a cross made of ash and placed on the forehead during *Ash Wednesday* by Christians. The Norse god Odin is known to have created mankind from an *ash tree* and in Hinduism we find *vibhuti* (sacred ash) smeared all over the body of Lord Siva, both as a sign of his divinity and his choice to mingle with the mundane world. The *vibhuti* in Hinduism is usually worn on the forehead but is often smeared over the entire body. In <u>Remembering the Kanji 1</u>, a book by James W. Heisig, the kanji symbol 自 is described as meaning "oneself." But it is the reason for this that is most interesting. According to James, this combination of the kanji symbols for "eye" and "drop of" can be remembered as a *"pictograph of the nose, that little drop that Mother Nature set between your eyes."* He adds, *"the Japanese refer to themselves by pointing a finger at their nose."* Pointing to the nose is the equivalent of sticking a *bindi* between the eyes. The Sanskrit for *bindi*, or bindú बिन्दु, also means point, drop, or dot. These points further signify that the human experience is but a single drop in the grand ocean of *maya* that adepts of the *mysteries* learn to walk upon. Mithraic initiates also had the Egyptian ankh placed upon their foreheads to signify spiritual resurrection. Since initiates had been killed and resurrected, the fact that they were *born again* relates directly to the meaning of the *Crux Ansata* itself - *The Life Bestowing*. They were likewise referred to as "lions" and there is some reference here to Daniel in the Den, and the strong grip of the "lion's paw" that raised the neophyte from symbolic death, as with Lazarus, within the sacred temples and pyramids.

It is believed that the directors of *will*, represented by the serpent, were not only familiar with, but also able to bend electricity, in some respect, to their *desire*. Through its understanding and application was termed *transcendental pyrotechny*, the mastering of *Celestial Fire*. The Greeks are thought to have been familiar with electricity, a knowledge acquired from Egypt. Manly Hall writes in <u>Lectures on Ancient Philosophy</u> of this seeming peculiarity:

> *"This accounts for the peculiar venerations accorded amber by the early priestcrafts, for this substance had been found to possess the quality of capturing and storing electricity."*

As per whether or not the electricity here is to be literal, metaphoric, or both, this author is convinced of the latter. Hall expresses similar feelings, stating that among the *Samothracian Mysteries* there are to be found images of what has been called the "electric head." The faces here are surrounded by bands of hair that are standing on end. They are very reminiscent of the gorgon Medusa; her head of serpents and ability to inflict her powers with a glance is once more related directly to the *uraeus*. Hall says this is symbolic of *"the concentration of the will upon the dissemination of the Great Work."* Another name for *will* is *faith*. It is by *faith* that many find comfort and strength in the name of God and are therefore able to accomplish much. For, as Hall puts it:

> *"Faith itself is a powerful constructive force which accomplishes its ends by natural and gentle means."*

Persistence of *will*, a key component of magic, if liberated from sensory illusions, and operated upon by the subduing of *desire* through rites and trials, allows for mastery of the elements. To attempt control of these magical powers by the unreasonable and rash will only serve to bring about destruction upon the practitioner like the collapsing walls of Jericho by the sound of trumpets in the Biblical book of Joshua, or the collapsing of the Temple from Samson pushing apart the pillars of balance and support. In Judges 16:19 is explained how Delilah removed Samson's powers:

> *"After putting him to sleep on her lap, she called for someone to shave off the seven braids of his hair, and so began to subdue him. And his strength left him."*

Samson's strength (hair) can be seen as the *electric head* of Hall's description and of the very obvious rays of sunlight which wax and wane as the *Wheel of the Year* turns. This *cosmic breath* or *Breath of the Sun* is akin to the breath we draw moment by moment. The underlying substance of the *mysteries* promotes learning this pulsation so that one may align the self with the *Divine Plan* through the understanding of *magnetism.*

Samson's seven locks of hair are the seven rays of solar manifestation, and like the *Twelve Labors of Hercules,* and the trials of life, the sun must traverse the twelves houses of the zodiac to be born again.

SOLAR RAINBOWS

First Iteration

As the creator, preserver, and protector of all within our macrocosmic solar system, the sun is inherently the ultimate emanation of divinity. On a blank sheet of paper if lines are drawn south from one point to seven specific other points there is geometrically depicted the seven original emanations from Source, or the *seven divine rays* that created all things. The *Seven Days of Creation* are the seven days of the week, each governed by their respected planetary intelligence. In the Northern Tibetan tradition, it was the meditation of the seven modes of consciousness, or *Adi Buddha*, by which the physical world is likewise made manifest.

Source is a single dot, the eighth originating point, and each day is one of seven lines or "rays" emanating outwardly: the symbolic day of *rest* for Christians and Jews. From *unity* stems all forms suspended in hypothetical *individuality*. The cube also has six square sides, and they *rest* on the seventh, or center position, as God *rested* on the seventh day.

Those with the spark of gnosis can glimpse at the higher pattern here, the harmony and order of the Universe, and will therefore be able to see beyond the seven days, or emanating rays, to *the Universal Logos*. They will find the eighth point from where fall seven divine rays to produce the cube in three dimensions. This cube is then expressed in two dimensions as a hexagon, with six rays directed outward and a single seventh point in the center.

The concept of an eighth sphere is based on the principle of emanation. God is the Source of the seven rays. The eight points are the eight yearly sabbats and the seven days are expressed with seven circles called the "seed of life" in sacred geometry.

These seven points are also found in the bodily temple of the head: ears, eyes, nose, mouth. David Fideler writes in <u>Jesus Christ Son of God</u> about this symbolism:

> *"The literal-minded, like the proponents of materialism, see the world as through the lower diagram and see no further: literalism reads the letter of the law but does not grasp its spirit; materialism holds matter to be the only reality, but does not see*

that it is merely the effect of a higher cause. Those with the spark of gnosis, however, catch an occasional glimpse of the higher pattern – the Universal Logos, the intelligent pattern of order and harmony which informs all existence."

The highly sacred number *seven* is therefore the basis of countless traditions and mysteries. In the *Xibalbian Mysteries* of the Maya there are seven Houses of initiation similar to those of ancient Egypt. Each house had an important symbolic meaning wherein an alchemical transformation was intended to occur. Here we are reminded of the seven grades of the Mithraic cult in Persia: corax (Raven), nymphus (Bridegroom), miles (Soldier), Leo (Lion), Perses (Persian), heliodromus (Courier of and to the Sun), and pater (Father). Initiates of the *Midewiwin*, or Grand Medicine Society of the Ojibwas, underwent near identical ritual initiations, the further projections also of masonic ordeals.

From the sacred *seven*, as we know, come our days of the week, which are named after the classical gods: Sunday is the day of the Sun, belonging to Mithra(s) and various other sun gods; Monday is the day of the Moon, belonging to Diana, Artemis and Selene; Tuesday is the day of Tyr, the God of War like the Greek Ares and Roman Mars; Wednesday is the day of Woden, a southern name for the northern god Odin in Norse mythology, and also the day of the Greek Hermes and Roman Mercury; Thursday is the day of Thor, the Norse god of weather, agriculture and homes, and the son of Odin and Frigga. Thursday is also the day of the Greek Zeus and Roman Jupiter. Friday is the day of Frigg (Frigga), Odin's wife and the mother of Thor, who is also known as Fria or Freya, the goddess of love and beauty, otherwise known as the Greek Aphrodite or the Roman Venus. Saturday is the day of the Roman Saturn or his Greek equivalent Cronus.

Second Iteration

Within the days of the week, as within the Source of the sacred number seven to reach out and *create*, we find a bridge between *that which is above and that which his below*. This connecting thread is also found famously in *The Sephirothic Tree* of the Kabbalists, running between Malkuth and Kether.

Wednesday is the day of marriage, a *bridge* connecting Sunday through Tuesday and Thursday through Saturday. It is a sacred day of *wedding* and thus the unifying of *what is above* with *what is below*. The term *bridegroom* is appropriate for men seeking marriage, since the word is a compound of *bride* and *man*. It is no wonder then that Hermes and Mercury, the messengers of the gods, are the foundation of this *wedding day*; for they unite the earth with the heavens, Saturn-day with Sun-day.

Third Iteration

It is on Sunday, wherein the triune forces were One, that *"God said, Let there be light."* This is probably why the Jews observe sabbath, or the day of rest, on a Saturday since this was the final day of creation when God rested. Christians hold Sunday as sacred but this likely has more to do with the blending of pagan solar elements into Christendom.

The sun can be divided into a *holy trinity* of material, spiritual, and intellectual. It may also be physically separated into its *septet* qualities by the trinity of refraction, reflection, and dispersion of light. Here we are referring to the manner in which light shines through water droplets resulting in a rainbow of many colors, like the *"coat of many colours"* made for Joseph (Genesis 37:3). As with the *seven days of the week* there are *seven colors of the rainbow*: red, orange, yellow, green, blue, indigo, violet. These colors may also carefully be related to the gods, as we have seen.

Rainbows are probably most famous for their Biblical significance. After *"God remembered Noah and all the wild animals and livestock that were with him in the ark"* he *"sent a wind over the earth, and the waters"* of the flood *"receded"* (Genesis 8:1). Immediately after, in Genesis 9:11-16, God promises to never flood the earth again, and says to Noah:

> *"'I establish my covenant with you: Never again will all life be destroyed by the waters of a flood; never again will there be a flood to destroy the earth.' And God said, 'This is the sign of the covenant I am making between me and you and every living creature with you, a covenant for all generations to come: 'I have set my rainbow in the clouds, and it will be the sign of the covenant between me and the earth. Whenever I bring clouds over*

the earth and the rainbow appears in the clouds, I will remember my covenant between me and you and all living creatures of every kind. Never again will the waters become a flood to destroy all life. Whenever the rainbow appears in the clouds, I will see it and remember the everlasting covenant between God and all living creatures of every kind on the earth.'"

According to the Incas, the rainbow symbolized Illapa, their god of rain and thunder. In Islam, all the hues of a rainbow express the qualities of the Divine Being made visible in the physical realm. In Hinduism, each color reflects one of the *Upper* and *Lower* worlds, of which there are seven each. In Norse mythology, the rainbow bridge connects *Asgard* (heaven) to *Midgard* (earth). That connection is severed when the *sons of the giants* come to destroy the earth. In Hopi tradition, spirits of the ancestors descended from the celestial *realm of the dead* to the *land of the living* by way of a rainbow. The Buddha also utilized a multi-colored stairway to descend from heaven to earth. One of the Eight Immortals of China is said to have transformed into a rainbow and coiled into a snake. A similar reference is made by the Australian Aboriginals, who say that a rainbow serpent created mankind and earth. In Japan it is the creator couple Izanami and Izanagi, who use a *rainbow bridge* to stir the primal sea and use the droplets to form matter. In Tibet, Buddhists see the rainbow, which connects the material and spiritual, as an intimation of spirit transcending nature so that the *rainbow body* can be reached through solitary meditation.

The Greek pantheon of gods even assign a specific authority to the rainbow by way of the goddess Iris. The word *rainbow* is a direct translation of *iris* from ancient Greek. An iris is likewise what gives our eyeballs color. Wearing her rainbow robes or cape, Iris is in direct communion like Hermes and Mercury with the gods. Acting a bridge, her authority brings information from *above* and *below*. The Akkadian and Sumerian goddesses Ishtar and Inanna were said to wear necklaces made of rainbow. In Norse mythology she is Freya (Freyja). Ishtar, Inanna, and Freya are all embodiments of love, fertility, and conflict.

The rainbow also has distorted connotations because of its inversion as a bridge to the abyss. The Hebrew demon Lilith, or Mesopotamian Lamashtu, wears the rainbow around her neck too. As the *mother of demons*, tempter of men, and aborter of children,

Lilith is the destroyer of innocence and life. She mocks God's Creation, or refuses to adore it like Lucifer, having been removed from the Garden for likewise refusing the dominion of Adam. Lilith is the perverter of all things sacred, from protection and preservation to birth and life. She is rot, abortion, and EFIL, and the chaos of unbridled tempest. In Hindu mythology a parallel to Lilith can be found in *nature spirits* called *Yakshas*, which are female and sometimes eat children.

Nevertheless, as with Japanese *kappa*, the stories told about these creatures are probably to warn children of the dangers of nature – in the case of *kappa*, to be careful in bodies of water. In ancient Greece we find the same concepts embodied in the child-killing demons of *Gello*, *Mormo*, and *Lamia*, or the Roman *Strix*, which derives from the Slavic *Strzyga* and perhaps even the *Baba Yaga*.

This may bring to mind the Mexican ghost *La Llorona*, who drowned her own children. Whereas the waters of Isis from the Nile were baptismal, the waters of Lilith are like a destructive deluge.

Izanami and Izanagi stirring the primal sea while standing on a rainbow bridge, from a hanging scroll by Nishikawa Sukenobu, 18th-century Japan.

Fourth Iteration

Noah's Ark is the *protector* of *Creation* from such *destructions*. Noah was given instructions by God to build an ark for himself and his family, but large enough to accompany two of every animal so that they may survive the coming flood waters. Genesis 6:20 relates:

> *"Two of every kind of bird, of every kind of animal and of every kind of creature that moves along the ground will come to you to be kept alive."*

In Genesis 7:1 the Lord *"said to Noah, 'Go into the ark, you and your whole family, because I have found you righteous in this generation'."* After several days of heavy rain most of Creation was washed away, leaving a desolate and mangled landscape. This is when Noah sent out a white dove (a symbol of peace) to find dry land. Eventually the floodwaters receded, and the ark came to rest on the top of a mountain.

This story is told in so many cultures that it should be a crime to relegate its popularity to coincidence or change. In the *Quest for the Golden Fleece* the Argo and Argonauts escape sure destruction from Clashing Rocks, the *Symplegades*, by the assistance of a dove. Edith Hamilton explains in her book <u>Mythology</u> that the old man Phineus gave the warning:

> *"If she [the dove] passed through safely, then the chances were that they too would get through. But if the dove was crushed, they must turn back and give up all hope of the Golden Fleece."*

The story of Gilgamesh, a character the Bible associates with Noah, is told in one of the oldest texts known to man, the *Epic of Gilgamesh*.

The Mesopotamian version of the deluge tells of how Utnapishtim was given instructions to build an ark and to save his family and animals from a coming deluge. After the floodwaters receded, he sent out birds in search of land. His boat came to rest on top of a mountain called Nisir. It was there he released a dove, swallow, and raven. Yet another story originating out of Mesopotamia is the story of *Ziusudra* and the "Great Deluge."

The god EN.KI felt much compassion for mankind, similar to the feelings of Prometheus, and decided to help them. He chose a man named Ziusudra and instructed him of the coming flood and on how to construct an ark to save his family. Ziusudra was also directed to take aboard "beasts and birds."

The Encyclopedia Britannica explains the story in the following outline:

> "Ziusudra, in Mesopotamian Religion, rough counterpart to the biblical Noah as survivor of a god-sent flood. When the gods had decided to destroy humanity with a flood, the god Enki (Akkadian Ea), who did not agree with the decree, revealed it to Ziusudra, a man well known for his humility and obedience. Ziusudra did as Enki commanded him and built a huge boat, in which he successfully rode out the flood. Afterward, he prostrated himself before the gods An (Anu) and Enlil (Bel), and, as a reward for living a godly life, Ziusudra was given immortality."

Other versions of this same story involve an Akkadian character Atrahasis, another survivor of a great flood. In the *Puranic* version of the watery deluge story, the fish god Vishnu warns a human named Manu of the coming flood and tells him to prepare the sacred scriptures in a safe place. Manu is considered an Indian version of both Moses and Noah. The sacred knowledge he was to preserve is the *seed* or wisdom. He is thus a lawgiver and the Father of mankind after a great flood. The *Mahabaratha* says he is a powerful sage or *rishi*. The sacred *Satpatha Brahmana* informs us that Manu was instructed by a tiny fish to *"make for thyself a strong ship"* and to *"embark in it with the Seven Sages and stow in it, carefully preserved and assorted, all the seeds"* known and described. The fish sent Manu a ship and told him to load it with two of every living species and the seeds of all plants. Later in this account the ship is brought to rest atop *"the highest peak of Himavat"* – the Himalayas. The *Bhagavata Purana,* which specifies that the fish is an incarnation of Lord Vishnu, informs us on how Manu was instructed by the god:

> "On the seventh day after this the three worlds shall sink beneath the ocean of the dissolution. When the universe is

dissolved in that ocean, a large ship, sent by me, shall come to thee. Taking with thee the plants and various seeds..."

Manu is later granted 64,800,000 years of life by the gods, or about seventy-one complete cycles of four *yugas*. Likewise, Ziusudra is also granted what amounts to eternal life:

"Life like a god they gave him; Breath eternal like a god they brought down for him."

Manu's relationship with Moses is strengthened by examining the flood story in further detail. The Vedic word for "boat" is NAU, a word also meaning DIVINE WORD. Thus, the *place of the binding of the ship - Naubandhana -* in the *Mahabaratha* also translates to the *place of the protection of the divine word*. It is here, atop the mountain like Moses, that sacred laws were handed down or, in the case of Vedic history, preserved by the Seven Sages.

In the mythological narrative from Mesopotamia, it is Utnapishtim who was told the same thing by the god Ea, to collect writings and bury them in the city of the Sun at Sippar. In another version of the same story Xisouthros is visited by God in a dream and warned of a coming deluge. He is then instructed to build a boat and gather sacred tablets for preservation at Sippar. Interestingly, it was the Egyptian Innu, or the Greek Heliopolis (City of the Sun), which was the storehouse of ancient wisdom and Ra's sanctuary. It cannot be coincidence that Ra is essentially the Egyptian name for the Hindu Rama, an incarnation of Vishnu, who warns of the flood.

In Central America it was a deluge which ended the Fourth Sun or Age. Aztec mythology tells of two humans who survived. Coxcoxtli and his wife Xochiquetzal were warned of the coming cataclysm and then instructed to build a huge boat which eventually came to rest atop a mountain. Another version tells of the *smoking-mirror* god of illusion and human sacrifice, Tezcatilpoca, imitating a great flood to wipe out mankind. A man named Tezpi was warned ahead of time in order to save his wife, children, and a variety of animals, grains, seeds, etc., with which to rebuild civilization after the flood waters receded. His vessel eventually came to rest on a mountain where he sent out a vulture to search for dry land.

In the Maya book *Popol Vuh* is described a massive flood which killed "wooden creatures," or the first men:

> *"The wooden figures were annihilated, destroyed, broken and killed."*

The surviving husband-and-wife pair, with their children and animals, were known to the Maya as the *Great Father* and *Great Mother*.

The Chibcas people of Columbia tell the story of an old man of a totally different racial type, with long beard, named Bochica. His wife Chia played the part of Tezcatilpoca in essence as she used her magical powers to cause the flood. Survivors fled to the mountains and survived at the highest places. Canarians in Ecuador talk of two brothers who escaped an ancient flood by finding shelter in the tall mountains. The Tupinamba Indians of Brazil talk about Monan, an ancient deity who created mankind and then destroyed the world with a flood and fire. The Araucnaians of pre-Colombian Chile talk of a great flood, with survivors once again finding refuge on a tall mountain called *Thegtheg*. In Yamana legend the flood was caused by a woman - as with the lady Chia – who was associated with the moon.

Such legends survive in North American Indian mythology with the Inuit, Luiseno, Montagnais, Sioux, and Dakota mythologies. In Chickasaw mythology a *single family was saved and two animals of every kind*. Hopi mythology and history detail how the first world was destroyed in fire, the second in ice, and the third in a massive flood. They believe that our present fourth world will only be shown mercy if its inhabitants abide by the plans of their Creator.

Similar stories of floods are found in Malaysia, Laos, Thailand, Viet Nam, and Burma. Information discovered by Jesuits in the Imperial Library of China detailed a colossal flood and massive astronomical changes occurring in the past. As reported by Charles Berlitz:

> *"The planets altered their course. The sky sank lower towards the north. The sun, moon, and stars changed their motions. The earth fell to pieces and the waters in its bosom rushed upwards with violence and overflowed the earth."*

Much like with the Yamana and Lady Chia, a funerary text from the tomb of Pharaoh Seti I tells of a deluge brought about due to man's wickedness. It was caused by the moon god Thoth:

> *"This earth shall enter into the watery abyss by means of a raging flood, and will become even as it was in primeval time."*

A tradition from the Amis tribe of Taiwan tells how four gods of the sea and two gods of the land, Kabitt and Aka, conspired to destroy the world and all mankind. However, two children named Sura and Nakao survived by embarking in a wooden mortar and floating eventually to the Ragasan mountain.

Avestic Aryans also believed in three ages of creation before our own. Indian, or the Indus-Sarasvati civilization, preserves similar notions within their mythology, theology, and history. Here we find four ages or *Yugas*. The *Krita Yuga* was a golden age of peace and harmony; the *Treta Yuga* saw the decline of virtues; in the *Davapara (Dvapara) Yuga* lying and arrogance spread further throughout mankind; and in the *Kali Yuga* man became his most wicked, only valuing degradation and chaos. Suffice to say it is the age of Kali that we currently reside. Each *Yuga* or Age ends with *pralaya*, a fire or a great flood, and every cycle of four *Yugas* ends in a larger cataclysm. Thus, at the end of these four ages is the *Kali Yuga*, a time when men are most wicked, and a time when God decides to bring judgement. The same idea is present in the Biblical book of II Peter 3:5-7, where we read a telling prediction of which much talk of the end of the world today is based:

> *"…the heavens came into being and the earth was formed out of water and by water. By these waters also the world of that time was deluged and destroyed. By the same word the present heavens and earth are reserved for fire, being kept for the day of judgment and destruction of the ungodly."*

The four Yugas relate further to the four ages of the Greeks, the gold, silver, bronze, and iron, which themselves share a relationship with Nebuchadnezzar's dream in the book of Daniel 2:32-33, *"The head of the statue was made of pure gold, its chest and arms of silver, its belly and thighs of bronze, its legs of iron, its feet partly of iron and partly of baked clay."* These immense periods of time further correspond to the head, shoulders, body, legs and feet of man, which are birth, growth, maturity, age, and death. The gold, silver, bronze, iron, and clay equate to the mental body, emotional body, vital body, and the upper and lower parts of the physical body.

Noah's Ark by Edward Hicks (1846).

Yet another story of creation involves Prometheus, his son Deucalion, and his wife Pyrrha, the daughter of Epimetheus and Pandora. When men grew wicked enough to attract the furry of Zeus, says one story, he called on his brother Poseidon, God of the Sea, and famous for his trident, to help bring about a massive deluge. Together they caused torrents of rain to fall, causing bodies of water to overflow and drown the land. Nearly all was submerged except for the topmost peak of the sacred mountain of Parnassus. Edith Hamilton writes of this deluge:

> "After it had rained through, nine days and nine nights, there came drifting to that spot [Parnassus] what looked to be a great wooden chest, but safe within it were two living beings, a man and a woman."

Those two living creatures were Pyrrah and Deucalion. Foretelling of the coming deluge, the wise Prometheus acted to protect his family, instructing his son to build a chest, fill it with supplies, and embark upon it safely with his wife. Much later in the story, after exiting the chest, the two used stones to create mankind anew.

Fifth Iteration

When examining these universal flood myths, we find the same themes present with gods, messengers, floods, arks, birds, mountains, and rainbows - covenants and promises - in one form or another.

The "ark" represents the womb and heart, perhaps even *Heka*, as a container for the physical and spiritual *seed* awaiting its moment of sprouting and birth. Noah's Ark is therefore another version of the *cosmic egg*. In fact, as the ark floats on the *lower waters* the rainbow shines in the *upper waters* as the flood recedes.

The ark below and the rainbow above represent the two halves of that universal *world egg*, which contains the seed of new life. That *seed* is watered with the deluge and fed with the photosynthesis of solar light which shines on the newly fertile and dry land.

Sixth Iteration

Finally, Genesis 8:4 says: *"the ark came to rest on the mountains of Ararat."* Mt. Ararat is the Greek Olympus, Hindu Mt. Meru or even the Japanese Mt. Fuji. The sacred mountain is that of Mt. Sinai where the Ten Commandments were handed to Moses, and like this later story we find that Noah's ark was the preserver of the cosmic *seed* and *germ.* Just as these elements are concealed in an ark so too are the heavenly laws preserved in the *Ark of the Covenant.* The mountain whereupon the ark came to rest is what Manly Hall describes as *"the first firmament or the heavens which are above the earth, that is, the sphere of the fixed stars."* The ark itself is thus the zodiac, or animal wheel, and the ship's mast is the polar axis. The deluge waters were not actual liquid in this case but instead a form of cosmic material.

Noah is the second Adam, a foster father to humanity, and a precursor to Jesus, who saves humanity from chaos like Noah saves his family from the deluge. His family is *life* itself and Noah, whose name means *rest*, is the preserver of the cosmic seed as life is temporarily withdrawal from the material world, put into a container, and retired.

In effect, Noah is the ego and his three children - Shem, Ham, Japheth - represent the principles of mind, emotion, and physicality. Their wives are the corresponding aspects of brain, heart, and reproduction.

The ark may also be seen as: a microcosm of the planet itself floating in a vast cosmic ocean of endless space; the illuminated individual protected from the chaos beyond; or the manger in which Christ Consciousness is born among a barn of animals.

When the flood waters finally recede and the cosmic egg reopens, God sets his "bow in the cloud" as a "token of a covenant" between heaven and earth. This *promise* is the symbolic *"releasing into manifestation the energy of the Logos,"* says Hall, *"through its seven principles - the Builders of the cosmos."*

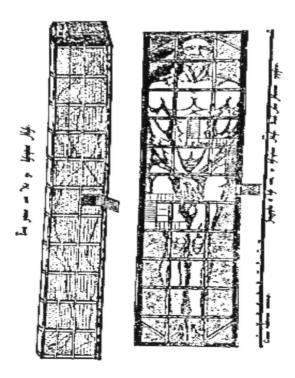

Noah & His Wonderful Ark, reproduced here from Manly Hall's book *How To Understand Your Bible*.

FOUR HORSEMEN

First Iteration

In Genesis 9:11 God says that He will never against "destroy the earth" with the "waters of a flood." In 9:17, He confirms that the rainbow *"is the sign of the covenant"* between heaven "and all life on earth." Perhaps not by water but the Bible does state in 2 Peter 3:7 that the world will be destroyed by fire:

> *"But the heaven we see now and the earth we live on now have been kept by His word. They will be kept until they are to be destroyed by fire. They will be kept until the day men stand before God and sinners will be destroyed."*

There should be no reason to fear these verses, particularly if you are religious. The same can be said about virtually every other religious "prediction" pertaining to the end of the world. Just as the "ark" of Noah is equivalent to a *seed* watered by deluge and fed by the sun, all of the countless doomsday verses of the Bible and Quran are in essence an almanac for natural occurrences. In Joel 2:30 we read another disturbing prophecy:"

> *"The sun will be turned to darkness and the moon to blood before the coming of the great and dreadful day of the LORD."*

However, since blood moons occur every few years, and since the sun weakens and dies in the winter every year, such darkness and lunar change predicts only the cyclical nature of the seasons and stars before the *white horse of the apocalypse* rides once again saving mankind from the cold and dark days of winter. The *Four Horses of the Apocalypse* can be interpreted in several ways, but for our analysis here we will identify them with the four major seasons and all other quaternary associations. They are revealed in Revelation 6:1-8 as such in relationship to the opening of the seals:

> *"I watched as the Lamb opened the first of the seven seals. Then I heard one of the four living creatures say in a voice like thunder, 'Come!' I looked, and there before me was a **white***

*horse! Its rider held a bow, and he was given a crown, and he rode out as a conqueror bent on conquest. When the Lamb opened the second seal, I heard the second living creature say, 'Come! Then another horse came out, a fiery **red** one. Its rider was given power to take peace from the earth and to make people kill each other. To him was given a large sword. When the Lamb opened the third seal, I heard the third living creature say, 'Come!' I looked, and there before me was a **black** horse! Its rider was holding a pair of scales in his hand. Then I heard what sounded like a voice among the four living creatures, saying, 'Two pounds of wheat for a day's wages, and six pounds of barley for a day's wages, and do not damage the oil and the wine!' When the Lamb opened the fourth seal, I heard the voice of the fourth living creature say, 'Come!' I looked, and there before me was a **pale** horse! Its rider was named Death, and Hades was following close behind him. They were given power over a fourth of the earth to kill by sword, famine and plague, and by the wild beasts of the earth."*

The *white horse* conquers the cold and dark of winter with warmth and light through the increasing strength of its rays - the sun; the *red horse* wages war on evil, or darkness, in the summer; the *black horse* brings about the decline and fall of the sun in autumn – the *fall of man*; the *pale horse* is ridden by death and followed by hell, i.e., darkness, cold and winter. The cycle then repeats.

All of this is precisely what we find described in Revelation 6:8, which says the "pale horse" was named Death, and *"Hell followed with him."* For reference to why Hell follows Death we can read Canto XXXIV (34) of Dante's *Divine Comedy*, which factually states that the underworld is a place void of light and warmth. It is, in effect, winter, or an ice palace:

> *How frozen and how faint I then became,*
> *Ask me not, reader! for I write it not,*
> *Since words would fail to tell thee of my state.*
> *I was not dead nor living. Think thyself*
> *If quick conception work in thee at all,*
> *How I did feel. That emperor, who sways*
> *The realm of sorrow, at mid breast from th' ice*
> *Stood forth; and I in stature am more like*
> *A giant, than the giants are in his arms.*

Dante Alighieri's *Divine Comedy* depicts Hell as a frozen infernal realm with the Devil/Satan stuck in ice.

Second Iteration

The four horses likewise signify the divisions of human life as seen in the table above as childhood (birth), youth, maturity, and age (death). Birth is the rider of the white horse coming forth to conquer; the impetuosity of youth is the red horse that takes peace from earth; maturity is the black horse weighing all upon the scales of reason like Lady Justice, Ma'at, Anubis, Saint Michael, Jesus, and even Santa Muerte; and the final pale horse is death, given power over a fourth part of the earth.

In the allegory of the four horsemen is symbolized the condition of man during each stage

Five Horses as the *senses*, from the Bhagavad Gita.

of the coming "out of" existence like leaves from a tree – the blossoming and wilting of life. One may also be reminded of these "horses" as they relate to the aspects of self and the senses - though there are five or more - in the *Bhagavad Gita*. These four aspects are: *individual, material, intelligence,* and *mind.* Commentary from chapter 6:34 relates how, *"the individual is the passenger in the car of the material body, and intelligence is the driver. Mind is the driving instrument, and the senses are the horses."*

These horses are usually red, black, pale yellow, white, and blue. The four directions and stages of existence also relate to the horsemen, as does the sun in its association with the four stages of existence: spring birth or rebirth, summer youth, autumnal maturity, and winter death. The sun is anthropomorphized as a baby during the new year of spring; a youth in the summer; a maturing adult in autumn when scales of reason must be applied in preparation for the death of nature; and an old man in winter. All of this can be gleaned from the above chart.

The horsemen and their associated seasons are also linked with the red and black colors of playing cards, signifying the divisions of a year during which the sun is north and south of the equator. Four suits in the deck relate to the yearly seasons, corners of the world, classical elements of fire, water, air and earth, the stages of life, ad infinitum. The symbols of the Tarot, and the four expressions of the Kabbalistic Tetragram, also relate to the quaternary aspects of the Four Horsemen: the *Wand* represents YOD; the *Cup* corresponds to HE; the *Sword* refers to VAU; and the *Pentacle* to the second HE.

Four Horsemen of the Apocalypse by Viktor Vasnetsov (1887).

Presented here is a table from my book *Occult Arcana* pertaining to the quaternary traits of nature:

Corners of Creation	East	South	West	North
Fixed Zodiac Signs	Aquarius	Leo	Scorpio	Taurus
Parts of Cherubim	Man	Lion	Eagle	Bull
Seasons	Spring	Summer	Autumn	Winter
Ages of Man	Childhood	Youth	Maturity	Age
States of Existence	Birth	Growth	Maturity	Decay
Parts of Man	Spirit	Soul	Mind	Body
Parts of Man (alt)	Spiritual	Emotional	Intellectual	Physical
Enochian Spirits	Hcoma	Bitom	Exarp	Nanta
Worlds of Elements	Aquatic	Infernal	Aerial	Terrestrial
Qualities of Elements	Cold	Heat	Moisture	Dryness
Qualities of Celestials	Agility	Light	Ethereal	Solidity
Rulers of Elements	Tharsis טרשיט	Seraph שרפ	Cherub כרוב	Ariel אריאל
Elementals	Undines	Salamanders	Sylphs (Slyphs)	Gnomes
Rulers of Four Corners	Gabriel גבריאל	Michael מיכאל	Raphael רפאל	Uriel איריאל
Perfect Mixed Bodies	Metals	Animals	Plants	Stones
Kinds of Animals	Swimming	Walking	Flying	Creeping
Horses of Apocalypse	White	Red	Black	Pale
Evangelists	Matthew	Mark	John	Luke
Agents of Alchemy	Mercury	Salt	Sulphur	Azoth
Scientific Elements	Hydrogen	Nitrogen	Carbon	Oxygen
States of Matter	Liquid	Plasma	Solid	Gas
Forms of Divination	Hydromancy	Pyromancy	Geomancy	Aeromancy
Metals	Mercury	Copper	Lead	Gold or Silver
Powers of Soul	Phantasy	Intellect	Reason	Sense
Judiciary Powers	Opinion	Faith	Science	Experience
Moral Virtues	Prudence	Justice	Temperance	Fortitude
Humours	Phlegm	Choler	Blood	Melancholy
Infernal Rivers	Styx	Phlegethon	Cocytus	Acheron
Senses	Taste & Smell	Sight	Hearing	Touch
Elements	Water כום	Fire אש	Air ריח	Earth עפר
Ichirei Shikon of Shintō	Nigimitama	Sachimitama	Kushimitama	Aramitama

Third Iteration

In these images we find *resurrection* of the dead savior-god in spring, his reign in the summer, the *fall of man* and the *apocalypse* (revealing) in autumn, and the *final judgment* in the *end times* of the year. Both the bible and Quran speak of the latter as *Judgement Day*

The book of Revelation 20:12 states:

> *"And I saw the dead, small and great, stand before God; and the books were opened: and another book was opened, which is the book of life: and the dead were judged out of those things which were written in the books, according to their works."*

The book of An-Nisā, verse 87 states:

> "Allah, there is no god worthy of worship except Him. He will certainly gather all of you together on the Day of Judgment — about which there is no doubt. And whose word is more truthful than Allah's?"

In the book of Ar-Rūm we also read in verse 19 how:

> "He brings the living from the dead, the dead from the living, and quickens the earth after it had died. So you will be brought forth (from the dead)."

The *Bhagavad Gita* 8:18 says something similar:

> "At the advent of Brahma's day, all living beings emanate from the unmanifest source. And at the fall of his night, all embodied beings again merge into their unmanifest source."

In the case of Brahma, however, we get a glimpse of the creator's brilliance as the solar god like Ra. In the next verse we learn that this process of living and merging with source is a daily occurrence:

> "Again and again, when Brahmas day arrives, all living entities come into being, and with the arrival of B'ahma's night they are helplessly annihilated."

What we learn here is that with every day, as the sun rises and saves mankind from darkness and cold with light and warmth, it will inevitably sink into the western sky in the evening. The same occurs in the spring, summer, fall, and winter. This story unfolds every single day, week, month, year, decade, ad infinitum, and reminds us of that of moment of creation when "God commanded, 'Let there be Light'," when the Creator said in the *Popol Vuh* "Let there be light, let there be dawn in the sky and on the earth," and when Ahura Mazda first spoke: "First I have made the Kingdom of Light, Dear to all life." Each morning we witness the microcosmic creation of the macrocosmic universe and the birth of man from a minor slumber. As we mourn separation from Source in the Garden of

Eden, we likewise awake (attend a wake) every morning (mourning) and become conscious once more of our physical bodies like Genesis 3:7 – *"Then the eyes of both of them were opened, and they realized they were naked; so they sewed fig leaves together and made coverings for themselves."*

In the *Zend Avesta* we read in the epilogue the following verse, which seems to share a relationship with the inherent nature of change and the purification it brings:

> *Evil exists not,*
> *Only the past.*
> *The past is past;*
> *The present is a moment;*
> *The future is all.*

Fourth Iteration

The "pale horse" referred to in Revelation as one of the *Four Horseman of the Apocalypse* does indeed have a color. Although pale, the final horse is named *khlōrós*, a word meaning green or yellow. Khlōrós is Greek for "green" and over time the word was used as a foundation for the French word *chlorophyll*, the green pigment in plants responsible for their absorption of light into energy through the process of photosynthesis.

When sunlight becomes scarce and temperatures fall in the latter half of the year, plants and trees are unable to produce as much chlorophyll, or none at all, and therefore their leaves turn yellow, orange, or red depending upon the type of tree. Grasping this concept means that one is able to comprehend the *apocalypse*, a word referring to the complete destruction of the world, or winter, and generally meaning *unveiling* or *revelation*. What is unveiled and revealed is the method of nature in its cyclical essence.

The "name that sat on him was Death" is a reference to what follows the horse and his rider, i.e., the *winter*, and therefore the death of nature and a cold, dark, icy world akin to Hell. The pale green-yellow horse is actually the changing of leaves which heralds the death of nature. Death's power is over the "fourth part of the earth" that we know as the fourth season and old age. Whereas spring, summer, and fall represent birth, maturity, and decay respectively, winter represents death before rebirth in the spring. This is true for humans as much as it is for *nature*.

Fifth Iteration

The Four Horsemen also correspond to the seven solar spheres and seven *Seals of Revelation*, with the remaining three seals likewise corresponding to planets and principles:

First Seal is the White Horse or Moon

Second Seal is the Red Horse or Sun

Third Seal is the Black Horse or Saturn

Fourth Seal is the Pale Horse or Venus

Fifth Seal is Mars or Blood

Sixth Seal is Jupiter or the Martyrs

Seventh Seal is Mercury or Silence

EXORCISING DEMONS

First Iteration

We return in this section to *kotodama* and *otodama*, defined in Japanese as the *spirit of words* and *spirit of sounds* respectively. There is much to be said about the words *exorcise* and *exercise*, far beyond their near identical pronunciation. The familiar term *exorcise* obviously is defined as the *driving out* of an *evil spirit* from a person or place. Originally from the Greek *exorkizein,* the word is reduced to "ex" and "horkos" - *out* and *oath.* To *exorcise* someone or some place is therefore to adjure a spirit to fulfill its oath to higher authorities and leave, hence why the Lord or some powerful divine force is called upon.

The term *exercise* is defined as a *physical effort, carried out to sustain or improve health and fitness.* While we use this word far more often than *exorcise,* the two have much in common. *Exercise* comes from Middle English for *application of a right,* which stems from the Latin *exercitium* and further from *exercere,* which means to *keep busy. Exercere* is reduced to "ex" and "arcere" in Latin - *thoroughly* and *to keep away.*

Both words thus request a spirit of manifest evil or illness to fulfill its oath, leave, and stay away. The fact we *exercise* to stay healthy is a direct descendent of the purposes of ancient *exorcisms,* i.e., *disease*s were what was usually being *driven out.* We also *exercise* to stay in *shape* so we do not become distorted versions of ourselves. These indwellers were sometimes seen as just *illness,* but like the *spirits* of alcohol such an *ailment* was thought to be caused by something *unclean* or otherworldly.

Just as knowing the name of a demon is supposed to give an exorcist, or even commoner, power over the unclean and corrupt, knowing the name of disease provides for the same power. As Roy Kotansky writes in a detailed essay called 'Greek Exorcistic Amulets', exorcists typically were "*adjuring demons directly by the name of the affliction they cause.*" Call them illnesses, ailments, diseases, demons, chaos, or the unclean, these forces are distortions of creation and thus "*do not belong in the realm of the living but of the dead.*" The domain of these things is the *Underworld* or *Parallel-world.*

Great proof of the existence of demons comes in the form of the internal conflicts we all face in our lives, some more significant than others. We all have the capacity for *good,* but we also have the same capacity for *evil.* As famed clinical psychologist Jordan Peterson points out, having also worked in the study of alcohol-related social issues: *"Continued use of an addictive drug therefore feeds the growth of what can be accurately conceptualized as a living monster in the user's psyche..."* That internal *living monster* is the *demon,* which must be exorcised. Hence, why we call alcohol *spirits* and say that drugs can induce possession. So can ideological conviction.

Second Iteration

Exorcisms were, and are today, done in a variety of ways around the world. The most common instruments used in antiquity were tablets made of wood or metal, gems, papyrus, and similar items. Magical inscriptions, powerful names for God, names of the angels, works of divinity, etc., were carved or etched and, as amulets and talismans, worn around the neck or placed into the pocket. The Syrian word *Abracadabra* has traditionally been used as a magical charm or amulet just as with the phrase *open sesame.* If inscribed on a medal it is considered a powerful defense against misfortune and disease. The word itself is said to come from Ab, Ben, Rauch, ACADosch – Hebrew for the trinity of Father, Son, and Holy Ghost. The earliest recorded account of its usage was in a poem called *Precepta de Medicina* by Q. Serenus Scammonicus, a second century Gnostic physician. Its usage was recommended as a preventative measure against fevers, in particular.

Interestingly, gingerbread has also been used in the same way - if written on and eaten properly it is believed to convey a medicinal benefit. Although there are many interpretations of *abracadabra* it is supposed to translate into something equivalent to *A – U - M:*

I WILL CREATE AS I SPEAK

If not inscribed on a medal it can also be written on a piece of parchment, paper, or whatever else is workable. The paper is to then be folded into the form of a cross and worn for nine days, then *"thrown backward before sunrise into a stream flowing eastward,"* according to author William J. Fielding. When *abracadabra* is worn in some manner next to the heart it is considered a protection against the influence of spells and enchantments. There are several ways in which it may be written, but it should always be done so in the form of a triangle to represent the Holy Trinity. As a symbol of protection, the triangle itself was used in evocations and countless other magical practices throughout antiquity. Today it is still an extremely recognizable magic symbol. If spirits were to be drawn from heaven, a magician is to place himself at the top of the triangle and place the altar of fumigations at the bottom. If the spirit is drawn from what some call hell, or the abyss, the magician should place himself at the bottom of the triangle and place the altar above. Francis Barrett writes in <u>The Magus</u> of the proper formulating of any kind of magical item if it is to be successful: *"…in forming of a charm, or amulet, it will be of no effect except for the very soul of the operator is strongly and intensely exerted and impressed, as it were, and the image of the idea sealed on the charm, or amulet; for without this, in vain will be all the observations of times, hours, and constellations; therefore, this I have thought fit to mention, once for all, that it may be almost always uppermost in the mind of the operator, for, without this one thing being observed and noticed, many who form seals, &c, do fall short of the wished-for effect."*

Here is shown the proper method of writing the *abracadabra* in descending order as per the drawing down of divine influences and for the dissipating of diseases:

ABRACADABRA
BRACADABR
RACADAB
ACADA
CAD
A

ABRACADABRA
ABRACADABR
ABRACADAB
ABRACADA
ABRACAD
ABRACA
ABRAC
ABRA
ABR
AB
A

Abracadabra also conceals the name of the Hellenistic deity *Abraxas*, who is often associated with the name of Demiurge, or IAO, the creator of the physical Universe – sometimes referred to Isis, Apophis, and Osiris, or *OM*. Typically, Abraxas is depicted with the head of a cock, which announces the return of the sun each morning.

Third Iteration

In Acts 19:13-17 we read about the driving out of evil spirits using the name Jesus:

> *"Some Jews who went around driving out evil spirits tried to invoke the name of the Lord Jesus over those who were demon-possessed. They would say, 'In the name of the Jesus whom Paul preaches, I command you to come out.' Seven sons of Sceva, a Jewish chief priest, were doing this. One day the evil spirit answered them, 'Jesus I know, and Paul I know about, but who are you?' Then the man who had the evil spirit jumped on them and overpowered them all. He gave them such a beating that they ran out of the house naked and bleeding. When this became known to the Jews and Greeks living in Ephesus, they were all seized with fear, and the name of the Lord Jesus was held in high honor."*

Whether Abraxas or Jesus Christ, the son and sun of God, we are dealing with the same motif. Exorcists work the same in any culture, for the most part, adjuring demons, putting them under oath, casting them out, driving them out, and setting them aside. Whatever the terminology it is important, as with magic in general, to recognize the power of *will* and its ability to help one overcome - be that a disease or a demon.

In the *Great Magical Papyrus of Paris*, phrases such as "I adjure you," "to come out of," and "stand away from" are used, along with a call to the "god of Abraham, Isaac, and Jacob," and an interpolation of "Jesus Christ, the Holy Spirit, the son of the Father." Much like the sacred names of Adonai, Jesus Christ, and Tetragrammaton are used to dispel evil spirits, we can also use the name of the Buddha - *Nembutsu* - to accomplish the same.

As for the term *demon* we find it relates to the working of chaotic forces from beyond. Demons are *evil spirits* that perform cruel, wicked, and forceful actions against both the *innocent*, who can be corrupted, and the *sinful* who have opened their hearts to such influences. According to Roy Kotansky in the essay mentioned above, to the Greeks these forces were *"a genie awakened from the dead to render service"* and to the Semitics they were *"an entity to be expelled from the sufferer."* We can add that to the Egyptians they were a ghost or spirit adjured to return to the land of the dead. Roy adds how, *"...'Greek' adjurations conjure up the underworld dead to serve. True 'Jewish' adjurations, on the other hand, cast out (i.e., 'exorcise') the demons represented as actually indwelling the afflicted."* Although Roy and many other scholars believe that the casting out of demons is birthed from Judaic tradition, and it very well may be in many ways, there certainly must be careful consideration given to other cultures and their customs. For although the Jews and Greeks, and others, may have developed many of the classical elements of exorcism as we know them, this only presumes that other cultures saw *illness* or *demons* in the same capacity. In Japanese culture, for example, Shintō professes that *all* evil and misfortune comes from *all* things crooked, including one's heart and mind. This is why we *exercise* to keep the former and latter in *shape*, instead of in a curved, jumbled, warped, and distorted form. The 'curved spirit' is called *magatsubi*, the cause of all evil deeds, diseases, disasters, misfortunes, and the like. In other words, the indigenous Shintō practitioners were certainly exorcising demons but by totally different parameters than the Jews.

Fourth Iteration

We acquire the word *demon* also due to the Greek concept of *daemon*, a name referring to a divine spirit of nature existing on a spectrum somewhere between earth and heaven. Within the human experience we find ourselves to be conscious, subconscious, and unconscious. Our *persona* is perceived by others, our *psyche* is within, and our *body* is the temple housing these sacred spiritual elements. In nature there are similar forces at work. Gnomes, Undines, Sylphs, and Salamanders collectively make up the elements of the earth, water, air or ether, and fire. These *elementals* relate to the four domains or directions of north, west, east, and south respectively. Today we call them carbon (earth), hydrogen (water), oxygen (air), and nitrogen (fire). Joseph Campbell also points out that the gods are simply agents of a masked mystery, essentially representing the mathematical nature of reality:

> "The gods themselves are simply agents of the great high mystery, the secret of which is found in mathematics. This can still be observed in our sciences, in which the mathematics of time and space are regarded as the veil through which the great mystery, the tremendum, shows itself."

It is from the *Gnomes*, those elementals of earth, rock, dirt, wood, etc., for which we get stories of goblins and their leader Gob.

The *Undines* occupy water and invoke imagines reminiscent of sirens and mermaids.

Sylphs are considered entirely intangible and invisible, but they provide us with the idea of the *great eastern wind*, as this was their creative domain.

Salamanders are elementals of fire similarly related to the fire-gods known to the Arabs as *Djinn*, and wherefrom we derive the idea of *genies*.

Manly Hall explains how, "*The Christian Church gathered all the elemental entities together under the title of 'Demon,'*" inverting simplistic Polytheism into a sophisticated monotheism with mandates that all but the true God be seen as his oppressors and false idols. As per the fire elementals, Hall says they work through our emotional nature by means of the *"body heat, the liver, and the blood stream."*

We can likewise extract similar associations with water, air, and earth. In describing the spirits that exercise control over the elements, Augusta Foss Heindel confirms, *"the spirit of water has its workers, the undines; the spirit controlling the winds works through the sylphs."*

Our emotions are driven by Undines, thoughts by Sylphs, and physical form by Gnomes.

We conclude Hall's commentary from <u>The Secret Teachings of All Ages</u> on elementals and their associations with demons:

> "The Christian Church gathered all the elemental entities together under the title of demon. This is a misnomer with far-reaching consequences, for to the average mind the word demon means an

evil thing, and the Nature spirits are essentially no more malevolent than are the minerals, plants, and animals."

Levi has a slightly different idea of elementals, suggesting that they are like phantoms. He says Kabbalists view elementary spirits in their *"most secret books"* to be *"the children of the solitude of Adam."* They were born of his dreams as he yearned for the companionship of a woman yet to be created by God. In other words, his ejaculations birthed demons perhaps not unlike the demons of Lilith. As suggested by Paracelsus, both the blood lost during menstruation by a female and the nocturnal emissions of male celibates created phantoms or larvae that were also known as *elementary spirits.* Levi says of these creatures:

"...such larvae have an aerial body formed from vapor of blood, for which they are attracted towards split blood and in older days drew nourishment from the smoke of sacrifices."

These monstrous creatures are said to be the *incubi* and *succubi* of legend and the vampires draining the vital heat or energy of healthy persons. Nearly all of us have experienced these individuals, perhaps without realizing the fact, knowing that we somehow feel drained of energy after spending a period of time with one of these creatures. If the life force or energy of a creature resides in the blood, as is commonly believed, then the *sucking* or *draining* of energy through an act of vampirism may be associated with the *drinking of blood.*

Fifth Iteration

At the core a *demon* or *demonic classification* is a cultural determinate of societal limitations and values. People falling outside these boundaries are thus seen as *cursed, possessed, crooked, wicked, demonic,* and certainly as *wizards, sorcerers,* and *magicians,* even if the actions of the latter are simply called *works of God* within other societal parameters. In other words, a *miracle* within a religious community is the divinity of God at work whereas outside that same religious group it is an act of wicked *magic* and condemned as *demonic.* Sarah Iles Johnston put it simply in her essay 'Defining the Dreadful, how in this paradigm, *"'normal' demonic behavior =*

abnormal human behavior." One of the best examples of this comes in the form of demonic female spirits or ghosts seeking to harm children.

It has always been considered part of the female duty, regardless of other employment, to bare children, raise them properly, nurture them, and protect them. This is not to say that the man does not have an equal role, because he does, but our focus is on the female for this commentary.

Motherhood provides the cornerstone and organization around which virtually every culture on the planet has aligned itself, i.e., the family. If a woman refuses or fails to have children, by her virginity or abortion, or due to her lack of interest in motherhood, then she becomes *demonic* in the eyes of most civilizations. Most cultures, and especially the Greeks, placed this woman on the boundary between life and death, forcing her to have, as Sarah writes, *"no recourse but to wander restlessly between the two."*

Yaksha
sandstone bracket
2nd-century AD

Here we find understanding for the story of *La Llorona*, the *weeping woman* who drowns her children out of her failure to provide. Whereas the purifying waters of Isis from the Nile River were healing and imparting of wisdom, the *weeping woman* uses feminine waters to commit treasonous crimes against nature. In Hindu mythology we find nature spirits called *Yaksha* that are known to harm and even eat little children. *Lilith* is the Mesopotamia and Judaic temptress of men and aborter of children. She steals their souls while they sleep in innocence and makes men ejaculate in their rest, using the semen to birth demons. Lilith is depicted as such because she refused to be submissive to the dominion of *man*, thus being exorcised from *paradise*, though returning to tempt Eve into abandoning *perfection*.

In Greece we have the demons Gello, Mormo, and Lamia. *Gello* died prematurely as a virgin and was thus unable to produce any children. *Mormo* birthed children but they died at a young age. In her anguish and envy of other happy women and mothers, she hunted down newborns and killed them like Lilith. *Lamia* is said to have eaten her own children, a story we can take to mean she failed to provide for them. In Greece and Rome, the female demon *Strix* can be equated with the Slavic *Strzyga* and perhaps even the *Baba Yaga*, both of which are vampiric, ugly, dwell in seclusion, and are known to harm children. The *Strix* is pictured as part woman and part bird, usually of an owl, like those taking flight with Lilith. Collin De Plancy writes in his 1863 <u>Infernal Dictionary</u> about a powerful and demonic creature fitting these descriptions. The monstrous entity is named *Stolas*, and he is a *"Great prince of the hell, which appears in the form of an owl."*

Associations such as these likely arise since birds of prey are swift and silent in catching their prey, particularly at night. Lamia, Strix, Lilith, and Lamashtu all certainly are depicted as therianthropes, having the body of a woman and the lower limbs of a nocturnal raptor.

The *Baba Yaga* likewise has a house with chicken legs, similar to the rooster legs of the demon *Deumus*. Lamia is also speculated to be a daughter of *Belos*, the Hellenized version of the Babylonian Baal, a grand duke of hell who was worshiped with human sacrifices by the Canaanites, Carthaginians, Chaldeans, and even the Israelites.

As with the distinctions between *magic* and *miracle*, Lamia was thought to have originated in Libya, Africa, a place bordering the outer limits of the 'civilized' Greek world. Lamashtu was said to dwell in foreign lands, too, particularly in the swamps, forests, or mountains. Sarah further adds, *"Egyptian child-killers are believed to come out of Asia."* All this suggest that like the distinctions between *magic* and *miracle*, the differences between *angels* and *demons* likewise depends on geographical location and cultural boundaries.

As the tempters and seducers of men these demonic *spirits of the night* are often depicted with body parts of a donkey rather than bird of prey. This likely signifies their role as seductress rather than a killer of the innocent, though they embody both roles. The same meaning can be derived as per why the Devil is depicted as a goat. The goat is a symbol of "evil" because these animals are notoriously difficult to manage, and as Sarah Iles Johnston writes, *"for a culture in which herding is important, therefore, the goat is a potent symbol of trouble and possible loss of livelihood."* In this capacity - the goat as a difficult animal - we see why Satan is seen as *oppositeon* or why the Hebrew śāṭān is an *accuser* and an *adversary*.

The Queen of Night in terracotta from Old Babylon. Commonly called *Lilith*, she wears a crown of lunar horns, a rainbow necklace, and stands between two protective owls with the feet of a raptor. Sometimes she is called *Ereshkigal*, the Sumerian goddess of *Kur*, or the Land of the Dead.

Apollonius of Tyana with his disciple Menippus: Here he exposed the youth's beautiful and wealthy bride as a flesh-eating vampire called Lamia. Published in *The Mirror of Magic*.

Stolas from Collin De Plancy's *Infernal Dictionary*

Deumus from Collin De Plancy's *Infernal Dictionary*

Baba Yaga by Ivan Bilibin, from *Russian Popular Fairy Tales*

Within these stories can also be derived the meaning behind *Hansel and Gretel*, the story of two siblings abandoned by their mother who is replaced by - or transforms into - a cannibalistic witch in the woods.

The Japanese yōkai named *Yamamba* is another perfectly terrifying example of women unable or unwilling to fulfill their civilizing duties. She is likewise a symbol of *mother nature's* wrath when not appeased. The word *yamamba* means "mountain old woman" in Japanese – *yama* alone means "mountain." She shares much in common with the *Hansel and Gretel* witch (their failed mother), and thus she has a proclivity for kidnapping both young women and young children from local villages. Her insistence on entering a home, usually with only young children inside, may be metaphoric of nature attempting to reclaim her own innocence in response to the encroachment of man. If appeased, *yamamba* can actually provide good luck and abundance so long as you do not venture too far into her woods. This means you should not take more than you need. It is from the

Yamamba by Shinonome Kijin, from *The Book of Yōkai*

mountains and valleys that we acquire food, water, wood, etc. By balancing what we take with what we give, and paying our respects, we may appease nature and live harmoniously within its fertile womb. If we are unable or unwilling to do so then there are monstrous *egregores* to contend with. Richard Cavendish, in his book <u>The Black Arts</u>, calls these forms *"fly-the-lights"* because they *"naturally never appear in the day-time."* The demon Beelzebub surely fits this description as his name means *Lord of the Flies*. Collin De Plancy writes that he is *"the prince of demons…the first for power and crime after Satan."* Cavendish adds of these terrifying monsters:

> *"These spirits are the medieval and modern survivals of the wide-spread primitive belief that all Nature is alive as man is, in trees*

and fields and hedgerows, in boulders, crags and caves. They are unpredictable and mischievous as Nature is, sometimes kindly but more often cruel."

Sixth Iteration

Women have traditionally been accused of practicing *witchcraft* or *black magic* far more often than men, and the reasons above are likely the cause of this historical fact. The *witch* is therefore likened to the horrible and demonic crimes of Lilith, Lamashtu, Gello, Lamia, and Mormo among others. These women have become physically ugly, too, and often bisexual. Sarah references the fifth-century comic poet Crates who portrayed Lamia with a staff symbolizing a penis. She explains how in the stories *"some women are busily disguising themselves as men; one woman shows the others the splendid [staff/penis] that she has stolen from her sleeping husband."* In addition, *"Like her ugliness and dirtiness, Lamia's bisexuality obviously runs counter to the standard of the desirable woman."*

Priests of the Cybele cult in Phrygia, which gained traction in Greece and Rome, performed similar proscriptions against themselves. The Galli, as they were called, allowed their hair to grow extremely long and they took donated women's clothing in exchange for providing fortunes. Galli stood in contrast to Roman gender norms since they paraded around dressed like women.

Far be it from a social commentary in contemporary times, this demonological record confirms that *demons of the night* were ugly, alone, promiscuous, pro-abortion, anti-life, dressed like men, and would even steal a penis to replace their own unused or mutilated sexual organs. The meaning here is that these female *black magicians* have abandoned their beauty and roles as creators and nurturers of life, instead becoming blasphemers against God. They are the defilers of innocence and perverters of nature like the powerful demon Volac, who Collin De Plancy describes as *"a great president of hell."* Nevertheless, the roles of these women were not so much abandoned but instead unfulfilled as a result of chance, such as the death of a child due to disease or the inability to give birth at all.

St. Hippolytus says that witches must recite the following verse, since they deny the Christian faith and withdrawal any allegiance to God, reserving it for the dark lord they now worship. Here is once more a denial of creation:

> "I deny the creator of heaven and earth. I deny my baptism. I deny the worship I formerly paid to God. I cleave to thee, and in thee I believe."

Acting on certain evil or immoral impulses is a sure proof of *possession*, especially for that person in a state of frenzy or emotional upheaval. This is why women were called *hysterical*, the word deriving from the Greek *husterikos - of the womb*. Today we have the word *hysterectomy*, a surgery to remove the uterus. Let none of this be misconstrued, however, to suggest that men cannot become beasts and demons by failing or refusing to fulfill their duties.

Seventh Iteration

Immoral behaviors are resultant from influences of intangible concepts that so often are anthropomorphized by demonic characters representing the qualities of pride, lust, anger, gluttony, envy, covetousness, and sloth. Joseph Campbell says that these deities are the *"personification of a spiritual power"* which *"are not recognized."* As a result, or even if they are recognized but remain unheard or unheeded, they *"become demonic and are really dangerous."*

Sarah explains further how demons change based on location, observer, and cultural vision, being malleable like clay:

> "Demons are clay with which people mold images of their fears and anxieties; in order to express the fears and anxieties of the moment effectively, that clay must remain malleable. It is not until those who stand outside of a community begin to make lists of its demons (i.e. demonologies) for their own purposes that any real consistency of traits and imagery is obtained, and it is artificial consistency, born form a scholar's desire to organize, a magician's desire to control or a missionary's desire to devalue and eventually overcome."

These are the same philosophical, anthropological, and sociological parameters wherein fall monsters, chimeras, hybrids, and generally assorted cyrtid-creatures which are, as therianthropes, associated with both altered states of consciousness and demonology. Because, for example, a *werewolf* fails to register as man or beast, it is both, and thus operating outside of comprehension and the natural world. Worse yet, it possesses the intelligence and viciousness of both wolf and man. The *werewolf* itself is real, for it represents the expression of the unstable emotions and apprehensions held by man. An angry and violent person may be said to have the influence of such animals coursing through their veins.

Monsters of this sort are also derived from very natural things like snakes and centipedes, the former of course having no legs and the latter having far too many for human comfort. This results in a type of non-human-conformity in which we see the snake as evil or the centipede as just another creepy-crawly. Although some may fear these creatures, it is an all-around different fear than if one were faced with their own internal demons. Japanese yōkai are constructed along both of the former and latter lines, usually in exaggerated and distorted forms. Contrarily, a *kaiju* is an enormous monster exhibiting the excessive qualities of the forces of nature.

The yōkai of today is a term that refers to what most of us call spirits, phantoms, specters, sprites, fairies, elementals, shapeshifters, demons (*oni*), aliens, monsters (*bakemono* or *obake*) etc. They are energetic personifications of crossroads, bridges, tunnels, of living on the edge of town or between villages, of the top of mountains, of deep inside forests, or in the depths of the ocean.

When we speak of *crossroads*, the *threshold of a* house, or secluded areas between destinations, dangerous entities are conjured for the simple reason that these places are not exactly ne one place or another. They exist in the *twilight zone* between worlds. What we speak of here can also be named *twilight forces*, those 'things' which appear most actively during the *witching hours*, usually 2-4 A.M., when night is the darkest, and as night begins to give way to the next morning.

These hazy, vague, transitional moments between night and day open a sort of gateway between worlds, much like the shifting changes of earth's seasons. As night breaks, or day breaks, definition and certainty return to physical reality.

Michael Foster describes in <u>The Book of Yōkai</u> how *yūrei* (ghosts) favor the earliest part of these hours, or a time called *ushimitsu*, appearing in *"the third quarter of the hour of the ox, about 2:00-2:30 A.M., when night was at its darkest."* Yanagita Kunio, who was one of Japan's most influential voices on folkloric studies, classifies *bakemono* and *yūrei* slightly differently, stating that the former *"generally appear in set locations"* and haunt a particular place, whereas the latter haunt a particular person. He adds, *yūrei* tend to arrive before the twilight time whereas *bakemono* prefer the *"dim light of dusk or dawn."*

Twilight Language is thus the undercurrent of our lexicon, a sort of *anāhata-śabda*, or sound beneath audible sound, which influences our perception of realty. It is essentially the power of sound (*otodama*) behind the spirit/soul of words (*kotodama*). This is why certain sounds and vibrations can both conjure and banish these forces of *twilight*.

The word *daemon* also comes from the archaic spelling of *demon*, though both relate to the voices we hear battling for supremacy within over whether our decisions be moral or immoral - not unlike the little *angel and devil* sitting on your shoulders feeding you contradictory advice.

We all have the power to *exercise* and *exorcise* these forces, even if we often need assistance in that *belief* to assist our *will* - as is the purpose of magical tools like wands, swords, and athame, offerings such as incense, salt, water, and so on, or certain ritual garb.

The *fear* we may feel for dramatic demonic representations is grossly misplaced, considering that these diabolic forces are conceptual images of internal struggles. When Proverbs talks about fearing the Lord, we find an interesting correlation with the fear we have for demons. Proverbs 9:10 says: *"The fear of the LORD is the beginning of wisdom, and knowledge of the Holy One is understanding."* It is a necessity in life, for worthwhile growth, to conquer the serpentine tempter and overcome the dragon to acquire the treasure of transformation – *philosopher's stone*. This is done by killing demons and sacrificing the animal nature to a higher purpose – i.e., sacrificing instant gratification for future benefit. The fear we have for the LORD, however, is to be wary of self-deception and misplaced fear, both of which distort and corrupt our basic instincts.

Eighth Iteration

The *Good Daimon* is traditionally the protective spirit of a house, individual, or an entire family. In Rome these household gods were called *Lar* and positioned within the home at the "center" of the family. Household protections were also found in a distinct form of *magical bowl*, which was an object of exorcism found most commonly in Mesopotamia. Jason David BeDuhn writes in an essay titled 'Magic Bowls and Manichaeans', that these *"bowls are related to each other in other ways, by scribe, client, or spell formulae. The spells on the bowls are concerned with 'sealing' the bodies, families, homes, and property of the clients. The 'seal' expels or blocks a host of demonic forces, including evil dreams and illnesses."*

An interesting parallel can be found here between *magic bowls* and both modern and ancient eastern *singing bowls*. The wonderful sounds these bowls produce, if utilized properly, are harmonious with the bells of a Church, Hindu temple or Shintō shrine, which are intended to protect against evil and also to inform kind spirits that there is an offering about to be presented. In case of the Church, they are meant to inform the people of a town that a service is about to begin. In other words, they exorcise the immediate area of all malicious energies while also invoking the angelic.

Ninth Iteration

King Solomon is probably the most famous of all exorcists, being acknowledged by Christians, Muslims, and Jews alike. He is known for having compelled legions of demons to complete construction on the Great Temple. Solomon reportedly obtained this power, according to 1 Kings, by requesting wisdom from the Lord instead of wealth or power over material enemies. God thus granted him with immense wisdom, along with wealth and honor. Collin De Plancy writes in the riveting <u>Infernal Dictionary</u> about Solomon as such:

> *"Philosophers, botanists, soothsayers, and astrologers consider Solomon or Soliman as their patron. According to them, God having given him his wisdom, at the same time gave him all*

natural and supernatural knowledge; and as part of the last one, to evoke spirits and genies, and to control them."

Solomon's wisdom was largely concentrated in the power of a ring which gave him absolute authority *"over all intermediate beings between God and man."* According to Plancy, *"the ring still exists; it is enclosed in the tomb of Solomon, and whoever will possess it, will become master of the world."* This "ring," however, is probably more akin to the 36,525 books written by Hermes - the number equivalent to the days in a solar year.

During the building of Solomon's Temple, three murderers known as Jubela, Jubelo, and Jubelum waited for the exit of their Grand Master from the unfinished *sanctum sanctorum*, where Chiram Abiff had gone to pray at high noon. Each stood at the gates of the temple ready to strike fatal blows upon their master if he refused to divulge the secret code of a Master Mason. In his refusal at each cardinal direction within the unfinished temple – south, west, east - they struck the Master dead in their own distinct ways with a with a gauge, square, and a mallet. This is metaphoric for the soul or spirit ascending from the underworld in the south to the land of shadow in the west, before being resurrected in the east. The three ruffians also represent all life divided into three distinct parts: growth, maturity and decay, or birth, life, and death. In this story each gate of the temple represents a position of the sun in relation to the temple of *Solomon* itself. The name *Solomon* has also been reduced by some authors and thus rendered as a triune compilation of words relating to the sun. The term *Sol* relates to *Solus* or *Solar* and means *sun*. In Sanskrit the term *OM*, or *A - U - M*, the Hindu sound of creation, refers to heat. A similar sound, *ON*, is an Ethiopic term referring to the solar principle manifested. The term *aum* is also similar to the Egyptian god *Amon-RA* or *Amen-RA*, Chief of the Gods and from whence we get the term *amen* said at the end of prayer. Jerusalem, the location of Solomon's Temple, also means *City of Peace*, and is referred to as the "Holy City." The word *Holy* is similar to the word *hely*, which is rooted in the Greek word *Helios*, which means *sun*. This also gives us the Egyptian *Heliopolis*, or the *city of the sun*, where RA had his sanctuary.

As the son of David, and considering his unmatched authority over demons, Solomon can be presumed responsible or most of the classical elements of exorcism in the Jewish tradition.

Roy Kotansky adds that *"given the reputation of Jewish practitioners for magical ritual, the calling up of the dead cannot have been excluded, along with other exorcist rites."* He says the *"calling up of ghosts from the grave must have derived from Jewish practice itself."* However, depending on how far one wishes to go into history and pre-history, and how much credit one wishes to give to the Jewish tradition, there are faraway lands to the west and east of Israel where the same exorcistic concepts are embodied.

Tenth Iteration

As we know, God is the *Logos* or *Word made flesh*, a concept expressed by the Japanese word *kotodama*. The ancient Japanese *Kujiki-72* text informs us, again, like all of the other Creation stories, how: *"The Creator rules over boundless infinity. Nothing existed before the Creator. No one ruled before the Creator. The Creator is without Form."* Unlike the specifics of the *Holy Bible* or *Holy Quran*, however, the *Kujiki-72* describes the creation of ALL as appearing in five forms called WEIGHTS. These *Five Weights* are *Kami, Kokoro* (Mind-Heart), *Principle* (Nature/Behavior), *Qi* (Vital Energy), and *Boundary* (State). Avery Morrow, in The Sacred Science of Ancient Japan, describes the *Five Weights* as: *"kami lives, the mind rules, principles preserve, qi determines our fates, and borders create form."* In books 53-56 of the same *Kujiki-72* we learn about how sickness is caused by disharmony in all things and how words, or vibrations, can heal. Avery explains the text from his translation:

> *"We learn the sickness is caused by a climate of dishonesty and untruth, that the people in the Age of the Kami avoided illness entirely through honest and frank attitudes, and that if anyone ever got sick their hearts were purified through healing kotodama and other methods, and they would quickly recover."*

Here we find ancient, and some believe pre-ancient, Japanese prescriptions of such a similar form to the Jewish tradition that one must wonder if the same *mysticism* operating among the Jews was not also operating in far-away India, where Jesus supposedly traveled for years to learn from mystics, and even as far away as Nihon - what we now call Japan. In fact, there is a legend in Japan that Jesus Christ died and was buried in Amori Prefecture, in the tiny village of Shingō. The story is based on the theory that Jesus spent at least some of his *missing years* in Japan. He later returned to Japan and died at the age of 106.

There is also proof of his tomb found in the 1980s, when a crew of construction workers discovered an ossuary in the south suburb of Talpiot, located in the Old City of Jerusalem. Known as the "Talpiot Tomb," it is believed Jesus and his family were buried here.

Although Solomon was born around 1010 BCE, and the oldest official Japanese text (Kojiki) is thought to only date to around 712 AD, the *Kujiki-72* and other similar texts are thought to stem from a far earlier time period - possibly emanating from the same *mystical cult* or *civilizing gods* who spread their *wisdom,* in the wake of a great deluge, from the Americas, Africa, and the Middle East, to India, China, and Japan. Readers interested in this subject should read my book *Occult Arcana.*

Eleventh Iteration

Officially, Christianity did not make it into Japan until 1549 when Francis Xavier arrived on a mission to convert feudal lords, and their people, to the faith. By 1587 there was a backlash against the new religion and an edict was issued banning any Japanese from holding the belief. By 1637 the 300,000 or so converted had been hunted down and either made to repent, were tortured, or were executed. The first major incident took place in 1597 when 26 Catholics were crucified. After the Japanese inquisition, the *shogun* closed the country to all but a few traders, probably Dutch and French, who had been allowed access to the country, in part, since Nagasaki Harbor opened in 1571.

In honor of the 26 dead Christians, who symbolized the first major persecution of Japanese converts, a church was opened in 1865. With the opening of Oura Church many Catholics emerged from hiding but were once again targeted for their outward expression of faith. It only took a few years until the Meiji Emperor reversed the ban on Christianity under intense criticism from the same Christendom in the west that had in the past issued its own inquisition against pagans and other forms of opposition. By 1940 there were more Japanese Catholics, who had that year been officially recognized, than there were in the 1600s. Japan's government and military, instead of repressing the growing movement during this time, decided instead to recruit Jesus Christ for the war effort.

Scholars equated Jesus with Confucius and Christians, including Christ, were aligned with the notion of *bushidō,* i.e., the *way of the warrior* in which an individual was willing to die for their belief. Just as eastern religions and philosophies are attractive to the west, we also find that in Japan Christianity was an equally fresh take on concepts which up until that point had been largely based on shintō. Although authorities attempted to hijack Christianity and force it into compliance with state-shintō, a distorted version of the ancient practice, just as paganism was forced to conform to Christianity, both practices shared a lot in common. It was likely because of this fact that the Japanese people took easily to the new faith; they recognized it as a new way of looking at already deeply held beliefs. By December 25, 1941, the 'Prayer for Victory' in World War II was mandated at mass.

The idea of ancestor and nature worship is certainly *pagan* to Christians but in shintō it is the equivalent of *everlasting life.* The creator in Genesis is really the *law of nature.* Personal *duty* in shintō easily fit into the Christian paradigm and the practice of *misogi,* or ritual purification, was the Japanese version of *baptism.* The practice of ringing bells at shintō shrines, much like those used in Christian churches, is twofold: to ward off evil and to alert the *kami,* or townspeople, to the intentions of worshipers. Since Japan was already a proud nation of four seasons, even their holy days would fit into the Christian-pagan calendar system.

The point of this historical overview is to point out that Japan was already aware of the doctrines of Christianity before it emerged; those doctrines were also the basis for many pre-Christian religions that if not related to shintō, certainly were a universal proof of human observation in God's creation. In other words, if Jesus had gone to Japan, as we are sure he traveled to Egypt and India, then he probably learned from ancient shintō what he learned elsewhere. The irony is that when the Church marched into Japan in the name of saving its people from damnation and heathenism, they were attempting to force a distorted version of *ancient teachings* on a people who, for all intents and purposes, were already living closer to the source of those *teachings* than the modern Church. It is doubly ironic that Christians and the Japanese shintō-state thus attempted to exorcise each other, since both views, in essence, share the value of openly accepting your neighbor.

Another interesting value shared was that of *exorcism*. In Japan these acts were performed by *Samurai*, the famous military nobility, with their sword. Using their weapon and a special prayer the evil demon was expelled by cutting the air above the head. The process is called *katana-kagi* and is meant to sever the connection of the unclean spirit to the body. In shintō this is called *harae*, or ritual purification, and it shared the same meaning thousands of miles away from Greece, Rome, Egypt, etc., in that of exorcising disease from within or without the body.

Twelfth Iteration

The fact that demons are typically described and depicted as *therianthropic* is perhaps more evidence that their physical manifestations are also, possibly, the result of visions had in altered states of consciousness. Or, like the werewolf, these demons represent unstable emotions and passions expressed through animalistic behaviors. These excesses, including *thought* and *emotion*, then birth creatures on the lower planes of the astral world which have the power to cause havoc. Therianthropic creatures, Egyptian Gods most famously, represent the merger of man and nature. They are proof of a multitude of conflicting forces operating within. *"It was for such reasons,"* writes Jordan Peterson in <u>Beyond Order</u>, *"that archaic people found it easy to believe that the human soul was haunted by ghosts - possessed by ancestral spirits, demons, and gods - none of whom necessarily had the best interests of the person at heart."* These *forces* have been further conceptualized by psychology as *"impulses, emotions, or motivational states - or as complexes, which act like partial personalities united within the person by memory but not by intent"* – see the werewolf. Carl Jung points out something similar: *"Whatever names he may give to these creative powers and potentialities within him, their actuality remains unchanged. No one can stop a religious-minded person from calling them gods or daemons, or simply 'God,' for we know from experience that they act just like that. If certain people use the word 'matter' in this connection, believing that they have said something, we must remind them that they have merely replaced an X by a Y and are no further forward than before."* In simple terms, these forces are the *demons in your head* or the *angel and devil* debating on your shoulders. The game Pac Man is representative of this, too, as the television show *Black Mirror* references: PAC is the Program and Control Man, stuck in a maze of consumption and pursued by ghosts/demons that are probably just in his own head. Even if he escapes the maze from one side, he reappears back on the other. It is a constant struggle to exorcise demons.

Thirteenth Iteration

The Bible is filled with exorcisms, as are many other religious and philosophical texts. As Gerald A. Larue writes in his book, The Supernatural, the Occult, and the Bible:

> *"David's use of music therapy might be classified as a form of exorcism in that it relived Saul of the evil spirit that possessed him. The action of the high priest on the Day of Atonement when the sins of the nation were transferred to a goat by the laying on of hands might also be recognized as a form of exorcism.... It is probable that in Israel, as in Babylonia, there were itinerant exorcists who expelled demons by using the name of one god or another. In Israel, exorcism would be performed in the name of Yahweh."*

Many people today simply use the English pronunciation of Jesus to expel negative energy or superficial demons, even without Biblical references to his ability to do the same. This is *faith* and the *power of belief*. In the book of Matthew, Jesus can use both his "word" and the "Spirit of God" to do away with devils:

Matthew 8:16

"When the even was come, they brought unto him many that were possessed with devils: and he cast out the spirits with his word, and healed all that were sick..."

Matthew 12:28

"But if I cast out devils by the Spirit of God, then the kingdom of God is come unto you."

~ PART IV ~

Magic in Sacred Scriptures

JESUS AS A MAGICIAN

First Iteration

The Bible is filled with *magic* in a variety of forms. Adherents to a strictly literal, and absolutely dogmatic interpretation of the text argue a caveat, though, that what would be defined as *magic* elsewhere is merely the *hand of God* at work here. These *miracles* are set aside from both the unnatural productions of *magic* as much as they are from works of *alchemy*.

First, we must address some of wondrous works found throughout the Bible and see how they compared to the otherwise vague definition of *magic*.

Second, we will look at how Jesus was viewed in his own time and after, as either a *sorcerer* or the true *son of God* who worked miracles.

Jesus performs his miraculous *seven signs* in the book of John, signifying his divinity, or connection thereto. His miracles include turning water into wine, healing a royal official's son, healing a paralytic, the dividing of fish and bread among 5,000 persons, walking on water, healing the blind, and raising the dead. Each of these stories are preserved below for easy reference, most almost entirely in full length.

~

Jesus Changes Water Into Wine (John 2:7-11)

"Jesus said to the servants, 'Fill the jars with water'; so they filled them to the brim. Then he told them, 'Now draw some out and take it to the master of the banquet.' They did so, and the master of the banquet tasted the water that had been turned into wine. He did not realize where it had come from, though the servants who had drawn the water knew. Then he called the bridegroom aside and said, 'Everyone brings out the choice wine first and then the cheaper wine after the guests have had too much to drink; but you have saved the best till now.' What Jesus did here in Cana of Galilee was the first of the signs."

Jesus Heals an Official's Son (John 4:46-54)

"Once more he visited Cana in Galilee, where he had turned the water into wine. And there was a certain royal official whose son lay sick at Capernaum. When this man heard that Jesus had arrived in Galilee from Judea, he went to him and begged him to come and heal his son, who was close to death. 'Unless you people see signs and wonders,' Jesus told him, 'you will never believe.' The royal official said, 'Sir, come down before my child dies.' 'Go,' Jesus replied, 'your son will live.' The man took Jesus at his word and departed. While he was still on the way, his servants met him with the news that his boy was living. When he inquired as to the time when his son got better, they said to him, 'Yesterday, at one in the afternoon, the fever left him.' Then the father realized that this was the exact time at which Jesus had said to him, 'Your son will live.' So he and his whole household believed. This was the second sign Jesus performed after coming from Judea to Galilee."

The Healing at the Pool (John 5:1-15)

"Some time later, Jesus went up to Jerusalem for one of the Jewish festivals. Now there is in Jerusalem near the Sheep Gate a pool, which in Aramaic is called Bethesda and which is surrounded by five covered colonnades. Here a great number of disabled people used to lie – the blind, the lame, the paralyzed. One who was there had been an invalid for thirty-eight years. When Jesus saw him lying there and learned that he had been in this condition for a long time, he asked him, 'Do you want to get well?' 'Sir,' the invalid replied, 'I have no one to help me into the pool when the water is stirred. While I am trying to get in, someone else goes down ahead of me.' Then Jesus said to him, 'Get up! Pick up your mat and walk.'

"At once the man was cured; he picked up his mat and walked. The day on which this took place was a Sabbath, and so the Jewish leaders said to the man who had been healed, 'It is the Sabbath; the law forbids you to carry your mat.' But he replied, 'The man who made me well said to me, 'Pick up your mat and walk.' So they asked him, 'Who is this fellow who told you to pick it up and walk?' The man who was healed had no idea who it was, for Jesus had slipped away into the crowd that was there. Later Jesus found him at the temple and said to him, 'See, you are well again. Stop sinning or something worse may happen to you.' The man went away and told the Jewish leaders that it was Jesus who had made him well."

Jesus Feeds the Five Thousand (John 6:5-14)

"When Jesus looked up and saw a great crowd coming toward him, he said to Philip, 'Where shall we buy bread for these people to eat?' He asked this only to test him, for he already had in mind what he was going to do. Philip answered him, 'It would take more than half a year's wages to buy enough bread for each one to have a bite!' Another of his disciples, Andrew, Simon Peter's brother, spoke up, 'Here is a boy with five small barley loaves and two small fish, but how far will they go among so many?' Jesus said, 'Have the people sit down.' There was plenty of grass in that place, and they sat down (about five thousand men were there). Jesus then took the loaves, gave thanks, and distributed to those who were seated as much as they wanted. He did the same with the fish. When they had all had enough to eat, he said to his disciples, 'Gather the pieces that are left over. Let nothing be wasted.' So they gathered them and filled twelve baskets with the pieces of the five barley loaves left over by those who had eaten. After the people saw the sign Jesus performed, they began to say, 'Surely this is the Prophet who is to come into the world.'"

Jesus Walks on the Water (John 6:16-24)

"When evening came, his disciples went down to the lake, where they got into a boat and set off across the lake for Capernaum. By now it was dark, and Jesus had not yet joined them. A strong wind was blowing and the waters grew rough. When they had rowed about three or four miles, they saw Jesus approaching the boat, walking on the water; and they were frightened. But he said to them, 'It is I; don't be afraid.' Then they were willing to take him into the boat, and immediately the boat reached the shore where they were heading.

"The next day the crowd that had stayed on the opposite shore of the lake realized that only one boat had been there, and that Jesus had not entered it with his disciples, but that they had gone away alone. Then some boats from Tiberias landed near the place where the people had eaten the bread after the Lord had given thanks. Once the crowd realized that neither Jesus nor his disciples were there, they got into the boats and went to Capernaum in search of Jesus."

Jesus Heals a Man Born Blind (John 9:1-7)

"As he went along, he saw a man blind from birth. His disciples asked him, 'Rabbi, who sinned, this man or his parents, that he was born blind?' 'Neither this man nor his parents sinned,' said Jesus, 'but this happened so that the works of God might be displayed in him. As long as it is day, we must do the works of him who sent me. Night is coming, when no one can work. 5 While I am in the world, I am the light of the world.' After saying this, he spit on the ground, made some mud with the saliva, and put it on the man's eyes. 'Go,' he told him, 'wash in the Pool of Siloam' (this word means 'Sent'). So the man went and washed, and came home seeing."

The Death of Lazarus (John 11:41-44)

"So they took away the stone. Then Jesus looked up and said, 'Father, I thank you that you have heard me. I knew that you always hear me, but I said this for the benefit of the people standing here, that they may believe that you sent me.' When he had said this, Jesus called in a loud voice, 'Lazarus, come out!' The dead man came out, his hands and feet wrapped with strips of linen, and a cloth around his face. Jesus said to them, Take off the grave clothes and let him go.'"

Second Iteration

All of these acts, if not allusions, can certainly be defined as acts of mystical power, i.e., *magic*. For it does not matter if the source is called *God* or the *Unknown*, we are dealing with the same otherworldly authority. So long as these acts were not performed with intent to harm or in the name of the *Infernal* they remain both *magic* and *miracle*. They may be classified as the latter strictly if it can be admitted that God is the *unseen force* working through nature and magician alike. The question of *intent* is associated with the *images* used by the magician, be them heavenly or infernal. As Reverend John Butler said about astrology, which was no doubt practiced by the Christians as it was the Jews and Muslims:

> *"And while I study thus I find that next unto Theology, nothing leads me more near unto the sight of God, than this sacred astrological study of the great works of nature."*

In other words, a practice condemned by science and religion alike today is nothing more than an observing technique of God's Creation, and of the works of nature mathematically manifest through square and compass of the Grand Architect.

It is only a connotation of *magic* and the dogma of institution which sees the word as unfit for Christendom in particular. However, if *magic* is not the appropriate word perhaps the *secret teachings* would suffice. The turning of water into wine, the *first of the signs*, is reference to rough ashlar being turned into smooth stone in masonry and the transformation of lead into gold in alchemy.

Dionysus and Bacchus were able to turn water into wine because it was the water, along with proper sunlight, which transforms the vine and produced *fruit*. Light penetrates our "eyes" and through proper fermination produces the fruit of enlightenment. Fermentation usually takes place in the dark, hence the seclusion of initiates in temples, pyramids, chambers, caves, etc., and the spiritual transformation that followed upon resurrection. These Greco-Roman deities are thus prototypes for Jesus Christ since they predate his birth by many hundreds of years. To be slightly more aggressive in our water-to-wine assertion: since alcohol was thought to contain *spirits* we can say that Jesus performed conjurations of the same.

Healing the sick and paralytic is reference to unmatched knowledge in the fields of medicine and perhaps *pharmaka*, the preparation of biological ingredients into medicine. Healing the blind is likewise a similar reference to the latter, but from the sick to the blind there is also reference to metaphoric conditions wherein the patient is blinded to *reality* or *truth*, even made sick by the pollution of corrupt *ideas*. When we read that Jesus *walked on water* (Matthew 14:29-31) the direct correlation to the healing of the sick and blind, who suffer from delusions about reality, becomes clear:

> *"Then Peter got down out of the boat, walked on the water and came toward Jesus. But when he saw the wind, he was afraid and, beginning to sink, cried out, 'Lord, save me!' Immediately Jesus reached out his hand and caught him. 'You of little faith,' he said, 'why did you doubt?'"*

The water here is illusion, or *maya*, and when Peter becomes afraid, he sinks into the illusion of *matter* just as the archetypical man is crucified on the *cross of matter* with *nails of illusion*. Overcoming fear, particularly that of death, was the central goal of the *mystery schools* of which Jesus was no doubt an initiate. Joseph Campbell adds that the essence of this story and of the miracle of walking on water *"is that as the spirit blows over the waters, so anyone who has entirely spiritualized himself can do the same."* The ocean is emotion and those able to calm that emotion, the disciples representing humanity in the boat, are worthy of saving. For truth, wisdom, and peace calm the ocean just as beauty calms the beast. Jesus and Peter are not the only two men to have walked on water outside of ancient Indian tradition. Krishna is carried across water as a baby just as Moses is placed in a basket on the Nile in identical fashion to the Akkadian King Sargon. The basket is the coffin of Osiris and the Ark of Noah. In the Druidic Mysteries an initiate would be placed in a small boat with no oars and floated out on a body of water. A Buddhist sage named Bodhidharma is also said to have walked across the China Sea.

Manly Hall's excellent work <u>The Mystical Christ</u> explains how these "miracles" are evidence of the power one has over their internal self to transform the personality:

> *"The miracles bear witness to the power of the internal over its own personality and finally become the revelation to all men. The man of soul transforms all things into the likeness of himself and into the fulfillment of his own substance by the miracle of love. By the God-power within him, man quells the tempest, heals the sick, opens the eyes of the blind, casts out evil spirits, and conquers death."*

The casting out of demons is not one of the *seven signs* performed by Jesus through the *hand of God*, but it is, as Hall says above, evidence of man's ability to transform by the *miracle of love* - the opposite of evil (evol). At the basis of *love* is also a requirement for *faith*, which Peter lost, for *doubt* and *distrust* cannot exist alongside God. They are works of *evil* and the *infernal*. The same story is told in the myth of Psyche and Cupid, that love cannot dwell where there is suspicion. In Matthew 8:28-34 we can read the story of how Jesus sent demons into pigs and then drowned them – if Jesus were not there to help Peter he would have drowned too:

> "And when He came to the other side into the country of the Gadarenes, two demon-possessed men confronted Him as they were coming out of the tombs. They were so extremely violent that no one could pass by that way. And they cried out, saying, 'What business do You have with us, Son of God? Have You come here to torment us before the time?'

> "Now there was a herd of many pigs feeding at a distance from them. And the demons begged Him, saying, 'If You are going to cast us out, send us into the herd of pigs. 'And He said to them, 'Go!' And they came out and went into the pigs; and behold, the whole herd rushed down the steep bank into the sea and drowned in the waters. And the herdsmen ran away, and went to the city and reported everything, including what had happened to the demon-possessed men. And behold, the whole city came out to meet Jesus; and when they saw Him, they pleaded with Him to leave their region."

Third Iteration

While the feeding of 5,000 has been analyzed as a mathematical metaphor by David Fidler in <u>Jesus Christ Sun of God</u>, the raising of Lazarus from the dead is another clear indication of a powerful *mystery* tradition. When initiates had spent three days in the temples and pyramids of ancient Egypt, they would be reborn through a process of *living resurrection* by being offered the hand of an Egyptian hierophant speaking the words *COME FORTH*.

Lazarus was also dead, albeit symbolically, for three days (raised on the fourth) in the tomb of materiality - the sacred maternal womb represented by the pyramid, cave, mountain, or mound - before being symbolically resurrected by the words "come out" or "come forth." Hence the reason that the classical *Egyptian Book of the Dead* originally goes by the name *Coming Forth By Day*.

We can also read confirmation of this in the story of Jonah and the Whale. When Jonah flees from the Lord he is swallowed up like Peter in the belly of the great fish, which after *"three days and three nights"* was commanded by the Lord to vomit *"Jonah onto dry land."* Cornelius Agrippa writes: *"Jonah was three days in the whale's belly; and so many was Christ in the grave."* Hall likewise informs us that the raising of the dead is a "mystical tradition" preserved by many secret schools within the original Christian communities:

> *"There is a mystical tradition that the raising of Lazarus described symbolically the establishment of a secret sect or school within the Christina communion. The religious mysteries of antiquity included in certain of their rituals a scene in which the candidates for initiation passed through a mystical death and resurrection. This ceremony implied a departure from worldliness and a rebirth in light and truth."*

Leading up to the resurrection of Lazarus we find Nicodemus in John 3:4-6 asking Jesus how someone could be born again:

> *"How can someone be born when they are old?' Nicodemus asked. 'Surely they cannot enter a second time into their mother's womb to be born!' Jesus answered, 'Very truly I tell you, no one can enter the kingdom of God unless they are born of water and the Spirit. Flesh gives birth to flesh, but the Spirit gives birth to spirit. You should not be surprised at my saying, 'You must be born again.'"*

For no person is born a second time by flesh! They are reborn in spirit, purified by truth and filled with wisdom.

He who possesses *truth* and *wisdom* will surely *live forever*, even when facing death, whereas those who may seem to live, if they do not possess truth and wisdom, are surely already dead. As Hall writes, *"Wisdom bestows immortality upon internal consciousness."*

The resurrection of Lazarus is of great importance in the works of Jesus, though other of his lesser resurrection miracles are just as significant. The motif of *"Lazarus, come out"* or *"Lazarus, come forth"* is also found in these other accounts too. In Luke 7 Jesus resurrects a man prepared for burial in the city of Nain. Upon touching the coffin, he says in verse 14, *"Young man, I say to you, arise."* In Luke 8 he restores to life the sick and dying daughter of a man named Jairus, a powerful member of the synagogue. When confronted with mourning of her death Jesus says in verse 52 that *"She is not dead but asleep."* When bringing the girl, who had only just died, back to life Jesus says, *"Little girl, arise."*

Jesus Raises a Dead Girl (Luke 8:40-42 & 54-56)

"So it was, when Jesus returned, that the multitude welcomed Him, for they were all waiting for Him. And behold, there came a man named Jairus, and he was a ruler of the synagogue. And he fell down at Jesus' feet and begged Him to come to his house, for he had an only daughter about twelve years of age, and she was dying."

"But He put them all outside, took her by the hand and called, saying, 'Little girl, arise.' Then her spirit returned, and she arose immediately. And He commanded that she be given something to eat. And her parents were astonished, but He charged them to tell no one what had happened."

Jesus Raises the Son of the Widow of Nain (Luke 7:11-15)

"Now it happened, the day after, that He went into a city called Nain; and many of His disciples went with Him, and a large crowd. And when He came near the gate of the city, behold, a dead man was being carried out, the only son of his mother; and she was a widow. And a large crowd from the city was with her. When the Lord saw her, He had compassion on her and said to her, 'Do not weep.' Then He came and touched the open coffin, and those who carried him stood still. And He said, 'Young man, I say to you, arise.' So he who was dead sat up and began to speak. And He presented him to his mother."

The "son of the widow" is without doubt a reference to Egyptian adepts who were resurrected as *Sons of the Widow*, i.e., Isis, *Mother of the Mysteries*, who is mourning over her husband Osiris. In these three above stories we find that Jesus can resurrect a girl who had just died, a man prepared for burial, and a man who had been dead for several days.

Fourth Iteration

Of serious note here is also Jesus and his relationship with both India, during his 'missing years', and the Hindu *Rishis*, who were, through intense austerities (*tapas*), meditation, and yoga believed to have obtained incredible powers that in Christendom are attributed solely to Jesus Christ. These include the ability to *walk on water*, *heal the sick*, and *restore the dead to life* like Lazarus. Their *tapas* include adhering to a strict diet, heavy introspection in solitude, and meditation in sacred locations. John E. Mitchiner details in his book <u>Traditions of the Seven Rishis</u> how sages *"performed tapas in order to escape death."* This is precisely the purpose of the *mystery* traditions around the world, from those made famous from Eleusis and Egypt to the Americas and Japan. The goal was to overcome the animal self, commune with the heavenly and infernal, and overcome the fear and uncertainty of death. Nowhere is this better documented than in indigenous shamanism. The title of *Seven Sages* was also known in Greece. There are many theories about the conspiracy to kill Jesus with a few suggesting that he became too great a threat to powerful *secret societies* highly displeased with his teaching of their *secrets* to the uninitiated. But for Jesus this was the point; overcoming the *animal self* and our *fear of death*, among other things, were not processes only for the wealthy, connected, or political and royal classes. Jesus was clearly a threat to the Roman establishment at the very least. As Ramsay MacMullen wrote about magicians and astrologers, etc., categories where we could easily group Jesus, they were *"enemies of the Roman order."* In Mark 3:2-26 we read that early on Jesus was accused of terrible things, namely that he was a sorcerer communing with demons like Beelzebub or the Canaanite god Baal: *"Then Jesus entered a house, and again a crowd gathered, so that he and his disciples were not even able to eat. When his family heard about this, they went to take charge of him, for they said, 'He is out of his mind.' And the teachers of the law who came down from*

Jerusalem said, 'He is possessed by Beelzebul! By the prince of demons he is driving out demons.' So Jesus called them over to him and began to speak to them in parables: 'How can Satan drive out Satan? If a kingdom is divided against itself, that kingdom cannot stand. If a house is divided against itself, that house cannot stand. And if Satan opposes himself and is divided, he cannot stand; his end has come'."

Even the Quran documents the accusations of sorcery against Jesus. In the book of *Formations* 61:6 we read:

> "And call to mind when Jesus, son of Mary, said: 'O Children of Israel, I am Allah's Messenger to you, I verify the Torah which has come before me, and I give you the glad tiding of a Messenger who shall come after me, his name being Ahmad." Yet when he came to them with Clear Signs they said: 'This is sheer trickery.'"

Jews and pagans accused Jesus of *sorcery*, which was never defined, but instead affirmed by Church fathers, who saw his power as emanating from a divine source, as *miracle*. Some Christians, however, such as Nestorius, Bishop of Constantinople (428-431 A.D.), saw any comparison between Jesus and God as therefore equating Mary to the Mother Goddess of ancient nature religions.

Stephen D. Ricks writes in an essay for <u>Ancient Magic and Ritual Power</u> that *"whether Jesus was viewed as a magician or not was almost solely dependent upon whiter he was seen as an 'insider' or an 'outsider'."* This is the still the case today, and although *magic* is not illegal it is certainly utterly inundated with fraud and ignorance.

The *miracle* is not so much witnessed by a community anymore, as it is now confined to the private experiences and thoughts of an individual seeking *signs* that God is present. Miracles today actually seem to have replaced the practice of *magic* as a social subversion. In some parts of the world, particularly governments hostile to religion or spirituality, *miracles* have become the new *magic* in how they are viewed by the dominate authority. In David Aune's essay, 'Magic in Early Christianity', he defines *magic* in antiquity as *"that form of religious deviance whereby individual or social goals are sought by means alternate to those normally sanctioned by the dominant religious institution."* But now it is fraudulent *magic,* which is sanctioned by the dominate institutions, to a degree, while *miracles* are cursed and mocked. All the while scholars, religious institutions, and faithful followers of numerous religions continue to debate and argue over whether their own prophets are *magicians* or *charlatans*.

But as with Jesus Christ most of them are forever neophytes seeking admission into the gates of the *Kingdom of Heaven*. To follow in their footsteps means that we take up the mantle of spiritual work for ourselves. If God is solar radiation and light, and Jesus is his Son, we are all therefore *little sons* of the Father. As *light* we represent like droplets in an ocean individual solar rays when we allow Jesus to enter our hearts - the domain of the sun in our bodies. We therefore become *suns of God*, rather than *sons* or *daughters* of man and woman.

The solar *rays* of the sun give the *Father* an ability to *raise* crops from the ground and to *raise* the dead back to life like Lazarus. Such power allows the sun to *raise* man out of the abyss and death and back into the true light of the *mysteries*. This is what is meant by being *born again*. The process of initiation into the mystical tradition involves a *resurrection* of the internal self within a physical body-temple by which one then becomes a *Son of God*. These bringers of light are the wise teachers who, like the sun overcoming physical darkness, dispel ignorance in the world and save mankind.

Fifth Iteration

In his book <u>How to Understand Your Bible</u>, Hall explains what is meant by the incredible *teachings* and *miracles* of Jesus Christ:

Preach the Gospel: *"to teach or inform those who were prepared to receive instruction."*

Heal the Sick: *"to remedy not merely the infirmities of the flesh, but those of ignorance, fear, and superstition."*

Raise the Dead: *"to recover souls from materiality by the word of Truth."*

Cast out Demons: *"to modify the passions, emotions, and appetites"* of the individual.

Cleanse the Lepers: *"to purify those who were unclean of thought and deed."*

MAGIC & MIRACLE
IN THE BIBLE

First Iteration

Throughout history, and particularly in the Bible, there is little different between *magic* and *miracle*. Stephen D. Ricks points out in an essay titled 'The Magician as Outsider in the Hebrew Bible and the New Testament', how *"both priest and magician thought their spells were more effective when pronounced in one place and at one time rather than another; both turned to the east to say them; and both thought that mere words could possess a magic virtue."*

Virtually every element of Catholicism is steeped in mysticism, secrecy, symbolism, and magic. As John Calvin wrote about Roman Catholics, they like to *"pretend there is a magical force in the sacraments, independent of efficacious faith."* From prayer and garb to the offering of incense and the practice of communion there is an underlying and powerful *magical* element at work. For the outside observer the Catholic Mass in particular it is nothing more than a ritual ripe with incantations, necromancy, human sacrifice, cannibalism, and blood drinking.

But even the Bible preserves *necromancy* as a practice sought beyond the assistance of what God would provide to King Saul. Necromancy comes from Greek for "corpse divination." It has two forms; one by evocation of prayer, perfumes, and magical objects, and the other by blood, curses, and sacrilege. Francis Barrett says that the two kinds of necromancy include, *"raising the carcasses, which is not done without blood,"* and sciomancy, *"in which the calling up of the shadow only suffices."* Of this practice all is worked by the carcasses of the once alive and their members, i.e., organs, blood; for in these are qualities friendly to spirits. Souls may love their bodies even after death, much like those souls having left their bodies by violence may not even be aware of their own death. Barrett explains further of necromancy:

> *"Necromancy has its name because it works on the bodies of the dead, and gives answers by the ghosts and apparitions of the dead, and subterraneous spirits, alluring them into the carcasses of the*

dead by certain hellish charms, and infernal invocations, and by deadly sacrifices and wicked oblations."

In his essay about King Saul, 'The 'Witch of En-dor, 1 Samuel 28, and Ancient Near Eastern Necromancy', Brian B. Schmidt points out the following:

> *"The affinities that 1 Samuel 28:3-25 shares with the mid-first millennium divination and (in particular) necromantic traditions from Mesopotamia are remarkable. These include the role of divination in dictating military strategy and in producing the outcome of royal engagement, necromancy's role in determining the fate of the royal dynasty, and the assistance of the gods in the retrieval of a ghost."*

In 1 Samuel 28:4-6 we find King Saul seeking these things first from God and then from a necromancer or witch in order to see what the future of battle holds:

> *"The Philistines assembled and came and set up camp at Shunem, while Saul gathered all Israel and set up camp at Gilboa. When Saul saw the Philistine army, he was afraid; terror filled his heart. He inquired of the Lord, but the Lord did not answer him by dreams or Urim or prophets."*

Saul then turns to the witch in verse 7-8:

> *"Saul then said to his attendants, 'Find me a woman who is a medium, so I may go and inquire of her.' 'There is one in Endor,' they said. So Saul disguised himself, putting on other clothes, and at night he and two men went to the woman. 'Consult a spirit for me,' he said, 'and bring up for me the one I name.'"*

King Saul is later informed by Samuel in verse 17 that his Kingdom has come to an end due to his treachery:

> *"The Lord has done what he predicted through me. The Lord has torn the kingdom out of your hands and given it to one of your neighbors – to David."*

It is well known, however, that even the Egyptians, famous for all manner of magic, never called upon the dead in this manner. Brian B. Schmidt explains how the Egyptians never called on the dead to *"dispense special knowledge concerning the fate of the living."* Instead, the deceased were merely, and only, petitioned to *"cease haunting the living"* or for the purpose of taking *"legal proceedings against a malevolent ghost, or to dispute knowledge about the underworld."*

Although King Saul is punished in 1 Samuel 28:19-20, as per the words of Samuel, we still witness the attempt at divining the future present in the Bible:

> *"'The Lord will deliver both Israel and you into the hands of the Philistines, and tomorrow you and your sons will be with me. The Lord will also give the army of Israel into the hands of the Philistines.' Immediately Saul fell full length on the ground, filled with fear because of Samuel's words. His strength was gone, for he had eaten nothing all that day and all that night.'"*

For some reason King Saul has committed blasphemous acts and treason against God here, but otherwise the use of oracles like Lots, Urim and Thummim (*light* and *perfection*), and the Ephod (an object connected with oracular practices) are perfectly acceptable in the Bible. Just as Stephen D. Ricks writes of *"whether Jesus was viewed as a magician or not,"* we can also factually state that divination and even dream interpretations are perfectly legal and permitted so long as one is an "insider" with God.

Other Biblical characters like Samuel were possessed with the ability to engage in what we today would call supernatural acts, or the ability to *predict the future*. All prophets fall into this category. We may therefore call these men seers or clairvoyants. Whether their predictions were a result of communicating with God, or are considered pure intuition, they are nonetheless magical (supernatural – beyond the natural world) in essence.

Some will certainly say that the opposite of a *miracle* is not only *magic* but the blackest sort of *sorcery*. But these exact same types of practices are carried out by priest and magician alike, and some prophets too. Simply saying that "the Bible is the truth" is no longer, if it ever were, a satisfactory explanation for the issue of *magic*.

Second Iteration

In Daniel 2:1-49 we read about the interpretation of King Nebuchadnezzar's dreams. Verses 1-2 relate:

> *"In the second year of his reign, Nebuchadnezzar had dreams; his mind was troubled and he could not sleep. So the king summoned the magicians, enchanters, sorcerers and astrologers to tell him what he had dreamed. When they came in and stood before the king."*

Unable to satisfy his demands, the King ordered his wise men to be put to death. In verse 19 we learn that *"the mystery was revealed to Daniel in a vision of the night"* and that he was soon brought before Nebuchadnezzar. Verse 26-28 relate the following:

> *" 'The king declared to Daniel, whose name was Belteshazzar, 'Are you able to make known to me the dream that I have seen and its interpretation?' Daniel answered the king and said, 'No wise men, enchanters, magicians, or astrologers can show to the king the mystery that the king has asked, but here is a God in heaven who reveals mysteries, and he has made known to King Nebuchadnezzar what will be in the latter days."*

The essence of this story is that, once again, what some do is a *miracle* and what others do is *magic*. For wise men, enchanters, magicians, and astrologers, etc., cannot correctly interpret the King's dreams, but Daniel is able to do so as a result of a *miracle* or *divine vision* received from God.

In Genesis 40:1-18 there is a story of how Joseph was able to correctly interpret the dreams of a cupbearer and a baker, both of which had been imprisoned. Verses 1-8 read:

> *"Some time later, the cupbearer and the baker of the king of Egypt offended their master, the king of Egypt. Pharaoh was angry with his two officials, the chief cupbearer and the chief baker, and put them in custody in the house of the captain of the guard, in the same prison where Joseph was confined. The captain of the guard assigned them to Joseph, and he attended them.*

"After they had been in custody for some time, each of the two men – the cupbearer and the baker of the king of Egypt, who were being held in prison – had a dream the same night, and each dream had a meaning of its own.

"When Joseph came to them the next morning, he saw that they were dejected. So he asked Pharaoh's officials who were in custody with him in his master's house, 'Why do you look so sad today?' 'We both had dreams,' they answered, 'but there is no one to interpret them.' Then Joseph said to them, 'Do not interpretations belong to God? Tell me your dreams.'"

In verses 9-18 Joseph interprets both of their dreams, correctly assessing that the cupbearer would be lifted up from prison and restored to his original position under Pharaoh while the baker would be killed. It makes little sense to suggest that if someone were to correctly interpret a dream without declaration of the assistance of God that they were a charlatan. In Genesis 41:15-16 Joseph is then brought before Pharaoh:

"Pharaoh said to Joseph, 'I had a dream, and no one can interpret it. But I have heard it said of you that when you hear a dream you can interpret it.' 'I cannot do it," Joseph replied to Pharaoh, 'but God will give Pharaoh the answer he desires.'"

Third Iteration

One of the most famous and infamous cases of magic in the Bible comes from the book of Exodus wherein we read about Moses, Aaron, and the court magicians of Pharaoh. Exodus 7:1-5 tells the story of God's threats upon Egypt:

"Then the Lord said to Moses, 'See, I have made you like God to Pharaoh, and your brother Aaron will be your prophet. You are to say everything I command you, and your brother Aaron is to tell Pharaoh to let the Israelites go out of his country. But I will harden Pharaoh's heart, and though I multiply my signs and wonders in Egypt, he will not listen to you. Then I will lay my hand on Egypt and with mighty acts of judgment I will bring out my divisions, my people the Israelites. And the Egyptians will know *that I am the Lord when I stretch out my hand against Egypt and bring the Israelites out of it.'"*

In Exodus 7:6-13 we read about the *miracles* performed, such as the turning of Aaron's staff into a snake:

"Moses and Aaron did just as the Lord commanded them. Moses was eighty years old and Aaron eighty-three when they spoke to Pharaoh. The Lord said to Moses and Aaron, 'When Pharaoh says to you, 'Perform a miracle,' then say to Aaron, 'Take your staff and throw it down before Pharaoh,' and it will become a snake.'

"So Moses and Aaron went to Pharaoh and did just as the Lord commanded. Aaron threw his staff down in front of Pharaoh and his officials, and it became a snake. Pharaoh then summoned wise men and sorcerers, and the Egyptian magicians also did the same things by their secret arts: Each one threw down his staff and it became a snake. But Aaron's staff swallowed up their staffs. Yet Pharaoh's heart became hard and he would not listen to them, just as the Lord had said."

Another *magical miracle* is noted in 1 Kings 17:1 when Elijah tells Ahab about the coming drought:

"Now Elijah the Tishbite, from Tishbe in Gilead, said to Ahab, 'As the Lord, the God of Israel, lives, whom I serve, there will be neither dew nor rain in the next few years except at my word.'"

Fourth Iteration

Despite all these *sacred writings*, invariably and blindly called "the truth," which speak of necromancy (even accompanied by punishment), dream interpretation, magicians, and human sacrifice, we read in Deuteronomy 18:10-11 the following about all the same practices termed *magic* or *sorcery*:

"Let no one be found among you who sacrifices their son or daughter in the fire, who practices divination or sorcery, interprets omens, engages in witchcraft, or casts spells, or who is a medium or spiritist or who consults the dead."

We find a similar prescription in Leviticus 18:21 against offering children to Moloch, the Canaanite god of fertility:

"And thou shalt not let any of thy seed pass through the fire to Molech, neither shalt thou profane the name of thy God: I am the Lord."

However, in Genesis 22:1-12 we learn about how God tested Abraham by convincing him to offer up his son Isaac on a burning alter. The fact that an angel stopped the sacrificial testing is not penance for the commandment:

"Some time later God tested Abraham. He said to him, 'Abraham!' 'Here I am,' he replied. Then God said, 'Take your son, your only son, whom you love – Isaac – and go to the region of Moriah. Sacrifice him there as a burnt offering on a mountain I will show you.' Early the next morning Abraham got up and loaded his donkey. He took with him two of his servants and his son Isaac. When he had cut enough wood for the burnt offering, he set out for the place God had told him about. On the third day Abraham looked up and saw the place in the distance. He said to his servants, 'Stay here with the donkey while I and the boy go over there. We will worship and then we will come back to you. Abraham took the wood for the burnt offering and placed it on his son Isaac, and he himself carried the fire and the knife. As the two of them went on together, Isaac spoke up and said to his father Abraham, 'Father?' 'Yes, my son?' Abraham replied. 'The fire and wood are here,' Isaac said, 'but where is the lamb for the burnt offering?' Abraham answered, 'God himself will provide the lamb for the burnt offering, my son.' And the two of them went on together. When they reached the place God had told him about, Abraham built an altar there and arranged the wood on it. He bound his son Isaac and laid him on the altar, on top of the wood. Then he reached out his hand and took the knife to slay his son. But the angel of the Lord called out to him from heaven, 'Abraham! Abraham!' 'Here I am,' he replied. 'Do not lay a hand on the boy, he said. 'Do not do anything to him. Now I know that you fear God, because you have not withheld from me your son, your only son.'

The Bible is filled with astrologers, wizards, wise men, magi, magicians, sorcerers, and prophets. Stephen D. Ricks describes that these words are defined dependent upon whether you are an *insider or an outsider* of the dominant cultural, political, and social cult. He thus references the usage of these words in the bible, particularly in their relationship with the Israelites:

> *"...three-quarters of the occurrences of the words refer, explicitly or not, to non-Israelite practitioners or activities... The remaining quarter of the occurrences of the terms for magicians and magical practices refer to prohibited Israelite practices or to Israelites engaged in these forbidden practices... Even in those instances where there is no strongly negative value to magic, magicians, and related words, they refer either to non-Israelites or to Israelites in a non-Israelite setting."*

RABBINCAL SORCERY

First Iteration

The subject of *magic* and *miracle* in Jewish tradition is as equally debatable as it is the Christian tradition. It, of course, consists of the Jewish Torah of Law, the Talmud, the Prophets, and much more, including the persecution of Jesus as a dangerous *sorcerer*. Here we are attempting to separate the *Judeo* from the *Christian* or *Roman Catholic* tradition.

According to the *Babylonian Talmud*, any judge on the Sanhedrin, the assembly of council members who became the *rabbis* after the destruction of the Second Temple, will not be allowed a seat *"unless they are wise men, men of vision, men of stature, elders, masters of magic, and knowledgeable in seventy language."* Jonathan Seidel writes in the essay, 'Charming Criminals: Classification of Magic in the Babylonian Talmud' how:

> *"It is in the Second Temple period, especially in the wake of the rhetoric and monotheism and diatribes against paganism, that sorcery and magic become part of the constellation of 'foreign' or polluting influences"* [against the ancient Land of Israel].

Brian B. Schmidt explains that *"crucial to deuteronomistic ideology was the general premise that the land and its blessings were dependent upon compete separation from foreign religious practice."* This is partly why some actions are classified as *magic* and others as *miracles*. The incorporation of necromancy, divination, and the like, into the various texts of *sacred scriptures* therefore *"epitomized both Israel's prostitution and pollution"* in these regards. In the Rabbinic tradition *magic* and *miracle* are separated by a very uncertain or faint line. In the *Mishnah Sanhedrin 7* we learn that *magic* is defined as an act of *sorcery*, whatever that may be, but a simple illusionist is never liable or deserving of the same punishment afforded the former:

> *"One who performs a real act of sorcery is liable, but not one who deceives the eyes, making it appear as though he is performing sorcery, as that is not considered sorcery... The one who performs*

a real act of sorcery is liable, and the one who deceives the eyes is exempt."

Seidel explains that to the rabbis the definition of *sorcery* varied but usually included "anti-social types" along with "sexual deviants, misleaders, and idolators." Once more we reference Stephen D. Rick's definition of *magic: "dependent upon whiter he was seen as an 'insider' or an 'outsider'."* For the rabbis saw Zoroastrian *magi* as malicious, but so too did the latter see the former as such, or as *Judaized magi.*

Second Iteration

Rabbis are famous for their seemingly *magical* ability to utilize linguistics to bring matter to life, as in the case of GOLEM. Seidel explains how rabbis *"may be able to animate anthropoids, as in the proto-type of the Golem myth,"* but says they lack the essence of the *"ultimate, divine magician."* In other words, they can manifest and distort, like *black magicians* in particular, but they cannot truly create life. Such an act of manifestation is arguably more diabolic than demonological works considering the latter are a polluted form of Creation, and the former are a pure abomination erected from God's Creation - and manifested through His Word.

In an essay titled 'Magical Piety in Ancient and Medieval Judaism', Michael D. Swartz also explains, as have Jewish historians, how:

> *"Rabbinic leadership in late antiquity cultivated practices that could conventionally be considered magical."*

Here we find the Jewish Virtual Library explaining in detail what a GOLEM consists of and where its essence arises:

> *"In Jewish tradition, the golem is most widely known as an artificial creature created by magic, often to serve its creator. Especially well known are the idols and images to which the ancients claimed to have given the power of speech. Among the Greeks and the Arabs these activities are sometimes connected with astrological speculations related to the possibility of 'drawing the spirituality of the stars' to lower beings... The Sefer Yezirah ('Book*

of Creation'), often referred to as a guide to magical usage by some Western European Jews in the Middle Ages, contains instructions on how to make a golem. Several rabbis, in their commentaries on *Sefer Yezirah* have produced different understandings of the directions on how to make a golem. Most versions include shaping the golem into a figure resembling a human being and using God's name to bring him to life, since God is the ultimate creator of life."

In the Biblical book of Psalm 139:16 we read likewise about the unmanifest creature:

"*Your eyes saw my unformed body; all the days ordained for me were written in your book before one of them came to be.*"

The word גלמי (*golem*) is used here and translated as "unformed body" or "shapeless man." Many believe, however, that the *golem* is nothing more than metaphor, something akin to Muhammed splitting the moon, i.e., Arab tribes. But it is highly likely that the golem was brought to life in some capacity since the history of rabbinical *magic* is not far removed from abominable *sorcery*.

In fact, as related in *Mishnah Sanhedrin 7*, rabbis were so aware of their traditional past that they actively sought to "*distance themselves and Jewry from what are clearly indigenous Jewish magical practices,*" says Seidel, particularly those described in the *Wisdom of Solomon 12:3-5*, which harshly lays out the barbaric history of that land and its varied people:

"*Those who lived long ago in your holy land, you hated their detestable practices, their works of sorcery and unholy rites, their merciless slaughter of children, and their sacrificial feasting on human flesh and blood.*"

Such terrible things relate to Levi's statement on the same:

"*The more difficult or horrible the operation, the greater is its power, because it acts more strongly on the imagination and confirms effort in the direct ratio of resistance.*"

Third Iteration

There is even greater irony present here since the Jews and pagans made terrible accusations against Jesus, and even Mary, when both groups have a barbaric past as bloody as any other. In fact, the Talmud of the Jews, who we know accused Jesus of a *sorcery* he learned in foreign lands, refers to Mary as a whore.

Sanhedrin 106b of *The William Davidson Talmud*, which certainly has been censored, state as fact:

> *"This woman was descended from princes and rulers, and was licentious with carpenters."*

Of Jesus himself, Shabbat 104b says as fact that Jesus learned magic from Egypt and that:

> *"They said to him: He was a fool, and you cannot cite proof from a fool."*

In tract 56b of the Talmud there is a conversation ongoing about the people who stand against Israel being called "chief." The verse says:

> *"Anyone who distresses [meitzer] Israel will become the chief."*

A man named Onkelos, who wanted to convert to Judaism, asked what the punishment was for these chiefs. In tract 57a we learn that, as with Jesus, anyone who "distresses Israel" will suffer the following:

> *"Every day his ashes are gathered, and they judge him, and they burn him, and they scatter him over the seven seas."*

The same tract goes on to say that *"Onkelos then went and raised Jesus the Nazarene from the grave through necromancy,"* a practice not uncommon for the Jews.

What Onkelos learns is that Jesus now finds the Jews to be "important" and that his punishment for doubting their authority is to forever burn in boiling feces. Anyone following in the footsteps of Jesus Christ is likewise to be punished with boiling excrement:

"Who is most important in that world where you are now? Jesus said to him: The Jewish people. Onkelos asked him: Should I then attach myself to them in this world? Jesus said to him: Their welfare you shall seek, their misfortune you shall not seek, for anyone who touches them is regarded as if he were touching the apple of his eye (see Zechariah 2:12).

"Onkelos said to him: What is the punishment of that man, a euphemism for Jesus himself, in the next world? Jesus said to him: He is punished with boiling excrement. As the Master said: Anyone who mocks the words of the Sages will be sentenced to boiling excrement. And this was his sin, as he mocked the words of the Sages."

In other words, Mary was a whore and Jesus was a wicked magician who is now burning in excrement. The Jews are *God's Chosen People* and all others are just *goyim*. This ideology, however, is by no means exclusive of traditional or magical Jewish history.

As Michael D. Swartz writes in an essay titled 'Magical Piety in Ancient and Medieval Judaism', the mystical *"Kabbalah was"* thus *"meant to be a stabilizing influence in relation to Jewish tradition."* Perhaps it was meant to make up for the perversity of the *Talmud* and similar beliefs of superiority.

Fourth Iteration

The *Kabbala* (also: Hermetic Qabalah) is a variety of mystical Jewish texts concerned with matters of the divine realms and how kabbalists may interact with those forces.

In the ancient Jewish mystical tradition, we find references to *magic* as being distinct from other wise men, which are said to have abused *natural laws*. Rabbis began to believe that *magic* was a violation of *divine law*, though such a "law" is irrelevant when viewing the godless cult of Zoroaster and its magicians – to the Jews.

Black Magic in this context is the action of destroying that which was decreed by God to be Created or killing that which is supposed to live. Is the action of creating a golem not an abomination of these divine laws? *Evil, Efil,* or *Evol* are indeed Live, Life, and Love inverted into chaos and disorder. As Seidel points out, *"while tools are taken into consideration in the legal discourse,"* of magic, *"it is intention that is weighed most significantly."*

Michael D. Swartz says we can identify three major themes in Jewish *magical* texts, which relate to typical *religious* behaviors. They include:

> *"(1) the emphasis on the power of the name of God; (2) the intermediacy of the angels in negotiating between divine providence and human needs; and (3) the application of divine names and ritual practices for the needs of specific individuals."*

All of these behaviors describe and define the numerous forms of *religious-magic,* be it found in the Bible, Torah, Quran, ad infinitum.

Fifth Iteration

As with magical traditions all over the world, the obtaining of great wisdom through memory spells and divine assistance was foundational in Jewish tradition too. There are memory spells in the *Greek Magical Papyri,* which is analyzed in the book <u>Ancient Magic and Ritual Power</u>, and as Swartz points out:

> *"...ritual memory practices where widespread in medieval Islamic and Jewish popular beliefs."*

As with *mystery* traditions all over the world, austerities were practiced by the rabbinical cult in order to bring about a clear channel of body and mind by which a practitioner could receive *divine inspiration* and *open the heart,* or *petihat lev* as the process was often referred. Swartz writes how:

> *"Dietary recommendations of the improvement of memory occur in the Babylonian Talmud. Jewish magical manuals also contain recipes and ritual formulae for improving memory... In one text, an Aramaic ritual text inserted into Ma'aseh Merkavah in one manuscript, the practitioner is to write magical names on a series of substances or objects and consume them, including a cup of wine, fig, and olive leaves, and an egg."*

These practices are called *rituals of ingestion*. Sacred names, words, and letters can be placed on food or in drink, then consumed to swallow the essence of what is desired. Magic of this type usually has the intent of acquiring better memory, but it can also be used for sexual endeavors too.

Rebecca Lesses explains in her essay 'The Adjuration of the Prince of the Presence', how the second most powerful angel, *Sar ha-Panim,* may be called on to *"come down to earth and reveal wisdom to human beings."* This can only be done through proper preparation, proper spoken words and names, fasting, abstinence for seven days prior, ritual bathing, and without conversations, particularly with women. The ritual is found in early Jewish texts known as Hekhalot literature, or Hebrew literature relating to visions of heavenly places. This ritual is very similar, and may be the source, for the invocation of one's Holy Guardian Angel in the western Hermetic Order of the Golden Dawn tradition.

Lesser magical assistants are found in the rabbinical "man of dreams," the angelic Maggid, and other supernatural assistants which provide wisdom and knowledge. In fact, in 1 Kings 3:11-13 we learn of how Solomon, for his reverence and desire for wisdom, was granted much more by the Lord:

> *"So God said to him, 'Since you have asked for this and not for long life or wealth for yourself, nor have asked for the death of your enemies but for discernment in administering justice, I will do what you have asked. I will give you a wise and discerning heart, so that there will never have been anyone like you, nor will there ever be. Moreover, I will give you what you have not asked for — both wealth and honor — so that in your lifetime you will have no equal among kings."*

Leda Jean Ciraolo's says in her essay 'Supernatural Assistants in the Greek Magical Papyri' that these supernatural assistants can be separated into four categories:

> *"…the divine, the celestial, the spiritual, and the material."*

In the *Greek Magical Papyri*, of which she discusses in length, she extracts various other names for these assistants, including 'mistress of the house', 'mighty angel', 'god of gods', 'mighty assistant', and 'aerial spirit'. They may also be associated with a star in the heavens or are *"disembodied former inhabitants of bodies."*

These "assistants" were invoked and conjured by the rabbis as much as they were by any other group. This fact further proves that the history of rabbinical magic and Jewish sorcery is, especially considering the Golem, Kabbala, and memory spells, a very real history filled with both *magic* and *miracle* of the *white* and *black* varieties.

Sixth Iteration

It is rarely debated that Moses was indeed a priest in Egypt. This fact would almost guarantee that he would have been learned in the subject of astrology, which only more recently became separated from astronomy. Astrology was without question cultivated and practiced in every ancient culture, including by the ancient Hindus, Chinese, and Jews. Manly Hall writes in <u>The Story of Astrology</u> of this fact:

> *"Much of the religious inspiration of Christendom is derived from the ancient Jews and it is not amiss to realize that astrology was greatly cultivated by the wisest among the ancient Israelites... even by Moses himself, who must need have been proficient in it because he was a priest of the Egyptians."*

He goes on to quote a Jewish Encyclopedia which states as fact:

> *"Abraham, the Chaldean, bore upon his breast a large astrological tablet on which the fate of every man might be read; for which reason - according to the Haggadist - all kings of the East and of the West congregated every morning before his door in order to seek advice."*

We can also assume, as was the case in Egypt, Greece, Rome, India, the Americas, and Asia, and probably everywhere else, that astrology was used to diagnose and even cure diseases, i.e., to *cast out demons.*

Seventh Iteration

In this final analysis of rabbinical sorcery, we will take a look at the sacred *Kabbala* in detail. Far from *sorcery,* the Kabbala is one of the most mystical religious and magical systems anywhere in the world. The Kabbalists divided the universe into *four worlds* and *four trees.* The *Sephirothic Tree* has 10 globes arranged in 3 vertical columns that are connected by 22 channels or paths. Each path is indicative of the 22 letters of the Hebrew alphabet by which through various combinations all laws of the universe are established. When combined the twenty-two paths and the ten globes, or first ten numbers, comprise the sacred number 32, relating to the *Paths of Wisdom,* and the 32nd degree of Freemasonry. According to Kabbalists, all of the keys to knowledge are contained in letters and numbers, and by a secret system of arrangement would reveal the *mysteries of creation.* At the very top is a globe separated by the two aspects of the white and black god, as depicted by the Great Kabbalistic Symbol of the *Zohar.* It is the *Horizon of Eternity* where the worlds of darkness and light were separated at Creation. The four central spheres are numbered one, six, nine and ten. The three spheres on the left are numbered three, five and eight. The three spheres on the right are numbered two, four and seven. The top sphere is *The One* and the first sphere to its right, number two, is assigned the position of *Fixed Stars.* The remaining eight are explained in the table below:

Name of God	Numeration	Intelligence
Eheia	Cether (essence of deity)	Metatron
Jod	Hochma (wisdom)	Raziel
Tetragrammaton	Elohim Prina (understanding)	Zaphkiel
El	Hesed (clemency)	Zadkiel
Elohim Gibor	Gebusach (judgment)	Camael
Eloha	Tiphereth (beauty)	Raphael
Adonai Sabaoth	Nezah (triumph)	Haniel
Elohim Sabaoth	Hod (honor)	Michael
Sadai	Jesod (foundation)	Gabriel
Adonai Melech	Malchuth (kingdom)	Metatron

Also described above are the ten names of God with their divine powers, His ten numerations called Sephiroth, which are instruments or agents exercising influence upon all creation, and the respective intelligences.

KETHER is the power of God, the initial emanation that produced all of existence. Within this Supreme Crown there were two principles, one active ad another passive, one male and another female. These are the twin forces of the universe. Below the uppermost sphere of the Tree of Life are an active force and a passive force.

The active force **HOKMAH** is positive and rests behind movement and growth. Hokmah is "wisdom." Its opposite is **BINAH**, the passive principle remaining stable and unchanging, and representing constant "understanding."

The mingling of these forces in the primordial waters brought forth life. Therefore, Hokmah is the Father of the universe and Binah is its Mother.

Beyond the three initial spheres are the trinity of father, mother, and child. Here we find **HESED**, a just and forgiving force, and its opposite, **GEBURAH**, also a symbol of authority, but a destructive force, too; a necessary evil. Hesed is "love" and Geburah is "power." Their equilibrium is **TIFARETH**, traditionally held as a sphere of the solar principle. Tifareth is the child of Hesed and Geburah, representing the urge to survive and the vital energy compelling life to continuously progress. Tifareth is "beauty."

David Conway explains in <u>Ritual Magic</u> that Tifareth attains adulthood and brings us to the next two spheres, or third triangle of the Tree. Here we find the male force of **NETSAH**, a force encouraging and urging survival. It urges a continuation of life despite hardships and represents passions, instincts, and primeval desires. Netsah is "triumph of endurance." Its opposite force here is the female principle known as **HOD**.

This power deals with mental activity while very little of its essence deals with sensory perceptions. Hod is "majesty." Creating equilibrium between the two previous spheres is **YESOD**, a force encompassing both of the previous in balance. Yesod is therefore "balance."

The final sphere at the root of the Tree is **MALKUTH**, the "kingdom." David Conway explains of this lower sphere:

> *"Its source, it is true, is lost in the light of the eternal, but we need not despair of reaching that light. We are a part of it. Indeed, being a composite symbol of the universe, the tree can be used to help us draw closer to the fountainhead. We can use it too as our guide to the astral world whenever we choose to leave the sphere of Malkuth; for by recollecting the pattern of the tree we may safely go ahead and explore the astral without any risk of losing our way."*

The Infinite or the All, as there are many names given to ALL POSSIBILITY, is named *Ain Soph* (ain = *nothing*) in the *Kabbala* – Hebrew for *tradition*. According to philosophical and occult tradition, as described in <u>The Tree of Life</u>, by Israel Regardie, this Infinite potential is not a *Spirit* or *Will*, but an *"underlying cause of both."* *Ain Soph* is not a force of matter but *"that which underlies them."* It is their fundamental *Cause*. Regardie provides one of the clearer and more precise descriptions of the *Life Tree* by breaking down the bulbs of the structure and explaining their relationship with numbers:

> *"It was the view of several Magicians that by the ideas expressed in number was Nature conceived in the bosom of infinite space. From these ideas or universals issued the primordial elements, the immense cycles of time, the cosmic bodies, and all the host of heavenly changes."*

It goes without critical analysis that zero represents the *Infinite Space* that gives way to various intelligences and branches of Sephiroth - the emanations are often referred to as spheres of light. The first emanations initiate manifestation and provides balance as the *Pillar of Beneficence*.

~

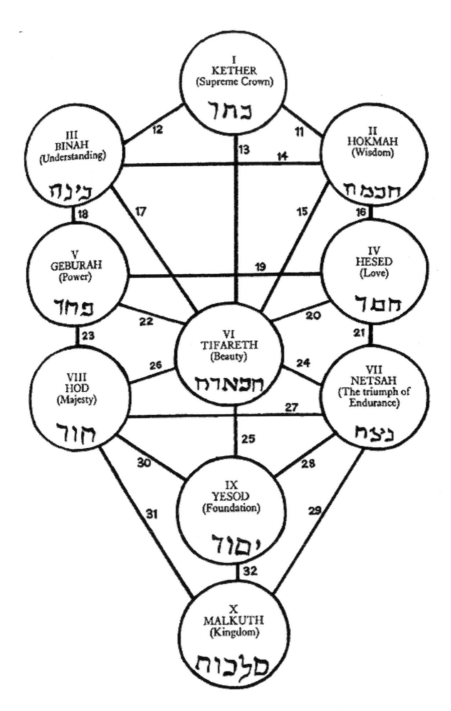

Tree of Life from David Conway's
Ritual Magic: An Occult Primer.

The "Cosmic Metaphysical Center" of this emanating "tree" is known as *Kether*, which becomes the first number (1). In the *Zohar* this center is known as *The Concealed One*. It is the central sphere of manifestation, the top of our Tree, from which all branches come out of. It is the *Logos* that we know as *order* and *knowledge*. As the branches grow downward the number (1) splits into duality, the two principles that become permanent throughout all lower spheres. In other words, the androgynous splits into what we refer to as men and women, or precisely speaking, the Father and Mother - Hokmah and Binah. *Kether*, the Crown, flows into the *Pillar of Mercy* where we find *Chokmah*, our number (2). Across the tree through the central pillar is a connection to *Binah*, our number (3), which initiates the *Pillar of Severity* as it flows from the Crown through the second sphere. Chokmah is 'wisdom' and the 'father'; Binah is 'understanding' and the 'mother'. Regardie explains that the four letters of YHVH, or Tetragrammaton, are associated with the father and mother principles. The former is given the letter "Y" to its name and the latter is given "H." From these two principles comes the child, or *"from consciousness and its vehicle are all things formed."*

All of these "things" are what we refer to as the *material world* and they form the world from the father and mother through the next seven spheres of light on the Tree. This is likely one of the main sources, or the source, for the sacredness of the number seven in relation to Creation. These first three spheres, (Kether, Chokmah, Binah) – a triad - are considered unique and "Supernal" in the sense that they have less relationship to the material world than any others. The fourth Sephiroth is known as *Chesed* and means 'grace'. It flows downward from *Chokmah* on the *Pillar of Mercy* through its number (4).

The fifth Sephiroth is known as *Geburah* and means 'might'. The fourth and fifth unite in flow to the sixth sphere. This sphere is known as *Tiphareth*, which in Hebrew means 'beauty' and 'harmony'. The harmony provided is the balance provided to the former forces. Regardie writes:

> *"...in the human being Tiphareth, the harmonious emanation of the Sun, is the Sephirah of the soul of Man, the center of the microcosmic system, and the luminous intermediary between the brooding spirit above and the body with the instincts below."*

Speaking on the Tetragrammaton, the third letter "V" is assigned to this sixth sphere of light. It comprises the second trinity of the Tree in that of *Chesed, Geburah* and *Tiphareth*. The first, of course, being *Kether, Chokmah* and *Binah*. The third triad is comprised first of *Netzach* (7), which means 'triumph' or 'victory'. The next sphere is *Hod* (8), meaning 'splendor'. Seven is male and eight is female. The third of this third and final trinity is the ninth sphere known as *Yesod*, which is "stability" in change. It is Lunar in nature and associated with *Astral Light*. All things form here before being crystalized in the final sphere. The final Sephirothic sphere is *Malkuth* (Kingdom), the tenth representing finalization and crystallization. It is tangible to the senses and *"all the qualities of the preceding planes."* Regardie refers to this tenth sphere as a Bridge and *"the Daughter, and the Virgin of the World."* It is the final letter "H" in Tetragrammaton. For every virtue of the ten Sephiroth, there are vices. The twenty-two paths of the *tree* are called *Navitoth*, and along with the 10 emanations form the Sacred 32 Paths of Wisdom. The *Sephiroth* are receptive and feminine, and the *Navitoth* are projective and masculine. Between the left *Pillar of Severity* and the right *Pillar of Mercy* is the *Middle Pillar of Mildness* known as THE WAY. Chic Cicero and Sandra Tabatha Cicero write in *Golden Dawn Magic* about the famed Serpent of Wisdom and the Tree:

> *"The Flaming Sword is the descending current of divine energy that facilitates the manifestation of the Universe. It is the Way of Involution of the descent of Spirit into matter. The Serpent of Wisdom, on the other hand, is the counterbalancing ascent of materialized energy. This is the Way of Evolution from matter back to its Divine Source."*

The Great Seal or Symbol of Solomon represents the micro-macro-cosm of the earth reflecting the heavens; the inferior reflecting the superior. The bearded Architect is depicted through reflections from the higher realm as we may recall from Genesis: *"God created man in his own image."* Also, the Kabbalistic symbol of the Zohar, the chief text of the Jewish Kabbalah, is an allegorical or mystical interpretation of the *Pentateuch*, or the first five books of the Hebrew Bible.

That God created "male and female" is synonymous with the androgyny nature of Source, or Unity, separated hypothetically into opposites. The description above the shaded area and triangle of the inferior sphere, and below that triangle of the superior sphere, reads from Latin something to the translation of: *As Above. So Below.* What is above is also similar to that which is below, something we can witness in the micro world of atoms and storms into the macro world, or higher celestial sphere, of solar systems and planets.

This symbol is the fusing of upward and downward triangles, or pyramids, often described as being the phallus and yoni, the passive and active principles united for the purpose of generation. When right side up the triangle represents man's attempt to connect with the heavens. When upside down the triangle expresses the interest of the superiors in the affairs of the lower world. At the very bottom is another triangle reaching above to touch the lower descending triangle. More abstractly these triangles represent the superior and inferior worlds touching at a point between which is often depicted a serpent, or staff, the umbilical cord linking man with heaven. The staff represents this link, which is why it is often carried by the wise, be it Moses or the Hermit. In the center of the image we find the Star of David or Saturn Star derived from the *Magical Square of Saturn*. Central in this symbol is the Maltese Cross. We find the intelligence of Saturn with human or godly attributes, commonly depicted with a white beard as *Father Time*, or the *Grim Reaper* with a scythe, relating to agriculture. The *Demiurge* is the Creator and Grand Architect as depicted in this Seal.

The Great Seal of Solomon

THE QURAN
& THE GOSPEL OF BARNABAS

First Iteration

The Quran shares in the same messages as the Bible and even the Babylonian Talmud on the subject of *magic* and *sorcery*. In the chapter called *Cow* 2:102-103 there is both a reference to the dangers of magic and to the corruption, prostitution, and pollution of those enemies of *"God and His angels and apostles, and of Gabriel and Michael"* (*Cow* 2:98). In surah 2:102-103 we read the following:

> *"And they follow what devilish beings used to chant against the authority of Solomon, though Solomon never disbelieved and only the devils denied, who taught sorcery to men, which, they said, had been revealed to the angels of Babylon, Harut and Marut, who, however, never taught it without saying: 'we have been sent to deceive you, so do not renounce (your faith). They learnt what led to discord between husband and wife. Yet they could not harm any one without the dispensation of God. And they learnt what harmed them and brought no gain. They knew indeed whoever bought this had no place in the world to come, and that surely they had sold themselves for something that was vile. If only they had sense. Had they come to believe instead, and taken heed for themselves, they would surely have earned from God a far better reward. If only they had sense!"*

With the perspective of the Quran, we may further conclude that *magic* is not merely a matter of the *insider* and *outsider* but an abuse of God's creation and authority. Nothing of this sort could even be done *"without the dispensation of God"* and a corruption of it henceforth. This is true in the Quran as it is in the Bible.

In the chapter *Rising Day* 113:1-5 we read what is meant to be said as an incantation:

> *"Say: ' I seek refuge with the Lord of rising day. From the evil of what He has created, and the evil of evening darkness when it overspreads, from the evil of sorceresses who blow incantations on knots, from the evil of the envier when he envies."*

Here we can read and interpret what once more is indeed a solar reference, i.e., the rising sun overcoming 'evil' in the form of "evening darkness." This *darkness* is likewise equated with the "evil of sorceresses" and the evil envy, which is also one of the *Seven Deadly* sins. The chapter called *The Most High* 87:1 directly states:

"Glorify the name of your Lord, most high."

In the Bible we read in the book of Psalm 97:9 almost the exact same text:

"For you, Lord, are the Most High over all the earth; you are exalted far above all gods."

The *Most High* could as easily be interpreted as a reference to God and Allah as it is to Jesus, the son, and the actual sun.

Buddha walked the middle path, Jesus was "the way, the truth, and the life" (John 14:6) and the crucified savior in the middle of two thieves, the Kabbala has the *Middle Pillar of Mildness*, and the indigenous Japanese practice called Shintō literally means *True Way*. In the Quran chapter *Muhammed* 47:5-6 we read that Allah will likewise show the *way*:

"He will show them the way, and better their state, And will admit them into gardens with which he has acquainted them."

Second Iteration

The Quran is also filled with references to Jesus, and books (chapters) on Abraham (14), Mary (19), and Noah (71). Muhammed is supposed to have performed similar miracles to Jesus, too, and others seemingly more miraculous such as splitting the moon. In the book called *Moon* 54:1 there is a note how the moon was split: *"The hour has come and split is the moon."* However, Muhammed is merely associated with the act, perhaps since he is the miraculous author of the Quran. The moon was primarily symbol of the Quraish, a group of Arab clans using the moon and claiming historical control of the holy site of Mecca, birthplace of Muhammed. Since these clans were the most dominate, their moon became a symbol of most Arab nations as a whole, even though the sun was an emblem of Iran.

After Islam formed there was a *splitting* of these clans and tribes, with some accepting the new religion and others remaining pagan. If Muhammed did indeed split the moon, it is likely a reference to the creation of Islam rather than a serious lunar anomaly.

A similar story can be found in the Biblical book of Joshua 10:12-14, which relates how the sun and moon were manipulated by the prophet:

> "Then spake Joshua to the Lord in the day when the Lord delivered up the Amorites before the children of Israel, and he said in the sight of Israel, Sun, stand thou still upon Gibeon; and thou, Moon, in the valley of Ajalon. And the sun stood still, and the moon stayed, until the people had avenged themselves upon their enemies. Is not this written in the book of Jasher? So the sun stood still in the midst of heaven, and hasted not to go down about a whole day. And there was no day like that before it or after it, that the Lord hearkened unto the voice of a man: for the Lord fought for Israel."

There is great irony in the fact that while Jews and pagans made horrible accusations against Jesus, it is well understood in Islam that Jesus truly was a miraculous prophet. In the chapter of *The Family of Imran* 4:45-51 we read of the angels speaking to Mary, the teachings of Jesus, and the middle pathway called the *straight way*:

> "And when the angels said: 'O Mary! Allah gives you the glad tidings of a command from Him: his name shall be Messiah, Jesus, the son of Mary. He shall be highly honoured in this world and in the Next, and shall be one of those near stationed to Allah. And he shall speak to men in the cradle and also later when he grows to maturity and shall indeed be among the righteous.' She said: 'O my Lord! How shall I have a son when no man has ever touched me?' The angel answered: Thus shall it be. Allah creates whatever He wills. When He decides something, He merely says: 'Be' and it is.

> "And He will teach him the Book, the Wisdom, the Torah, the Gospel, and he will be a Messenger to the Children of Israel.' (And when he came to them he said): 'I have come to you with a sign

from your Lord. I will make for you from clay the likeness of a bird and then I will breathe into it and by the leave of Allah it will become a bird. I will also heal the blind and the leper, and by the leave of Allah bring the dead to life. I will also inform you of what things you eat and what you treasure up in your houses. Surely this is a sign for you if you are true believ-ers.

"And I have come to confirm the truth of whatever there still remains of the Torah, and to make lawful to you some of the things which had been forbidden to you. I have come to you with a sign from your Lord; so have fear of Allah and obey me. Surely, Allah is my Lord and your Lord; so serve Him alone. This is the straight way.'"

The only major difference between Islam and Christianity, outside of the terminology applied and cultural issues, is that Muslims do not believe Jesus was the true manifestation, or son, of God. As blasphemous of a notion to Christians as this is, since it otherwise makes their denomination unique, the Bible itself is ripe with confirmation of this Islamic view.

Take the book of John 5:16-28 for example. Here we learn that because of the *miracles* or acts of *magic* that Jesus was performing, the Jewish leaders sought to "persecute him." In these verses we learn that Jesus as the "Son" is powerless without knowledge of the "Father," meaning that Jesus as a person is only acting through the power he derives from God - the implication is that he is not God. He even separates himself from his Father's work. We also learn that the dead will "hear the voice of the Son of God" and as a result live. Here we once more have reference to the notion of the profane being lame, deaf, blind, and dead, and in need of being resurrected by the *mystery* tradition and the words *come forth*:

"So, because Jesus was doing these things on the Sabbath, the Jewish leaders began to persecute him. In his defense Jesus said to them, 'My Father is always at his work to this very day, and I too am working.' For this reason they tried all the more to kill him; not only was he breaking the Sabbath, but he was even calling God his own Father, making himself equal with God. Jesus gave them this answer: 'Very truly I tell you, the Son can do nothing by

himself; he can do only what he sees his Father doing, because whatever the Father does the Son also does. For the Father loves the Son and shows him all he does. Yes, and he will show him even greater works than these, so that you will be amazed. For just as the Father raises the dead and gives them life, even so the Son gives life to whom he is pleased to give it.

"Moreover, the Father judges no one, but has entrusted all judgment to the Son, that all may honor the Son just as they honor the Father. Whoever does not honor the Son does not honor the Father, who sent him. 'Very truly I tell you, whoever hears my word and believes him who sent me has eternal life and will not be judged but has crossed over from death to life. Very truly I tell you, a time is coming and has now come when the dead will hear the voice of the Son of God and those who hear will live.

"For as the Father has life in himself, so he has granted the Son also to have life in himself. And he has given him authority to judge because he is the Son of Man. Do not be amazed at this, for a time is coming when all who are in their graves will hear his voice and come out – those who have done what is good will rise to live, and those who have done what is evil will rise to be condemned. By myself I can do nothing; I judge only as I hear, and my judgment is just, for I seek not to please myself but him who sent me.'"

Others will argue what is in John 8:58, wherein Jesus claims: *"'Very truly I tell you,' Jesus answered, 'before Abraham was born, I am!'"* Here he is referring to himself as the Almighty God - I AM. But these sorts of claims are precisely why Jewish leaders began persecuting him in the first place, i.e., he claimed to be the ALL incarnated in flesh. Such a notion is blasphemous to nearly every religion with a concept of GOD ALMIGHTY at its core. The term "I AM" was exceedingly offensive since it is how God named Himself to Moses through the burning bush in Exodus 3:14, which reads:

"God said to Moses, 'I am who I am.' This is what you are to say to the Israelites: 'I am has sent me to you.'"

In John 14:6, Jesus says, *"no man cometh unto the Father, but by me."* Far be it from an intended declaration of his position in relation to God, but such a verse implies that the Son of God is merely walking in the footsteps of his Father. This verse is nearly identical to the inscription of Isis and her "veil." Joseph Campbell explains that when Jesus refers to himself as "I AM" he is simply saying: *"I have identified myself with the all."* Such an idea is more understood in the east than it is in the west, but even today *"anyone who says, as Jesus is reported to have said (John 10:30), 'I and the Father are One,' is declared in our tradition to have blasphemed."* Matthew 26:39 seems to offer further confirmation of these facts, as Jesus speaks to the Father as a separate part of himself: *"Going a little farther, he fell with his face to the ground and prayed, 'My Father, if it is possible, may this cup be taken from me. Yet not as I will, but as you will'."*

Third Iteration

According to the Quran, which some Christians refuse to open, just as some Muslims refuse to open a Bible, it was actually Judas Iscariot who was arrested in the dark when Roman soldiers came to arrest Jesus. The Quran 4:157-158 relates:

"And they did not kill him and they did not crucify him, but it appeared so to them. And surely those who disagree about it are certainly in doubt about it - they have no knowledge about it except that they follow speculation. And they did not kill him for certain - but God took him up to Himself. And God was every Mighty, Wise."

As Muhammad 'Ata' ur-Rahim and Ahmad Thomson write in their book <u>Jesus Prophet of Islam</u>:

"If the Romans did become aware of the true identity of their prisoner when he was brought before Pilate, the Roman Magistrate, then it is possible that the dramatic turn of events may still have satisfied everyone. The Romans would have made an example of someone - whoever that someone was - which was sure to act as a deterrent. The majority of the Jews would have been happy for, due to a miracle, the traitor was standing in the dock instead of Jesus. Even the pro-Roman Jews would be happy, for,

with the death of Judas, the proof of their guilt would be destroyed. And furthermore, with Jesus officially dead, he would be far less likely to come out into the open to give them trouble."

Our contention here is in no way to confirm that Islam is correct and Christianity wrong. Instead, we seek to point out that rather than rejecting Christianity, Islam almost entirely accepts the same doctrines and narratives with exception to the supernatural resurrection of Jesus - which in all likelihood was birthed as a dogma through trickery and fraud.

According to some sources it was the gnostic mystic Cerinthus who was crucified in place of Jesus. This story was told by the Egyptian Basilides, a disciple of Matthias.

Nevertheless, there is more to the story than the Muslim record of history. The last name *Iscariot* literally means "man of cities" and since he *sold out* Jesus for thirty pieces of silver, Judas becomes the Devil in Matthew who offers the savior *all the kingdoms (cities and wealth) of the world.* He is Scorpio the backbiter, the Egyptian Typhon, and the destroyer of truth. In the book of The Slanderer (104) from the Quran we find a similar warning about men like Judas in verses 1-4:

> *"Woe to every slanderer, back-biter, who amasses wealth and hordes it. Does he think his wealth will abide for ever with him? By no means. He will be thrown into Hutama."*

Despite how difficult it may be for some to even consider that a fragment of truth exists in the Quran, a quick examination of the Bible suggests that its authors were entirely ignorant of what happened to the *betrayer.* In fact, it is quite clear that the canonical Bible has no definitive answer whatsoever as per the mystery of the whereabouts of Judas. Matthew 27:5 and Acts 1:18, provided below in order, tell completely different stories:

> *"So Judas threw the money into the temple and left. Then he went away and hanged himself."*

> *"With the payment he received for his wickedness, Judas bought a field; there he fell headlong, his body burst open and all his intestines spilled out."*

Fourth Iteration

The *Gospel of Barnabas,* named after Bare Nabe, a Jew from Cyprus who became a leading disciple after Jesus disappeared, is a very intriguing text. It documents several things that, if forgery, speak to one of the most well concealed fraudulent conspiracies of all time. On the other hand, if real, the hiding of this gospel from mainstream Church doctrine is perhaps the single greatest concealed conspiracy of all time.

In chapter 218 we learn that the body of Judas, after the crucifixion, was stolen to spread word that Jesus had risen.

In chapter 219
we learn about Mary returning to Jerusalem to find her son. Eventually she discovers that Jesus is indeed still alive.

In the very next line from chapter 220 we learn that Jesus had *"not been dead at all."*

In the following chapters 221-22 we learn that Jesus informs Barnabas to tell the truth about Judas so that *"everyone may believe the truth."* Jesus then proceeds to provide Barnabas with John and Peter *"who saw everything,"* so that they could provide the author with all the details of the death of Judas. Jesus then *"reproved many who believed that he had died and risen again"* before being taken up to heaven by four angels. As the disciples departed for different regions, the gospel informs us that "evil men" perpetuated a falsehood that is the cornerstone doctrine of Christianity, i.e. that Jesus died and rose again and that he was the "Son of God."

Others preached falsehoods that Jesus had died and never rose again. These things, Barnabas writes, were preached by men *"pretending to be disciples."* It is difficult to see the modern Church, particularly the Vatican, but any demonization thereof, as anything expect *pretend,* filled with *false prophets* making false profits.

The *Gospel of Philip* from the *Gnostic Bible* also confirms what Islam and the *Gospel of Barnabas* say about the controversy surrounding Jesus:

> *"Some say the lord died first and then ascended. They are wrong. He rose first and then he died. Unless you are first resurrected, you will not die. As god lives, you would already be dead."*

This rejected gospel [Philip] goes even further, igniting controversial questions and plenty of fictional accounts that may be based on something tangible:

"And the companion of the Savior is Mary Magdalene. But Christ loved her more than all the disciples and used to kiss her often on her mouth. The rest of the disciples were offended by it and expressed disapproval."

Within the *Gospel of Philip* is further described the companionship of Mary and Jesus:

"Wisdom, who is called 'barren,' is mother of the angels. The companion is Mary of Magdala. Jesus loved her more than his students. He kissed her often on her face, more than all his students, and they said, 'Why do you love her more than us?'"
The savior answered, saying to them, *"Why do I not love you like her? If a blind man and one who sees are together in darkness, they are the same. When light comes, the one who sees will see the light. The blind man stays in darkness'."*

We shall conclude this part of our study with a statement attributed to the prophet of Islam: *"This Jesus was a good and holy man, a teacher among the Jews, but one day his disciples became mad and made a god of him."*

Fifth Iteration

Here are presented chapters 218-222 from the Barnabas Gospel:

Chapter 218

Then returned each man to his house. He who writes, with John and James his brother, went with the mother of Jesus; to Nazareth;.
Those disciples who did not fear God went by night [and] stole the body of Judas and hid it, spreading a report that Jesus was risen again; whence great confusion arose. The high priest then commanded, under pain of anathema;, that no one should talk of Jesus of Nazareth;. And so there arose a great persecution, and

many were stoned and many beaten, and many banished from the land, because they could not hold their peace on such a matter.

The news reached Nazareth how that Jesus, their fellow citizen, having died on the cross was risen again. Whereupon, he that writes; prayed the mother of Jesus; that she would be pleased to leave off weeping, because her son was risen again. Hearing this, the Virgin Mary, weeping, said: 'Let us go to Jerusalem to find my son. I shall die content when I have seen him.

Chapter 219

The Virgin returned to Jerusalem with him who writes, and James and John, on that day on which the decree of the high priest went forth. Whereupon, the Virgin, who feared God, albeit she knew the decree of the high priest to be unjust, commanded those who dwelt with her to forget her son. Then how each one was affected! God who discerns the heart of men knows that between grief at the death of Judas whom we believed to be Jesus our master, and the desire to see him risen again, we, with the mother of Jesus, were consumed.

So the angels that were guardians of Mary ascended to the third heaven;, where Jesus was in the company of angels, and recounted all to him. Wherefore Jesus prayed God that he would give him power to see his mother and his disciples. Then the merciful God commanded his four favourite angels, who are Michael, Gabriel, Rafael;, and Uriel, to bear Jesus into his mother's house, and there keep watch over him for three days continually, suffering him only to be seen by them that believed in his doctrine.

Jesus came, surrounded with splendour, to the room where abode Mary the Virgin with her two sisters, and Martha and Mary Magdalen, and Lazarus, and him who writes, and John and James and Peter. Whereupon, through fear they fell as dead. And Jesus lifted up his mother and the others from the ground, saying: 'Fear not, for I am Jesus; and weep not, for I am alive and not dead.' They remained every one for a long time beside himself at the presence of Jesus, for they altogether believed that Jesus was dead. Then the Virgin, weeping, said: 'Tell me, my son, wherefore God, having given you power to raise the dead, suffered you to die, to the shame of your kinsfolk and friends, and to the shame of your doctrine? For every one that loves you has been as dead.'

Chapter 220

Jesus replied, embracing his mother: 'Believe me, mother, for truly I say to you that I have not been dead at all; for God has reserved me till near the end of the world.' And having said this he prayed the four angels that they would manifest themselves, and give testimony how the matter had passed.

Thereupon the angels manifested themselves like four shining suns, insomuch that through fear every one again fell down as dead. Then Jesus gave four linen cloths to the angels that they might cover themselves, in order that they might be seen and heard to speak by his mother and her companions. And having lifted up each one, he comforted them, saying: 'These are the ministers of God: Gabriel, who announces God's secrets; Michael, who fights against God's enemies; Rafael, who receives the souls of them that die; and Uriel, who will call every one to the judgment of God at the last day. Then the four angels narrated to the Virgin how God had sent for Jesus, and had transformed Judas, that he might suffer the punishment to which he had sold another.

Chapter 221

Jesus turned himself to him who writes, and said: "Barnabas, see that by all means you write my gospel concerning all that has happened through my dwelling in the world. And write in a similar manner that which has befallen Judas, in order that the faithful may be undeceived, and every one may believe the truth." Then answered he who writes: "I will do so, if God wills, O Master; but I do not know what happened to Judas, for I did not see it." Jesus answered: "Here are John and Peter who saw everything, and they will tell you all that has passed." And then Jesus commanded us to call his faithful disciples [so] that they might see him. So James and John called together the seven disciples with Nicodemus and Joseph, and many others of the seventy-two, and they ate with Jesus.

The third day Jesus said: "Go to the Mount of Olives with my mother, for there I will ascend again to heaven, and you will see who shall bear me up." So they all went there except twenty-five of the seventy-two disciples, who for fear had fled to Damascus. And as they all stood in prayer, at midday Jesus came with a great multitude of angels who were praising God: and the splendour of his face made them greatly afraid and they fell with their faces to the ground. But Jesus lifted them up, comforting them, and saying: "Do not be afraid, I am your master."

And he reproved many who believed that he had died and risen again, saying: "Do you hold me and God for liars? I said to you that God has granted to me to live almost to the end of the world. Truly I say to you, I did not die; it was Judas the traitor. Beware, for Satan will make every effort to deceive you. Be my witnesses in Israel, and throughout the world, of all things that you have heard and seen."

And having said this, he prayed God for the salvation of the faithful, and the conversion of sinners and [then], his prayer ended, he embraced his mother, saying: "Peace be to you, my mother. Rest in God who created you and me." And having said this, he turned to his disciples, saying: "May God's grace and mercy be with you." Then before their eyes the four angels carried him up into heaven.

Chapter 222

After Jesus had departed, the disciples scattered through the different parts of Israel and of the world, and the truth, hated of Satan, was persecuted, as it always is, by falsehood. For certain evil men, pretending to be disciples, preached that Jesus died and rose not again. Others preached that he really died, but rose again. Others preached, and yet preach, that Jesus is the Son of God, among whom is Paul deceived. But we - as much as I have written - we preach to those that fear God, that they may be saved in the last day of God's Judgment. Amen.

THE WAY OF ISA

First Iteration

The name *Jesus* is very similar to the Greek *Zeus*. *Jesus Christ the Messiah* is without question a title applied to a person or many persons. His real name would likely have been something closer to *Joshua*.

Jesus or *Jeshua* was also a very common name held by dozens of different people during the Biblical time period, and after, as it is still in some parts of the world today. The letters IHS stand for the first three letters of Jesus in the Greek alphabet (IHΣΟΥΣ). They come from the Aramaic name *Jeshua* and the Hebrew *Joshua*. IHS is furthermore another name for the sun and wine gods Bacchus or Dionysius, all three of the former having performed wine miracles. In the *Gospel of Philip* we learn that Jesus is a hidden name altogether and merely a title:

> *"Jesus is a hidden name, Christ is an open one. So Jesus is not a word in any tongue but a name they call him. In Syriac the Christ is messias, in Greek he is Christos. All languages have their own way of calling him. Nazarene is the revealed name for what is secret."*

The accepted name or title of "Jesus Christ" was not even officially used until after the Council of Nicaea in 325 A.D.

The word *Christ* is thought to be an actual name, although it is more widely known to be a title too. Christ or Christos was the title applied to priests of Judah and various other "savior" gods, including Krishna of the Hindu pantheon. Krishna was an incarnation of Vishnu, who was associated with the sun, much like Jesus, or Mithra, the son of Persian god Ahura Mazda (Ormazd), the creator spirit of Zoroastrianism. Vishnu was also protector of *dharma* - moral and religious law - and had ten Avatars, reminiscent of the five pairs of Poseidon's children, who ruled Atlantis. The ten Avatars of Vishnu, and Poseidon's progeny, correspond numerically to the *Sephiroth* of the Kabbalah, the emanations surrounding the Infinite, that are depicted by ten spheres. Vishnu was, like Jesus, born of a virgin in his incarnation as Krishna, known as the *Christos* or Christ. His annual festival was held in August under the sign of *Virgo,* the Virgin.

The title *Messiah* may even come from Egypt where Pharaohs were anointed with oil from the fat of a crocodile. This substance was literally called *messeh* and after application a Pharaoh literally became an *anointed one.* According to Joseph Campbell, the entire idea of a Jewish Messiah *"had nothing to do with the end of the world"* but instead with a *"king who would reestablish Israel among the nations."* D. M. Murdoch writes in <u>The Christ Conspiracy</u> of titles relating to the anointed one:

> *"...anyone anointed would be called 'Christ' by the Greek-speaking inhabitants of the Roman empire, who were many since Greek was the lingua franca for centuries...in Greek, Krishna is also Christos, and the word for 'Christ' also comes from the Hindu word 'Kris,' which is a name for the sun, as is evidently 'Krishna' in ancient Irish."*

There is a further correlation between *Jesus* and female deities like the Egyptian *Isis* or the Japanese *Amaterasu.* In Arabic the name for Jesus, and thus the name used in the Quran, is ISA. Just as RA, the sun god, had his sanctuary at Heliopolis, Amaterasu has her sacred temple at *The Grand Shrine of Ise.* The name ISE relates to ISA, both Jesus in Arabic and the Egyptian Isis, in various ways. Priestesses of the Ise Jingu shrine were known to use a rattle that bears striking resemblance to the sistrum used by priestesses of Isis, and even by name to the ISTAR (Ishtar) instrument of the Hittite people. The two goddesses also share other striking attributes; both were married to a husband-brother, which signified the sacred alchemical marriage; both were repositories of divine wisdom; and both oversaw a yearly inundation that brings fertility to their land. In Egypt this inundation was that of the Nile River and in Japan it was the rain that assured a descent rice harvest. The waters that flood the land are like the baptismal waters that flood the body and bring about purification, healing, and resurrection. Buddha walked the middle path, Jesus was "the way, the truth, and the life," the Quran says Allah *"will show them the way"* (Quran 47:5), and the Japanese practice of Shintō literally means *True Way.* By extension, the adherents of Amaterasu practice *The Way of Ise* secluded in a lengthy ritual space called *Place of the Way.* The famous inscription of Isis expresses the heart of these *mysteries*: *"I, Isis Am All That Has Been, That Is Or Shall Be; No Mortal Man Hath Ever Me Unveiled."*

The phrase "no mortal man" means that the profane (deaf, dumb, blind, lame, etc.) are not allowed access to the secrets of the Universe and that no one has ever simply been bestowed wisdom for no good reason. As Manly Hall stares: *"Wisdom is not bestowed, it is achieved"* and *"No man may justifiably demand anything except the fruitage of his own labors."* Likewise, as Jesus says in the Bible: *"no man cometh unto the Father, but by me"* (John 14:6).

Though we tend to associate nearly all human history with the male character, since after all it is *His Story*, the *mysteries* of life were always preserved in the waters of a woman's body and womb. For true students of history will also acknowledge that most primitive and even advanced societies also worshiped the goddess, or bringer of life. Perhaps this is why Jesus loved Mary *"more than all the disciples"* (Gospel of Philip) and why goddess worship was, and remains, so prevalent throughout the world. Yet the history of mankind is still a collective record of the entire human race which cannot be reduced to male and female, as the *mysteries* teach. For it is through the *mystery of marriage* that *the existence of the world depends.* But the MAGNA MATER is nevertheless central because she is the gateway to heaven.

The Way is taught by both wise men and wise women, but ultimately is only a path to be followed internally. This is what clinical psychologist Jordan B. Peterson points out in his book <u>Beyond Chaos</u>:

> *"The way - that is the path of life, the meaningful path of life, the straight and narrow path that constitutes the very border between order and chaos, and the traversing of which brings them into balance."*

Second Iteration

The Sumerian goddess of love and fertility, Inanna, was often depicted with reddish sunbeams radiating from her body like Amaterasu. Known as Ishtar in Babylon, Inanna was considered a "sacred woman" and called *Hierodule*. This was also a title awarded to a Sumerian high priestess presiding over the most sacred ceremonies in the *bridal chamber*. From their positions as "sacred women" they administered the final rites of initiation, leading the candidate to *come forth by day* – i.e., *living resurrection*.

Human priestesses called "bees" oversaw the temples of the Greek goddess Aphrodite, who had the honeycomb as one of her symbols. The *souls* of her priestesses were said to also inhabit the bodies of *bees*. These women were called *Melissae*, a word rooted in the source of bees and honey. A *Melissa* was a title like *Christ*, applying to a group of bee nymphs that held the duty of teaching civilization and assisting initiates with *living resurrection* within *bridal chambers* that were often modeled in the fashion of a beehive. Nymphs are a personification of the female creative force, and the Greek root of *Nymphe* also means "veiled," which relates to that famous inscription of Isis.

It is said that like the Grand Masonic Master CHiram Abiff, who refused to unveil the *secrets* of the *Master Mason,* when a *Melissa* refused to reveal the secrets of initiation, she was torn to pieces, her remains birthing a swarm of bees. Teardrops from the Egyptian sun god RA also turned into bees as they struck the ground.

The significance of the bee pertaining to the illuminating deity RA is that they represent a form of redemption acquired through initiation: *see* the redeeming blood of the Mithraic bull, Attis, Jesus, Odin, Bacchus, Dionysius, and others. Those teardrops of RA are *solar rays* and *alchemical gold* personified in the *golden honey* of the beehive. Thus, we refer to the phrase: *Dat Rosa Mel Apibus,* or *The Rose Gives Honey to the Bees.*

The rose is a symbol of the *mysteries* and the *bees* are the *initiates*. We are likewise reminded here of a *land flowing with milk and honey.* Bees and beehives are a cornerstone in Masonic symbolism because of these facts. They are a Greek symbol of work and obedience, and in tradition they also erected the second temple at Delphi.

In Orphic teachings, and Indro-Aryan and Moslem tradition, the migration of bees from a hive in swarm was representative of the swarm of souls emanating from Source. In Minoan symbolism - a Bronze Age civilization centered on Crete (c. 3000–1050 BC) – the Goddess appears as half woman and half bee, or therianthropic. The honeycomb is thus a symbol of community, work, personal insight, divinity, and harmony within nature. J. E. Cirlot's <u>A Dictionary of Symbols</u> says the following about the bee in Egypt:

> *"In Egyptian hieroglyphic language, the sign of the bee was a determinative in royal nomenclature, partly by analogy with the monarchic organization of these insects, but more especially because of the ideas of industry, creative activity and wealth which are associated with the production of honey."*

The officiating party over the Greater Mysteries of Demeter at Eleusis were known as *crier*, but more properly called *hierokeryx*. In Egypt it was Isis who used *beeswax* to fashion a phallus for her husband Osiris, and therefore to impregnate herself immaculately with the solar-savior Horus.

Third Iteration

Just as Horus and the *sun of God* offer salvation to mankind, the reddish sunbeams of the goddess, and both the *reddish blood* of menstruation and birth, all share an obvious relationship. Robes of the *high priestesses* (hierodule) were *scarlet* to represent *ritu* (Sumerian for *truth*), from where we may derive the word *ritual*. Before the Bible was translated into English the word *hierodulai*, from whence *hierodule* (like *hierokeryx*) is derived, was mistranslated into *harlot*. A *woman in red* then became identified with promiscuity and prostitution. Inanna and Ishtar thus became individually known as the *"Whore of Babylon"* while those like Mary Magdalene were even called *whore* and *prostitute*.

In fact, the *Talmud* of the Jews, who we know accused Jesus of a sorcery he learned in foreign lands, even references Mary as such. Sanhedrin 106b of The William Davidson Talmud, says she was *"descended from princes and rulers, and was licentious with carpenters."* Shabbat 104b refers to Jesus as a wicked magician and a "fool." In punishment for his perversity tract 56b of the Talmud calls him, and anyone *"who distresses Israel,"* a *"chief"* who is, according to tract 57a, burned in *"boiling excrement."*

In other words, Mary was a whore, and Jesus was a wicked magician who is now burning in excrement.

Fourth Iteration

As with the *baptism* of the Christian Church, the purifying rites of the Templars, Muslims, Jews, and of the Shintō practices of purification (*harai*) called *misogi*, the waters of Isis, associated with the Nile River, are used to save the life of the infant Horus, who is burned in the *Egyptian Hieratic Papyri* spells:

"Your son Horus is burnt in a place where there is no water."

These "waters" are the birthing fluids, but also associated with the saliva and urine of the goddess, which flow as the Nile River itself. In a similar spell from Babylon it is water drawn from the Tigris and Euphrates which carries the weight of purification. As Christopher A. Faraone writes in his essay titled, 'The Mystodokos and the Dark-Eyed Maidens':

"This use of Nile water to 'save' living patients from disease and discomfort has also been connected with the use of Nile water in the mysteries of Isis, where water apparently played an important role in protecting an individual from the fires of the underworld."

Bees and the waters of Isis provide absolution and salvation.

Fifth Iteration

The name ISIS also plays an interesting role relating to the Pyramids of the Giza Plateau. Considered a place for *ascension*, the Great Pyramid contains the most dominant of all *bridal chambers*, or those sacred locations for the *alchemical marriage* to be performed. Such a thing is described in the *Gospel of Philip*:

Great is the mystery of marriage!
Without it the world would not be.
The existence of the world depends on marriage.

It was here that an initiate was to have communion with spirits and after deep introspection be *born again*. The Great Pyramid itself is thought to have been built on a much older – pre-ancient – chamber cut into the lower bedrock, and water is thought to have surrounded or run under the structure at one point in the past. The historian Herodotus documented that this chamber had been connected to the Nile via a channel. He writes of Khufu, *"for the underground he caused to be made as sepulchral chambers for himself in an island, having conducted thither a channel from the Nile."*

Although the Giza complex was possessed and marked by many leaders and peoples over millennia, it was from some point used as a temple complex to perform rituals of a mysterious and almost supernatural nature. It acted as a doorway to the underworld and a gateway to the heavens, as is the case with similar facilities in the Americas built over caverns or water.

The sarcophagus in the King's Chamber acted as the *body* and the individual initiate acted as the *soul*, the same being told in the story of Osiris being entombed in a golden casket and set afloat on the Nile River... of souls which blended with the Milky Way. The Cherokee peoples of the Americas call the Milky Way "Where the Dog Ran," referring to a myth about a dog that ran away with a meal dripping from his mouth. The trail became *Sky River* and the dog certainly refers to Anubis and Canis Major, positioned behind the Great Hunter Orion, the personification of Osiris in the sky.

Upon emersion in the physical and rough tomb - the material body - the initiate would undergo a dark and isolated process of reflection within self (below) and communion with the divine (above). This entire ritual process, which included other steps, is further told in the story of Osiris and Set.

The rough ground and polished walls and ceilings of these spaces represented the earth and heavens. Tight and cramped passageways opening into grander areas represented the *ups* and *downs* of life, the good and bad, the breath of living. Such maneuvering was required as a physical representation of the soul's journey in the corporeal body, the purpose of which was to reunite with Source. Everything culminated in a *resurrection* by which the initiate would be *reborn*.

Red walls in the King's Chamber bear a striking resemblance to the megalithic sites of Ġgantija on the island of Gozo and the Hypogeum on the nearby island of Malta, which is subterranean and womb-like. Red within the confines of such rooms likely represents the pain and blood of *birth*. A parallel could thus be found here with the *Land of the Rising Sun*, Japan, which sees the bloody red sun appear over the horizon (Horus) of its ocean-locked islands. Japan still uses the red sun on their pure white flag.

Other temples contain at their core natural subterranean crypts or artificial chambers that mimic the womb itself. Some structures, perhaps including the Osireion, located under the Temple of Seti I, contain water by intention due to its link with birth and especially the Nile.

Conceptually the red is a symbol of blood, which is taken from the lamb to purify. The blood of Christ and the *Paschal Lamb* washes away our sins. The blood of menstruation and birth give us new life.

Initiation into the *Mystery Religions* around the world involved the color red in the various chambers mentioned above as a symbol of the womb. After days of gestation a person would be reborn as a "sun" of God. What is meant by "sun" here is that they would be bright, pure, washed clean, etc. They were a miniature sun, with a fire burning inside - the soul.

The Japanese sun-goddess Amaterasu is the *light of heaven*, the Judeo-Christian God is the *Most High*, and each of us is an individual expression of that light. Perhaps the red hats on Rapa Nui (Easter Island) Moai are a sort of solar corona, as is often used to depict Jesus, Horus, and countless other god-like figures.

Sixth Iteration

From the word GIZA we can further extract "iza," "isa," and "ise." The letter "G" relates to earth, which was formed on the potter wheel of Ptah and by the geometrical and mathematical designs of Saturn. Otherwise known as the *Great Architect*, he is represented by the "G" inside the Masonic *square and compass*. From these tools the *natural laws* of existence were calculated. From the letter "G" can also be derived Geb, lord of earth, and Gaia, mother of earth. The pyramid itself is a tomb which symbolizes the *Womb of the Earth*. Therefore, the Gisa or Giza plateau literally embodies the essence of the goddess and her womb that is the ultimate *bridal chamber*, acting as a sacred location for *living resurrections* to be performed. From the Japanese ISE and Arabic ISA, to the African IZA, the solar light and cleansing waters of the Nile or Baptism prepare an initiate for being reborn – *born again* – and returning to the *Garden of Paradise* from the *Garden of Hallucinations*.

The Goddess Amaterasu Emerging from Earth by Utagawa
Kunisada, woodblock print, 1860.

Coming to such *realization* should trigger a *desire* to *know
thyself* and to *know God*. It is the epitome of the *Divine Plan* by which
the cycles of man and nature can be put into harmony with one
another. For this is the ultimate goal of the *mysteries*, to follow in the
footsteps of the *Son of God* and to be *born again* as a *Sun of God*.

The *Virgin Birth*, or the mythological motif of the *search for
the unknown father*, occurs within one's own heart as we begin to live
a spiritual life called *Christ*. On this journey to discover our father
we become *reborn*, something traditionally carried out in puberty
rites wherein the little boy symbolically dies and is born again as a
young man. The *Virgin Birth* is also the *Parousia*, or *Second Coming*,
that unfolding and sprouting of the *seed within*. This is the moment
in Matthew 17:2 when Jesus *"transfigured before them. His face shone
like the sun, and his clothes became as white as the light."* A *baptism*
functions to purify and water this internal *seed* while awakening the
individual to their *destiny*, which, as Joseph Campbell points out, *"is
the secret cause of your death."* Baptism is thus attempting to *"pull
something out of you."* This concept of *death* as a fulfillment of life
"underlies the sacrifices of the great planting societies" and *"the idea of
the Crucifixion of Jesus."* As per the *mysteries*, Campbell adds:
*"...when you have identified yourself with the consciousness, the body
drops off. Nothing can happen to you."*

It is the *realization,* not of *consciousness* itself, but of the *unconscious* that sets you free. As with the Greek maxim of *know thyself* the Sanskrit maxim *tat tvam asi* says *"though art that,"* referring to an individual's relationship with the *Absolute.* In other words, the *Kingdom of Heaven* is within each individual, and the *Promised Land,* as Campbell points out, is therefore *"not a place to be conquered by armies and solidified by displacing other people."* The *Holy Land* of legend, myth, and theology is thus *"a corner of the heart, or it is any environment that has been mythologically spiritualized."* Heaven is of similar consideration.

The *Dormition of the Virgin* and the ascension of Jesus in Acts 1:9 both refer to a *heaven* that is internal and the place from whence we originally were born *out of* at the moment of temporary *spiritual death,* or the *Little Birth.* What we term the *Great Birth* is our passing from the physical body into *infinity.*

The path of this descension and ascension can be seen in Athanasius Kircher's <u>Œdipus Ægyptiacus</u>, which depicts a scarab moving between the *above* and *below* worlds - the alchemical key according to the Egyptians. Here is depicted the path of *seed* through each planetary body until, reaching the center, it is *perfected* for return to *source* or prepared for another *incarnation.*

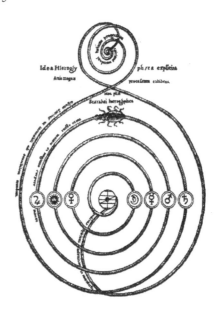

The *path* is symbolic of the transition of spirit/souls from the spiritual world into the physical world during the *lesser physical birth* – the *great spiritual death.* The *second great birth* is symbolic of man's liberation from the material world, as he arises from the tomb into the heavens to experience the *great spiritual birth* – the *lesser physical death.* This Egyptian symbol is identical to the Buddhist *unalome,* which represents the spiraling *path* of individual transcendence.

~ AMEN ~

EPILOGUE

THE DIVINE PLAN, GNOSTICISM, & JESUS THE NAZARENE

First Iteration

Following the path of ISA is, in the final equation, to be equated with that hermetic axiom: *as above, so below*. What is below is DNA, what links it to the heavens is the caduceus, and what is found above is the ancient art of astrology. Until relatively recently this art form and mathematical delineation of the stars was the second serpent on the staff, entwined with his brother astronomy. In prior times of antiquity, we even learn that astrology was the basis for astronomy, or its father. Astrology and astronomy could further be likened to magic and science.

To follow in the footsteps of *The Way* is to understand the code of life on earth and the code of life beyond. For the planets orbit and rotate with the equivalency of the double helix. Furthermore, what is *below* is a subatomic realm, wherein electrons buzz around the nucleus of an atom, not in any way dissimilar to the manner that planets orbit a star.

Astrology was not merely an ancient magical practice based on ignorance, but one that incorporated mathematics, geometry, and science into the same category. It is not, except by ignorant and uninformed opinion, a superstition. Those seeing it as such must be of the children of atheism wherein *fear of creation,* i.e., responsibility and logic (God), is replaced by a willful ignorance that sees the body as a distinct and separate unit apart from a nature they believe exerts no influences on the former. However, astrology is certainly inundated with charlatans and wishful thinking. For it to have any value whatsoever the calculations must be precise and a person's knowledge of the heavens at least considerable. If these conditions are not met, then astrology is nothing more than fanciful role play and trite banality. As the mystic H. P. Blavatsky wrote: *"Astrology is a science as infallible as astronomy itself, with the condition, however, that its interpretations must be equally infallible..."*

That astrology was practiced by every civilized society is by no means a fact of ignorance in antiquity any more than it is proof of modern scientific advancement. As Manly Hall writes in The Story of Astrology:

"Astrology was practiced by the earliest civilized peoples of the earth, and in every period of philosophic and spiritual enlightenment was accorded a place of honor by those of high birth and great learning."

It was in the Garden of Eden where Adam, or the first man, was reportedly instructed in astrology. By this tradition we might suggest that man was given a certain authority over the stars in order to understand *God's Plan* and live in harmony with the same. In fact, as Genesis 1:27-28 states, man was given "dominion" over all living creatures on earth:

"So God created man in his own image, in the image of God created he him; male and female created he them. And God blessed them, and God said unto them, Be fruitful, and multiply, and replenish the earth, and subdue it: and have dominion over the fish of the sea, and over the fowl of the air, and over every living thing that moveth upon the earth."

We may say then that all the fish, fowl, and *"every living thing that moveth"* could comprise both the physical creatures below and those symbolic creatures above in the form of the *Zodiac*. These stars do appear to live and move, and the word "zodiac" itself comes from the Greek *zōidiakos*, which means "animal figure." Being granted "dominion," from the Latin *dominium*, or master, over these creatures thus gave mankind the knowledge of the *animal wheel*.

These matters are, of course, evidence of the mind and creative influences of God. Astrology is a signature of the angelic and divine, making itself known to man through scientific observations, mathematical calculations, and sacred geometry, i.e., all the things in philosophical and occult sense equate GOD. Perhaps this is the reason that this ancient science acquired the name *Rule of Kings* since the stars were consulted for everything from royal births and coronations to war and the death of a monarch. As a representative of the *Kingdom of God* on the *Kingdom of Earth*, a king likewise extracted his authority from *above*. Astrology is also called the *Mother of Science*. Sir E. A. Wallis-Budge reported on astrology as such:

> *"The Sumerians and Babylonians believed that the will of the gods in respect to man and his affairs could be learned from watching the motions of the stars and planets, and that skilled star-gazers could obtain from the motions and varying aspects of the heavenly bodies indications of future prosperity and calamity. They therefore caused observations to be made and recorded on tablets, which they interpreted from a magical and not astronomical point of view, and these observations and their comments on them, and interpretation of them, have formed the foundation of the astrology in use in the world for the last 5,000 years."*

From the Chaldeans and Egyptians to the Indians and Chinese, astrology was used in nearly all affairs of society and state. Halls reports on its antiquity in India as having been developed before the writing down of the sacred *Vedas*. The Brahman priests were most efficient.

In China the rules of state and family were governed by the same science used in Greece, Rome, and in the worlds of Christendom, Islam, Judaism, and the like.

Even the Aztecs used astrology to divine the future of newborn children among other things. Hall reports further:

> *"The scriptures of the Brahmans, Taoists, Lamas, and other Oriental sects are replete with allusions to the influence of the heavenly bodies; and from the stars that fought against Sisera to the morning star of Revelation, the Bible of the Jews and Christians lends its testimony to the validity of astrology and astronomy."*

Astrology is still consulted today my members of Wall Street and, of course, by common people who acquire their knowledge from countless bookstores that carry numerous volumes on the subject. From Kings and Queens to Pharaohs and Popes to Emperors and Empresses, astrology has been consulted throughout human history for the same reasons that dreams were interpreted in the Bible. Alexander of Macedon, Julius Caesar, Nero, Tiberius, Cleopatra, Genghis Khan, and Napoleon I would all attest to the science as largely accurate. Queen Elizabeth I of England was famous for employing Dr. John Dee in her service and Charles the First of France was advised by Sir Cornelius Agrippa. Hall also adds of numerous Popes:

> "*Pope Julius II had the day of his coronation set by astrology; Sixtus IV arranged his audiences according to planetary hours; and it is said of Paul III that he never held a consistory except when the heavenly bodies were propitious.*"

He adds of even the founding of the United States:

> "*A man who is known to have been proficient in astrology was present in an advisory capacity at meetings attended by George Washington and Benjamin Franklin.*"

As H. Flanders Dunbar said: "*The ego, created directly by God, in its connection with the body comes under stellar influence, and at birth is stamped like wax by a seal.*" This should remind us that astrology is a language of God discernible through the messages it sends us like those found in DNA. As Sir Francis Bacon points out:

> "*In the traditions of astrology, the natures and dispositions of men are not without truth distinguished from the predominances of the planets.*"

When Edmond Halley, for whom the comet is named, made disparaging remarks about astrology it was Isaac Newton who supposedly and famously said: "*I have studied the subject, Mr. Halley; you have not.*"

Second Iteration

Manly Hall also refers in his astrology essay, mentioned above, to an entry in the Schaff-Herzog <u>Encyclopedia of Religious Knowledge</u> which notes the birth of the savior in relation to the stars:

"The Star of the Magi (Matthew ii) was probably a conjunction, in the sign of the Fish, of Jupiter and Saturn in the year of Rome 747, a coincidence which Abar Danel stats was recorded by Jewish astrologers as an indication of the Messiah."

Matthew chapter 2 is a reference to the verse which reads: *"When they saw the star, they rejoiced with great joy."* In his book <u>Thou Art That</u>, Joseph Campbell explains something similar:

"Saturn is the star of Israel, after whom Saturday is named, and Jupiter is the star of kingship, and the conjunction of these in the sign of the fish - Pisces was extremely vivid on May 29, 7 B.C. - identifies this star as that which the story of the Magi refers."

We know the arrival of the *magi* today by the common image of the *Christmas Nativity*, which depicts zodiacal characters and the *wise men*. Manly Hall says these men represent with their gifts of gold, frankincense, and myrrh the essence of mind, emotion, and body respectively.

Campbell documents how the first carvings of this scene were found on a sarcophagus of the second and third centuries, and that *"one of the earliest shows the little child in the crib, surrounded by the ass, the ox, and the Magi."* What can be extracted from this is the relationship that the ass and ox have to Set and Osiris respectively, and to the entire Egyptian religion, along with astrology in general.

In the Egyptian Mysteries priests surrounded a candidate for initiation while wearing various animal masks. These masks and symbols are of the *Nativity* and representative of the temptations that a neophyte will repeatedly face. The manger itself is a trough from which the animal consumes grain, which is a motif dating to primitive agricultural cults. That Jesus rode an ass is a similar motif told of the Greek Bacchus, god of wine miracles, who also rode a donkey. When Horus, the son or incarnation of Osiris, kills the red Typhon (Set), or Devil, he also conquers and rides the great ass. Hall adds of Osiris, and the Greek Orpheus, that both were dark skinned men *"from the East, who brought the knowledge of the sacred sciences from a race or order of sages who passed an almost fabled existence amidst the highlands of northern Hindustan [India]."*

These *sacred sciences* were juxtaposed to one of the most prominent, i.e., astrology. The Brahminic *sciences* were supposedly derived much like the Egyptian sciences, and countless other resurrected societies post-deluge, *"by a line of antediluvian patriarchs who, perfected in all human virtues, communed with the Gods."* These men were called *Rishis* and the greatest among them were called *Maharishis.* They share a relationship with men like Noah, Abraham, Jacob, and Moses. Not only is one of the oldest horoscopes in the world found in the Hindu *sacred sciences,* that of Rama, an avatar of Vishnu, from 3,102 B.C., but a complex astrological narrative can be extracted from these facts.

The name *Rishi,* one who taught astrology and other sciences, means *to shine.* The word *Risksha* is a *shiner* and a *constellation,* and since the word *Maha* means *great,* we are talking about *great shiners,* or stars. This is almost surely why the *Seven Rishis* are identified with the Seven stars of Ursa Major, or the Great Bear. Since navigators relied on the Pole Star, discovered by way of the Great Dipper, the *Rishis* point the way and the Bear guarded the Pole. Hall says they *"dwell together in the Polar Shamballah – the City of the Gods."* These gods and shining ones came to earth to teach civilization and impart wisdom, sharing *sacred sciences* in the millennia before Jesus Christ – another shining teacher from the heavens.

Third Iteration

The story of Jesus is an allegory of "astronomical" proportions. Jesus is said to have been betrayed by Judas with a "kiss" before dying on a cross and being placed into a tomb for three days, whereupon he was resurrected in a celebration later referred to as Easter.

Each year the physical sun is reborn in like manner, from the cave of the earth. Due to the tilt and wobble of the earth this solar orb seems to pass through the twelve houses of the zodiac. It does this as part of a yearly cycle, and a much larger cycle lasting roughly 26,000 years, or more specifically 25,920 years, wherein the sun rises in each zodiac house for a division of said time. Interestingly, humans are said to breath on average 25,920 times per day, the number of years in a great Platonic year, and the specific number of years it takes for the sun to complete one full precession of the zodiac. Upon its completion a new cycle begins: the wheel continues turning.

Throughout the solar year the sun grows in age, strength, and light, to overcome the cold and darkness of winter. From birth and youth to maturity and death the sun is anthropomorphized as a man. In some cases, the sun is considered as a penis, going from flaccid to erect until ejaculation before becoming flaccid once more. After reaching its strongest point during summer, when the sun is *Most High*, it begins to lose strength as it sinks lower in the sky in the proceeding months. The full demise of the sun is realized in autumn, and it is said that the light of the world eventually will be extinguished, in part, during winter. In mid-December the sun lowers into the lowest portion of the northern hemisphere and symbolically dies; it ceases visual movement for *three days*. At this point it rests near the *Southern Crux* constellation, from a certain point of view. After three days the sun begins moving northward again, but only by a few degrees, until it is reborn on December 25th.

From this astrological fact it can be determined that the sun/son dies on the Southern Cross, or zodiac wheel, remains dead for three days in the tomb of earth, and is then resurrected or reborn upon the conclusion of the winter solstice.

~

The story of Jesus details his birth to a virgin in a manger surrounded by animals. His birth took place in Bethlehem and was signaled to the *magi* by a star. This is the same Burning Star, or Eastern Star, that is met through initiation into the *mysteries* upon exiting the Temple to greet the rising sun. For magicians it is the Great Arcanum and for Kabbalists the sacred pentagram; that symbol marked ascending on the idol Baphomet for which the Templars were said to kneel in worship; they were accused by a man named Esquian de Horian of worshiping this graven image, spitting or trampling upon the cross, and eating roasted babies.

The star signifying the birth of a divine child may also be interpreted as Sirius, others say Saturn, while the three Wise Men or Magi are likely the three stars of Orion's Belt, which, on December 25th, partly aligned so that it is possible to follow them to Sirius in route to the birth of the sun rising northward.

When the sun is born, reborn, or resurrected, on December 25th, it resides in the constellation *Virgo* - the Virgin. This interpretation is debatable depending upon where you view the sun during that time of the year. It would be made more universal to express the virgin birth as an infant coming out of the world and into what we call life. But such a birth was not necessarily literal, though it could be both literal and figurative. However, as Joseph Campbell points out, Mary probably *"gave a normal birth to Jesus, who became the vehicle of the Logos at that particular moment."* This birth is symbolic of a renewing of the earth, a virgin world to be experienced by new life. The anthropomorphized image of the constellation is a virgin holding a sheath of wheat, thus relating to bread.

The reason bread is important is because *Bethlehem* translates to become the zodiacal *House of Bread*. The "house" is one of the twelve divisions of the zodiac constructed by God, and his son Jesus, both of which are architects and carpenters. The animals in the nativity are the other *houses* of the "animal wheel" or zodiac. The *wheat* used to make bread is a powerful symbol with consideration for the Eucharist and the agricultural *Killing of the King* ritual. It also refers to the bread consumed at the *Last Supper* by the disciples of Jesus, one of which betrayed him, the infamous Judas. In *Sleeping Beauty*, he may be associated with the seventh fairy placing a curse on the birth of the royal child. Astrologically he is the constellation *Scorpio*.

As the sun makes its journey through the sky it obtains full strength during the summer solstice, after which it begins losing strength before being declared dead upon the zodiac cross on the winter solstice. This astrological occurrence is described in Mark 14:43-46 of Judas and his betrayal:

> *"While He was still speaking, Judas, one of the Twelve, suddenly arrived. With him was a mob, with swords and clubs, from the chief priests, the scribes, and the elders. His betrayer had given them a signal. 'The One I kiss', he said, "He's the One; arrest Him and take Him away under guard'. Then they took hold of Him and arrested Him."*

The twelve disciples are the houses or signs of the zodiac and Judas is called the "betrayer," he who kisses Jesus to alert the Roman guards of his identify. This is a strange incident considering the relatively small size of such a town at the time, and considering the presence of Jesus whose whereabouts would likely have been known already. Either way the betrayer played by Judas signals the upcoming death of Jesus. The constellation *Scorpio* takes the place of Judas astrologically and Jesus is the sun.

Scorpions have a tail stinger and are also known to leave a second puncture mark from another part of their tail. This dual sting is a symbol of two lips. The approach of the summer solstice is preceded by *Scorpio,* and the "kiss" bestowed upon Jesus was thus the *kiss of death*. Since the scorpion stings from behind it is known as the "backbiter," from where we derive the word "backstabber." Judas backstabbed Jesus and "kissed" him, marking him with death, much like *Scorpio* marks the sun with imminent death upon beginning its decline after the summer solstice.

However, Judas should not be viewed as an entirely dark force since he is responsible for both the death and resurrection of the sun and son. Joseph Campbell says that Judas is selected by Jesus because he is the *"most developed of the lot"* and therefore *"eligible for that assignment"* as the *midwife of salvation*.

Therefore, the sun/son was born on December 25th of the Virgin/Virgo in Bethlehem, the House of Bread, or Constellation Virgo. The three Wise Men/Orion's Belt then followed a bright star, Sirius, Venus, or the pentagram, to the birth of the sun/son on that significant Solstice/Yule date. Astrologically it is also relevant that the sun enters each sign of the zodiac at 30 degrees and as such the ministry of Jesus begins around age 30. In her book <u>The Christ Conspiracy</u>, D. M. Murdoch explains the metaphor of Jesus as a carpenter:

> *"The Sun is the 'Carpenter' who builds his daily 'houses' or 12 two-hour divisions."* She adds, *"As the mythos developed, it took the form of a play, with a cast of characters, including the 12 divisions of the sky called the signs or constellations of the zodiac. The symbols that typified these 12 celestial sections of 30 each were not based on what the constellations actually look like but represent aspects of earthly life. Thus the ancient peoples were able to incorporate these earthly aspects into the mythos and project them onto the all important celestial screen."*

~

Thus is the study and field of *astrotheology*. The often difficult to separate fields of astrology and astronomy are merely different ways of observing and learning from God's creation. Although these subjects, especially astrology, are reduced to new age-isms today, they were vitally important for our ancestors in determining planting and harvesting times. In <u>The Supernatural, the Occult, and the Bible</u>, author Gerald A. Larue explains the importance of one star in particular to the Egyptians:

> *"The Egyptian year began when Sirius appeared on the horizon at dawn, July 19. At that moment, the Egyptians knew that the inundation of the Nile was about to begin. This mighty river, fed by rains at its headwaters in the Mountains of the Moon in central Africa, annually swelled and overflowed to revitalize the black soil bordering its banks in Egypt. The event was heralded by festivals dedicated to the goddess Isis."*

Isis is the patron goddess of water as it relates to femininity, birthing fluids, and new life. Her ankh is a symbol of life, which she nurtured just as the Nile River was the protector of the Egyptian people. In this way, Isis was the savior and redeemer of her people, as would be her son Horus, and the later Jesus.

We also read in the book of Judges 5:20 how the stars of heaven fought against a Canaanite general named Sisera, meaning that God gave his favor to the Israelites over the Canaanites of Palestine – this was determined by the stars:

> *"They fought from heaven; the stars in their courses fought against Sisera."*

Fourth Iteration

Since *astro* relates to the stars and *theology* is the study of nature and God, astrotheology, like astrology, is truly the observation of a *Divine Plan*. For GOD is not a man with a scepter, or any other anthropomorphized figure, nor is HE a *male, female* or an *it*. As Joseph Campbell wrote, *"God is beyond duality."* In the east we find the incarnation of Buddha, for example, as a *"model through which to realize the mystery of incarnation in oneself."* Although western models separate heaven and earth, God and man, teaching that the divine is not within you, His essence can still be found externally in the nature below and nature above. This is why nature has been poisoned with sin and all things natural are considered sinful in large parts of the west.

This is not to say the east has perfected spiritual understanding, for there is much corruption present there as well. As a matter of fact, the east is just as guilty as the west in selling *enlightenment* as a factual *feeling* that can be purchased with idols, mantras, or religious-like labels. However, there is a difference between tribal gods like the one found in Jewish tradition and the nature gods and goddesses found all over. *"When your principal god is your tribal god, no other tribe can possibly possess the same theology,"* wrote Campbell. This breeds conflict. But when the general laws of nature are observed, be them above or below, or both, they are visible to all of mankind. They are *"local, historic, and specific."*

Fifth Iteration

It is evident that tribal and institutional gods have done much through their emissaries to destroy the *mysterium tremendum et fascinans*. The *Gnostics*, an early Jewish and Christian mystical sect, are known for their spiritual wisdom, which was held outside the authority of the state and religious institutions as far back as the first century CE officially. According to the *Encyclopedia of Britannica*, the English poet Henry More (1614-1687) first applied the term *gnosticism* to religious

Demiurge

groups known as *gnostikoi*, or those who have *gnosis - knowledge*. The Greek *gnostikos* was first used by Plato to describe the intellectual, rather than practical, manner of learning.

Some of these early Gnostic-Christian writings were found in 1945 near the Egyptian city of Nag Hammadi. The *Gnostic* story of creation is peculiar and quite fascinating. They say that *Sophia*, goddess of wisdom, accidentally, or without knowing, gave birth to *Demiurge*, who falsely took credit for what she had created. Being unable to truly *create*, the *Demiurge*, or Ialdabaoth (Yaldabaoth), became not only a malevolent usurper of creative authority, but was the author of schism and distortion. It is Ialdabaoth that many call YHWH, and it is the latter whose authority is still worshiped today in institutional religions. Although images vary, Yaldabaoth typically has the head of a lion and body of a snake.

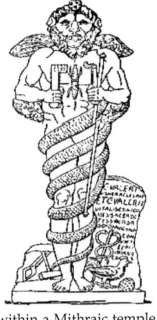

The Greco-Egyptian circular amulet inscription probably depicts the rising of consciousness through the erection of the human spinal cord – some say *kundalini* – that is to say, a serpent with human or lion head, not dissimilar from the Roman snake god Glycon.

Other depictions of this lion-headed figure mirror those of Phanes, both of which have a human body entwined by a serpent. In an image found within a Mithraic temple in Italy, the figure holds what appears to be a square and compass, as the grand architect, and is flanked by a caduceus and a cock (bird), which represents the sun. The Greek deity *Abraxas,* who has serpentine legs and a cock's head, is symbolic of the 365 spheres, or days in a solar year. The sum of *Abraxas* (Ἀβραξας) in Greek is: A = 1, β = 2, ρ = 100, α = 1, ξ =60, α = 1, and ς = 200, equating to 365. Abraxas, therefore, is symbolic of the 365 Æons or *Spirits of the Days* that bring about new life and health with each cycle. The Gnostics called him *Great Archon.* Collin De Plancy's *Infernal Dictionary* depicts him as a sort of grotesque goblin king with serpents at his feet and a giant belly:

> "ABRACAX or ABRAXAS: One of the gods of a few Asian theogonies, from whose name one drew the phylactery abracadabra. Abracax is represented on amulets with a rooster's head, dragon's feet and a whip in his hand. The Basilidians, heretics of the second century, regarded him as their supreme god. As they found that the seven Greek letters that made his name added to 365 in Greek, which is the number of days in the year, they subjected to him several genies who presided over the three hundred and sixty-five skies and to whom they attribute dthree hundred and sixty-five

virtues, one for each day. The Basilidians also said that Jesus Christ, Our Lord, was only a benevolent ghost sent to Earth by Abracax. This was a deviation from their leader's dogma."

Some Gnostics saw this Demiurge *trickster* as a misleading god who wished to keep humanity in bondage to his whims. Much like Lucifer and Satan, the *Demiurge* distorted human perception and inverted it downward from *above* to *below*, focusing *The ALL* into individual and separated elements concerned only with their own *desire*. The *Demiurge* and his architects known as *archons* are thus *false prophets*, *tricksters*, and *distorters* of creation. They are also *necessary evil*.

Abracax - from Collin De Plancy's *Infernal Dictionary*

In the Gnostic text <u>On the Origins of the World</u>, the *Demiurge* has the audacity to claim: *"I am God, and no other one exists except me."* To this his mother replies, *"You err, [blind god]. An enlightened immortal humanity exists before you!"*

In his intriguing text <u>The Secret Books of the Egyptian Gnostics,</u> Jean Doresse explains how the Gnostic sect known as the Naassenes explained the creation of Man:

> *"At the beginning of the universe, as the Naassenes imagined, there had been a Man and a Son of Man, both androgynous. To the honor of that primordial Adam they composed numerous hymns."*

The Gnostics believed in an internal and physical truth and wisdom, rather than an external expression of faith. They saw the body itself - a temple - as corresponding to many popular spiritual and theological motifs:

> *"In their anthropological speculations, the brain corresponds to Eden; the membranes enveloping the brain, to the heavens; the head of man, to Paradise, etc."*

According to the Philosophumena, attributed to the theologian Hippolytus of Rome, the *Rivers of Paradise* described in Genesis 2:10-14 correspond likewise to the body and brain:

"This river, flowing out of Eden [i.e.,out of the brain], divides into four branches. The first river is called Phison; it is this which flows around the whole land of Evilat, where gold is found... it is there also that one finds the carbuncle and the emerald; this refers to the eye, as the value and the colours of these precious stones suggest. The second river is called Geon, it is this which surrounds the whole land of Ethiopia; that river is the ear, for it resembles a labyrinth. The third river is called the Tigris; it is that which flows near Syria; a river of the most impetuous current, which is the nostrils. It flows over against Syria because, in our reparation, the air breathed in from without rushes in with violent impetuosity to replace that which has just been breathed out..."

It is as 1 Corinthians 6:19-20 states:

"Do you not know that your bodies are temples of the Holy Spirit, who is in you, whom you have received from God? You are not your own; you were bought at a price. Therefore honor God with your bodies."

In Manly Hall's book How To Understand Your Bible there is reference to the two great aspects of the human body, referring to the arterial and nervous systems, which also represent the Edenic trees:

"The tree of life, which is the arterial with its roots in the heart; and the tree of the knowledge of good and evil, i.e., the nervous system which has its roots in the brain."

Literal interpretations aside, the facts being stated here are twofold: (1) the *Kingdom of Heaven* is within you; (2) the "price" is both the one that Christ paid but also the *separation* of the *One* into *Many*, which causes pain and suffering.

Another interpretation of the heavens and Rivers of Paradise comes in the form of Ezekiel's Wheel which features four strange creatures called cherubs. Each cherub has four heads and six wings, relating to the number of hours in a day, and the four directions, seasons, and rivers flowing out of Eden making the mundane world fertile. The wheels and eyes in Ezekiel's vision relate to the planets, stars, constellations, and zodiac. The solar system is a wheel which turns within the greater wheel of the cosmos. Within the midst of these powers rests God, i.e., the Ancient of Days or the Most High.

Part of Ezekiel's Vision, reproduced here from Manly Hall's book *How To Understand Your Bible.*

The Sethians, one of the main currents of Gnosticism, imagined that heaven and earth were a pregnant woman's belly. They say that the first principle engendered was a wind, born from water, which stirred up waves and created vegetation. This is Genesis 1:2 told in a different way:

> "And the earth was without form and void, and darkness was upon the face of the deep. And the Spirit of God moved upon the face of the waters."

The "wind" is what drives the "Spirit of God" to move *upon the face of the waters.* It is as Joseph Campbell writes of the miracle of walking on water: *"as the spirit blows over the waters, so anyone who has entirely spiritualized himself can do the same."*

The waters, now worked up by a blowing wind, turned to waves. Jean Doresse says, *"the movement of the waves... is comparable to the efforts of the full womb to bring forth."* Even today we still say that birth *contractions* come in *waves.* The blowing of wind also, according to the Gnostics, resembled the hissing of a serpent. Jean writes how *"it was, then, from the Serpent that generation began."*

At this moment we know that Adam and Eve have been sent from the *Garden of Paradise* into the *Garden of Hallucinations,* separated from God and forced to earn what they needed or desired by the *sweat of their own brow.* Jean describes further in his book the relationship between light, spirit, darkness, and the serpent in Genesis:

> *"And when the Light and the Spirit from above entered into contact with the dark and disorderly Matter, then the Serpent (the wind issuing form the waters of the abyss) penetrated it and begot man. The Serpent, they said, is indeed the only form that is known and loved by this impure Womb. For that reason, the perfect Word of the Light from on high, when he wished to come down into the material world, took on the frightful form of the Serpent in order to enter this impure Womb under that deceptive appearance. Such was the necessity that obliged the Word of God to come down into the body of a virgin."*

However, this *Perfect Man* or *Word* which had *"penetrated the body of a virgin, and relieved the anguish that prevails in the Darkness,"* was not enough. For *"after having entered into the shameful mysteries of the womb, he cleansed himself, and drank of the cup of living water that must imperatively be drunk by whosoever wills to divest himself of the servile form and put on a heavenly garnet."*

Sixth Iteration

Gnostic tradition suggests strongly that Jesus was a member of the community of *Essenes,* another mystical Jewish sect. By the name of the Gnostic, or early Christian, *Nazarenes,* he became known as *Jesus of Nazareth*. This secret society wore white robes, lived in relative seclusion, and practiced ritual baptism. They also believed that John the Baptist was the *Real Christ*.

Jesus was no doubt a masterful teacher, preaching *mysteries* that were great threats to man's worldly powers. Jean Doresse documents his teachings about the *Treasury of Light*, which upon death is said to *"pilot the soul out of the body, through all the aeons of the invisible regions, and lead it as far as the Treasury; how they release it from sins and turn the soul into a pure light."*

According to the <u>Bruce Codex</u> the soul is then brought into the *Three Amens, Triple-Powers, Five Trees* and the *Seven Voices*. These *mysteries* were considered sacred and secret, and as Jesus says:

> *"These mysteries I am revealing to you, take care not to tell them to any man unworthy of them. Do not give them away to father or mother, nor brother or sister nor to any relatives; disclose them not for food or drink nor for a woman; neither for gold nor silver."*

He goes on to reference the 72 Demons of Solomon and the 72 Secret Names of God, which Hebrews call YHWH, i.e. Ialdabaoth, commanding that the *mysteries* be given to no person working with these forces:

> *"Transmit them to no woman, to no man who is found acting upon any belief in the seventy-two Archons, or who is serving them; never reveal them to those who worship the eight powers of the great Archons."*

These "eight powers" refer to, as Jean writes, *"certain sectaries who practised, upon such pretexts, veritable orgies and impure rituals while pretending to possess the true Gnosis and to adore the true God."* Jesus goes on to say about these false prophets: *"their god is evil; he is the Triple-Power of the Great Archon, and his name is Taricheas, the son of Sabaoth the Adamas. He is the enemy of the Heavenly kingdom; he has the face of a wild-boar, his tusks project from his mouth; and from behind he has another face with is that of a lion."*

The son referred to is one of Ialdabaoth's progeny, who, like Saturn, overthrows his father. *Encyclopedia Britannica* explains: *"When Sabaoth realizes that there is a higher realm, he undergoes a kind of conversion, condemns Ialdabaoth, and is enthroned above him."* The boar spoken of is absolutely related to the one that kills Adonis and Tammuz, and the meal, or pork, that results in Buddha's death.

Jesus then announces, after he warns his disciples to never reveal these *secrets*, that he will administer three baptisms consisting of water, fire, and spirit, and then disclose the *"mystery of the spiritual anointing and the secrets of the Treasury of the Light."* After instructing a few disciples to bring small containers of wine and specified plants, which are placed on an altar, a magical prayer is recited:

> *"May these powers come, and may they baptize my disciples with the water of the Life of the Seven Virgins of Light; and may their sins be forgiven, and may they be cleansed from their iniquities, that they may be numbered among the inheritors of the Kingdom of the Light."*

Jean says the *"wine in the cruet on the right changes into water, and the disciples approach Jesus, who baptizes them. Then, by means of analogous rites, Jesus administers, one after another, the baptisms of Fire and of the Holy Spirit."* Jesus then teaches them passwords and signs by which they will make themselves known to the powers guarding each gate of the heavens. This is similar to the *lost keys of Freemasonry* and identical procedure to the afterlife spells found in Egypt, whereby a Pharaoh would be instructed in passcodes and gestures to pass through the afterlife gates.

Learning of this it is no surprise, then, why the orthodox Jews and the Romans both saw Jesus as a *sorcerer* and a threat to their power. The accusations of Jesus having learned *magic* in Egypt (Shabbat 104b) seem to be quite accurate too.

Seventh Iteration

As Talmudic legend preserves, there is a curious story about a man named Jehoshua Ben Panthira, born 120 B.C., who also traveled to Egypt. To escape persecution of rabbis under the Jewish King Alexander Jannes, and to hopefully learn magic and become a miracle worker, Jehoshua visited the mysterious Nile land with his master Ben Prachia. An old manuscript quoted by Hall extends the verse from John 6:42 where it is written:

"And they said, Is not this Jesus, the song of Joseph, whose father and mother we know? how is it then he saith, I came down from heaven?"

That manuscript adds: *"Is it because he has dwelt among the Greeks that he comes thus to speak with us? What is there in common between what he has learned from the Egyptians and what our fathers have taught us."*

Hall says further of the Jewish tradition that Jehoshua was reportedly *"stoned to death as a wizard in the city of Lydda, and afterwards his body was hung on a tree. His death occurred about B.C. 70."*

Although Jehoshua Ben Panthira may have escaped persecution under King Jannes like Jesus escaped the infanticide of King Herod, we also know that in the latter case said king was dead in 4 B.C. before the birth of the savior baby. Likewise, as few scholars point out, the only registration of the Jews during Roman times took place under Quirinus in 6 A.D. In other words, the Christian tradition is loosely based on one, or perhaps many, historical figures, but is invariably mixed with excessive literary liberties, mythological motifs such as the virgin birth, archetypes for the sun, and without doubt the *secret teachings* of the ancient *mystery* traditions. We are indebted to Manly Hall for his life's work, and it was his conviction that the Christian religion was *"built upon the teachings of certain Syrian sects, partially the Essene and the Nazarene."* The truth embodied in this most assured fact is that the *Christian Mysteries* are a sort of drama like those performed in the *mysteries* of Greece and Egypt. The symbols and archetypes embodied by Christianity speak to the unconscious in a universal way – as with many religions.

In Egypt it was the story of Isis and her immaculately conceived son Horus. As with Mary and the mother of Quetzalcóatl, Isis was informed by the Holy Ghost that she would have a son named Horus, a reincarnation of her husband Osiris. But upon birth, the evil principle called Typhon sought to kill the child, like Set had attempted to destroy Osiris, and so Isis hid him away among the reeds near the edge of the Nile like Moses. Horus thus escaped this destruction and eventually led an army in a final battle against evil, vanquishing Typhon completely. Here is the Egyptian version of Armageddon and another version of the stories told of

Krishna and Jehoshua Ben Panthira, and the murderous Kings Kansa and King Alexander Jannes.

Horus in this story symbolizes *wisdom* and Isis is the *veil* behind which it is concealed from the profane forces of Typhon.

Osiris was born in his son Horus so that he may avenge his own death; the Son Jesus is God the Father. Osiris is also the Holy Spirit who presides over the dead in the *Hall of Judgement*. As with the relationship between Bacchus and Christ, be that their wine miracles or the riding of an ass, like Horus conquering the red ass Set, Bacchus is said to maneuver a chariot drawn specifically by panthers; the name Jehoshua Ben Panthira means *son of the panther*.

It is furthermore interesting, at least, to note that since Jehoshua was supposedly stoned as a wizard his death would more factually align with how Roman Law was carried out in Judea. Crucifixions were only reserved for great thefts and murders, whereas civil offenses like religious crimes were punished by the sword or stoning. Since Judas essentially stole his thirty pieces of silver by selling *wisdom* for worldly possessions, it is no surprise that the Muslims, and at least one Egyptian tradition, are assured Jesus did not die on the cross and that instead the man crucified in his place was actually the *betrayer* himself. Even the Bible itself is uncertain of what happened to Judas, who in the *Gospel of Barnabas* is hanged for his transgression and theft.

Whatever the true history and origin of these facts and myths there was a man hung between Gestas and Demas, and on either side of this crucified man were these *thieves* of contradiction, the two hemispheres of the brain, *abstract mind* and *concrete mind*.

These polarities may also be classified as the *Pineal Gland* for male (Adam) and *Pituitary Gland* for female (Eve).

The Wheel of the Zodiac is comprised of twelve houses separated by a cross into four quadrants of three. The outer portion contains the symbol of each sign, the next circle expressing the name of that zodiac section. Below that is another concentric circle with the astrological sign of each house.

In the center is the sun crucified on the cross, the points expressed as the four corners of the world and the four directions.

Each division signifies one of the four seasons: winter, spring, summer, and autumn.

The term *Zodiac* comes from the Greek *zōidiakos,* and from *zōidion,* meaning a sculptured animal figure. The wheel itself is known as the *animal wheel.* These "animals" were those attending the birth of Jesus, the sun/son of God, when he was born after the Winter Solstice in the House of Virgo, the Virgin - *Bethlehem.* They are also the animals Adam is given dominion over in the Bible.

Hieroglyphic Plan of the Ancient Zodiac
from Kircher's OEdipus Ægyptiacus

    The inner circle of this diagram contains the hieroglyph of Hemphta, the triform and pantamorphic deity. Emanating outward from the center are six concentric bands explained as follows: (1) lists the number of zodiacal houses in words and numerals, (2) the modern names of each house, (3) Greek and Egyptian names of the deities assigned to each house (4) characters of the zodiac represented by animals, objects, hybrid beings and anthropomorphic beings, (5) each symbolic sign of the zodiac, (6) the number of subdivisions under each sign.

    There are four quadrants each containing three houses of the zodiac. Each house is further divided into three subdivisions for a total of 36 throughout the entire diagram.

The Egyptian Zodiac from <u>The Gods of the Egyptians</u>,
E. A. Wallis Budge, 1904

Our lives are in the hands of the Grand Architect of the Universe,
here seen as the Devil spinning the Wheel of Life or as God
Supporting the entire world.

Indian Wheel of Life *

Tibetan Wheel of Life*

Japanese Wheel of Life*

God Supporting the World

*Reproduced from Paul Carus

By Buonamico Buffamalco

KEYS OF THE MYSTERIES

First Iteration

The sum of our assessment is the realization that God exists within and without all things, and that "He" cannot be defined as *male* or *female*, or even *it*, nor as a particular deity with humanly attributes. That God is *androgynous* and *hermaphroditic* says nothing of "His" appearance, sexuality, gender, and the like. God's indeterminate appearance speaks to the reality of "His" *Oneness* and *Unity* splitting into *Many* once the process of Creation had begun. In Genesis 1:1 we read the following about creation:

"In the beginning God created the heavens and the earth."

This verse, with its many translations, is ineffective at conveying the subtler values that are found within. GOD is actually *ELOHIM*, a term which is both plural and androgynous; the HEAVENS and EARTH are to be understood as *spirit* and *matter*; and the word CREATED implies that something must be in existence that can be ordered and manipulated into FORM. Therefore, what Elohim created in the BEGINNING was really a MANIFESTATION and FORMATION of eternal materials arranged into a new *order*, i.e. what the Masons call *ORDO AB CHAO*.

What can be inferred here is that Genesis contains a far more scientific approach to the BEGINNING than most believe, one that marries science and religion rather than divorces the two. The same meaning can be derived from Genesis whether we say GOD CREATED or the FORCES OF NATURE CREATED. Manly Hall explains the same of this sacred text, writing:

"...the creative forces of nature brought forth sequentially the super physical bodies of the solar system, then the material planets; and then, shifting perspective to the planet earth, unfolded the life upon it up to its present state."

He adds that *"if the reader can take such a statement as 'And God created' and read instead: 'And the forces of nature, over a great period, caused to manifest' – most of the difficulties will be overcome."*

~

The kabbalistic concept of *infinity* is embodied in AIN SOPH, the Boundless form of God before manifestation. According to the Egyptians the UNENDING ONE is triune in nature: being, life, and light. The first manifestation of AIN SOPH is known as the *Opened Eye* and called KETHER, or the crown, by the kabbalists. Within this *Eye of Providence* was manifested the polarities of ABBA, the father, and AIMA, the mother, or the MANY from the ONE. Hall says that from this *"union of Abba and Aima, energy and substance, was produced form,"* and it is from the *"union of life and matter"* that the creator-gods, or ELOHIM, were born.

From the unfolding of consciousness and the crystallization of matter to the development of man there is an ever-existing juxtaposition between *that which is above* and *that which is below*. For MAN is a miniature universe and the universe is the BOUNDLESS MAN. This pattern is found in everything: atoms, elements, minerals, plants, animals, humans, and the universe. According to Hall's <u>How To Understand Your Bible</u> the *Rivers of Paradise* correspond not only to the body, but also to the physical kingdoms:

> *"The four rivers are the four streams of ether or energy which sustain the four kingdoms of the physical world – mineral, vegetable, animal, and human."*

Philosophers believe that these vital elements nourish man's physical body today, but in THE BEGINNING, they formed the etheric body. When the physical earth was forming, Hall says it *"floated in a sea of superphysical humidity,"* or what the Greeks called *aether*. Within this non-physical sphere beyond the earth's surface were evolving the forms that would later descend upon the planet. In this interpretation we find that our GARDEN OF EDEN is not in the physical world or of the physical body, but *"in the higher etheric element which encloses the earth in a globe of translucent energy."* The area we call PARADISE was identified by the ancients as being the North Polar area of the etheric globe, a fascinating notion considering that cells impregnated with sperm are believed to first develop from their northern polar areas, and *"the same is true of planets and all of the cosmic planes."*

~

In Genesis 6:2 we learn: *"the sons of God saw the daughters of men that they were fair; and they took them wives of all which they chose."* From this story it can be inferred that as the earth cooled the gods came down and liberated the elements so that they could develop as a fetus grows in the womb. These "sons of god" were the *ego* and *consciousness* which took "wives" of the "daughters of men," i.e., the *material bodies* being formed. Hall explains in further detail:

> *"When the vehicles or bodies built up first from the more subtile [thin] parts of the physical globe reached a certain degree of development, the spirits dwelling in the ether above, and called in the Bible the 'Sons of God,' flowed downward and into the new bodies, which are called the 'daughters of men'; or more correctly the daughters of MANAS or mind – the mind – formed bodies; for the word man literally means mind."*

The FIRST MAN we know as ADAM is for certain not a singular individual, but instead a sort of species, race, or new kind of *vehicle*. In other words, ADAM is the development of a new means of consciousness unique and separate from the elemental, mineral, vegetable, and animal kingdoms. He is ADAM KADMON who is formed of the RED EARTH, a substance relatable to the fiery essence of the early cosmos.

~

The place where the first man and woman, ADAM and EVE, dwelt was a location uncontaminated by physical matter and desire, i.e., PARADISE. It is the place that, as Hall relates, *"all exiled humanity is seeking."*

Genesis 3:24 explains how God "drove man out" of paradise and then placed *"cherubim and a flaming sword flashing back and forth to guard the way to the tree of life."* Whereas the *Tree of the Knowledge of Good and Evil* represents the human nervous system, which reflects the vegetable body of roots and branches, the *Tree of Life*, which has the same roots and branches, is symbolic of the heart wherein Jesus is said to enter. Solomon also placed Cherubim with flaming swords on the doors to his temple.

Eden is thus the *Holy of Holies* contained in every bodily temple. As the microcosmic MAN the body can be seen as a miniature universe, which itself is a garden paradise where planets and suns blossom like sacred fruit. As physical *matter*, however, the body is also a vessel and living tomb which acts as the alchemical container and the putrefying material that comes from the PRIMA MATERIA.

Second Iteration

In Genesis we learn that Adam and Eve have a child named Cain. Genesis 4:1-2 relates that when she birthed her child, Eve said, *"I have acquired a man from the Lord."* In tradition it is the first child of man who is actually the progeny of Samael. Eve then gives birth to another child, a brother to Cain, named Abel, who was *"keeper of the sheep"* like Jesus, Mithra(s), Hermes, and Orpheus. In the next verses, 3-5, we read:

> *"And in the process of time it came to pass that Cain brought an offering of the fruit of the ground to the LORD. Abel also brought of the firstborn of his flock and of their fat. And the LORD respected Abel and his offering, but He did not respect Cain and his offering. And Cain was very angry, and his countenance fell."*

When Abel brings a firstborn lamb to the Lord we are reminded of Abraham and his only son Isaac from later chapters in the book of Genesis. The *lamb* represents the *animal* self being sacrificed, thus signifying one of the *keys* to the *mysteries*. Since Cain brings *fruit*, or the workings of the external world, the Lord rejects his offering. As the story goes, Cain is so angry that he eventually kills his brother Abel. What this story preserves are the conflicts between light and darkness, or right and wrong, that battle between the little angel and little devil. It is a war with ego within the soul akin to the battle between Lucifer and Michael the Archangel in heaven.

~

The great age mentioned in the Bible of Adam, who lived over 900 years, is reference to the duration of a lineage, just as Cain and Abel represent two distinct *races of man*. These are the *root races* of Madame Blavatsky.

The third race is known as Lemurian in the esoteric history, the child and lineage of Seth, and it was this race which replaced the former creatures and monstrous forms which were destroyed for having no ability to contain the spirit-soul-mind. Here again we witness the *creative* process of *evolution*.

The fourth race was that of the Atlanteans, a story which is both physical and symbolic, possibly preserving the story of creation in the form of an advanced spiritual people being swallowed up by the waters of *illusion* like the prince that becomes a beast and must be saved by beauty.

Third Iteration

Next, we read about Israel, Moses, the Exodus, Ten Commandments, Ark of the Covenant and Tabernacle.

The name *Israel* literally translates to *God is a Warrior*, a term therefore signifying the power of God manifesting throughout the entirety of Creation. The nation of Israel is not made of a singular people but of all mankind and nature. For MANKIND is God's CHOSEN PEOPLE. The *Twelve Tribes* are thus the signs of the animal wheel or Zodiac. Hall explains in <u>How To Understand Your Bible</u> what the term ISRAEL means:

> *"When we think of Israel, therefore, we have not only to consider a people or a tribe or nation, but of the whole life of nature, the gods of heaven whose shadows are upon the earth...The common notion that the twelve tribes of Israel make up the Jewish nation is quite incorrect, as Israel means all life; the tribes of Israel are all living things. Israel is a generic term for humanity as a collective whole, regardless of race or nation."*

As a collective people – all of humanity – Israel becomes ADAM. When the Twelve Tribes or Houses are wandering in search of the *Promised Land*, that internal place called the *Kingdom of Heaven*, they represent the collective of humanity searching for truth while growing and developing through a slow process of evolution.

The word Israel, like Solomon broken into three distinct words for the sun, may also be broken into separate parts; IS represents Isis, RA represents the sun god Ra (and also, his son Osiris), and EL is symbolic of the angELic realms and ELohim.

In fact, the name Moses is itself an arrangement of letters which, according to Hall, *"form the word Shemmah, which means the Sun."* It is most appropriate that Moses, the teacher, is associated with the horns of Jupiter (Jew Peter) Ammon, which symbolize the celestial Aries who leads the heavenly flocks.

The *Milky Way River* connects with the *Egyptian Nile* and from these waters, life pours forth. The same is said of Jesus Christ and of Moses when he strikes the rock at Horeb with the staff that had touched the Nile. The Lord tells Moses in Exodus 17:6 that he is to *"strike the rock, and water will come out of it for the people."* The place where this occurred is named Massah and Meribah, words that mean *testing* and *quarreling*, a reference to the Israelites. *Massah* is obviously very close to Messiah too.

Whereas Christians find grace in the crucifixion and resurrection of a savior, Jews, due to their rejection of Christ, continue to suffer, only finding salvation in a sort of religious catharsis called *EXILE*. It is only with the coming messiah and the End of Days that the Jewish people can find peace – as many believe. But *exile* shares a metaphoric origin with general term *Israel* and the *Promise Land*.

The mythos of exile has a few origins, but largely originated as a Christian story explaining the presence of Jews living beyond their homeland - this was considered proof of Jewish guilt and sin. Professor and author Shlomo Sand goes further in his book <u>The Invention of the Jewish People</u>, explaining that the word for *exile* - GALUT - has a meaning closer to *"political subjugation rather than deportation."* He adds, that much like the Promise Land, as described by Joseph Campbell:

> *"Exile, in fact, was anywhere, even in the Holy Land. Later the Kabbalah made it a central attribute of the divinity, for the Shekhinah (the divine spirit) is always in exile... Exile, therefore, was not a location away from the homeland, but a condition that is not salvation. The anticipated salvation would come when the messiah king of the seed of David arrived, and with this, a mass return to Jerusalem. Salvation would include the resurrection of the dead, who would also congregate en masse in Jerusalem."*

Sand's extremely controversial work explores the myth of exile in far greater detail, exposing the fact that there are no Roman records of deportation dating to the Siege of Jerusalem in 70 CE. Not only did the Romans keep immaculate records, but they never deported entire peoples even if certain officials or groups were forcibly moved by other powers, such as the Assyrians or Babylonians:

> "Even if we accept the unrealistic figure of seventy thousand captives, it still does not mean that the evil Titus, who destroyed the Temple, expelled 'the Jewish people'. Rome's great Arch of Titus shows Roman soldiers carrying the plundered Temple candelabra – not as taught in Israeli schools, Judean captives carrying it on their way to exile. Nowhere in the abundant Roman documentation is there any mention of a deportation from Judea. Nor have any traces been found of large refugee populations around the borders of Judea after the uprising, as there would have been if a mass flight had taken place."

Although captive fighters may have been shipped away while others fled, still there was no exile then nor after the uprising in 132 CE.

There is a similar issue of 'missing records' relating to the *Final Solution* during World War II. Even the *Holocaust Encyclopedia* online, in a page on the Wannsee Conference - where the plan was supposedly devised - admits that there is no record of such a plan. Sources like this allude to a "code name" and imply that it was secretly agreed to carry out such a policy with no written record, even though the Nazi regime, which certainly killed Jews and millions of others, was, we are told, proud of their actions:

> "The 'Final Solution' was the code name for the systematic, deliberate, physical annihilation of the European Jews. At some still undetermined time in 1941, Adolf Hitler authorized this European-wide scheme for mass murder.... The men at the table did not deliberate whether such a plan should be undertaken, but instead discussed the implementation of a policy decision that had already been made at the highest level of the Nazi regime."

Sand has no relationship to the above statement, but he does go into the depths of history to record that like the EXILE, the EXODUS is also fabricated. In fact, during the 13th-century BCE, *"the purported time of the Exodus, Canaan was ruled by the still-powerful Pharaohs."* This presents an interesting question: *"Moses led the feed slaves out of Egypt... to Egypt?"* There is no written record or of millions – hundreds of thousands of warriors and their families - wandering the desert for forty years, an event that alone seems entirely impossible. Such a historical fact should have left some sort of archeological record too, and this is perhaps the most significant fact. Sand writes, *"Yet there not a single mention of any 'Children of Israel' who lived in Egypt, or rebelled against it, or emigrated from it at any time."* As with the above question pertaining to Moses: *"If at the time of the supposed Israelite conquest the country* [Canaan] *was ruled by Egypt, how was it that not a single Egyptian document mentioned this?"*

Archeological research also *"failed to find any traces of an important tenth-century kingdom, the presumed time of David and Solomon. No vestige was ever found of monumental structure, walls or grand palaces, and the pottery found there was scanty and quite simple... no trace has been found of the existence of that legendary king, whose wealth is described in the Bible as almost matching that of the mighty imperial rulers of Babylonia or Persia."* Despite the grand theological and mythological nature of such stories, Biblical authors clearly merged parables, legends, and myths, with real locations as with any good science-fiction or fantasy story about Earth. The same may be said of Biblical heroes, kings, judges, priests, prophets, etc. There was possibly a tenth-century Judea presence, likely of a small tribal kingdom and a fortified stronghold called Jerusalem, possibly even ruled by a House of David, and Sand says that the *"kingdom of Israel under the Omride dynasty was clearly greater than the kingdom of Judah under the House of David."* This former kingdom was hated by the authors of the first five books of the Hebrew Bible (Pentateuch), whom were Judean monotheists. It is likely that these authors were *"no less envious of their legendary power and glory."* When attempting to create a consistent religious community by drawing on the glory of history, countless ancient authors sought to create a "cult center in Jerusalem," which Sand explains as such:

"Concerned to isolate it from the idolatrous population, they invented the category of Israel as a sacred, chosen people whose

origins lay elsewhere, in contrast to Canaan, a local anti-people of hewers of wood and drawers of water."

As we learned earlier of the *House of Israel* - a term referring to the twelve houses/tribes of the zodiac and all living things in general - they were accused in Acts 7 of taking up the "tabernacle of Moloch" and the star of "Remphan." Today we refer to that symbol as the Star of David, but this is incorrect since the "Jews" did not have a star, besides the one they adopted in the wilderness as a false idol –Chiun (Saturn), Apis (an Egyptian bull deity), and others as the brass bull-headed deity Molech.

Those extrapolating the 1948 State of Israel with the Biblical Israelites need to be careful, for these and other reasons. The *"invented…category of Israel as a sacred, chosen people"* bears a similar weight to the pseudoscientific concept of a *Master Race*. Whether they are called Frankists, Sabbateans, or Zionists, 1948-Israel is less aligned with Biblical Israelis and more aligned with Revelation 2:9, or the *Synagogue of Satan*: being comprised of people claiming to be "Jews" in "poverty" when they are neither:

> *"I know thy works, and tribulation, and poverty, (but thou art rich) and I know the blasphemy of them which say they are Jews, and are not, but are the synagogue of Satan."*

Israel was founded through the British establishment, home of modern eugenics, and the Nazi party of Germany. The 1917 *Balfour Declaration* announced the establishment of a "national home for the Jewish people" on the heels of the 1933 *Haavara Agreement*, which began the transfer of Jewish property to Palestine. A coin was even minted in 1934 to commemorate the joint Zionist-Nazi agreement (fed partly by Zionist boycotts of German goods), having a swastika on one side and a Star of Remphan on the other.

The United States Holocaust Memorial Museum says this of the coin:

> "The coin was struck in 1934 to memorialize the journey of Baron von Mildenstein, a Nazi party member, to Palestine. The trip resulted in a pro-Zionist report encouraging Jewish emigration, published in the nationalist newspaper, Der Angriff."

In 1992, the *Chicago Tribune*, along with a few other sources, published the following about the death toll at Auschwitz, which was two separate camps – one was a work facility and the other was for sick patients, hence the higher death toll:

> "*Jewish and Polish scholars of the Holocaust now agree that the Auschwitz death toll was less than half the four million cited here for four decades. The actual number was probably between 1.1 million and 1.5 million-and at least 90 percent of the victims were Jews.*"

While the atrocities of the communists have largely been ignored in all educational centers, Nazis are blamed for everything – having lost the war officially, this is commonplace. The 100-million dead of all races, religions, and the like, slaughtered by communists, particularly in Russia and China - not to mention the 9 million dead from the Holodomor in Ukraine – are almost entirely ignored while the 6-million figure of supposed discriminate killing is used to justify crimes, war, genocide, and financial shakedowns even into the 21-century – *see* Norman Finkelstein's The Holocaust Industry. As with the HOLOCAUST narrative, a term that simply means 'mass death, usually by fire', the EXILE and EXODUS myths are used to likewise justify the same. Shlomo Sand puts it simply:

> "The Jews were not forcibly deported from their 'homeland', and there was no voluntarily 'return' to it."

Israel is all of God's Creation, the **Promise Land** is internal, and the **Exile/Exodus** is that of the eternal spirit wandering in the wilderness and seeking salvation.

Modern Jews are some of the biggest critics of the Israeli state, too, and for good reason: Israel is highly discriminatory of its own people - and those they consider to not fit into the definition of Jewish - and is therefore extremely conceited of its own importance to the determinant of anyone who questions its politics. Israel has been rightfully accused of hiding behind Jews to wage war, genocide, etc., against its stated enemies – often at the behest of the United States. They hide behind Jews, the Holocaust, the Exodus, and the mythic exile; they exploit real Jewish suffering.

Few realize that the term *semitic* relates to a family of languages that include Hebrew and Arabic, meaning all Arabs are semitic but not all "Jews" fall into this category. The term *antisemite* is not only overused, but also nearly useless and erroneous. Victims of its use should declare *anti-gentile*!

Shlomo Sand ends his book with a commentary in response to his critics. His responses are very objective and when asked the question, *Are the Palestinians the Descendants of the Ancient Jews?*, he says:

> "For my own part, I believe that today's Palestinians derive from a variety of origins, just like all contemporary peoples.... it is quite likely that an inhabitant of Hebron is closer in origin to the ancient Hebrews than are the majority of those across the world who identify themselves as Jews."

~

Some researchers have pointed out that the tribal God of Moses may be significant proof itself that the great Biblical character was really the Pharaoh Akhenaten, who shifted the Egyptian pantheon from one of polytheism to monotheism (Akhenaten came to power around 1353-1351 BCE and the Exodus occurred roughly 1290 BCE). For further context on this history, it is vital to read about the Hyksos dynasty, which was of Palestinian origin. Between 1630 and 1523 BCE, these people ruled northern Egypt as the 15th dynasty. According to Jewish historical Flavius Josephus, the term *Hyksos* means "king shepherds" or "captive shepherds." Josephus also identified these people with the *Hebrews* of the Bible, a word itself which is translated by some authors as "desert wanderers" - and like Hyksos, "rulers of foreign lands." The Hyksos are Palestinian in origin and have Semitic names, but according to the Encyclopedia Britannica they are *"almost certainly designated the foreign dynasts rather than an ethnic group."*

Josephus, quoting Manetho, concludes that the expulsion of the Hyksos resulted in the building of Jerusalem:

> *"After the conclusion of the treaty they left with their families and chattels, not fewer than two hundred and forty thousand people, and crossed the desert into Syria. Fearing the Assyrians, who dominated over Asia at that time, they built a city in the country which we now call Judea. It was large enough to contain this great number of men and was called Jerusalem."*

~

When Moses says in Exodus 4:10 that he is *"slow of speech and tongue"* we have yet another reference to his status as an Egyptian priest, for certain esoteric secrets cannot be easily divulged. This is why the god Harpocrates, the Egyptian keeper of silence and the *mysteries*, is depicted with a finger to his lips. As we already addressed the story of Moses and Aaron in Pharaoh's court there is no need for a recap here. Suffice to say that Aaron's staff, which many have recorded, represents *truth* and in its serpentine form *wisdom*. Truth and wisdom then devour the *false truth* of the material court magicians of Pharaoh. Hall summarizes this story in his book:

> *"But like the Pharaoh, regent of the dark sphere, is not thus easily converted. Like a rich man or a great prince he clings to his world possessions and denies the laws of the universe. As infirmity and misery come to the rich and the powerful, so the plagues descended upon the Pharaoh; but he remains adamant until his own son is stricken."*

In other words, he *"permits his whole land to be laid bare and he does not relent; but when his own is afflicted he cries in terror for mercy."*

The exodus of Moses and his people is representative of all mankind, not just the Jews (Hyksos), escaping from the bondage of that material *desire* realized in the Garden Paradise. The Red Sea, like the RED EARTH from whence man was formed, thus represents instead the emotional state which must be overcome. We read in Exodus 14:21 the following:

"And Moses stretched out his hand over the sea; and the Lord caused the sea to go back by a strong east wind all that night, and made the sea dry land, and the waters were divided."

Here we find the wise teacher reaching his hand out to calm *emotion* (em-ocean), a process which takes "all that night," but one that eventually leads to the waters being divided. One could relate this "night" to the *Dark Night of the Soul*, that final stage in self-purification and surrender to the *Divine Plan*. Shortly after in Genesis, Moses receives the Ten Commandments on Mt. Sinai, that sacred mountain where the gods dwell:

"When the Lord finished speaking to Moses on Mount Sinai, he gave him the two tablets of the covenant law, the tablets of stone inscribed by the finger of God."

These commandments are the essence of wisdom itself which are brought down by Moses from, as Hall puts it, *"the height of his own realization down to the valley where mortals dwell who cannot see the light."* The two tablets, as with the sons of Noah and the Rivers of Paradise, likewise correspond to the body. Each tablet is given over and inscribed to either the left or right hemisphere of the brain respectively. The tablets therefore correspond further to Gestas and Demas.

When Moses breaks the commandment tablets, he substitutes them for rough stone tablets, a story which symbolizes the *laws of materiality* replacing those of *divine truth*. In mystical tradition Moses receives three distinct laws upon the mountain from three separate ascents and descents. These include the Torah, the Mischna, and the Cabala.

~

The *Ark of the Covenant* protected the rough stone tablets of Moses and was itself concealed in the *Tabernacle* - a moveable shrine constructed after the temples of Egypt. As man below represents the microcosmic universe above, the Tabernacle is likewise a symbol of the living temple found above and below. It is simply put, *the sun*. In more complex terms the tablets of Moses are the hemispheres of the brain, *abstract mind* and *concrete mind*, and the human head is the

Tabernacle we call the *temples,* where the skull bones fuse, which houses the *Ark of the Covenant.* Our head is therefore the vessel for the *sanctum sanctorum.*

The physical structure of the Tabernacle consists of three parts - which enclose the Holy of Holies - like the physical, intellectual, and spiritual aspects of the Most High. Tabernacle rites relate to the three states of consciousness expressed by the multitudes of people, priests, and the high priest. They are ignorance, knowledge, and true wisdom, or those of the unconscious, subconscious, and conscious mind.

The triune principles are found in the entered apprentice, fellow craft, and master degrees of the Blue Lodge of Freemasonry and are present in the subterranean chamber below the Great Pyramid at Giza, and the subsequent Queen's chamber and King's chamber above.

Within the Holy of Holies is the ark-body and within that container was preserved a pot of manna that fell from the sky, the rod of Aaron, and the commandment tablets. Hall says that these triune objects *"represent the spiritual, emotional, and physical nature of man and the mysteries thereof."* He goes on to explain what the rest of the Tabernacle represents in his book:

> *"The altar of burnt offerings represents the earth; the laver of purification the water; the candlesticks and the shewbread are ascribed to fire representing the two extremes of the emotional nature; the altar of burnt incense is the air; and the Shekinah which hovers over the Ark of the Covenant is the akasha or ether."*

On top of the ark, we find the two cherub with wings outstretched and touching each other over the center of the container. These two angelic beings represent the four elements and fixed signs of the Zodiac. Shekinah is the fifth substance or element, juxtaposed to the virgins Mary or Sophia. Here is the *Mother of the Mysteries,* whereupon only the high priest may gaze upon the face of the infinite and live. This is identical to the veils of Isis: *"No Mortal Man Hath Ever Me Unveiled."* Hall goes on to further explain the significance of the garb worn by a high priest in the Tabernacle:

> *"The white linen garment is the purified physical body, the long colored garment the vital body, the ephod the emotional body, the*

helmet the mental body, the jewels the seven senses; and the twelve jewels of the breastplate the twelve celestial or zodiacal principles which reside in every human soul."

The *Ark of the Covenant* at the center of this *mystery* is the golden coffin of Osiris, the ark of Noah, and the macrocosmic universe *above* expressed through the miniature universe of the microcosmic man *below*. The ARK in all its forms is equated to the everlasting house of Solomon, or *Solomon's Temple*, a more true and solid form of the symbolic universe.

~

Whereas the *Tabernacle in the Wilderness* was transient the temple of Solomon was not. The three men overseeing the temple's construction were Solomon, the solar principle, Hiram of Tyre, the earth, and supplier of material necessities, and (C)Hiram Abiff, the masonic grand master architect, and the energy of creation. Although the temple was a real structure at some point the story told in 1 Kings is of a solar or universal temple. Hall once again provides us with an understanding of the themes present in this story:

"It requires seven years to build the Temple, that is, seven periods or cycles are necessary to perfect the earth. The thousands of workers are the forces, energies, and atoms. The masters of the workmen are the laws of life, and the finished Temple, so symbolically small, represents the physical Universe itself..."

Just as the universal macrocosmic temple is under construction so too is the societal temple, with each illuminated member a brick in the everlasting unfinished pyramid. Man himself, of course, is the microcosmic unfinished temple, and his accomplishments, those of refined character, emotion, desire, and mind, are the bricks by which it will be completed. For the *"Holy Place of man is his mind, and the most Holy of Holy Places is the heart."* The *wisdom* of men supports the *mind* and *heart*, or temple, by providing *knowledge*, i.e., the upright *beam*.

Fourth Iteration

When an initiate exited the physical temple, they were *born again* of the veiled virgin, or *Mother of the Mysteries*, square, upright, and polished like a true masonic stone or the gold of the alchemists. Their knowledge and wisdom secured the personal, bodily, societal, and secret temples. They became *Sons of the Widow*, born of the veiled virgin, who mourns her husband's loss in the glitter of material but celebrates his rebirth with the birth of Horus, i.e., her *Son of the Hawk*. For Isis is the Virgin Goddess like Mary.

In fact, MARY comes from the Latin word *mare*, meaning *sea*, and *virgin*, which means *pure*. Mary is thus the *pure sea* or *pure waters*, symbolized by the Nile, Ganges, and Milky Way; she is the VIRGIN MARE by which initiates receive their baptisms and are awarded the *keys of the mysteries*. She is also the universal *matrix* or *womb*, the *dark goddess* or dark side of Ishtar, Astarte, Mylitta, Diana, Kali, and Isis. The name *Mary* has also come to signify the role of a person who is raised in a monastic environment.

On a similar note, *Magdalene* is often translated as *magdal-elder*, or the one who is a *watchtower of the flock*. In the *Kujiki-72* the universe is regulated by five constitutions comprising seventeen ways. Whoever embodies these *Ways* comes to embody *The Way of the Protector*, and if they choose to be a teacher of neophytes, *The Way of the Watchtower*.

We still use these *mystery* terms today, interestingly, in the form of our words: *college*, *gymnasium*, and *alma mater*. COLLEGE refers to a society bound by vows, a GYMNASIUM is a temple of wisdom, and an ALMA MATER is the virgin mother of its graduates.

Fifth Iteration

The *Great Mystery of the Seed*, which we derive from the ancient mystery traditions, is that of *germination* and *growth*. Descent of seed into the ground and its growth and resurrection provides man with salvation and *daily bread*. Just as the green god Osiris is raised as a pillar in the land of a foreign king, and Moses is raised in the royal household of Egypt, a seed, if raised properly, will sprout, and rise, like the sun, to maturity. The sun passes into the western land and is conquered by darkness until it resurrects the next day bringing warmth and light back to a cold and dark world.

The *seed* and *sun*, particularly as they relate to bread and wine, were the prototypes for the savior god myths. When a harvest failed, famine, disease, and death followed. It was therefore important to preserve a certain part of a successful harvest, usually a tenth, to be kept in reserve. This is the agricultural origin of tithing ten percent to the church.

Luke 8:11 says, *"Now the parable is this: The seed is the word of God.'* The WORD is planted in us and if we water it with purification and let the light of our hearts shine on this little seed then it will grow into a mighty tree. The seed pod itself is the tomb of Christ, the coffin of Osiris, the Ark of the Covenant, and the Ark of Noah. Since Mary means *pure waters* she is what Manly Hall calls the *"mistress of growing things, the very symbol of the humid principle that brings forth life."*

The *Parable of the Sower* in Mark, chapter 4, preserves this same motif in that of the seeds which fell in different places or were disturbed otherwise. The *seed* is truth and as Manly Hall explains:

> *"Some receive the truth and others reject it; some distort it, and others permit it to be plucked out by impulse and words; by weeds are to be understood the appetites and passions of the lower emotional nature; by the birds of the air, thoughts; by the sun, pride; and by the stony ground, such as are not yet ready to receive the law."*

Sixth Iteration

James M. Pryse writes in <u>The Apocalypse Unsealed</u> how the *apocalypse* was once subjected to historical interpretation, but without any evidence of such past records *"it was next interpreted as a history of the future, that is prophecy."* In some ways it can be both history and future, internal and external. He says that it is *"unintelligible to the conventional scholar"* and we know that countless *faithful* today sell it is a sort of explicit physical exaggeration of spiritual matters. For it is indeed *"veiled in symbolic language"* and thus *"relates to the Mysteries of the early Christian Society, the esoteric teachings which it was not lawful to reveal."* The Revelation of St. John is truly a masterful work in esotericism which acts as a preservation of early Christian and Gnostic thought against institutional dogma. This secret doctrine is carefully concealed *"under the most extraordinary symbols, checked off by a numerical key and by similar 'puzzles,' so that the meanings could be conclusively demonstrated from the text itself, and concluding it with a dread imprecation against any one who should add to or take away anything from the book."*

It therefore gives the key to *gnosis* in every age while transcending faith and philosophy. It is the *"secret science which is in reality secret only because it is hidden and locked in the inner nature of every man, however ignorant and humble, and none but himself can turn the key."*

~

The two crossed keys of Roman Popes and St. Peter are representative of the exoteric and esoteric religions. The silver key unlocks the *mysteries* of the mundane and the gold key unlocks the *mysteries* of heaven. These keys also unlock the *mysteries* of the Old Testament and New Testament. It is the keeper of keys, JANUS, the two-faced god, who unlocks the esoteric tradition. Since the esoteric teachings are  represented by a head the exoteric teachings are represented by the body, John the Baptist is decapitated, like Orpheus being ripped to pieces, a story symbolic of the loss of great wisdom. But this wisdom can still be found. It is not exclusive to any one religion or philosophy but preserved within all, like a *seed* or *egg*, despite corruption and distortion, because the *mystery* resides within man. '

Although Peter is the rock - PETROS - upon which the Church was built, and thus is the orthodoxy of Christianity and a mostly literal system of belief, Saul of Tarsus (Paul) helped to preserve the mystical nature of Christ's teachings. As Hall says, *"To Peter, the Christian 'mystery' was that of God made flesh. To Paul, it was flesh made God."*

St. John's Revelation is what theologians might call literal prophecy, what occultist may call the *mysteries*, and what explorers of thought may call an altered state of consciousness beyond that of the typical mystical experience. Perhaps the latter two possibilities are one and the same. It is rarely debated anymore that John even wrote the book, with some suggesting that a Gnostic named Cerinthus, who some say took Christ's place on the cross, was the author, a possible fact which would certainly explain its deep occult themes.

When John ascended by way of a symbolic ladder comprised of *seven churches*, he took the shamanic *sky rope* or *Jacob's Ladder* into the heavens.

These seven churches are not institutions but representations of the continents, holes in the head, days of creation, and creative rays. Revelation 4 tells the story of what John sees in Heaven:

> *After the vision of these things I looked, and there before me was an open door in heaven. And the same voice that spoke to me before, that sounded like a trumpet, said, 'Come up here, and I will show you what must happen after this.' Immediately I was in the Spirit, and before me was a throne in heaven, and someone was sitting on it. The One who sat on the throne looked like precious stones, like jasper and carnelian. All around the throne was a rainbow the color of an emerald. Around the throne there were twenty-four other thrones with twenty-four elders sitting on them. They were dressed in white and had golden crowns on their heads. Lightning flashes and noises and thunder came from the throne. Before the throne seven lamps were burning, which are the seven spirits of God. Also before the throne there was something that looked like a sea of glass, clear like crystal.*

> *In the center and around the throne were four living creatures with eyes all over them, in front and in back. The first living creature was like a lion. The second was like a calf. The third had a face like a man. The fourth was like a flying eagle. Each of these four living creatures had six wings and was covered all over with eyes, inside and out. Day and night they never stop saying:*

> > *'Holy, holy, holy is the Lord God Almighty.*
> > *He was, he is, and he is coming.'*

> *These living creatures give glory, honor, and thanks to the One who sits on the throne, who lives forever and ever. Then the twenty-four elders bow down before the One who sits on the*

throne, and they worship him who lives forever and ever. They put their crowns down before the throne and say:

> *'You are worthy, our Lord and God,*
> *to receive glory and honor and power,*
> *because you made all things.*
> *Everything existed and was made,*
> *because you wanted it.'*

St. John says he was "in the Spirit" having an experience beyond the physical. He saw the "throne in heaven" and the person seated there was like "precious stones."

The surrounding twenty-four thrones and elders are the hours in a day.

The *lightning flashes and noises and thunder* emanating from the throne relate to the power of the internal and the eternal. They are evidence of the *second coming,* i.e., the awakening of consciousness.

The *seven lamps* and the *sea of glass like crystal* witnessed on his journey are symbolic of the same septet symbology, but particularly the planets, along with the water above the firmament. In other words, the manifest heavens.

From the four living creatures, or the four directions, seasons, horses, etc., being "covered all over with eyes" is to be understood the shining stars in heaven; they are creation which *"day and night"* repeat *"holy is the Lord God Almighty."*

Therefore, it is to be understood that *"the One who sits on the throne"* is spirit, which is what John says he is "in," and the description of this Holy One as "precious stones" is clearly indicative of the *Philosopher's Stone,* alchemy, and masonry.

When all bow to the One and say "you are worthy" we are to understand that the spirt of man, like the seed planted in each of us, is the *mystery* and subsequently, if properly prepared, ready to receive the *revelation* of the *mysteries* by lifting the veil of Isis and peering into the Holy of Holies. The *revelation of St John* is thus the ritual of *living resurrection,* i.e., being *born again,* as is evidenced from Revelation 20:6 which states:

> *"Those who are raised from the dead during this first time are happy and holy. The second death has no power over them."*

In Revelation 20:13 it is said that the dead will be judged, a fact taken directly from the *mysteries* of Egypt, among others, wherein the heart of the dead is judged, or weighed, against a feather. The *sea* is, of course, illusion, and the *dead* are uninitiated:

> *"And the sea gave up the dead which were in it; and death and hell delivered up the dead which were in them: and they were judged every man according to their works."*

Seventh Iteration

The *REVELATION* is the *Kingdom of Heaven*, or the city of the Sun, like Heliopolis, existing in the *Garden of Paradise* from whence man *fell* into the *Garden of Hallucinations*. The *base* of the spine is the *fruit* of sexuality and procreation, or the *Tree of Knowledge of Good and Evil*, while the *crown* of the spine is the skull or temple, the *Tree of Life*, where Christ was crucified at *Golgotha*, i.e., the Hebrew *gulgoleth*, which means *skull*. From the *fruit of desire* to the revelation of *eternal life*, the human spinal column, or tree, with its mystical *thirty three* stacked vertebrae, is the *cross* that man is crucified on by the *nails* of the senses and perception, i.e. physical illusion. The body itself is a temple, even below the head, and remains forever unfinished. The *Third Eye* oversees this construction from realms beyond the physical kingdom of *malkuth*. This "eye" is the *Pineal Gland*, or Adam, and it oversees the positive (giving) forces of man, whereas the *Pituitary Gland* is Eve and controls the negative (receiving) forces of female. Manly Hall, in his book <u>Man: Grand Symbol of the Mysteries</u>, writes of how the brain and spinal cord offer keys to the mysteries of nature:

> *"The pia mater (that delicate membrane which invests the brain and spinal cord, forming as it were an inner garment) offers a definite clue to the anatomical arcana of the philosophers. Many scientific terms now in general use have been appropriated from older orders of learning, often with little understanding and less appreciation of the original meanings. Pia, for example, is the feminine of pius (pious), meaning 'godly' or 'devoted to Deity,' while mater is the 'mother'. Thus, pia mater is the Holy Mother, the Sophia-Achamoth of the Gnostics, containing within herself the foetus of the Heavenly Man. Mater, also interpreted as the*

origin or the source of, when read cabalistically indicates the brain to be the place where the gods are generated, or where piety or godliness has its seat. When the Cabalists declared the Heavenly Man to be androgynous, they stated only that which is testified to by the inner structure of man himself and by the early development of the embryo. Thus, the foetal creature within the womb of the Holy Mother (pia mater) is the celestial hermaphrodite, whose parts and members may be faintly traced in even the modern terms used to identify the parts of this amazing organ which we call the brain."

Regarding Hall's assessment, we find Augusta Foss Heindel making a similar statement as per the head, brain, and already mentioned glands:

"There is but one fountain of youth, one elixir of life, and that is our food and our thoughts. If we live a pure and simple life of unselfishness, eating lightly of vegetables and fruit, keeping close watch over our desires, then we need not sacrifice the life of the animal to replenish our wasted energy. Ponce de Leon sought the fountain of perpetual youth in far-off lands, while he had two tiny cups within his own brain which, if he had only paid the price of making an exchange of the worldly life of the senses for the spiritual life of purity, would have given him the elixir of life."

To this end, the Swiss physician and alchemist Paracelsus once said:

"The physical body itself is the greatest of mysteries because in it are contained in a condensed, solidified, and corporeal state the very essences which go to make up the substance of the spiritual man, and this is the secret of the Philosopher's Stone."

We may thus conclude that the *Fiery Red Dragon* of Revelation 12 is far more than an actual monster. The dragon is the hopeful devourer of a newborn about to be birthed by the *"woman clothed with the sun, with the moon under her feet, and on her head a garland of twelve stars."* In Revelation 2 we learn that *"the dragon gave the beast his power and his throne and great authority,"* and by his fact alone it becomes clear what the dragon and beast, and that newborn, really represent. The baby is our REBIRTH or RESURRECTED SOUL. The *RED DRAGON* is the EGO, and the BEAST is the ANIMAL SELF.

The ABYSS (formless and empty) of Genesis is both an oceanic depth and a dry desert and filled with all manner of predators like the serpent or dragon (danger). In Job 41 there is described a terrible beast, a "king of the ocean, king of the deep" that we also know as Leviathan, a creature easily associated with Ouroboros, the snake consuming its own tail. Both creatures signify the boundary of creation and limitless potential, even if the POTENTIAL is limitless within the bounds of CREATION. These monsters are also *necessary evils* which hold back the DARK from fully consuming LIGHT – it is a rhythm and breath like night and day. Manly Hall once wrote, as described earlier, that the potentiality of creation itself stems from darkness in the same way that Jordan Peterson writes, *"everything that emerges from the realm of possibility in the act of creation (arguably, either divine or human) is good insofar as the motive for its creation is good."* Both good and evil, like man and woman, come from darkness - as does light.

These are complex subjects that relate as much to the physical world as they do to the various layers of the human body and mind. For demons and monsters are not merely an expression of internal conflicts, they are spiritual and psychological forces operating in the same predatory manner - necessary evil - as the great serpent of Eden, which is always tempting us with the sin of transgression against divine authority – GOD'S PLAN. That *sin* is unmanifest potential and a LIE, which is the opposite of the TRUE WORD of God. Jordan Peterson writes further:

> *"The Word - the tool God uses to transform the depths of potential - is truthful speech. It appears necessarily allied, however, with the courage to confront unrealized possibly in all its awful potential, so that reality itself may be brought forth."*

From this point of view, psychologically speaking, *Original Sin* is our proclivity to reject creation, i.e., the manifesting of our potential, in favor of sinking into the expansive oceanic or desert abyss - being swallowed by the whale like Jonah. For the essence of reality, as Peterson concludes, is *"an eternal treasure house guarded by an eternal predator,"* which represents the *"way you are wired to react to the world at the most fundamental depths of your Being."*

From this point of view, psychologically speaking, the *fear* we should have for the LORD, as mentioned in Proverbs, is the corruption of our instinct through the pollution of deception.

So many of these esoteric themes help to preserve the *keys of the mysteries*, but when utilized as an ideological dogma they create immense confusion and distortion. There really is great danger in perverting the *mysteries*.

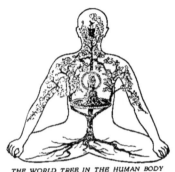

THE WORLD TREE IN THE HUMAN BODY

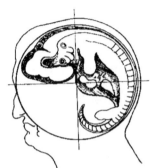

THE BRAIN IN THE FORM OF AN EMBRYO

Thus, we must come to understand the Holy Trinity of body, mind, and spirit (psyche). We must come to understand the demons and monsters within, and then overcome them. We must come to understand the nature of the Red Dragon and Beast from Revelation, as they relate to the ego and animal nature – that this metaphor exists likewise in nature and the world man has created. Jordan Peterson explains in further detail the meaning here:

> *"If the Dragon of Chaos and the paired Benevolent and Evil Queen are representatives of potential and of the unknown, the Wise King and the Authoritarian Tyrant are representatives of the structures, social and psychological, that enable us to overlay structure on that potential."*

We must recognize the archetypes of hero and adversary – like Satan. We must come to grasp that nature of both a Kind mother and Evil Queen or Witch – that nature should be preserved but that it is also there for our use so that we can build protections against its more wicked side. We must come to likewise grasp that society, institutions, etc., are comprised of a Wise Ruler and Evil

Tyrant, parallel to the mother and witch – that institutions are necessary for civility and order to exist but that too much order creates chaos (and too much chaos eventually inspires order).

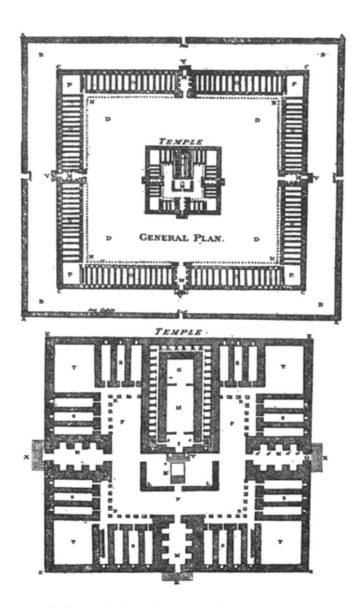

Solomon's Temple, reproduced here from Manly Hall's book *How To Understand Your Bible*.

St John's Vision of Christ,
woodcut by Albrecht Dürer (1497-98).

St John and the Twenty-four Elders in Heaven,
woodcut by Albrecht Dürer (1497-98).

About the Author

Ryan Gable is a veteran radio personality and producer for his weeknight show *The Secret Teachings*. His broadcast focuses on the synchronicity and objective analysis of para-politics, pop-conspiracy, para-history and history, the occult (occulture), the paranormal, symbolism, health, anthropology, theology, and etymology. He attempts to use this knowledge to analyze both historical and contemporary events with objective reasoning. Spending much of his life on air, and having written several books, Ryan has also been a guest on dozens of other radio shows and podcasts, and has had his broadcast aired on a variety of networks - from WPRK and CBS to Dark Matter Radio, LNM, the FringeFM, and Ground Zero Radio. He was a frequent guest on the *Kev Baker Show* until Kev's passing and is now a frequent guest on *Ground Zero* with Clyde Lewis. Despite this success, all achieved with near-zero capital, his broadcast has also been removed from various networks over the years for his refusal to censor content. He has also been banned from attending some conferences for speaking on subjects considered too controversial or for exposing con artists within the industry.

Ryan and *The Secret Teachings* are not aligned with any specific ideology so that they may stay fluid with information as it is unveiled. He holds himself to the same standards and recommendations suggested on air or in his writings, in relation to food or study. This involves an approach to *kaizen*, or the method of always improving. He focuses on critical thinking and objectivity as keys to understanding, utilizing, and appreciating *The Secret Teachings of All Ages*.

His other books are:

Occult Arcana, The Technological Elixir, Liberty Shrugged, Food Philosophy

You can find more information on his website or by email:

www.TheSecretTeachings.info

rdgable@yahoo.com - or - tstradio@protonmail.com

Notes

Printed in Great Britain
by Amazon